THE HANDBOOK OF
Family Dispute Resolution

■ THE JOSSEY-BASS LIBRARY OF CONFLICT RESOLUTION ■

THE HANDBOOK OF
Family Dispute
Resolution

MEDIATION THEORY AND PRACTICE

Alison Taylor

JOSSEY-BASS
A Wiley Company
www.josseybass.com

Published by Jossey-Bass
A Wiley Imprint
989 Market Street, San Francisco, CA 94103-1741   www.josseybass.com

Jossey-Bass books and products are available through most bookstores. To contact Jossey-Bass directly call our Customer Care Department within the U.S. at 800-956-7739, outside the U.S. at 317-572-3986, or fax 317-572-4002.

Jossey-Bass also publishes its books in a variety of electronic formats. Some content that appears in print may not be available in electronic books.

Library of Congress Cataloging-in-Publication Data

Taylor, Alison, date–
The handbook of family dispute resolution: mediation theory and practice/
Alison Taylor.
p. cm.—(The Jossey-Bass library of conflict resolution)
Includes bibliographical references and index.
ISBN 0-7879-5639-2 (alk. paper)
1. Family mediation.   2. Family counseling.   3. Dispute resolution (Law).
4. Domestic relations.   I. Title.   II. Series.
HQ10.T28 2002
362.82'86—dc21   2001006852

Printed in the United States of America
FIRST EDITION
HB Printing   10 9 8 7 6 5 4 3

CONTENTS

PREFACE

Starting this work in earnest in January 2001, I am reminded that the first month is named for the two-faced Roman god, Janus, who looked backward and forward at the same time. This book seeks to look in both directions at the same time with one mind—looking forward to providing new and currently practicing family mediators excellent concepts, processes, and specific information so they can continue to define for themselves their best way of practicing mediation, while also looking backward to capture and weave into the future the things of value from two decades of my own and other people's work.

I came to this field in the early days, when so much needed to be learned, built, and done by enterprising entrepreneurs and pioneers. In the past few years, with the convergence in professional organizations and national uniformity of laws and practice that may eventually lead to certification or licensure of family mediation practice, I find that some ideas worthy of being saved or at least noted in the development of this field are being lost, forgotten, or discarded, like indigenous practices and certain species. Although this evolutionary process can help weed out unhelpful or archaic ideas and practices, the worry is always that what is best may be lost in the urge toward uniformity.

Some ideas and ways of approaching family mediation practice are destined to be classics that will continue to be used because they still have something of value to offer. Others will be proven to be fads that fade or good ideas that did not stand the test of time or no longer speak to newer ways of thinking and doing. Evolution comes with a price, and with gain must come loss. To modify the famous quotation, those who remember the past are no longer doomed to repeat it, repackage it, or reject it.

This sorting, ordering, and categorizing process, which can be tedious but is necessary, is often called a history-and-systems course in academic disciplines: students learn about the past because it informs the present. It is about remembering contributions, concepts, and practices that may still be useful or that mark the discipline's growth and knowledge.

Although family mediation, as part of the alternative dispute resolution (ADR) movement in our justice systems, is part of and affected by larger societal changes, it may not yet qualify as a profession until the majority of practitioners know an organized body of information that they continue to pass along, contribute to, and maintain, for that is the essential element of a profession or discipline. This book is one step toward this goal; I hope it gives readers an integrated overview of the topics, issues, and information.

OVERVIEW OF THE CONTENTS

This book is divided into three parts. Part One looks at issues of basic theoretical understanding that mediators need to know about families, conflict, and the mediation process for family disputes. These first four chapters are critical to understanding the uniqueness of family mediation, which is different from other uses of mediation, such as business disputes and small claims mediation. These are understandings that attorneys and therapists may not have gotten in an organized way in their original professional training or even during their short mediation training courses.

Chapter One focuses on a systemic approach to families rather than seeing the parties as separate individuals who are disconnected. It looks at the development of the family as a system and the likelihood of certain disputes' arising within families because of individual and family developmental stages. Chapter Two looks at how family conflict is manifested. Because of the level of interdependence, many family conflicts have been covert for years and are extremely anxiety producing when they are overtly expressed. Families can experience normal conflict as deep betrayals, and family secrets are often revealed during mediation efforts.

Chapter Three asks family mediation practitioners to assess their own model and approach, how they got it, and what it has as advantages and disadvantages, so that they can make a more informed choice regarding their own training and services and therefore be more accurate and clearer with their professional disclosure to clients. Chapter Four reviews the interventions that grow out of the models and approaches. It reviews some examples that show how a practitioner from one perspective and model may act very differently in practice from a mediator using a different model. The basic presumption is that family mediators act as they think. This chapter focuses on the specific behavior of the mediator during sessions.

Part Two explores complex issues that family mediators must recognize and that require some additional attention. Family mediators, more than labor- or business-oriented mediators, need to understand the unique dynamics of abusive and drug-affected families, the cultural dimensions within families, and the complexity of working with family cases. These understandings are about the context of family mediation practice that requires practitioners to offer more than generic mediation. The issues brought up in these chapters may be reasons that mediators, no matter which model they use or what type of dispute the family is having, must assess the case and perhaps modify their usual or standard practice in mediating it.

Chapter Five looks at the issues of special concern to family mediators that happen all too often in these kinds of disputes: domestic violence, drug use, and other conditions. These are the conditions that may indicate that family mediation is inappropriate or needs to be modified to make it a fair and safe process for all participants and those who are affected by it. Chapter Six discusses a family mediator's ethics and special duties to provide a safe haven for the dispute to be discussed. It looks at the reporting requirements when a mediator is unsure if he or she must divulge information outside the mediation session.

Chapter Seven introduces the notion that mediation practice must be informed by and modified to match the cultural needs and expectations of the people it serves. It starts, but does not end, the discussion of how culture affects the mediators themselves, the participants, and the culture of mediation that is conducive to best practices. Chapter Eight acknowledges that mediators are on a continuum of services that the disputants experience. It looks at what family mediators need to do to minimize disruption for their clients while not overstepping the boundaries of the family mediation practice.

Part Three outlines specific applications of the mediation process to common disputes that arise in families. Services have often been oriented around the type of dispute it is—that is, who is involved or the manifest issues being decided. This part is organized into chapters that look at what is current practice and special knowledge that a practitioner would need to know in handling cases of that type.

Chapter Nine focuses on the use of mediation for marital disputes when the family does not want to divorce but needs to solve important problems and disputes, as well as the use of mediation for prenuptial agreements. Chapter Ten is a review of the most heavily addressed aspect of family mediation: divorce and custody issues. Because this is the area in which I have spent most of my professional career, I state what I believe is most important; my assumption is that readers have already come to terms with their own model and theory base.

Chapter Eleven looks at a relatively new development: the use of mediation practice to help with parent-teen problems within families. This chapter looks at how parent-teen mediation services can work with existing divorce or family mediation services. The change of families by adoption and external placement by child protective agencies and courts is the subject of Chapter Twelve. Because these disputes often involve allegations and actualities of abuse, neglect, and other disruptions, the reader needs to have absorbed all of the previous chapters. A growing area of practice for family mediators covered in Chapter Thirteen is the disputes that arise for families when a loved one is ill, disabled, temporarily or permanently incapacitated, or needs ongoing adult supervision, or when there are divisions within the family about extreme, end-of-life, or urgent medical care.

Each part sets out the ideas, references, and information that have been helpful to me and other mediators as we have moved through the professional development process. These ideas, skills, processes, and approaches should not be left behind in the evolution of the practice of family mediation. As new clearinghouses, databases, programs, and applications are developed, family mediation practitioners should review their own need for updating, and publications such as this must continue to incorporate the best practices that are upheld by solid research and user satisfaction. Our new professional organization, the Association for Conflict Resolution, should be helpful in facilitating the sharing of relevant information.

My guess is that readers will be tempted to select only the chapter in Part Three that they are interested in and bypass the earlier chapters. I urge readers not to skip Parts One and Two. They provide the foundation of understanding necessary before getting to specifics. The chapters throughout this book are sequential, and the effect is cumulative. Readers who do not read Parts One and Two will find Part Three incomplete and inadequate to provide the necessary support to be effective. All readers should take the time to start at the beginning, to augment their information and understanding. Mediators working with families need to read across the disciplines of social work, social and personal psychology, cultural anthropology, and child development, as well as negotiation and conflict resolution.

PURPOSE OF THE BOOK

The goal of this book is to summarize the current state of family mediation theory and practice as part of the creation of ADR programs and services. The book has been written with two audiences in mind: those who come to the field from a legal ADR perspective and those who come from a therapeutic or clinical orientation, since those are the most common paths that converge in family dispute resolution. The goal has also been to organize, summarize, compare and contrast, and make recommendations about the often conflicting and incomplete theories and practices, so as to make them available in one place.

This is not strictly a textbook, but it may need to serve as such for those who are already in family mediation or ADR practice and those who need to expand their practice to include additional types of disputes within family mediation. It should be helpful to beginning mediators, who are just starting to find out how to do family mediation, and to seasoned veterans, who have been practicing for a while but are thinking of expanding or clarifying their practice. If this book has met its goal, readers will reach for and refer to it often as they work with new types of challenging cases. It will provide readers with more self-understanding as well as practical information they can use in their work. This book is a work in progress, as is the reader's mediation understanding and practice.

Hillsboro, Oregon   Alison Taylor
December 2001

ACKNOWLEDGMENTS

Life is short, the art long, opportunity fleeting, experience treacherous, judgment difficult.
—Hippocrates, *Aphorisms,* sec. I

There are in fact two things, science and opinion; the former begets knowledge, the latter ignorance.
—Hippocrates, *Law,* Book IV

If I have seen further, it is by standing upon the shoulder of Giants.
—Sir Isaac Newton

We all have teachers and mentors who help shape our thoughts and actions as we are moving through the process of personal and professional development in the direction of artistry. This book is not only my own understanding of the theory and practice of family mediation after twenty years of practice; it is also based on the thoughts and actions of others who have contributed to the field as it is today. They will continue to be the shoulders on which all of us may stand to get a better view of the work we do.

I would like to acknowledge two men whose broad shoulders helped me: Stan Cohen and Nolan Jones, whose pioneering work and support of innovation at Clackamas Family Court Service in Oregon created the conditions for me and many others to develop ourselves and the uses and practices of family mediation. In that place and on that same path were other kindred souls who have shaped and influenced me and many others. Vana O'Brien's understanding of couples and family dynamics in conciliation and mediation are unsurpassed. Barbara Lee in Lane County is another successful graduate of the Clackamas internship program, whose careful and thoughtful approach to difficult legal and political issues as well as concerns about domestic violence and appropriate policies have been a help to the thinking within the field. Mary Ann Zaha, who has focused on the emotions beneath our work, has moved our perception from the businesslike negotiative approach to the understanding of the need to deal fully with the emotional issues in family disputes. Amy Swift helped develop parent-teen programs that integrated with other forms of family mediation, and her model of including teenage mediators has been highly useful in making knowledge of mediation transferable.

In addition to my local sages, my view of the larger world of family mediation has certainly been enhanced by the involvement of nationally known thinkers and doers. Jay Folberg, with whom I had the honor of teaching law students about mediation as part of one of the first alternative dispute resolution (ADR) classes at a law school when people were still asking what mediation was, held a wide-angle lens to the development of this field for me and many others. Michael Lang's development of an individualized master's degree program for those who would work with interpersonal disputes has helped produce and support cadres of practitioners who think reflectively and interact sensitively rather than automatically or prescriptively. John Haynes, whose videotapes show us a smooth master and whose prolific writings on important topics serve as a first foundation for this field, is the intellectual grandfather to whom we all owe a debt.

Robert Benjamin's creative writings and forceful opinions have served the field as the gadfly that makes us stop to think in different ways. Larry Fong has shown us over the years how to blend therapy with mediation to make both strong. Donald Saposnek, whose quiet presence has graced many conferences, continues to provide the good questions and seek the answers. Empirically minded researchers such as Joan Kelly have reminded us of the need to hang our hats on what is real and provable rather than what we might surmise or just hold as an opinion. Practical educators such as Isolina Ricci have given us and our clients the information needed.

This field is constantly in progress, and we need those who will take what we do know and continue to apply it to new areas or in new ways. Gregory Firestone, Jeannie Etter, Bernie Meyer, and others are developing new frontiers, such as the use of mediation for adoption and placement. The recent work of John Winslade and others in adapting narrative therapy to mediation has added new ways of thinking and working. And many other ordinary heroes of family mediation are silently doing this work, expanding the uses in their own sphere of influence.

From the writings and practice of these and other current thinkers and forerunners, we have been educating those who would do this important work of developing family mediation as a separate but integrated field that has depth and breadth, science as well as opinion, theory as well as practice. In bringing together some of these best thoughts and trying to organize and synthesize them, my hope is that as an interdisciplinary field of endeavor, we can coalesce what we know and what we need to find out. The need now is to organize this information personally and as a profession—not as rigid codification or as global generalizations but as composites made of our separate experiences that will continue to contribute to the larger understanding. A further hope I hold is that a shared reality of basic information we all can use will help all of us continue to improve what we do uniquely and separately.

There is more work to do in order to help develop organized internships and apprenticeship training opportunities for those who want to develop their own and their system's expertise. I would like to acknowledge the role of educational institutions such as Antioch, Portland State University, Marylhurst University, and Northwestern School of Law at Lewis and Clark, where I have been connected, in moving toward a more comprehensive way of providing opportunities for learning and teaching potential practitioners and potential participants in interpersonal and family mediation. I also acknowledge the important role of the publishers and professional organizations that work as allies and help isolated practitioners get up-to-date information. I look forward to the future, when I hope that there will be a merging of these three major forces of educational systems, professional organizations, and Internet and new technology publishing to work together to create even higher platforms for development of this information sharing.

There are many others to whom I owe a debt of gratitude for their work and contributions. I acknowledge the help I have gotten from my editor, Alan Rinzler, and colleagues with whom I have consulted while preparing the manuscript of this book. I appreciate the indulgence and support of my family and friends as I worked on this while trying to maintain active and full involvement with my teaching, workplace, and family obligations, all of them very important to me. I hope I have accurately interpreted and represented the concepts and practices I have included in this book. I am grateful for the help and support I have received along the way so far and look forward to going further in good company, to continue to develop this richly complex, challenging, and hopeful use of ADR in family disputes of all kinds.

A.T.

THE HANDBOOK OF
Family Dispute Resolution

PART ONE

PRACTICAL THEORY

CHAPTER ONE

Understanding Family Dynamics

What is true about family mediation is that first and foremost, it is about families, and secondarily, it is about mediation and dispute resolution processes. Family mediators help families change from what does not fit to what will work better. Therefore, it is absolutely critical for family mediators to understand how families work, and when and how they do not. Because family mediators come from all types of professional backgrounds and all kinds of families, it is imperative to start with a thorough investigation of how families are constructed, how they operate, and when and how they will or will not make changes that will lead to continuing conflict or more peaceful and harmonious relationships. The place that family mediators must start in understanding their work is with an understanding of how families operate in order to provide dispute resolution when conflicts occur. Whether the professional is acting as a *mediator,* a third party brought into the dispute to intervene in the conflict, or a *facilitator,* who simply helps conduct a dialogue, this understanding of the life cycle and functionality of behavior within a family can help the practitioner explain to himself as well as those in the conflict not only how the conflict started but what maintains it and what has to be done in order to let the conflict go. Mediators need some theoretical perspectives on the ways that families function that help make sense of the struggle. They need to understand why there often is apparent resistance to change in ways that appear to be so patently easy and beneficial.

Everyone who works with family-related disputes needs to understand how families work. The limits of a practitioner's theory are the limits of that person's understanding of what and why things are happening in the interaction. Mediators who understand systems theory and other concepts that explain family dynamics will see their constellation of theory expand, with an expanded capacity to use that theory at critical moments during interactions with disputants (Lang and Taylor, 2000).

Family mediation rests on four major pillars of knowledge and skill: family law, which contributes the frame in which the parties can legally negotiate and sets the boundaries of rights and responsibilities that are important to society; mediation and other conflict resolution theory and skills, which is the medium in which we work; an understanding of family, adult, and child development, each as separate knowledge that contributes to understanding the general field in which we operate; and specific information about the processes and structures involved in the specific dispute (for example, custody, parent-teen, reunification), which provides enough starting information to ask good questions and understand the specific dispute dynamics (Taylor, 1994). There are a few basic concepts in adult and child development that family mediators can draw from the broader study that are particularly relevant. Family mediators must understand the context in which the family conflict is embedded, and this context often relates to the stage of development of the parents and the children in the family, as well as the stage of development of the family as a unit.

This chapter sets out the essential understandings about family dynamics that those doing dispute resolution for families need so that they can understand and respond more consistently. This is particularly important for family mediators who have come to this work from legal or financial backgrounds or fields other than human services. Law courses will have provided attorney-based mediators with an understanding of where the family is standing relative to the legal requirements, obligations, and rights afforded them by law. This is the frame in which the picture of the family is bound. It is extremely important to know the boundaries of the law in order to understand the reciprocal bonds of rights and requirements. But knowing all the relevant family law rules will not give the family mediator a complete enough picture or fully describe the family. Knowing what the individual and group and reciprocal rights and obligations should be will not explain to the family mediator what happens when the rules are not followed or why the family did not follow the standard social contract. An understanding of family law is certainly critical to an understanding of the family dispute in question and forms one of the four foundations of the work of family dispute resolution. However, this understanding is incomplete without the theory and practical implications of how families maintain themselves, change, communicate, and function on a daily basis.

In order to understand the nature of families better, mediators need to have practical theory, based on clinical experience and research, that explains what is and is not going on. This helps them make sense of what often appear to be illogical, chaotic, or inexplicable in the thoughts and behaviors of family members and their interactions. The theory should give answers to the following questions:

- What are essential understandings about how families as systems operate before, during, and after conflicts arise?

- How and why do different members of the family respond differently to the same situation or conflict? What can the mediator do about their reactions?

- How does each family member's need for maintaining his or her self-concept help to fuel the conflict, and how can mediators recognize and deal with this issue?

- How is the past affecting the current dispute, and what can and should a mediator do about this positive or negative legacy?

- What would be the elements of a resolution of the conflict that would create or maintain family and individual health? What elements would not contribute or even actively work against the concept of health and healing?

- How can a mediator understand the underlying issues that family members bring to the current conflict?

ASSESSING THE FAMILY FROM THE SYSTEMIC VIEW

All families, whether they themselves or outsiders describe them as happy, maintain patterns of interaction that either lead to functionality (and therefore a perception of happiness) or are not helpful to one or more members of the family (and therefore lead to unhappiness by some members). Those patterns of interaction can be changed by the awareness and change of one or more members of the family. This statement depicts the family from a systemic point of view. It includes the basic construct that families operate like all other systems. It also indicates that change for the system can happen when only one person makes a change in his or her perception and behavior. Family mediators help families by creating conditions for that change.

There is a very practical reason to begin this book on family conflict resolution with general systems theory. An understanding of systems theory can provide family mediators with a way of explaining and making meaning of conflicts and their solution, and it can provide for broader problem solving and more creative solutions (McDermott and O'Connor, 1997). Particularly for mediators who come to family practice from other dispute resolution practices, such as workplace and business disputes, knowing general systems theory and being able to analyze a family based on these principles can lead to an understanding of the dimensions of the problem. By deconstructing the more generalized systems problems inherent in a particular case, the family mediator can demythologize the problem and apply universally recognized approaches to it.

Family therapists and social workers who deal with family systems have noted the practicality of understanding this systems perspective, which has become a dominant paradigm shift in the past twenty years in all of the helping professions (Becvar and Becvar, 1998; Nichols and Schwartz, 2000). Systems theory reminds practitioners that they must always look not only to the individuals involved in a conflict but also to the systems in which the conflict is embedded in order to manage or resolve that conflict.

General Systems Perspectives

We begin with the essential elements of all systems, not just families as systems. This is called *general systems theory* and is used to explain the functions of mechanical and other physical systems in nature. Systems thinking has revolutionized many disciplines in the hard sciences, as well as the human sciences of psychology, social work, and therapy. It is important to discover what is the same and what is different about families as systems when compared to other general types of systems.

According to Anderson and Johnson (1997), all systems, whether they are human families or mechanical systems, share the following principles:

- All of the system's parts must be present for the system to carry out its purpose optimally.

- A system's parts must be arranged in a certain specific way for the system to carry out its purpose.

- Systems attempt to maintain their stability despite fluctuations and adjustments.

- Systems require feedback loops between parts to convey vital communication.

- Systems are part of larger systems and structures.

Putting these principles into a family context, families obviously work best for doing the instrumental tasks of maintaining the survival and well-being of the family as a whole when all members (the mother, father, children, and extended family members) maintain ongoing relationships with each other and support each other by doing their part. When fathers or mothers are emotionally absent, drug affected, or incarcerated, when children skip school or run away, and when family members will not talk to each other or shun each other, the family system is not functioning optimally. These types of missing component problems create ongoing problems and conflicts, and family members often define these conflicts requiring the help of a third party.

In line with the second principle, a family's parts must be arranged in certain ways in order for it to be functional. For example, divorcing parents must know when they will pick up and deliver children, and adult children dealing with ailing parents must cooperate to maintain the family home. Despite fluctuations of job layoffs, illness, and moves, families attempt, albeit sometimes less than adequately, to adjust to externally and internally caused changes in their family system. Very important in all of this is the communication, or feedback loop, that lets everyone know how it is going for each member in the family. Finally, families are parts of and must relate effectively to larger structures, such as their schools and neighborhood, their community, and their nation. They are also influenced by larger systems, like the legislative, judicial, and economic systems, and by entities such as the media, religious groups, and unions. Families are complex and dynamically changing systems swimming in even larger complex and dynamic systems.

When analyzing a system, the analyst should start by witnessing the current events that are happening and then measure and track the patterns of those events. By noticing the events, then the patterns, the analyst can find the root causes in the structures of the family. In this way, the analyst will be better able to predict the future. It is also necessary to understand how the system fits into larger structures and systems and whether it has intangible components, such as the family's available time to communicate or their motivation to share information. As conflict resolvers, mediators and others working with families must first analyze the conflict and the systems that are part of it. Thinking about families and the conflicts they are experiencing as a systems analyst may be new to mediators and dispute resolvers who were trained to think of themselves as lawyers, therapists, or mediators, yet they do this analysis even if they do not recognize the function. When family mediators start by analyzing the family systems dynamics, that process helps both mediator and family define and understand what patterns and structures of the family system are functioning beneath the events of the dispute and what outside influences are doing to the family.

Systems Archetypes

According to general systems theory (Anderson and Johnson, 1997), because of the commonalities of elements within systems, different types of systems can start to demonstrate amazingly similar patterns, which are called *systems archetypes.* Following are three common archetypes translated into the context of family systems:

- *Drifting goals.* There is a gap between the goal and the actual condition. There is pressure from inside and sometimes outside the system to take corrective action, but the choice is whether to lower the goal or reinforce the high goal. When the gap between actual conditions and the goal becomes large and the system keeps lowering the goal, it leads to even lower performance. *Example:* The family has a goal of high achievement in education, but the child is having problems, which the parents correct for by lowering the goal.

- *Escalation.* The actions of one member of the system reinforce the perception of threat to the other, who in turn engages in behavior that is perceived as threatening to the first. This mutually increasing perception of threat grows exponentially. *Example:* Divorcing parents tell each other that they are going to take custody of the child away from the other parent. The mutually escalating perception of threat can lead to kidnapping or parents' going underground or a series of restraining orders issued by judges.

- *Fixes that fail.* Attempts to repair one problem have unintended consequences that make the initial problem worse. The problem symptom diminishes at first, then returns to its previous or even higher level over time. *Example:* A parent has attempted to prevent her child from feeling stressed by withholding the other parent's visitation or access to the child. But this situation leads to increased stress for all parties when the closed-out parent gets the custody agreement reversed or the court orders him or her an even longer parenting time.

Jervis (1999) has written about how unintended systems consequences happen in large societal fixes that fail. He points out that a person cannot understand a system by just looking at the attributes and goals of the interconnected elements. Following this premise, family mediators cannot understand a family just by counting noses, seeing that a father or mother is absentee, or having them tell us their family values and goals. Jervis also notes that many unintended effects are significantly delayed and indirect, so we often lose the causality connection. For example, parents may be perplexed by their teenager's self-destructive behavior; they have forgotten or not made the connection between the sexual or physical abuse that the teenager suffered as a child and the delayed effect now showing up as self-destructive behavior. Although therapists are often aware that victims and survivors have symptoms years later, general systems theory would indicate that a family mediator should look at the larger family system to see how this one person's problems are affecting the entire family.

Jervis (1999) also points out a general systems truth that seems to hold true in families: the relations between two people are often determined by each person's relations with others, not just themselves. This theory explains why the former marital partners seem to get along so well in the mediator's office, yet the agreements they make are not durable because of interference from and alignment with their new spouses or partners. Jervis notes another truth about general systems: the regulation of systems is difficult. Regulation of families as systems is certainly difficult, which is one reason that attorneys, judges, law enforcement officers, and therapists have tried to institute more mediation efforts into justice systems rather than more rules, regulation, and enforcement. Mediators can see the difficulty of forcing families to meet external regulations imposed on them by larger systems. It can be difficult to try to help the family members become more self-regulating and follow through on agreements to do what they have promised. Mediators cannot and should not become enforcers or regulators of families; instead, families must take this on themselves.

BASIC TENETS OF FAMILY SYSTEMS THEORY

Once mediators embrace the basic tenets of families as systems, they can look at the particular family in their office, considering the following premises that systems therapists use in assessing families:

1. A system needs to be stable and yet be able to change or be flexible.
2. Families, like individuals, go through developmental stages.
3. The family needs to be both an open and a closed system.
4. Family members need to be individuals and yet feel like they belong.
5. Communication is feedback and this information exchange is the energy that maintains the system.
6. A family system is composed of subsystems with roles which logically complement each other. (Becvar and Becvar, 1998, pp. 101–102)

Mediators who understand these principles and properly assess the dynamics that are operating for a particular family can help the family change in ways that are realistic and durable.

Stability and Change

Therapists have developed tests to help describe the differences of families in regard to the need for structure and closeness. One standardized test, based on the Circumplex Family Functioning model (Olsen, 1993), helps place families along two separate sets of axes: one about the level of the family's flexibility and one about the family's level of engagement and closeness. On the flexibility axis, the continuum moves from low to high in the following sequence: rigid, structured, flexible, chaotic. On the engagement continuum, the terms from low to high are disengaged, separated, connected, and enmeshed. In this way, families are sorted into quadrants and levels to help identify the issues they are having as a social unit. Families that are at either end are less balanced than those in the midrange, demonstrating a pattern of overreaction or underreaction, overinvolvement or underinvolvement.

Over its life cycle, the family's rating can and should adapt to different needs and stresses. For example, we would expect a newlywed couple to be more enmeshed and families in later life to be a bit more separated to enable the couple to pursue their own separate interests they had deferred. Similarly, families with young children often do best in child rearing if they are in the structured category, preserving clear naptimes and bedtime routines, while parents with teenagers often must move to a more flexible stance regarding house rules. Families demonstrate different levels over time, and individuals within the family can expect or be concerned about the levels the family is experiencing. When parents or children disagree about the appropriate level of these factors, these concerns are often part of the underlying conflict in family mediation cases.

Families need some level of stability to provide consistency and predictability for members. When they are lacking that, we often see many problems in satisfaction and parenting. A quick and effective way to get some sense of how stable or how chaotic a family is is to ask the members questions about how a typical day goes. What time do they get up? Who wakes whom? When is dinner served? Who plans for it and makes it, and how is it eaten? When is bedtime? Who locks the home and puts out the garbage? Family mediators must often ask these clarifying questions to be able to assess the family's former functioning in order to determine what the new problem is and what might be a realistic solution. Families that have been historically chaotic will not be able to maintain complex or rigid mediated plans without considerable change.

Chaotic families often cannot even relate to these questions. For them, each day is different; no one has specific responsibilities to do tasks, or else they have tasks but do not do them. When families are highly chaotic, there is no dependable structure, and some or all of the members of the family may be experiencing vast amounts of stress and anxiety, unable to predict even the most basic things of life. Children growing up in chaotically structured families often develop coping skills to help them deal with these feelings and often also develop survival-based behavioral patterns, such as always eating quickly, hoarding food, binge eating in case of scarcity, or reacting out of anger.

These behaviors and patterns are often unconscious and tenacious and can carry over into adult lives and parenting behaviors, either as the same or opposite reactions. For example, an adult who was raised in a chaotic family may insist on having a rigid dinner protocol or bedtime routine. The mediator may find that such strongly held rules are part of the sticking points in divorce negotiations or other family conflicts. Family members who had to survive in chaotic families of origin often develop patterns of competitiveness or use injuring, rejecting, or other negative behaviors in order to control their worlds. This also can lead to the current dilemma that is being presented in family mediation.

In contrast, families that are too rigidly constructed may not be able to respond to the needs of growing adolescents and family members who need space or need to change patterns that were effective in earlier family life stages but now impinge on their need for different rules. Mediators working with parent-teen conflicts often see this dynamic at work underneath the conflict that is brought to mediation. The teenager is asking for reasonable accommodations to her new peer group and activities, and the parent is resisting and reissuing the family rules. Elderly parents whose adult children are trying to make hard decisions in mediation about out-of-home placement may also be operating out of these rigid rule systems and therefore not be receptive to otherwise reasonable changes and options.

Mediators who do not understand this conflict dynamic may be confused or have a tendency to label the less flexible members as being resistive or poor negotiators. Family mediators who understand that families must redefine the levels of change and stability they need at different stages of family life are able to help the parties articulate the differences of approach and need without labeling or blaming. This is often part of the reframing process that happens in family mediation efforts.

These same concepts have also been used as the basis of several brief screening instruments for mediators—for example, Family Modes (Mathis and Yingling, 1998), which screens divorcing families into quadrants similar to Olsen's, and the Divorce Mediation Assessment Instrument (DMAI) (Tan, 1991), which evaluates readiness of a family to mediate based on six factors. The current thinking behind this type of family assessment is that it helps the mediator know which types of historical patterns are at work. In fact, the usual mediation efforts and processes may be less productive with families that are too extreme in their chaotic or rigid conditions; the extremes are not as receptive to or capable of making changes to the family system. Chaotically structured families cannot get to the mediator's office consistently or immediately fall out of agreements because they cannot, by their very structure, hold to rules and agreements. Rigidly structured families want no change to the rules and structure, and so are less likely to cooperate with the negotiative process inherent in mediation efforts. While some family mediators may resist on principle or because of logistics and cost to test their clients, using questions to get clients to self-assess their family in regard to these factors of flexibility and closeness, both historically and currently, is often the key to understanding what started and what is underneath the conflict.

Developmental Stages

The patterns of interaction and the needs of members of families are different depending on what stage of family life they are in. Courting couples need a lot of togetherness with each other and have to spend a lot of time making the adaptations necessary to become an effective couple. Families with young children find they have to become more highly structured than before, since naps and bedtimes and the need for babysitters impinge on spontaneous adventures, freedom, and the ability to respond immediately to desires for sex and intimacy.

Families with teenagers have to keep some control yet allow for the adolescents' need to start to pull away, and families with adult children who are leaving home have to reformulate and reencounter their coupleness while still trying to release the young adult with appropriate support, a difficult dance of trying to create autonomy while also maintaining connectedness. Couples facing retirement are also facing the deaths of their parents and often their own siblings and the losses and changes of work and home, and they are grappling for some sense of meaning and support between them when the attractions of sex and status change and lessen. They have to figure out the new role of grandparenting and how to become the oldest members of their family.

In each of these stages, the particular balance of life is different. Some therapists working with both individuals and couples have proposed that the basic emotional needs of individuals, which they try to meet both as individuals and as couples and family systems, fall in four areas: affection (including both intimacy and sexuality), belonging, fun, and freedom. Each individual has a different optimum level for these four factors, and each couple or family must negotiate these as they proceed through the phases of family life. Two other important factors can be added to these first four because they are involved in many decisions regarding the adequacy of couples and family relationships: companionship and a sense of meaning. These naturally are in addition to physical safety and security needs and physiological needs.

Consider that these are both individual and relationship targets and goals and that each individual in a family is striving to have these needs met in a way that is unique to that person. Then consider the changes that family systems must go through over the cycle. In courtship (the process of finding and pursuing a partner and becoming a couple) and early relationship (the first six months to two years after the pair has established themselves as a couple or social unit), affection and belonging, fun and freedom, companionship and meaning are so high that the partners want to make a lifelong commitment to each other. By the family life stage when partners are experiencing the wonderful crisis of childbearing and infants, usually affection (and almost always sexual expression) has decreased in frequency and intensity, belonging can be affected by feeling left out or being overly involved, fun must be redefined in the light of child care and responsibilities, freedom seems nonexistent, companionship has usually suffered losses due to the time and energy demands of parenting, and the meaning of the relationship may be changing for one or both partners.

Contrast these necessary changes with the family life stage of parents with teenagers, in which the sense of affection and belonging through sexual and other intimate encounters has dwindled and become routinized, lacking passion or verve. Regarding belonging, families by this stage often have either a sense of family solidarity and belonging to a unique family or a sense of displacement and disconnection on the part of one or both of the couple or their children. Sometimes the major affiliation and belonging has switched from the nuclear family to a larger system, such as a religious community, a corporation, or a lifestyle. Fun and freedom may be increasing for the couple, or they may have stayed at the lowered level they were accustomed to during the years when their children were young. Companionship issues become important again as the couple tries to reestablish itself separate from the rest of the family. The sense of meaning—"Why should we be together?"—may well have changed over the years, and the answer, "For the sake of the children," may no longer ring as loudly.

Mediators may be asked to work with families having crises or disputes at any of these stages of the family life cycle. Understanding that certain issues are common and normal can often help defuse the need of family members to personalize or vilify their family member for creating situations that they are experiencing. Family mediators who understand and can relate to the necessity and normalcy of such changes during the life cycle can often impart this understanding to their clients in such a way that the disputants see the problem in a different light.

The Need to Be Both Open and Closed

This apparent paradox of a family to be simultaneously open and closed as a system is easier to understand when considered in terms of a real-life dilemmas. Being open and capable of accepting influence would be an adaptive response to families referred to helping professionals, such as therapists, social workers, and mediators. When a family is open to accepting the influence of these helpers, the helper can create change through intervention. Some families as a whole system, or some subsystems within the family, are often more open than others.

For example, in a divorce case being brought to mediation, the mediator might hope that the parental system is open to input regarding the best interests of the children (such as the recommendations of child development specialists for custodial and access patterns that are more conducive for certain ages of children) and the input from parent education classes for divorcing parents now routinely offered or even required in some jurisdictions. The mediator might also hope that the parents are closed in some ways and to some extent, especially when it comes to making choices that might violate the family's core values or changing patterns that work well. Given that same divorcing couple, we might hope that the parents will not separately or jointly listen to and be influenced by media or by friends who insist that they got a better deal when they went to court and that the parent should get the "standard visitation" or what "everybody else gets" when they divorce.

Families that are too open to outside influences forget what they uniquely want and need, but if they remain too closed, they do not benefit from important new information that can be helpful. Family mediators, unlike other more neutral third parties or mediators in other dispute resolution types, often have to be the ones providing families the information and education they need. Having the skill to understand the difference between a closed family system as opposed to a family or parent who just does not want to hear a particular piece of information can help the mediator in the case know whether to proceed or back off.

Belonging and Individuality

Belonging and feeling secure in our primary relationships are deep individual and family needs in both intact and functional families and those that are not functioning well or even break apart. Children in divorcing families often express concern about disloyalty to parents or siblings, and these loyalty conflicts can create great personal hardship for children, requiring strong intervention by therapists, family mediators, and court systems to prevent or lessen the emotional damage (Johnston and Roseby, 1997). One of the many crucial tasks of divorcing families is to maintain the right of children to continue to belong and express love for both parents without having to exclude or be excluded. Belonging in the family by adapting to the general family system and yet having individual needs met is the task for intact families as well as those that are renegotiating their family contracts and understandings due to divorce, relocation, illness, abuse, incarceration, or other triggering events.

Belonging requires some level of loss of freedom as parties submit to the rules. Families that have closed boundaries experience a dichotomous world of "us and them." Healthy belonging can allow someone to belong to several systems simultaneously: a parent can belong to her family of origin as an adult child, while at the same time belonging to her own selected partner and family of choice, and even have a sense of belonging to her partner's larger family system. When belonging becomes unbalanced, distorted, and unhealthy, a person must make a choice and can belong to only one such group at a time—a "you're with us or against us" or friend-or-foe dichotomy. Many children in highly conflicted divorce situations feel exactly that us-versus-them mentality and need help in securing their right to belong to all the parts of the system. Family mediators working with disputes about the care of elderly parents often see this need to belong as crucial to whether a plan works or fails. Belonging is a strong survival instinct for humans.

Cults and groups, and even families, that do not allow the individual members the right to be themselves or to have some form of individuality in method or behavior become repressive, emotionally fascist societies that cost too much emotionally and do damage to the members' self-esteem. Repressive, coercive, and vindictive families can repress individual members' right to be themselves. Such families must often exert tremendous pressure and coercion in order to maintain their belonging. This can then become part of the continuum that can lead to serious domestic violence—from controlling, to abusive, to violent behavior by one or more members of the family toward the others. The concern for the safety and well-being of all members of a family is of utmost priority to a family mediator. (Chapter Five discusses the implications of control, abuse, and violence for family mediators.)

Communication as Feedback

Some of the questions a mediator might ask a family in conflict are about the style and effectiveness of their family communication. Because families have rules that often distort or make communication ambiguous, a family mediator who is working with a theoretical knowledge of family systems can ask questions to find out how the family communication patterns reduce, maintain, or enflame the conflict situation. Many postdivorce visitation or access problems are the result of incomplete, oblique, or misleading communication. Many family mediators routinely include in their parenting plans negotiated agreements about expectations for family communication, such as who will communicate with whom, when, and about what. This is an attempt by the mediator to try to help the family make changes in what they have all assessed as past or current communication problems that can interfere with the successful working of the mediated agreements. Family mediators working with parent-teen problems or family reunification issues also need to look at past, existing, and potential future communication strengths and weaknesses.

If there are historical or current problems in how often or in what way family members communicate, it is important to note the three principles of communication that family systems therapists accept as guidance:

Principle One: One cannot *not* behave.

Principle Two: One cannot *not* communicate.

Principle Three: The meaning of a given behavior is not the "true" meaning of the behavior; it is, however, that individual's personal truth. [Becvar and Becvar, 1998, p. 19]

Everything that is said and not said, everything that is done and not done, forms each person's communication. When family mediation clients say, "We just don't communicate," the mediator should not assume that the person is stating an observable fact that there has been a complete cessation of all verbal and nonverbal communication. What the client is describing is his own personal truth regarding his dissatisfaction with the level, type, or frequency of communication. Silence, the lack of response to a question, or looking away and not responding *is* a communication, and it is loaded with meaning. All family communication from a family systems perspective is drenched in meaning by the context in which it is conveyed. A descriptive statement, such as "The kids are always asking for food when I arrive," can change its meaning based on whether the prior discussion had been about roles and responsibilities of the parents, the nutritional needs of the children, or a dispute about whether a parent is legally fit to continue having custody.

Virginia Satir (1972) proposed that all communication in families contains information about three elements beyond the content: something about the self, something about the other, and something about the context. Family mediators who are not listening with this in mind may hear the content of the message and start to work only with the face-value statement instead of being sensitive to the additional information being conveyed in these three elements. In this way, a parent who says to the other, "You can have joint custody," not only is communicating overt content regarding her position on the custody issue, but is also conveying information about how she views herself (capable and coequal) and the other (capable and coequal) and the context (depending on the state laws, mandated or voluntarily choosing this option). Each communication made in family mediation accumulates, and the mediator must work diligently to listen openly to what is said and what is not said. Following is a set of reflective questions that family mediators should ask themselves to evaluate and deal more effectively with the levels of communication by both the family members and the mediator in the interactive process of family mediation:

- What is the "meta-message" of their and your communication?
- How flowing or hesitant, formal or informal is it?
- What is self-defeating about their or your communication style? What could improve it?
- What are the patterns that they and you use? Should they be changed?
- How do blockages occur, and how do they and you handle them? [Lang and Taylor, 2000, pp. 169–170]

Satir also points out that family communication settles into routine roles that support the role assignments and functions of that family member in the family structure and system as it has been. Table 1.1 shows Satir's concepts of four common patterns of communication that serve functions within the family yet can be negative for self-growth and full involvement, and the pattern that both disputants and mediators could strive for.

Family patterns of direct and indirect, clear or vague communication, and the rules of who tells what to whom and under what circumstances are issues that will either confound the family mediator or be facilitative of the mediational process. Because direct verbal and nonverbal communication is the

Table 1.1. Common Patterns of Communication Within Families

Role	Purpose or Function	Meta Message	Nonverbal	Example
Placater	Agree: So the other won't get mad at you	Lowered body, eyes averted, squeaky or whining voice	I am worthless, helpless, dependent.	"Whatever you want is fine— I just want to please you."
Blamer	Disagree: Other person will see you as strong and go away; defense	Loud, posturing, intimidating gestures, hitting objects	I am the boss (inwardly, I am lonely and unsuccessful).	"You never do anything right; what's the matter with you?"
Computer	Ultrareasonable: Shows no feeling; above it, logical	Flat tone, big words, stiff posture, unmoving	I never make mistakes, so I am not at fault (inwardly, I am vulnerable).	"If one would look carefully, one might notice the work-worn hands of someone here."
Distracter	Irrelevant: Makes no sense, doesn't follow the topic	Constant movement, stares, ignores questions, yawns	Nobody cares. This is no place for me.	"What did you say? Oh, what do you think about . . . (other topic)?"
Leveler	Direct, open: Is specific, congruent, attentive	Eye contact, body relaxed yet mobilized	I can handle it; I am free to make choices; I am responsive to change and others.	"I understand what you said, but I want to try another option."

Source: Adapted from Satir, 1972, pp. 63–70.

medium that the family mediator uses, it is important to step back from the communication to determine the qualities and quantities of communication that are being used during a family mediation session. Who talks for whom? What are the "unsayable" words or concepts? Is silence screaming? (Chapter Three provides more information about interactive processes during family mediation.) The communication qualities and amount of communication during the mediation session are one of the elements of interaction that the family mediator must monitor and change in order to bring about change for the family system.

Subsystems and Complementarity of Roles

Families are made up of many complex relationships among family members. Family systems theorists tend to look not only for dyads—the husband and wife, for example, or the two children—as separate units, or subsystems, but also to see if a subsystem has brought a third person in as an assistant or ally. This process of triangulation is an attempt—often a harmful one—to stabilize the system and provide a safe focus for the tension of the conflict. How many family mediators have seen cases where the mother and father's relationship has deteriorated and is conflictual, so both of them focus on a child as the "troublemaker" or reason that they are having the conflicts? Or a grandparent, sibling, or therapist has been brought into the conflict to serve as a stabilizing force, only to be co-opted into taking sides.

The complexity of doing family mediation is in understanding the geometrical proportion of the relationships within the family. A family of two parents and two children (in fact, a small percentage of all families) has at least six different dyadic relationships, plus each person's relationship to the family as a whole. When triads have been formed due to conflicts in a dyad, there is a strong potential for as many as four triangles:

Mother/Father/Child 1

Mother/Father/Child 2

Mother/Child 1/Child 2

Father/Child 1/Child 2

When these are mapped out, it is often easier to see who is in alignment with whom, who has dual citizenship between two households, and which family members have formed triads. It is important for the family mediator to understand whether any of these triads has already been formed or is being created during the mediation process, and whether they can or should be maintained as part of the mediated agreements. A family mediator might ask the following questions about a client family.

- Does one (or both) of the parents rely on a particular child, or the children as a group, for emotional support?

- Are there major differences in role, authority, and power between the parents and the child subsystem?

- Are the grandparents used in a dependency relationship by the parents or grandchildren or in place of the parental subsystem?

- Are there historical alliances that the family mediator needs to know in order to understand the current conflict?

Knowing each person's answer to these questions will help the family mediator understand more about the context of the dispute. (The issues of when to gain this information and how much information are discussed in Part Two.)

THE CHANGE PROCESS FROM A FAMILY SYSTEMS PERSPECTIVE

Therapists and others who work with families know the basic dictum of systems theory: *A change in one part of the system changes the entire system.* Think of the conflict as a rubber band, which represents the simplest part of the family system, the dyad, which is placed around two objects, which represent the people involved in a family conflict. If those two objects are moved in diametrically opposed directions, the tension on the rubber band (family system) increases until the entire system breaks from that tension.

For example, if a parent and teenager are locked in a family dispute over the cleanliness of the teenager's room or the person she is dating, the tension between the two family members increases. If you add the system archetype of escalation, the behavior of the parent will create an increasing perception of threat by the teenager, and the teenager's ongoing messy behavior will continue to increase the perception of belligerence and threat on the part of the parent. Family mediation and other intervention efforts are most effective in preventing the damaging consequences if the mediation can be started before the relationship is severed or broken by one person's behavior or position. Even if the bond has been broken and one person will not speak to the other, or even if one party has ended the relationship tension by running away, family dispute resolution and mediation efforts can still provide the systems perspective because the two are part of the larger family unit. The effort of family mediation can still name the problem and counsel a first step toward getting both parties to deescalate and search for fair and workable solutions. The change of behavior that either one will do will change the entire system and also change each party's view of the conflict.

When looking at conflict resolution within families from this perspective, the family mediator can work with all members of the family to produce change. Even if one side of the dispute is recalcitrant, undifferentiated, or fragile, a change of response, role, or function by another member will ultimately affect everyone else within the family system. Reminding disputants of this fact will help them regain some appropriate power and control for themselves, even if they cannot negotiate effectively with the other members. Each person within the family structure has the capacity to make individual change that will move the family in a different direction. This realization can be empowering without the mediator's doing much else but reminding the family members about it.

How Families Create, Maintain, and Change Boundaries

Boundaries are the set of invisible rules and barriers that help regulate the amount of contact between members within the family and between the family and larger systems. A mediator can get a sense of the lack of boundaries in a number of instances: when parents are being interrupted in their conversation by their children and no one cares; when divorcing spouses want to be able to drop over at the other parent's home any time without calling or asking permission; when grandparents come in to tell the parents what to do; when a parent is offended and angry because his teenager read his mail but feels justified in confiscating and reading the teenager's mail. These are all examples of boundaries that are either being respected or crossed, and they also show some situations where the family itself does not know where their boundary is or should be. Some boundaries need to be permeable or diffuse, meaning that generally they are in place but can be overridden under certain circumstances. This is the concept of having a fence with a gate that generally remains locked, yet sometimes the gate is unlocked for certain reasons and time periods.

An example of a permeable boundary is a family rule that the children can walk into the parents' bedroom if they are sick or hurt or scared, but only if they knock or only if they really need help and support. If the parents have a very loose boundary around this issue, the children could walk in at an inopportune time, thus preventing the parents from having any privacy for sexual or other communication. Loose boundaries or constant boundary violations serve an often unnamed function within the family for someone. When there are no boundaries or no consequences for intrusion or boundary violation, even inadvertent, people do not feel safe or respected. When this happens, high levels of conflict and injury to self and others can happen.

Newly married or recently cohabiting couples must make these boundaries for themselves as part of the process of becoming a couple. Because most people know only their own family of origin's rules and boundaries, there is a tendency on the part of new couples to bring to their current relationship the legacy of their own past relationships or of their family of origin—their own unique family culture. Larger cultural issues can also be at work here. Many couples whose partners are from other cultures (used here in the broadest sense to include gender, nationality, religion, and other affiliations) often find they start with a different set of assumptions and expectations about boundaries between subsystems. For example, in many cultures, children sleep with their parents until they are in elementary school; for other families, this would be considered not just a boundary violation but abnormal. An American woman who marries an Iranian man might discover a great boundary clash in the issues of how much closeness they are expected to maintain with her mother-in-law. Remarried or blended families often find that the boundaries they assumed from the former family no longer work or fit, and families can outgrow the need or usefulness of certain boundaries. Children in divorced families have to learn and practice very different boundaries in each household where they spend time.

Each family is a complex web of such boundaries between each of the members. When boundaries have been crossed, members feel betrayed and vulnerable, confused and indignant, violated and upset. This reaction is even more intense if the person believes that the boundary violation was an intentional, willful act. This reaction is often what the family mediator sees when the clients walk in: all members are reacting to the breaking of the code by one or more members. When family mediators listen to the client's narration of the "the problem," they often hear under the words the issues of inappropriate or nonexistent boundaries, or boundary violations that have left family members with often unvoiced emotional reactions. As part of the mediation effort, the parties can co-create a new boundary that is more acceptable, or apologize and acknowledge the often inadvertent or even intentional breach of the personal boundary.

At the heart of family mediation negotiations is the reformulation of the boundaries within the family. Through the conflict, family members are able to renegotiate less rigid or outgrown boundaries and often break long-standing patterns of interaction that have formed into the dichotomous and complementary patterns of boundaries, such as the pursuer-distancer, active-passive, and dominant-submissive interactional patterns. Although shades of these patterns exist in most couples and families, the pattern itself becomes dysfunctional and unhelpful when it becomes so enlarged and rigid that deviation from it is unacceptable. By noticing the pattern and asking questions about the emotional reaction to it, the family mediator can elicit discussion about what would constitute more acceptable limits and how to react if they are not requested.

For example, when couples have developed a dominant-subordinate pattern of interaction and this becomes the only way they can interact, the boundaries have become too rigid and unhelpful. It is hard for the two to break out of the pattern, and conflict ensues. These conflicts can lead to a perception of the inability to change the pattern, which then can lead to the divorce mediator's office, with the parties alleging "irreconcilable differences leading to irremediable breakdown of the marriage." In parent-child relationships, this pattern of complementarity can create conflicts that the participants bring with them to the family mediator's office.

If a parent has maintained a high level of dominance over the years or is trying to reestablish it now when she feels the teenager is getting "out of control," the teenager may no longer be receptive to playing the complementary role of being subordinate and obeying. Teenage rebellion is often a cry to change these rigid or outgrown boundaries in the relationship between the teenager and the parents. Adult siblings who are trying to make complex money and social arrangements regarding an aging or incapacitated parent may find that they must work through their hardened interactional patterns prior to being able to complete the business regarding their parent. Perhaps the eldest was dominant over the other siblings, who were expected to go along with the will of the oldest.

How Family Mediators Can Perceive Boundaries

Family mediators who are listening to and asking questions of their clients regarding the past patterns of interaction between members of families can get a wealth of knowledge regarding the type of boundaries each had and the level of rigidity and discomfort with the patterns. This will give the mediator clues as to the reempowering of the client who needs some intervention in order to break out of a complementary role that is no longer functional or acceptable. In this way, a divorce mediator might hear that a spouse has taken on the passive role in the marriage regarding the making and distribution of money (this single breadwinner and stay-at-home housewife used to be a common expectation), yet now needs to change that role from passive to active as the divorce looms, costs rise, and the need appears that both parents must become economically self-supporting. Understanding the wife's "resistance" to finding a job might include how this change from passive to active changes all the boundaries they had maintained and why the change to getting a job may seem overwhelming and wrong to the spouse who had adapted to the complementary role. Understanding the process of complementarity can reduce the family mediator's perception of personal pathology of a client.

Family mediators who do not understand and see these changes as important in the unwritten rules of the family system will miss important information. A mediator who does not understand and work with how hard it is to change these boundaries and learned and co-created patterns of interaction between the family members will not understand their levels of surprise, distress, and dislike of change. Simple negotiation and positional bargaining are only on the surface of these disputes. The creation and maintenance of these boundaries and complementary patterns help explain why straightforward problem solving and clearly workable positions fall on deaf ears for the clients. Until or unless they are ready to make changes in their boundaries and patterns, no amount of creative problem solving by the mediator will be acceptable. In this way, family mediators are often called on to help the parties transform their boundaries and patterns before problem solving can happen (Bush and Folger, 1994).

Watching for the Unwritten Rules

Families are systems made up of unique individuals with unique histories and concerns. To pay attention to the individual or to both parties without noticing what is happening to the family system as a whole leaves an incomplete picture. Also, any resolution must meet the need of the system as a whole, as well as the need of the individual, if it is going to be adopted and used effectively and be maintained by the system. If the solution creates unintended systems effects, the durability of the agreement will be negatively affected. It therefore makes good sense for family practice in dispute resolution to focus on the family systems needs. The more effective the family mediator is in discerning the complementary rules and roles, the violations of those established patterns, and the emotional responses to potential change, the more effective the family mediator can be.

NORMALCY, HEALTH, AND DYSFUNCTION

As a family mediator, would you be able to recognize when you are working with a healthy family in a situational conflict, as opposed to an unhealthy or dysfunctional family embroiled in a sick contract or complex web of ongoing crises? Would this assessment make a difference in the way you should approach the conflict and its resolution?

A mediator who is working with family disputes should be able to analyze not only the family systems dimensions of the conflict and proposed solutions but also the family from the perspective of how well the family system is performing for all members of the family. Sometimes the behaviors of families who are experiencing deep disputes about their members indicate the extent of their distress, anxiety, and fear. These signs of stress, however, may not be symptoms of pathology or illness at all, but helpful signs that tell the family mediator where to focus attention.

Normal and *abnormal, healthy* and *sick, functional* and *dysfunctional, cohesive* and *chaotic* are descriptors that may or may not be helpful to the understanding and working of the case. They are, after all, external judgments placed on the family by those outside. Mediators are cautioned against making premature and often inaccurate, unnecessary judgments about their clients' families. They must remember that their highest ethical stance is to allow the clients to be self-determining. These labels of *dysfunctional, sick,* and *abnormal* are not usually judgments that families would put on themselves. Any label, and particularly these, can be pejorative and unhelpful in creating the kind of relationship that family mediators need to have with the families they work with and for. Wise family mediators will examine these terms to determine which ones are useful to their own practice of family mediation and will suspend judgment without giving away discretion and truthfulness.

What Is Normal?

When Walsh (1993) explored this issue of how terminology reflects the practitioner's view of families, and therefore how therapists work with families, she looked at the different ways that the term *normal* is used in describing and understanding families. One connotation is *normalcy-as-health.* This concept comes from a theoretical understanding shaped by the medical, empirical model. In that view, an organic system is healthy if it shows no symptom of pathology.

By definition, conflict in families always shows as a disturbance even if it is unacknowledged by one or more of its members. Families experiencing internal conflict between or among their members usually do show signs of stress and distress, and so their behavior often reflects those negatives; this can at times look "pathological." The term *pathology,* borrowed from the medical worldview, refers to diseases and conditions that, left unchecked, can seriously impair the functioning of the organism, to the point of becoming lethal. Certainly, unresolved family conflicts, left without intervention, can escalate in severity of behavior that creates harm and even life-threatening conditions for some or all members of the family. Domestic violence, elder abuse, and child abuse or neglect come instantly to mind to a mediator who thinks of family pathological behavior using this conceptual framework, since in these conditions, the family has done harm to itself as a system and to members within it.

But the converse is not always true: If a family does not have any threat of harm or violence in its history, is it healthy? The absence of these conditions cannot be used as the sole determiner of the health of the family, just as a person who does not suffer a heart attack, stroke, or other life-threatening condition is not necessarily healthy. This view of normalcy-as-health seems be incomplete or misleading as the only concept to guide the family mediator.

Normality can also be thought of as *normalcy-as-averageness,* that is, thinking in statistical terms—a norm or median frequency of typical traits and patterns that are demonstrated by a high percentage of families. If we use this definition, then families in conflict or having conflicts and disputes are certainly the norm, since conflict in families is endemic and statistically frequent. Some sociologists believe that the family is defined as a system in constant conflict and that the absence of such conflict is the true mark of abnormality. It is much more likely that a family is going to have conflicts and disputes, either within itself or between it and other systems, than that it will not have such conflicts. So from this perspective, family conflict and disputes are normal, healthy, and statistically probable. Why then do most people in our society think of families with conflicts as unhealthy and abnormal, and therefore unacceptable? Why do families who are having conflicts carry shame and guilt for having them? This definition of *normalcy-as-statistically-average* also leaves out something.

Another definition of normality is the utopian or *normalcy-as-idealized*. If the standard to which all families subscribe is the "A + " version, then most families will not achieve this self-actualized or ideal condition. If normal equals typical, then most families are in the vast middle. Graded on a curve, only a small percentage of families would have this ideal standing, or the opposite of it. And on what factors would that evaluation have been done, and by whom? Conflict and dispute among members of the family are certainly typical. But are they necessarily unhealthy? If we do not manage to live to the ideal, does that make the family abnormal? Since ideas of what is ideal change over time and are culturally taught and shaped, the social constructivist view would indicate that the ideal is unattainable and constantly changing. It is a moving target that most families cannot and will not be able to achieve. So this definition of *normalcy-as-ideal* may make all the families in conflict look abnormal, and therefore it is not the best view.

Perhaps a better way is to look at families in conflict from the systems perspective we just covered: *normalcy-as-sufficiently functional*, or the "good-enough" family. Families that attend to all their members' needs, maintain the stability and functions of the family in both instrumental tasks, such as gaining and distributing financial resources to meet the physical needs of the members, and also attend to the expressive tasks, such as meeting the family members' emotional needs, are acting as good-enough families. Families need to care for the needs of the youngest and oldest members and those whose personal needs have changed, and to adapt to the fluctuations imposed by external forces.

Under this view, then, a normal family is one that functions effectively enough as a system for all members of that system. This combines the concept of normalcy and functionality, so that a normal family is functional in most things. The opposite would be a family that is dysfunctional in some ways or to some degree. The only thing missing from this definition is a way of measuring the level of function and dysfunction and acknowledging the different perspectives each person in the family will have on those levels and items that are or are not functioning. In this way, the family system will look very different to each member of the family and can be understood fully only when all members' perspectives are understood. It cannot and should not be labeled as abnormal or dysfunctional on the basis of one member's view alone.

Hallmarks of Adjustment

Fogarty (1976) has outlined the hallmarks of a well-adjusted family, another term that describes a family that is doing well from a family systems perspective.

1. Emotional balance and the ability to adapt to change.
2. Emotional problems are seen as existing in the whole group, with components in each person
3. There is connection across the generations to all family members.
4. They solve problems with a minimum of fusion (over-involvement of enmeshment) and distancing, not having to be over- or under-involved.
5. Each dyad can deal with the problems between them without bringing in a third.
6. Differences are respected and tolerated, and sometimes even encouraged.
7. Each person can deal with all the others on both a thinking and an emotional level.
8. Each is aware of what each person gets from their relationships with the others, so there are no major secrets being kept.
9. Each person is allowed his own emptiness, and others do not have to rescue them from it.
10. Maintaining a positive emotional climate becomes more important than doing the right or popular thing.
11. Each member would declare that it's a pretty good family to live in.
12. Each member can use the others for feedback and learning, but not as emotional crutches. [p. 150]

These might well serve a family mediator as mental bins into which the data from the family being helped should be placed.

The old model of Cartesian, binary, dichotomous thinking would place all families on the rack of polar opposites: good or bad, adequate or inadequate, functional or dysfunctional, normal or abnormal. In this new millennium, we have a chance to rethink our paradigms. Family mediators can choose to reject these constructs in favor of a view that takes into consideration the fact that most phenomena are on a gradient scale relative to themselves and others.

When thinking about how well a particular family is able to meet members' needs, a mediator using a family system perspective needs to think in terms of the continuum between these pairs of opposites. Families can be functional on some levels in some ways and dysfunctional in others, and they can function differently at different times. Families as systems may be able to care for the unique needs of one member but not another; they may be able to care for a member in some ways but not in other ways. They may be able to care for a member to a greater or lesser degree at this unique point in time, and that may be different from what it was in the past or will be in the future. Thinking in terms of gradient or scale is the idea that will enable family mediators to understand, empathize, and remain nonjudgmental yet discerning.

On each of Fogarty's twelve points, some members of a family may be better or worse off than others at this point. For example, a decision to have split custody may care for the needs of the father to be an active parent, while not supporting the need of one of the children or of the siblings together as a unit. Also, each member may have a different perspective relative to how well the family is doing this at any point in time. If you ask the divorcing family how well they are taking care of the needs of the child, the father may have a radically different view from that of the mother or the child; similarly, if you ask the members of a family trying to make decisions about an aging parent how the elder is able to care for herself independently, each member of the family might have a radically different view. This fact, since it is based on the different perceptions of all the members of the family, itself can be the source of family conflict.

Evaluating a family based on how well it functions to meet each member's needs assumes that such needs are able to be met within the resources of the family. This assumption breaks down when we think of cases where the needs of the individual are beyond the scope of the family. When teenagers need a positive peer group, a job for income, a positive personal and sexual relationship, and an opportunity to test themselves, it is not always within the power of the family to muster those resources. When a family needs to place an elder in a medical facility or reunite drug-affected parents with their children, it often runs headlong into social security, welfare, insurance, and financial rules and realities that make it impossible to meet that family member's needs. Families as systems are affected positively and negatively by larger societal systems. If the family responds to those outside resources and forces in certain ways, such as anger and frustration or delay, they can look dysfunctional, even when all they are trying to do is maintain what they perceive as an adequate balance or boundary.

The New Paradigm of Family Strengths

In summary, the concept of normalcy, functionality, and healthiness needs to be expansive enough to move the practice of family mediation into new paradigms. Family mediators must practice from a perspective that families are complex, dynamic systems that change constantly and cannot and should not be labeled based on only one factor or one task or one reaction. Family mediators who see the levels of normalcy, health, strength, and resilience in even the most troubled and conflicted families they encounter can bring that perspective to the family itself, and by doing so, change the level of awareness, which then will automatically change the family system. When family mediators can see what does work as well as what will not, they can share that with the family to promote the best response. This moves the family's view of itself as having problems to a view of capabilities and responsiveness to change.

DYNAMICS OF PERSONAL AND FAMILY DEVELOPMENT

While it is true that families operate as dynamic, changing systems that evolve over time and have internal processes that control the relationships within and the family's relationship with outside forces, it is also true that families comprise individuals who are also evolving and changing. In order for family mediators to work most effectively with families, it is imperative that they have at least a basic understanding of adult and child development, because it is happening within the context of the family life cycle. Parents in a custody dispute are often arguing over the "right" plan for their child, with little solid information about the needs, capacities, and problems for children of different ages. Parents themselves are growing and changing, and they may be unaware of the normalcy of their developmental urges and needs as a person in early adulthood, midlife, or approaching retirement. Family mediators who understand the normalcy of certain stages of development and dynamics that happen between family members can share these understandings with family members, changing their perception of the conflict.

The concepts of attachment, differentiation, and codependency are about how individuals within a family system develop themselves as individuals. Each of these dynamics may be functioning beneath the awareness of the individuals. The family members do not consciously want to have insecure attachments, to be incompletely differentiated, or to demonstrate codependency, and yet if these dynamics are present for members of the family, the conflict and its resolution will be affected by the dynamic.

Attachment Theory

Attachment theory is the developing branch of knowledge that crosses over child and adult development to study when and how we develop nurturing and appropriate social bonds of expectations and the resulting behaviors. This study started by looking at when and how children form emotional bonds with their caretakers and what happens when they are abandoned, are disappointed by, or lose their primary attachments to people (Bowlby, 1969, 1973, 1980, 1988). The history of the development of this theory is a fascinating story full of professional rivalries, competing ideologies, and disturbing findings that contradict our current social trends of care for children (Karen, 1994).

How Attachment Is Developed (or Not) in Children. Children learn to develop attachments to their caregivers at very early ages, since this is a survival-related activity. Researchers found that children form consistent patterns of behavior and that they exhibit these patterns when they are faced with new challenges. Because adult development is based on child development, these patterns tend to continue over the life of the individual, although they can be changed with conscious self-awareness and therapy.

Securely attached children form a secure base with their warm and sensitively attuned caregiver, who responds quickly to their needs, and so these children are able to be flexible and seek and get reassurance from the parent when in a strange situation. In preschool, they make friends easily and tolerate the separations needed from the caregiver, remaining open to new opportunities. By age six, they are warm and enthusiastic, able to relate and accept physical contact. In middle childhood, they form close friendships and appropriately join in larger groups. These children tend to turn into secure adults, who have access to the full range of their own feelings and memories and can work through negative experiences. They tend to have securely attached children, and they parent in the same way they were parented.

For *ambivalently attached children,* the caregiver is often unpredictable or chaotic, inattentive, or not very aware of their needs and feelings. These children cry a lot, seem clingy or demanding or angry, and do not tolerate separations. They tend not to explore the world. In a strange situation, they are difficult to soothe and give the caregiver the mixed message of wanting comfort yet being angry at that person. In preschool, these children are easily overcome by anxiety, can act immature, and may become victims of bullies or become overly dependent on the teacher. By age six, they can develop this confusing mixture of wanting intimacy and giving hostility into patterns of affected cuteness or people-pleasing behaviors. By middle childhood, there are patterns of difficulty in sustaining friendships or working cooperatively with peers. When they are adults, they often become *preoccupied adults,* who are still embroiled in the anger and hurt they have with their parents and are unable to take on responsibility in their own relationships. They tend to dread abandonment or lack of commitment in their adult relationships. They often have ambivalently attached children.

Avoidantly attached children have often been parented by a rejecting or emotionally unavailable parent who does not like the child's neediness or requires independence too soon. By the end of the first year, the child does not seek physical contact, is randomly angry toward the caregiver, and is unresponsive when held but does not want to be put down. When these children encounter strange situations, they do not seek help or support from the caregiver and cover their feelings or seem emotionally flat. By preschool, these children are often isolated, disliked, and aggressive or defiant. They withdraw when in pain and often hang around the teacher, who in turn can become controlling and angry at the child. By age six, these children continue to show no feeling and do not accept or give warm physical contact. By middle childhood, they are isolated; they are not accepted by the larger group and either have no friends or their friendships are characterized by intense jealousy. They often turn into a *dismissive adult,* who minimizes the importance of love and connection. They may idealize even abusive parents and have little self-reflection. They often have avoidantly attached children (Karen, 1994).

No matter how the research eventually classifies the disruptions of attachment, it is clear that when a secure attachment is not formed or when there are early separations and losses, profound effects occur in the development of the individual's view of how to form and maintain relationships later in life. These effects converge into patterns that can be detected and tend to continue over time for an individual.

An Internal Map of the World. According to attachment theory, children develop an internal, preverbal understanding about the world and the reliability and support they can expect based on these early interactions with their caregivers and the environment (Bretherton, 1990). This becomes their internal working model, which then becomes the pattern of expectation and response for future relationships with peers and larger systems. It becomes an almost self-fulfilling prophecy: a child who is securely attached expects all subsequent relationships to model after this, but if the child has problems, such as actual separation or loss of caregivers that creates anxiety, mourning, and rejection, then the expectation system becomes patterned to expect or even recreate these separations, losses, and rejections in subsequent relationships. "The working model is viewed as resistant to change, particularly if interactions with the caregiver were negative, as defensive processes are instituted to maintain the view that the relationship with the caregiver was adequate" (Levitt, Coffman, Guacci-Franco, and Loveless, 1994, pp. 237–238). Because this internal working model is so deeply embedded in the person, it tends to be consistent over the life of the person.

A Secure Base. The task of the parents and other caregivers in all stages of the child's development is to provide the child with "a secure base from which a child or an adolescent can make sorties into the outside world and to which he can return knowing for sure he will be welcomed when he gets there, nourished physically and emotionally, comforted if distressed, reassured if frightened. . . . Yet should one or the other parent become ill or die, the immense significance of the base to the emotional equilibrium of the child or adolescent or young adult is at once apparent" (Bowlby, 1988, p. 11).

Although many families instinctively know that this is the ideal, they have been unable to provide that secure base consistently over the life of the children in the family. When families have experienced major traumas from outside forces, such as discrimination, emigration, acculturation, violence, war, natural disaster, or internal problems such as domestic abuse, drug and alcohol issues, or mental illness, these factors can influence the child's and the family's collective level of security and attachment.

The extent to which the family and caregivers of infants and children are able to provide this secure base determines the level of personal resilience and personal emotional and social interactional patterns and security for children. "It is not difficult to understand why patterns of attachment, once developed, tend to persist. One reason is that the way a parent treats a child, whether for better or worse, tends to continue unchanged; another is that each pattern tends to be self-perpetuating." (Bowlby, 1988, p. 168). Secure children are easier and more rewarding to attend, while an anxiously ambivalent child is whiny and clingy and an anxiously avoidant child is difficult to parent due to his or her negative, bullying behavior. Each of these children then co-create with the parent an interactional cycle that becomes the usual relationship pattern and emotional expectation.

The Child Within the Adult. This interactional pattern of emotional security or insecurity is true not only for children in the current family but also for adults who are no longer living with their family of origin. "The pathways followed by each developing individual and the extent to which he or she becomes resilient to stressful life events is determined to a very significant degree by the pattern of attachment he or she develops during the early years" (Bowlby, 1988, p. 172–173).

Family mediators must remember that the ambivalently attached child can still be functioning emotionally inside the functioning adult. Recent studies have shown a close correlation between these early childhood attachment categories and the types of attachments people form as adults. Some theorists propose that people's choices of mates are to some degree influenced by the type of attachment they had as a child and what they have grown to expect. Adults' behavior in relationships is also affected by the level of security they feel in themselves and in the current relationship. Since a relationship is by definition a dyad, both partners bring to the couple their own level of inner security, ambivalence, and avoidance. The individual's internal working model—the internal schema that is based on the childhood and adolescent attachment level—filters and interprets information about the suitability of forming or maintaining a current relationship. That internal working model also interprets what is going on during the interactions in formed couples and families. An individual who came from a secure base will react differently to an event in the current couple or family than if he has ambivalent or avoidant attachment orientation in his past.

There is a major difference between adult-to-child interaction in the parent-child dyad compared to the adult-to-adult interaction in couples and families.

In the former, the adult's behavior helps create and maintain the child's internal working model, and the relationship is expected to be a unilateral, one-way street of giving and caring for the child without expectation of equal return from the child. In adult-to-adult relationships, both parties already have a solid internal working model based on their past, and they usually expect to have some responsibilities to provide caregiving to the partner as well as to receive caregiving, protection, and nurturance in return from their partner. The expectation is for reciprocity, so the two-way nature of adult relationships requires that both be able to comfort and be comforted. If one member of the couple is unable to respond to the other at times of stress due to anxious fears or emotional withdrawal patterns learned in early life, the couple will have more stress and conflict. Relationships where one person becomes the sole or ongoing parent-like caregiver and nurturer to the other partner, with no reciprocity, are usually not healthy. Patterns of insecurity and avoidance by one or both of the couple are usually counterproductive.

Similarly, families with adult children can have vast differences between the levels of secure base among the adult children simply because their experience of the family was so different due to external factors. Although they are brothers and sisters and lived in the same family, some siblings may have experienced their mother as providing a secure base and had no separations or losses, while others did not and lived in a very different family emotionally. Often, these separations and losses of parents due to illness, family emergencies, and external factors are forgotten by the siblings who felt secure, but are very present for the insecure or avoidant sibling who is still being affected by the results in his or her internal working model. Families who are experiencing conflict between adult children can still be playing out unconscious insecure or avoidant patterns with their siblings and aging parents.

Triggers of Attachment Issues. There are several life situations and concomitant emotional reactions that bring out either the inner security or the ambivalent or avoidant behavior that an adult learned as a child. When adults perceive that there is danger or threat to self or the others they care about or when there is potential for loss of proximity or responsiveness from the person they have grown attached to, they usually will respond from the level of attachment they had as children; if they were securely attached, they will be more resilient as adults.

For example, when a spouse or girlfriend is trying to leave the relationship, when a fairly long departure is required for work or due to illness, or when there is lack of accessibility to the partner for any reason, adults can lapse into very old insecurity-based behavior. If the partner is not there to provide the secure base or comfort for the insecurely attached member of the couple, the question becomes whether that person can use self-comforting behavior and change the pattern of insecurity. Any threat of separation or loss, or sense of danger to the relationship or self can lead to a full-blown anxiety reaction by one or both of the members.

A person who finds a partner and becomes part of a couple might form an anxious romantic attachment, which often includes strong insecurity, sexual jealousy, and even obsessive behavior. This is an adult form of the emotional dependency and clinging behavior similar to the ambivalently attached pattern of children. Researchers such as Julie Rothbard and Phillip Shaver (1994), Nigel Roberts and Patricia Noller (1998), and Kate Henry and John Holmes (1998) have tried to see what factors are predictive of this pattern in adults, and the findings are consistent with the basic premise of attachment theory: that the early experiences in the family of origin are still operating beneath the attempts of adults to find and maintain couples and families, and to some degree determine whether the current adult relationships will be stable, domestically violent, or emotionally satisfying.

Any current loss or separation can rekindle seemingly healed old wounds for adults. For many adults, the thought of divorce or separation from their current partner or their children engenders a huge crisis that indicates a need for therapeutic help and support to cope with the loss. Couples may find that the patterns of security and insecurity show up when the couple has conflicts, because they predict that this may lead to separation and loss.

The existence of any conflict can be a highly anxious time for couples when one or both of the partners have insecure attachment issues from the past or with each other. When couples have conflicts, they can find themselves trying to end the conflict by accommodating the partner to resolve the conflict or by withdrawing from the conflict, which can lead to increased anxiety by the other. They may become more dominating in an effort to take back control and power, which unchecked can lead to hostility, abuse, and violence. When researchers tested whether attachment is related to couple violence, they found that "both men and women were more likely to use violence against partners if they, themselves, feared abandonment, and women were also more likely to use violence against partners who were anxious over abandonment" (Roberts and Noller, 1998, p. 335). Even strategic small withdrawals meant to reduce conflict and tension in the relationship can become the occasion for couples to interpret such behavior from the lens of insecure attachment, and thus ironically increase the likelihood of abuse that really will lead to a reduction in commitment and long-term attachment.

Similarly, the withdrawal of teenagers from the family unit can bring on increased tension and even abuse and violence, triggering insecure or avoidant attachment behavior by the parents and the children who are involved. The healthy, age-appropriate need of adolescents to separate themselves from the parents can again bring to the light the insecure or avoidant reaction of the parents, who are reacting more out of their own insecurities than the child's needs. An adolescent who will not detach appropriately when it is time to leave home can also be showing the clinging behavior characteristic of earlier attachment issues.

Attachment and bonding are created in our first families by the interactions we had with our parents and other caregivers. The patterns are very deep and can influence the rest of our interactions as we become part of a couple and form our own families. Family conflicts bring insecurity, which can open huge wounds from the past and can be highly triggering patterns of avoidance and insecure behavior. The family conflict throws everyone back to the base level of intrapersonal security, or lack of it.

The Effect of Attachment on Bargaining in Mediation. When family mediators are dealing with family conflicts, they need to understand that each person in the conflict has a different level of inner security, often developed by the very people with whom they are now in dispute. Family members are often unaware of their own or their partner's deep patterns of emotional response, even though it is operating. Each person has an internal working model that functions like a turtle's shell—a place they come from and retreat to when under stress.

Activation of those attachment response patterns can create seemingly unpredictable bargaining and positions. In an example, when grandparents get involved in their adult child's custody and parenting dispute, the stress of the threat of loss of grandchildren can trigger deep emotional insecurities and activate the avoidant responses or the anxious ambivalence they feel rather than a more balanced, logical response to the situation. In parent-teen mediation cases, the teenager may still be responding out of the ongoing emotional withdrawal stance to parents who were not emotionally available to the teenager when he was a young child. The past is always with us and part of us, and it continues to operate covertly until we are able to acknowledge it and decide whether this is the response we choose to make in a given circumstance.

Because these are learned response patterns, there is hope that parents, couples, and families who are acting out old insecure or avoidant emotional patterns can change these to be more appropriate. Family members have learned to expect certain behaviors and reactions from each other, often based on these very early and continuing patterns of interaction over years of family life.

The possibility for change in behavioral patterns exists. Family members can have transformative experiences in family mediation often because the setting allows them to convey their anxiety and fear of separation and loss in new and more socially acceptable ways, which can form the basis for agreement.

When mediators voice the deep longing and need to avoid loss that is present under hardened positions, that action of giving voice in a different way often dispels the need for the old behavior to continue. As agents of change, family mediators can help family members understand in a different way what the needs are and see if parents and children, couples, and other family members are ready to change these old patterns. When they do, a new sense of interpersonal security can be developed to replace the anxious attachment or emotional blunting that has preceded the mediation event. Change of even deep levels of personal attachment and security can and does happen as part of the mediation effort when family members can recognize and accept their own past and make choices for the future to become the adult they wish to be.

Differentiation

The concept of differentiation, which originated with Bowen (1978) as part of his family systems perspective, speaks to a person's ability to use reason and solid self to maintain separateness even during highly reactive and emotional times. Rather than reacting to the other partner's discomfort or demand, differentiated marital partners are able to maintain their own emotional stance relative to the issue. They do not get sucked into the other person's annoyance, frustration, or anxiety. "The goal of Bowen's therapy became the differentiation of self of key family members, so they could help the whole family differentiate. This emphasis on differentiation, meaning control of reason over emotion, betrays Bowen's psychoanalytic roots" (Nichols and Schwartz, 2000, p. 123).

Family mediators can find this concept very useful in framing their formulations or hypotheses regarding members of families. A husband and wife who are well differentiated can tolerate the other person's feelings without sharing them. As full selves, they are able to experience themselves as separate, capable people. Poorly differentiated partners tend to be like half-selves who have formed a symbiotic relationship. If one feels angry and upset, the other becomes equally upset and angry. This dynamic often plays out in couples who married or started living together very early, before they had formed a full self. Mediators may also find this problem of poor differentiation when they are dealing with individuals who have experienced major disruption in their family of origin or experienced major trauma such as abuse early in life. Because their growth and development were interrupted at a critical stage, their lack of development or capacity leads them to seek and find partners at similar levels of differentiation. With the possible exception of very young couples who are simply immature, family therapists find that if one member of a couple is at a certain level of personal development and differentiation, so is the other.

Growth Creates Conflict. Individuals and couples can and do grow and increase their level of development and differentiation with conscious self-awareness and some support. This takes courage and perseverance to refrain from falling back into old behaviors and patterns associated with poor differentiation, such as being highly reactive to minor complaints of the partner or other family members. Some benefit greatly from therapy as instructive support while they try to make changes in this pattern. Often when a person recognizes this pattern and starts to change it, the change leads to an unequal state between the partners, which can be very difficult on the relationship. Many times the spouse making the change can no longer tolerate the other spouse's dependency and response and starts pulling away from the marriage. At this point, if the less differentiated spouse cannot or will not change, the growing spouse may decide to divorce in order to extricate herself from the other spouse, who remains less differentiated. It's not just in divorce mediation cases where the level of differentiation may make a difference in the mediation effort. If one or both of the parents in a family are poorly differentiated, they cannot help the children with this task and cannot model the process.

This issue of the level of differentiation of each person in a dispute is also a factor in family mediation cases involving children and parents, such as in dependency cases, adoption, and family reunification after abuse or neglect. Understanding the dynamics of how the parent's level of differentiation is affecting the conflict will give the mediator great insight. If the parent is not well differentiated, the child or children are often treated as objects or possessions to be gained or lost. The undifferentiated parent cannot separate his own needs from the needs of his child and may bargain inappropriately or make terrible parenting decisions as a result.

Differentiation Affects Negotiation. Parents with a low level of differentiation tend to project onto the child their own wishes and feelings rather than see the child as separate from themselves. They often form enmeshed relationships with children, who become caretakers to and for the parent. The unhealthy message is that the parent needs the child to meet the parent's needs, rather than the other way around. This message is conveyed overtly or covertly. The "need to be needed" message is so strong that it often forms a codependency for the child or an unhealthy triangular relationship with the child stuck at the center. If the parent needs the child in the home for the parent's own narcissistic or physical needs and relies too heavily on the child in ways that do not allow the child to focus on his own needs, this situation prevents the child from doing the necessary age-appropriate differentiation and development. When this happens, we see children acting as the functional decision maker and caretaker, a status that has been called the *parentified child.*

When children are the power brokers of the family or when they do most of the instrumental or emotional tasks, they and the parents are maintaining an unhealthy dependency. This forms what Bowen (1978) called an "undifferentiated ego mass" state, where everyone speaks and feels for everyone else and each is like a shadow of the other. Each person is unable to function separately without the other symbiotic partner. Dynamics like these need to change for every person's growth and development in the system.

Codependency

A member of a family who is fragile emotionally or not well differentiated may experience great distress and anxiety at any mediated solution that would provide levels of independence and power to the others in the dispute, such as a child or spouse. If the family member had problems during childhood and has insecure attachment issues, this often creates the conditions where family members hold on tighter when they fear loss or emotional pain. Also, a family member who is codependent will believe he must rescue all other members from any negative feelings, must be open and available at all times and in all ways, and will be ignoring his own needs for stability and reliability from others. Codependent people say they want change from the other but, paradoxically, do not allow them to change. They want responsibility from the other but support and reward irresponsibility. They most often do not see their own role in maintaining the homeostatic condition of the family until they recognize their role and function as the codependent.

Overfunctioning and Underfunctioning. In alcohol- and drug-affected family systems, we usually see this problem of codependency. The person with the drug or alcohol problem unconsciously and covertly entraps the others in a web of helping that enables and supports the problematic behavior. The person with the problem often becomes more dysfunctional in order to draw others in and to keep the others involved with him, even if the involvement and interaction seem negative. In this strange way, codependent behavior is functional because it helps the person better meet his needs by using external resources and people. Many books and programs such as Al-Anon and Alateen are aimed at helping family members and children recognize these patterns of interaction that foster helplessness and dependency. (More will be discussed on how to work with drug-affected family systems in Chapter Five.)

Patterns of codependency are systems dynamics that can be learned and unlearned in families that are not experiencing drug and alcohol concerns. Patterns of over- and underreaction, of being irresponsible and rescuing, are not exclusive to drug abusers. Finding a balance point between over- and underinvolvement, between helping and taking over, between cutting off entirely or being too involved, is a struggle to find appropriate interdependence, a goal for healthy and functional family systems. Finding that balance point for any member of a family can be a struggle.

Codependency is not helpful to the individuals involved because it robs the underresponding persons of their chance to make it on their own, and it keeps the helper more entwined than is necessary. Codependent patterns are learned behaviors and changeable dynamics, and so they can be modified by awareness, information, and practicing new skills by either or both of the parties involved.

For example, a diabetic child who uses diet and insulin to control her disease needs specialized care by parents when she is young to ensure that she eats proper amounts and types of food at the right intervals. Families must adapt to the special needs of the child. As the child develops, a healthy family will put more and more of the responsibility for controlling her food intake and doing the insulin injections on the child as she is ready to take on the task.

Families that stay stuck, who do not pass these tasks to the most appropriate parties, can unwittingly develop learned helplessness and codependency issues, where parents become overresponsible and overcontrolling of the child to prevent problems, and the child becomes underresponsible by undermining the diet or control of the parents. These same codependency dynamics can happen in situations of elderly parents and their caregivers, or divorced families between the parents and their new partners in two households. A hallmark of codependency is when the person being overly burdened and used is still actively making excuses for the other person, is not honoring her own boundaries, and is feeling resentful or even vindictive toward the person she is helping while she bends over backward to help that other party. Many family conflicts involve these dynamics.

When codependency occurs, the goal of personal change for the member is to help the family members reject inappropriate roles and functions and understand and respect their own boundaries so they can demand this of the other party who is acting irresponsibly. Having the codependent person change her responses to the other person's irresponsibility and helplessness makes change within the system dynamic. When one member of the family stops supporting the inappropriate dependency and irresponsibility of the other, the system must change, and the irresponsible behavior becomes less functional to the maintenance of the system as it had been.

The Goal: A Full and Healthy Self in Relationship to Others. The need to change from a codependent stance to a differentiated, empowered, and interdependent stance is the essence of the full realization of the self within the context of the family system. A good example of this dynamic and its resolution comes from a common problem in custody and visitation mediation. When a parent continually picks up the child very late or does not show up at all, the usual response by the child is distress, worry, or emotional rejection of the tardy parent, along with anger or disruptive behavior toward the custodial parent. Being left or continually experiencing abandonment contributes to insecure attachment issues for the child, so naturally the custodial parent wants the problem to stop. The custodial parent is understandably upset also. He does not want the child to suffer the disappointment, nor does he want to experience the consequences of his former wife's irresponsibility or maintain a codependent relationship. The parent in this situation often says that he wants to change the situation by either preventing the visitations completely, to avoid the conflict, or by trying to get the irresponsible parent to become more responsible by cajoling or creating negative sanctions when she is late.

When the divorced family as a system recognizes the problem and stops acting codependent as a system, they stop covering for or excusing the parent's inability to pick up the child reliably and on time. This helps the child see the reality of the irresponsibility, and the child often has an emotional reaction to that irresponsibility, which helps him learn and grow. If the custodial parent stops acting codependent, he stops protecting the child from the hurt of not being picked up and also stops protecting the visiting parent from receiving the consequences of the child's reaction in their relationship. The parent neither overreacts nor underreacts to the situation, but instead helps the child cope with his feelings and does not buffer the visiting parent or vindictively try to hurt her.

In this way, the parent's lateness or abandonment no longer becomes a codependency issue of conflict between the parents, even though it remains a challenging situation that needs to be solved for the family system. A custodial parent who cannot get the visiting parent to make active change must make change himself. Changing his own response is often the only thing he has any control over. When that control is applied to controlling his internal response and his response to the child, instead of attempting to make excuses for or control the irresponsible parent, the conflict and the family change and the codependency issue evaporates. The custodial parent may still be annoyed with his former wife, but he can do other things about this than he could if he were maintaining a codependent stance. For example, he can attempt to mediate from a healthy, empowered stance and change the visitation expectation to something that is more likely to work for the visiting parent and the child. This is a perfect example of how a different response to events by one member of the family can change the entire family pattern and dynamic.

Family members in healthy, functional families have the right to have separate responses and realize that they are not in control of the other members. They work on their own individual responses and empowerment rather than trying to control the responses of others. For many families, this concept is new. When the family mediator helps the parties in dispute sort out their past patterns of individual response and helps them decide whether they are operating from their own sphere of influence and personal power, the family members can then make a choice as to whether they wish to respond differently even if they cannot appear to change the others in the conflict.

This orientation to helping disputants see the dispute differently and understanding their own power base is common in mediation practice, but in family mediation, it often takes the form of reflecting the codependencies of the past, with the question for change. Family mediators cannot and should not be telling their clients what needs to change, since their highest ethical principle is client self-determination. When the family mediator asks questions to examine the patterns of codependency and response by the individuals, the family members can make their own choices as to whether change is needed.

ALLIANCES, LEGACIES, AND SECRETS

All families have some jokes, myths, speech patterns, history, and nonverbal patterns that they share that are unique to the family, usually created by the high levels of intimacy and shared experiences. Most families also find that there are some natural groupings that just seem to happen among the family members, because of age, interests, generation, or personal affinity. Although it is normal and functional for families to create subsets of family members and although there are naturally occurring and positive affiliations and groupings within families (such as "the parents" and "the children," "the girls" and "the guys," or "the younger kids" and "the older kids"), groupings sometimes become part of a more dysfunctional or negative subset of the family system. When this happens, alliances with and coalitions against others have formed. Family systems theory describes how and why these alliances form and in what way they serve the needs of the family.

Triangulation: The Dynamics of Threes

Two family members who are in conflict tend to pull others into their situation to defend themselves, buffer the conflict, create strength in numbers, and provide more stability. If a father and son are in conflict, one or both of them will often try to pull the mother into the fray. Brothers who disagree on what to do about their aging parent will try to convince the sister of the rightness of their position. Children who do not like their new stepfather band together to create problems, testing to see if their mother will jump in to stand by them or maintain solidarity with the stepfather. The struggle is for power and control. This is the concept of *triangulation,* which is the term given to triads that are formed by bringing others into the conflict in negative patterns to try to gain help and support. Triangulation is done by the parties on an unconscious level rather than as the active step of going to a designated third party.

Not all triangular relationships are negative. Triangles are also naturally forming occurrences and serve social and culturally supported functions, such as the primary mother-father-child threesome. In many organizations and professions, the concept of the mentor underlies a helpful and socially supported threesome that also includes a boss and an employee. In professional development, graduate students rely on their supervisor-supervisee dyadic relationship to form the active and positive third element to the work environment. Threesomes can in many ways be positive experiences in families too, with grandparents who know how to take an appropriate and supportive third seat in teaching and developing children. However, conflicts brought to family mediators more usually contain the negative patterns involved in triangulated relationships.

Forming Triads from Dyads. Dyads tend to bring in third parties in the search for stability and harmony. When dyads are strained, the original conflict resides within them. The stress of these dyads grows so great that the participants then find a willing (or unaware or unwilling) third person to enter the conflict and create the stabilizing triangle. In marital conflict, the unhappy wife has an affair or calls a former boyfriend, bringing some level of comfort to one side of the equation while bringing distress to the dyad or the other party.

The inclusion of a third person in the conflict can serve to mitigate the conflict or exacerbate it. The third person tries to provide balance. Both sides tell their dilemma and feelings to the third, who then soothes and calms both or takes sides and performs some function for the conflict. Some parties are brought in to serve the role of intercessor, which has strong cultural and even religious backing. In different cultures, that role may be taken on by various people, depending on the cultural expectations of the society. For example, aunts and uncles, godparents, the priest or rabbi, the village headman, or the grandparent often serve as informal or formal mediators in many cultures.

In North American culture today, people in conflict go to therapists and other helping professionals, clergy, friends, or their attorney. Court-appointed and private sector mediators have become part of the list of options in the past twenty-five years. The judicial system supports the use of mediation for this function, especially since the informal and traditional roles are often missing or unavailable for sizable percentages of the population.

Whoever is selected and by whatever means the society provides, that person becomes the family mediator—the helpful third party brought in to stabilize the conflict.

Mediators as Positive Third Parties. Family mediators form the third party in the situation, but in healthy and supportive ways rather than the negative, collusive way that is meant by the term *triangulation*:

> In contrast to triangulation, clear triad formation is intentional, methodical, and purposive. The participants know that the triad is a temporary arrangement designed to clarify and strengthen the dyadic relationship through reconciliation of its difficulties so that a third party will be unnecessary and undesirable. The

third person of a triad is committed to neutrality, to availability to each person, to flexibility in offering interventions, and to equal justice for all concerned. Effective mediators, who can form triads without triangulation, are recognized by disputants in every culture. The wise person who can maintain a median position and mediate from the centered stance is prized, honored, and trusted, whether in Asia or Africa, Australia, or the many cultures of Latin America. [Augsberger, 1992, p. 154]

Because families may have used triangulation as their usual conflict resolution strategy, they may unconsciously try to get the family mediator to collude or create an unhealthy alliance with him or her. It is important for family mediators to understand that some families will not even be aware of their attempts to collude with the mediator or each other, because it is so ingrained as a personal, family, or socially supported dynamic.

It is very important that family mediators themselves not be drawn into the conflict or form coalitions with one client against the other—and yet it is natural for families to try to put family mediators into this role, since by definition and function, the family mediator *is* the third person in the room. When family mediators are aware of the healthy and unhealthy use of the third-party role, aware of the differences between positive triads and negative triangulation, and aware of how a mediator may be co-opted to form unbalanced alignments, it is more likely that the mediator can avoid ethical and process errors.

Unhealthy Triangles and Coalitions. According to Jay Haley (1991), a leading family therapist, when families maintain unhealthy or "perverse" triangles, it is a setup for continuing conflict. We find that such dynamics coincide with the negative consequences of conflict, such as abuse and violence, acting out, and other forms of negative behavior by individuals within the system, and even disruption and demise of the family system itself.

In Haley's terminology, an alliance is a bonding between two people for reasons of affinity or mutuality. Two people in the family feel similar due to personality, common interests, or other factors. An alliance is a joining, not an exclusion. Alliances can be naturally occurring or formed for specific strategic reasons. They can be secret or open, are usually based on mutual interests, and need not have a third member involved. For example, a grandchild and a grandparent may form an alliance because both like to watch baseball. The intent and purpose is not to exclude others but to maximize their own interests. Those two might advocate together for baseball tickets if the family is making vacation plans.

Coalitions, in contrast, are bonds between family members in order to exclude a third person. They are bonds that form to provide exclusion. These then become a "perverse triangle," according to Haley, because the intent and process is negative. A coalition has the following characteristics:

- It contains two people from the same level in the hierarchy, and one person from a different level or generation (a father and mother, and a son).

- The two who are in the coalition are on different levels, against the third. (The father and son against the mother; or the mother and son against the father).

- The existence of the coalition must remain hidden, and behavior that indicates its existence will be denied. [Hoffman, 1981, p. 108]

Rigid Triangles and Deflecting the Conflict. In the 1970s, Salvador Minuchin, a seminal thinker in the field of family therapy, saw problems when he encountered families with rigid triads. When working with families where the children were exhibiting psychosomatic disorders, such as asthma, diabetes, and anorexia nervosa, he often found that the children were being used by the parents to deflect or obscure the conflict between their parents. Minuchin analyzed four patterns of such rigid triangles:

- *Triangulation,* where the child has positive bonds with each parent but is stuck in a loyalty conflict and becomes the focus of each parent's attention, because they maintain a conflict between themselves by excluding each other

- *Parent-child coalition,* where the child and parent collude to leave the other parent out

- *Detouring-attacking triad,* where the parents blame the child as bad and band together to control the child, but often disagree between themselves how to do this

- *The detouring-supportive triad,* where the parents mask their differences by showing overprotective concern and focusing in on a child labeled as sick (Hoffman, 1981, pp. 150–151)

These patterns of negative triads are generalizable to many conflict situations, not just parent-child conflicts. Grandparents stuck in a bitter custody battle with their adult children form a triangle that often follows one of these negative triangulation patterns, although it need not do so.

These early studies formed the basis of what has been called structural family therapy, and the work of Cloé Madanes (1991) and others has looked at examples of these unhealthy family connections from what has been called the strategic perspective. Both structural and strategic family therapy models try to intervene on negative interactional patterns that have become rigid system rules or bind family members to unhealthy alliances or negative triangles or roles within the family. "One set of goals for strategic family therapy is to help people past a crisis to the next stage of family life" (Madanes, 1991, p. 20). By changing the sequence of reactions and adding more complexity and alternatives to each member of the family, a strategic family therapist changes the way in which the family system plays out its problems.

The task of the family mediator is to recognize the patterns that might be operating in the dispute and see if some level of intervention by the mediator, as the positive, intentional, temporary third party, can help unstick the parties. The mediator can change the interactional patterns and roles by bringing them to everyone's awareness.

Acting Out of Control in Order to Control the Situation. Suppose a child develops symptoms and problems when she feels insecure about her parents' conflicts or threat of separation, and in response, the parents minimize the conflict or the threat in order to deal with their daughter's acting out. But once the child starts to act more normal and stable, the parents return to the conflict or imminent divorce. As a result, the child quickly learns to act out of control or symptomatic in order to maintain the equilibrium of the family. This can also be true in other family relationships—for example, when an ill or ailing parent's symptoms suddenly become worse when adult children quarrel.

The dynamic of acting out is similar to triangulation but is done in the interactional realm. Instead of putting the conflicted person between two other people, as in triangulation and coalitions, this dynamic puts the conflicted person between two equally important but mutually exclusive requirements, each with strong negative consequences. The dynamic can represent a tortured and impossible "Sophie's choice" of family interaction, as in the film *Sophie's Choice,* in which the protagonist must choose to save only one of her children from death at the hands of the Nazis. The dynamic forces the conflicted person, often the child, to choose between personally healthy behaviors or keeping the family together. The person is in effect triangulated between what he or she is overtly supposed to do that is positive and covertly supposed to do that is negative; either option brings unfortunate results for the person or the family. For many, this becomes an impossible choice. Because the inner conflict is acted out in observable, problematic behavior, the family may well present the conflicted person to the family mediator as the source of the conflict.

In unhealthy and highly troubled families, the very structure or social construction of the family requires the child (or even the parent) to act out in order to keep everyone together. The child (or other family member) performs the assigned role, even though it is not helpful to him personally. The family system seems to require that someone become the symptom bearer or the officially sick or black sheep member of the family in order for the family to continue. In some very troubled family systems, if the designated problem bearer becomes healthier and is no longer willing to act out his or her part in the drama, then the family will induct another family member into this now-empty role, because the system is constructed in such a way that someone must perform this function.

Family mediators may well be faced with families whose conflict dynamics include this level of negativity. When they recognize it, they can often help the family by getting the members the therapy they need. The family therapist can intervene, and the family will not need to reproduce the same dynamic for another member of the family. Although family mediators need not become family therapists, it is important to understand these negative dynamics enough so that they can get the family to the resource that is required.

Vicious Patterns and Vendettas. In some families, one parent tries to form a coalition with a child against the other parent. Johnston and Roseby (1997) have written eloquently regarding the dynamics and treatment implications of several forms of negative patterns that are often triangular in nature, such as parental alienation syndrome, children caught in loyalty struggles, and high-conflict families. These forms of divorce problems show this negative triangulation process in its most vicious form. Coalitions and alliances have often formed before the mediator is asked to enter the conflict, and they are now the dynamic underlying the manifest conflict or the dispute that was referred for mediation. The triangulation and alliance-coalition system dynamic is a deeper layer of the conflict that must be dealt with if family mediation is to have any long-lasting effect on families caught in these dynamics.

The family mediator needs to be able to recognize when a family has pre-existing patterns of interaction that have become so ingrained as to be unconscious and operating covertly. When these alliances and coalitions, dyads and triads are functioning, the family members often show problems that they do not seem to recognize. Simple problem-solving approaches to conflicts are doomed to fail unless these deep patterns of interaction are brought to the light. A family mediator who does not understand the alliances, coalitions, and history of conflict within the family will miss an important dimension that can either be harnessed to help the family change or will be used as an excuse and rationale for noncompliance with mediated agreements. Seeing these patterns underneath the presenting problems is like being able to see the skeleton inside a person with an X ray. These are the deep structures that hold the family up in some ways and down in others. When family members make new decisions in mediated conflicts, the pull of old alliances and coalitions may be overpowering unless the mediator can help the family members bring them to conscious awareness and determine whether and how to change them.

Legacies—Positive and Negative

The concept of legacy is important in understanding the multidimensional and multigenerational nature of families. Legacies are what we are bequeathed by the former generation that are either sufficient to support us or are burdens. They come to us as rules and ways of doing things, which we mostly got from our parents and other family members. Because so much of life is learned from our experiences, our parents, as our first teachers, brought their own parents into the child-rearing process. If the now-adult parents were spanked as children, then it is likely they will spank their children. The culture of the family, separate from the larger cultural context in which it exists in society, is handed down in this social learning process within the family unit, through modeling, identification, and overt teaching.

When the interactions in the current family are not working or when there is a lot of conflict and chaos in a family, it can be very confusing to the family. One parent may well blame the other, who brings a very different family legacy. When family conflicts are brought to the mediator, each side has hardened its position and presents its actions and methods as the right ones. There is often little room for making new choices, as each demands to fall back on the past.

For example, if a couple has conflicts over discipline methods or bedtime routines, sometimes the solution is a simple matter of making a mutually acceptable blend of both parents' expectations and practices. The current family creates its own unique blend of his and hers, perhaps by consulting the latest book by the current well-known child development specialist or enlisting the help and support from other acceptable authorities, such as school personnel, doctors, and trusted friends. In healthy families, this identification of problems, seeking resources, and open negotiation *is* the legacy, because they saw their parents do this. Other parents caught in the same dilemma may not have a rich legacy on which to draw. Their parents were absentee, inconsistent, or self-absorbed, or they had power and control issues that prevented them from consulting with others or accepting influence from others.

Patterns of interaction are part of the legacy we receive from our original family. How the family of origin treated people inside and outside the family, handled conflicts (or did not), raised children, handled money, and what they valued are all part of the complex mix of the legacy for each of the family members. When the conflict, such as a marital conflict or blended family problem, is between current family members who did not come from the same family of origin, it is very tempting for the disputants to see the conflict as a black-and-white struggle between the respective families. Young couples conflicted about parenting responsibilities can discount any advice or support from the other parent's extended family members. The conflict can be framed as an us-versus-them dispute.

When the conflict is within a family of origin, such as siblings trying to decide how to deal with their aging or ill parent, the dispute is often framed as a dispute between the upholder of the family values versus the traitor, and family members can take on the characteristics of the seemingly disparate family values and methods that were the family legacy. For example, if all the siblings saw their father get angry to get his way and the mother try to pacify and give in, this pattern of interaction is the family legacy. In a dispute, it is likely that some of the siblings will take the angry bluster role, while others will take the placating self-sacrificer role. When family members have seldom or never thought about their meanings and values, interpretations and interactions, they may tend to operate out of them without full awareness.

Another form of legacy everyone receives from his or her original family is emotional rather than interactive. Because people build their self-concept and view of the world in their families first, then later in their schools and activities and larger community, concepts of shame, worth, and respect for self and others are also part of the legacy. These feelings about self and other can be severely affected by poverty, immigration and acculturation factors, trauma, and other external social and economic factors and the meaning that the family places on those realities. Examining the emotional legacy each participant carries can help the disputants understand their own and the other person's thoughts and beliefs.

The goal of understanding family legacies is to support the current family members to remember their own legacy, respect and find out about the legacy of the others involved in the dispute, and make choices about whether to follow the patterns and choices dictated by the legacy. In order to help disputants have full self-determination in mediation, they must be free to accept or reject some parts of their own legacy as well as that of the other disputant in order to make fully informed and self-aware choices during the mediation process.

Family Secrets: The Elephant in the Room

Family conflicts often involve the darkest parts of family life. Unacceptable feelings and behaviors are packed away by family members in a remarkable process of selective forgetting and personal and collective amnesia. Unacceptable events and behavior, by others toward the self and by the self toward others, become covered over by mental and emotional processes as self-protection. Over the years, the concepts promulgated by Freud and other psychologists about defense mechanisms—those ways of covering and keeping material unconscious—have become widely known in the general population. People involved in family conflicts are often well versed enough in these concepts to accuse or judge each other as using defensive processes, such as projection (ascribing the unacceptable behavior, thought, or feeling to others), sublimation (taking the unacceptable urges and modifying them to serve a socially useful status), and denial.

People use various ways to cover their own awareness of unacceptability. It is so common to hear each person in a conflict defend himself or herself and his or her actions and blame the other person, at least initially, that it is almost unnecessary to state this obvious fact. The secret material by definition must remain underground. The usual way is to minimize or deny the problem, conflict, or the person's own involvement in the behavior or event. The unacceptable material—whether a thought, urge, feeling, intention, or actual behavior—is kept covert, and it is therefore unable to be examined and discussed openly by the one who did it or the one who witnessed it or was the recipient or victim.

Thinking errors, or the reconstruction of reality in order to preserve a positive self-image, are typical of those who are keeping secrets. Typical personal defenses against the truth include not only open denial and minimization, but also reaching to higher authorities, such as regulations, laws, rights, religious invectives and mandates, or prevalent beliefs that support the unacceptable. People also blame the victim and do character assassination against the victim that justifies their actions. In their work with divorcing parents, Johnston and Campbell (1988) called this process the "vilification of the other" and found that divorcing spouses often did this re-creation of the marital story because they needed to explain to families and themselves why it was so bad that they had to make the decision to divorce and uproot the children. Some people in conflict create the rationale for their actions and thoughts by blaming external forces, such as poverty and racism, or they blame their parents or the lack of social or economic opportunity. They can also go through a complex set of rationalizations that tell the story differently and explain that what they did was not really a violation or an unacceptable behavior but instead a way of helping. Sexual abusers often tell themselves and their victims the remade story that they are not abusing, just helping the victim enter into the realm of sexuality in the best of all possible ways. Thinking errors like these often go hand in hand with thinking failures, such as the inability to understand or empathize with the victim and the failure to have compassion.

When one or more of the participants in mediation is engaged in this kind of behavior during the session, it is clear that they are not feeling ready to take personal accountability. Because mediation requires some level of personal accountability, as well as the kind of climate that is conducive to full disclosure, there can be great tension for one or more family members to tell or not tell. Ambivalence is often maintained until the disputant believes he or she is both ready to divulge and will have no negative repercussions for doing so from either the family mediator or the other participants in mediation.

Kottler (1996) describes the process people must go through when they choose to release the other from this blame and take more personal accountability. The fact that almost everyone starting family mediation engages in some of these thinking errors and tries to keep some material hidden speaks to the inherent need for not only confidential but privileged communication in family mediation. (Chapters Five and Six further discuss the ethical and practice issues to consider when clients divulge secret information.)

There are controversies in the family therapy field about the process of recovered memories, the term used to describe the process in a sequence of stages when the self allows itself to remember past events that were terrifying, abhorrent, and unacceptable. A similar process also exists when people strip away their defenses and realize the enormity of their own perpetration on others. Because so many people have experienced some form of emotional or physical trauma, a sizable percentage of family mediation participants bring this legacy of pain with them into the room. Family mediators must be sensitive to the fact that the current dilemma or conflict may be triggering thoughts and emotions for disputants that are really more about the past abuse than about the current conflict. This is true whether the people involved in the conflict were or are currently also involved in the trauma, abuse, or violence or whether they are unaware of and not implicated in the past traumatic events.

The process of reexperiencing traumatic or unacceptable past events has been called *emotional flooding.* As the term implies, people experiencing it flounder mentally and emotionally and are swept away by the torrent of their own inner process. When this happens, they usually cannot stay involved in the here-and-now discussions and often must go for intensive crisis-preventive therapy to help them overcome these overwhelmingly hard rushes of feelings and thoughts. People who are flooded cannot do a rational-analytic task; they can even become depressed and suicidal, incoherent, or totally out of control with rage. It is an important breakthrough for them but also an emotionally vulnerable time. People who have started this process of recovering their memories independent of the conflict may suddenly stall out or behave differently. Those who are dealing with the trauma as part of the hidden material involved directly in the conflict being mediated are even more vulnerable to experiencing major psychological and behavioral shifts.

Family mediators must understand the signposts and behavioral antecedents, such as defense and thinking errors, involved in the process of keeping secrets and then must make choices regarding the mental and emotional well-being of participants when pursuing family mediation cases. Family mediators who understand the dynamics of hiding and uncovering and the emotional response to both can watch for and respond appropriately should this become an uninvited part of the family mediation case.

RESILIENCE AND THE CURRENT DILEMMA

Why does one family faced with a conflict or dispute seem to do so much better in resolving it than another? Why does one person in a family dispute crumble and have such a hard time emotionally with the family conflict while another member who is equally affected seems to go through the conflict unscathed? Why is a family conflict, resolved or unresolved, so devastating to one member and not another? All of the information previously described about family life stages, levels of attachment and the internal working model of each member of the family, and the functionality of the conflict given the structure of the alliances helps to explain something about how a particular family may be responding. Another part of the answer is the concept of resilience—the set of qualities that allows people to emotionally survive very difficult situations. This question and the concept of personal and family resilience are particularly important for family mediators, because the nature, longevity, and severity of the conflict can seriously affect the emotional and psychological well-being of all those affected—not only the direct disputants but also the secondary parties.

Resilience as a personal characteristic is either supported or hampered by family, educational, and larger community systems and has been studied internationally and cross-culturally, as well as longitudinally. Resilience is a measurement that is particularly useful for families and individuals, especially children, who are trying to grow up in environments where large-scale political or environmental impacts, like war, poverty, or natural disasters, have taken place, as well as those whose tragedies are more personal, such as in families where mental illness, alcohol and drug abuse, criminality, or pervasive verbal, sexual, physical, or mental abuse has taken place. Both personal and family resilience is tested and becomes especially important at times of conflict and stress. Family mediators thus see families who are not only in conflict but also in crisis. How the individual family members manage that crisis will show the level of resilience they have.

Some life span studies have documented that half to two-thirds of children stuck in terrible situations overcome the traumatic circumstances and overcome the adversity to demonstrate successful adaptation and transformation. "Resilience research validates prior research and theory in human development that has clearly established the biological imperative for growth and development that exists in the human organism and that unfolds naturally in the presence of certain environmental characteristics. We are all born with an innate capacity for resilience, by which we are able to develop social competence, problem-solving skills, a critical consciousness, autonomy and a sense of purpose" (Benard, 1995, p. 1).

Children and adults who can mobilize their inner resources in times of adversity seem to have some factors in common that had developed prior to the traumatic situation. They usually had some ability to elicit positive responses from others, to have empathy for others and gain that empathy from others in kind. Resilient people seem to have flexibility—the ability to move between different cultures or elements within society—as well as good communication skills and often a healthy sense of humor that allows them to overcome the adversity or see it in a different perspective. All of these factors form a body of social competencies that help mitigate the current dilemma because the person is able to reach out to others and get help.

Wolin and Wolin (1993) have identified seven factors that seem to be common among people who maintain higher levels of personal resilience: insight, independence, relationship, initiative, creativity, humor, and morality. Whether these are the antecedents of doing well in adversity or the consequence of having survived is debatable. Given that for many people in family conflict, the dispute itself is a test of their personal resilience as well as the resilience of the family, it would be good for the family mediator to support any personal or systemwide moves in these directions.

Many cultural traditions support resilience-building activities. For example, Evans (1995) has noted that these seven resilience factors are very similar to and cross-supportive of the seven principles of Kwanzaa, the celebration of African American culture founded by Maulana Karenga in 1966, which promotes the following seven principles: (1) Umoja (unity), (2) Kujichagulia (self-determination), (3) Ujima (collective work and responsibility), (4) Ujamaa (cooperative economics), (5) Nia (purpose), (6) Kuumba (creativity), and (7) Imani (faith). When mediators are aware of and speak to existing concepts in a person's values or culture, they help support the development of family and personal resilience. This is one way to support the family's value structure while encouraging change.

Young children have not had time to develop these abstract concepts fully, but they have different levels of self-worth and caring from infancy. The type of attachment that is formed with parents and other caretakers helps to form the level of resilience the child will carry into future relationships and situations. Self-concept and personal resilience are developed in the numbers and types of encounters. Because of this, children are in many ways more vulnerable targets when negativity and the destructive elements of family conflict ensue. Supporting and maintaining a child's personal resilience become part of the global goals that parents and family mediators might have for all cases, a goal that does not prevent client self-determination or override particular family values and structures. Just as children form attachment patterns that continue to shape their adult development, they also start to develop the elements that indicate their level of resilience, and this level develops over time.

One of the informal assessments that family mediators may need to make about their clients is how resilient they are in this moment in this conflict. Mediators should look for some of the hallmarks of resilient adults and informally assess their participants' resilience by using the following criteria, which were developed by studying people with high levels of resilience.

- They establish and maintain relationships marked by a high degree of reciprocity and concern for the other as well as the self.

- They develop and actively participate in relationships that can withstand (or even thrive on) conflict, disappointment, frequent anger, and frustration when the needs of either person in the relationship are not met. These conflicts are actively and successfully negotiated throughout each relationship.

- They relate to others in a way that, in general, does not sacrifice the accuracy and empathy with which they perceive other people; that is, they make consistent and generally successful attempts to recognize the needs and characteristics of other and to differentiate those needs from their own. [Higgins, 1994, pp. xiii–xiv]

Many resilient children learn long-term coping strategies to deal with severely troubled families who are in constant chaos and crisis, or conflict, or both. Some of these strategies become so automatic that they can be termed "overlearned" and must be "unlearned" when they are no longer needed, because they can interfere with openness and responsiveness later if the pattern becomes immovable. For example, resilient children caught in a drug-affected household have often overlearned how to become capable of meeting their own and others' needs, to the point that they can be identified as developing patterns of overresponsibility and becoming parentified children. Part of their resilience is to maintain the will and capacity to survive and help others, no matter what it requires of them.

Another feature of people with strong resilience is that they have a sense of autonomy and some level of self-control. They feel competent and sense their own ability to master tasks and requirements. They have a strong level of inward control and tell themselves positive messages about their own abilities. They often have developed the skill of resistance. They do not listen to disparaging remarks, put-downs, or other negative messages about themselves and do not accept these comments internally, thus not allowing themselves further psychological wounding. They also practice a level of detachment that serves to distance and therefore protect them from the negativity.

Along with the ability to ward off negatives, resilient people have a strong sense of purpose, worthiness, and meaning. They believe deeply that things happen for a reason, that things will work out in the end, and that they are connected to a larger meaning. This belief leads to a sense of optimism, goal direction, and hopefulness. When added to persistence and perseverance, these mental and emotional strengths develop synergistically to create and maintain a very strong person who can withstand many obstacles. Resilient people have a vision of themselves they do not abandon despite negative feedback and problems. "Resilient adults do not take people, themselves, or life at face value. Striving always to understand, resilient survivors process their experiences, look for meanings hidden beneath the surface of events, and confront themselves honestly" (Wolin and Wolin, 1993, p. 81).

Resilient children who grow up in terrible situations tell themselves something positive about themselves and see the problem as real but survivable. Many of them develop a secure base and an internal working model of belief in themselves and others before the crisis, conflict, or trouble begins, so they are able to maintain that worldview despite the problems they are encountering.

> Resolved not to repeat their parents' folly, they have become highly skilled at conflict resolution and dedicate themselves to maintaining emotional clarity with others. Although they struggle with an underlying, nagging sense of their own "basic badness," they simultaneously maintain high self-esteem regarding their own executive and interpersonal competence, believe that they deserve to be loved, and feel that their trials made them far more than they might have been otherwise. These commingling, apparently contradictory convictions capture the complexity that is so characteristic of a resilient life. Over time these people have become more integrated, reducing their discrepant views of themselves and achieving consistently higher self-esteem. [Higgins, 1994, p. 21]

Like most other concepts presented in this book, resilience should be seen as levels and a continuum rather than as a factor that a person has or does not have. All people have some level of resilience, but it can be severely lowered by temporary events, ongoing intractable conflicts, and physical conditions. Like all other dynamic factors, levels of resilience one day may be different than they are on another day, yet the baseline level remains in a similar range. Family mediators can get a sense of the level of resilience that each member of the family has by asking them some background questions and bringing up the topic as part of the definition of the mediation process.

External Factors That Promote Resilience

The presence of at least one person who cares, shows compassion, and understands that the person is doing the best he or she can is a hallmark of environments that establish and maintain resilience for others. When a family has severe problems, it is often isolated, and children and adults cannot make or keep these vital connections with others. Even in the most abusive families, children or adults who maintain positive contacts with someone they know likes or loves them maintain their resilience. When siblings in an abusive family are taken out of the home, these caring connections can be unnecessarily broken, leading to further erosion of the child's resilience. This also explains why siblings may differ in their level of resilience. If one child has a caring friend, scoutmaster, teacher, or other outside resource such as friend's parent, this support can contribute to the child's resilience; another child in the same family unfortunately lacks that source of nurturance, through no fault of his or her own. This is why we need not ascribe blame or permanency to the condition of resilience. Unlike basic personality, which is fairly well established by an early age, resilience is dynamic and developmental and is dependent on variables such as access to resources that are beyond the control of the individual.

Sometimes the family mediator becomes this linking person who provides emotional support and caring about the person stuck in the conflict and thus improves the person's resilience. A family mediator who creates a caring, supportive climate or facilitates a referral to those who can provide this support concurrently with the mediation effort (therapists, social services, clergy, and others) provides these necessary conditions to support personal resilience.

Research has also shown that when the environment stresses high expectations for the child or adult, these expectations overcome the negative messages about self that the child or adult is experiencing. If somewhere in the person's life there is a message that communicates that "you can do it," that voice of positive expectation counteracts the negative self-image that has been delivered from the trauma or problem. Thus, some schools and environments are giving children who are burdened with poverty or other hardships the message that they can and are expected to achieve, despite the disenfranchisement or disturbance. Some families also set achievement as a family value and stress that temporary problems, conflicts, or disputes should not and will not stop them from maintaining their integrity as a social unit. Just because a family experiences conflicts or problems severe enough to require mediation does not prevent it from holding itself accountable and working toward a positive outcome, while maintaining the resilience of the family and the individuals within it.

Disputes as Opportunities for Resilience

Because people in conflicts tend to see the world negatively and project that negativity into the future, it is important for family mediators to help reinstill hope and aspiration in their clients. Although mediators cannot and should not impose their own values on the family, they can help the family work toward creating and maintaining resilience even during the crisis or conflict. When family mediators convey the clear expectations that families can make appropriate decisions for themselves to solve the conflicts, they are acting along with the concept of accountability and encouragement found in the research.

Resilience is also fostered by participation in the processes and structures that surround the individual, since participation gives back some level of power and control that had been lost in the negativity of the situation, which was usually beyond the person's control. Because family mediation requires full participation (after the normal reluctance and resistance during the initial session is overcome), it is a venue that helps support emotional resilience. Family mediation is consistent with the need to control what is manageable in situations that seem beyond control. The concept of reempowerment in mediation speaks to this issue of building and fostering resilience.

The more that family mediators allow children's concerns and wishes to be part of the mediation effort in some way, even if the children cannot or should not be making the final choices, the more the family mediator is setting a stage that supports the child's resilience to deal with the negativity of the conflict. The same is true with any other participant in mediation whose resilience seems lowered. Instead of allowing the child to be disenfranchised and unheard, family mediators can help parents realize the importance of including information directly or indirectly about the needs and desires of the children rather than just allowing distributive bargaining between the parents as the legal decision makers. Many parents give lip-service to wanting to help reduce the negative aspects of a family conflict yet resist including the children in the mediation process on any level. The research on resilience supports the notion that appropriate participation can help reduce problems and support the creation and maintenance of the personal resilience of children during family conflict.

Maintaining Mediator Resilience

Working with families in conflict after conflict, where there is constant anger and tension or the mediator feels the lack of recognition and emotional support from the service delivery system or his or her own family, can take a toll on the personal resilience of the family mediator. Especially if the mediator overcame personal obstacles in becoming a family mediator, his or her resilience can also be maintained or negatively affected by the same three factors: caring relationships, high expectations, and opportunities to participate in processes that will affect him or her. In this way, family mediators might see themselves becoming overly involved in a case, dreading a particular family's coming in, or other signposts of emotional response to their work.

Mediators might label their resistance, reluctance, or overinvolvement as countertransference, which means an overidentification with the clients. When this occurs, the therapist inappropriately and unconsciously takes on the problems or processes of the client or works on his or her issues using the clients to represent his or her own unresolved issues.

Another similar concept is called parallel process, where the client's level of functioning affects the clinician's level of functioning. This is characterized by the clinician's engaging in the same type of behavior or showing the same level of functioning as the person with the problem rather than maintaining the secure base for the client.

The same process may happen in looking at resilience: family mediators who are surrounded by clients with lowered personal resilience may find themselves functioning at the same level of despair and hopelessness as their clients. They may start to feel that their personal resilience is threatened by the negativity of the family or the larger legal or social system's response to the progress (or lack thereof) in the case. "Know thyself" becomes the dictum to remember here. If the family mediator came from great adversity or a troubled family, or is experiencing problems similar to those of clients, his or her personal resilience and ability to be fully present in the interaction may be severely compromised.

❧

Families are dynamic small systems that create groupings and special bonds of loyalty and function. They are constantly changing, and individuals within these small groups can change the entire family process and structure by taking independent action. Because of the interconnectedness, each action creates reaction, and a change in one member creates change in the whole. Conflict within families is inevitable, and families develop rules and roles regarding who, how, and when they deal with conflict. These patterns of behavior form part of the unique culture of the family and serve as models of adult behavior for the children growing up within the structure. These patterns contribute to either the constructive or negative aspects of the conflict and along a scale of positive to negative for each member within the family.

Families show patterns when compared to themselves at different family life stages or when compared to other families. Some families tolerate and encourage closeness, while others are more distant. Some are more rigid and others more flexible. Different stages of family life require different responses by the family in order to provide the members what they need as individuals. When family patterns become solidified into unhelpful triads, problems can ensue. Similarly, when family members maintain roles that are complementary but not helpful, such as codependency or over- or underfunctioning, either side of the dyad can make changes that will change the functioning of the family.

Because family members have both a personal and collective history, children and adult family members can have a solid basis for vastly different perspectives on past events. They can have very different responses to the same situation. They can be controlling for attachment or loss, maintaining the status quo or working for change. They can continue to maintain unhelpful legacies or family secrets, and produce alliances and coalitions that maintain stability but do not foster growth and development of one or more of the family members, or the family as a unit, or be aware and interested in revision and repair. Families as units and family members as individuals provide social learning environments, and are either more or less skilled in certain aspects, such as communication and instrumental and emotional tasks.

Families are where we live. We learn how to be people in our families. People bring their total selves to the family conflict, with all their past and present and hope for the future, with all their skills, deficits, and motivations. Children and adults are products of their families yet also co-creators of them. They can make bold changes that affect the very existence of the family as they have known it. Family rules and structure and behavior can be very tenacious, despite everyone's recognition of a need for change.

Family conflicts touch people at a deep level and deserve to be mediated in ways that preserve what is best and most valued and needed by each member.

When family mediators remember the primacy of this social, educational, economic, emotional, and physical entity and realize the complexity and uniqueness of each family, as well as each member in the family, they can humbly offer the mediation process to help family members redesign their future. When they remember all the processes that have already gone on to create the family they see before them, they should work for constructive change.

CHAPTER TWO

Understanding Family Conflict

T he dynamics of family conflict operate in some ways as all other conflicts do, and yet there is a vital difference. Family conflicts are perhaps the most personal of all conflicts. Although people spend lots of time in their workplaces and communities and have many disputes with others in the normal course of living, they live in their families. Family disputes therefore affect a person's social and personal identity in a way that no other type of conflict can. The level of self-involvement in the conflict and the impact of its outcome are huge. Family conflict is not only about the self-identity of the disputants, but also about the identity of all the others affected by the dispute, such as children, grandparents, and other relatives. A dispute in a family affects not only the identity of the individuals but the identity of the family as a social, economic, and interpersonal system:

> To creatively manage a conflict when individual and group identity is at stake,
> core concerns—survival, recognition, dignity—must be surfaced and addressed.
> When conflict is rooted in the protection of identity needs, the stakes are greater
> than in interest-based conflict born out of competition over resources. In identity
> conflict, groups struggle for their basic physical and moral survival. Accordingly,
> the potential for destruction is strong. [Rothman, 1997, pp. 8–9]

Family conflict is not only about tangible items but the intangibles of what makes the family unique and special in their own and others' eyes. It is about the intrinsic qualities that make them distinctive and bonded to each other. It is about each person's level of inclusion or exclusion from the family system.

58

THE MULTIPLE LEVELS OF FAMILY CONFLICTS

Any family dispute can have simultaneous elements of all four levels of conflict described by Lewicki, Saunders, and Minton (2001, pp. 12–13):

- Intrapersonal conflict—they are of two minds in themselves
- Interpersonal conflict—they are in dispute with one or more members of the family
- Intragroup conflict—factions within the family have formed
- Intergroup conflict—the family is in dispute with other outside groups or entities

A termination of parental rights case that is being mediated might have component parts for each of the participants as follows:

- Intrapersonal level: The internal struggle of "what kind of parent gives up her child?" versus "I know I cannot handle the child and it is best for her to go to a good home"
- Interpersonal level: The father who wants the termination so his new wife can adopt the children versus the mother who is not relinquishing parental rights
- Intragroup level: The grandmother who wants the mother to fight to retain her parental rights as well as her grandparental contacts versus the mother's new spouse, who is counseling her to let go
- Intergroup level: The protective services agency worker and the probation officer who are making a recommendation for termination based on the past abuse versus the mother and her current therapist, who are recommending family reunification based on the mother's capacities after treatment

Family mediators need to map out all the layers of conflict for each person in the conflict, since family systems are complex and family conflicts are even more so. A family mediator who knows all of these levels of conflict for each member who is mediating will understand the conflict situation much more fully.

Each person in the family may have a different context for understanding and relating to the conflict. And yet family conflict is uniquely painful because it is not just about the self against outside forces, that is, "me against them" but about "us against us" or even "me against us." It is less easy to distance oneself from the conflict and achieve a level of dispassionate reason about issues that touch so deeply. It is particularly wounding when the people with whom we have been so close and so intimate, on whom we have based our lives, start doing the adversarial framing of blaming, polarizing, attributing negative characteristics, and projecting unacceptable traits from themselves to the others in the conflict. It creates intense loyalty and betrayal issues for those caught in the conflict.

Family conflicts have the potential for constructive or destructive processes and outcomes. They are opportunities for positive change for individuals and the entire system, or destruction of what is most important. As Kreisberg (1998) points out, any social conflict can be characterized by the sequences of constructive to destructive qualities in the way in which they are dealt with or waged, how long they last or how prolonged the conflict is, and what the outcome ultimately is. A family conflict that finally has a positive outcome after many years of dispute may have been very destructive in the way in which it was handled, and so leaves a legacy of distrust, indignation, or avoidance even though the outcome seems fair, workable, and positive.

In family conflict, the way in which the conflict is discussed and handled will be at least as important to the family members as the specific terms and agreements listed in the outcome document of the mediation process. This is one of the factors that makes family mediation a very different context for those used to standard distributive negotiation in business, commercial, or other forms of mediation and conflict resolution. Family mediation is messy business, dealing with self-concept, face-saving, high emotions, crisis, past background, and identity issues for all participants. This chapter provides practical understandings of the dynamics of conflict in general and family conflict specifically.

CONFLICT EMERGENCE AND INTERVENTION

It has been said that mediation is a practice in search of a premise, and yet there is extensive work in many fields that directly affects the nature of conflict as it manifests in families. While much of the literature base of conflict resolution has looked at larger-scale social conflict, many of the foundational constructs about conflict can and should be taken from that literature base. The fields of social psychology, individual psychology, sociology, and cultural anthropology have much to tell us about how families dispute and what the basis of dispute is.

Conflict as Powers Meeting and Balancing

R. J. Rummel (1976, 1991) outlined in descriptive, linked principles how conflict develops and asserts itself in individuals, groups, and larger societies. Starting with the microcosm of self and then generalizing to the larger society, he saw conflict as developing whenever individual or societal powers meet and balance. He believed that each person (or group entity or system) has its own unique blend of thoughts, feelings, history, values, status, and meaning, which he called their *sociocultural space.* This fact in itself can lead to interpersonal conflict as each unit encounters others who do not understand, tolerate, or respect their sociocultural space. He also saw that some conflicts are structural in nature, because built into the system is conflict due to the opposing tendencies of the roles, functions, or intentions of individuals or entities. These naturally occurring oppositions can lead to a situation of conflict, where the individuals or entities involved realize their differences but are unwilling to do anything to change the situation.

Eventually, a trigger event happens: these opposing tendencies come out in ways that mean they can no longer ignore, deny, or minimize the level of conflict. This trigger event, or series of events, leads to a state of uncertainty, where everyone who is involved consults with others to determine what they will or will not do and what that will take. Sometimes they try some status quo testing, to see if they can return to the condition they had before the trigger event and go on without much change. If it becomes apparent they cannot, then the disputants enter into the process of balancing their relative powers.

Methods for Balancing Power. Rummel identified three major processes through which individuals attempt to balance their power:

- *Coercive force:* Physical, social, financial, or legal intervention where the decision is made by parties other than the disputants or the disputants themselves. It can be socially acceptable, as in an appeal to courts, restraining orders, and other social and legal processes, or not socially acceptable, such as manipulation, persuasion, intimidation, threat, or actual abuse or violence.

- *Accommodation:* Mutual behavioral change done by agreement between the disputants by means of direct dialogue and negotiation.

- *Noncoercive processes:* Mediation, facilitated dialogue, and other conflict management processes where disputants make their own decisions

In family situations, it is common for disputants to start with direct negotiation and resort to noncoercive methods like mediation because it is required prior to the institution of judicial and other coercive processes. Partners having difficulty may try to talk to each other but resort to restraining orders and other redress of law when they will not or cannot converse without harming each other or without violating the restraining order or judicial order of no contact that has been imposed. Sometimes they resort to the coercive system before any harm (or threat of harm) has been made in order to secure a tactical upper hand in the balancing of their relative power. This brings up the questions as to whether mandatory mediation efforts become just another coercive force and do not retain the noncoercive methodology they are meant to embody and whether mediation can maintain its status as a true alternative dispute resolution method when it becomes the required response.

Families in dispute often use all three methods, sequentially or randomly. They try direct negotiation and accommodation, switch to coercive methods by filing legal documents, then try noncoercive mediation, then get court orders that coerce and require certain things, then return to mediation efforts, which may return them to a status of direct negotiation and accommodation. Whichever methods are used, a new balance of power is created that rests on the interests, capability, and credibility of the disputants to enact it. Over time, there is often a gap that widens between the newly created expectations of the disputants and the reality that follows. This expectation gap leads to a continuing cycle of conflict, which then reemerges as another conflict situation or a trigger event. The goal is to create a new balance of power that is truly anchored to the interests and capabilities of the parties. In this view of conflict, each set of relationships between the disputants and others in the family is viewed as a socially constructed group of negotiated agreements or an interpersonal contract between the parties that must seem fair to each disputant in order for each one to want to implement and continue the agreements.

In Rummel's view, the durability of any new balance of power, including mediated agreements, would depend not only on the skill of the mediator and the clarity of the new balance of power but also on the unavoidable changes that might occur following the mediation. Children grow up, people get laid off work, move, change partners, and make new decisions, which can start to affect their ability to comply with the terms of the mediated agreement, the court orders, or the verbal understandings they had.

Another goal of mediation following this view is to help disputants understand the cyclical nature of dispute and predict likely gaps, or times and circumstances under which the agreements will no longer work. When participants understand this cyclical nature of conflict and the inexorable drift away, they do not need to blame the mediator or the other participant for this. It depersonalizes a process that is essentially beyond their control. They can then choose where and when to return to balance their power. They need not wait until a devastating trigger event in order to restart the process of response to conflict; they can choose to return to a noncoercive process, thus mitigating the destructiveness of the cycle.

Many family mediators routinely discuss this issue of how future predictable and unpredictable changes and conflicts will be handled. They include a remediation clause as part of the original mediated agreement, which will specify the criteria for return and whether that return to mediation should or must happen prior to initiating the coercive legal remedies. By making a choice for the noncoercive processes like mediation for the future, the disputants are making a choice for reducing stress and destruction while still acknowledging the need for flexibility for the future. Understanding the cycle of conflicts obviates the need to conflict in the same way and can lead to more cooperative efforts.

A Divorce Example. To illustrate Rummel's cyclical conflict model, we will look at a husband and wife, each with a very different sociocultural space: different understandings of the nature of marriage, different styles of conflict resolution, different levels of attachment that lead to different internal working models of relationship and patterns of closeness, and different expectations, goals, and methods for parenting. The structure of conflict they find in married life is that both have to go to work daily, returning with little time and energy to maintain an adequate relationship or parenting. This can be true for quite a while in a state of predispute conflict.

Then a conflict situation develops—regarding time spent with each other, parenting, sexual matters, money, or something else. This situation of conflict leads to an awareness by one or both partners that their relationship is drifting and is becoming less satisfactory. This stage may last for months or even years. Then a trigger event occurs: one partner has an affair or overspends, or hits the partner or child; the other is shocked and upset; things happen (one partner moves into a friend's apartment or packs up the household and drives to the family of origin's home to stay). At this point, the couple can no longer deny the long-standing family conflicts. Although to outsiders it may appear that this conflict came out of nowhere, it had actually been in existence for quite a while, but the family's defenses (denial, minimizing, ignoring, projecting, and other conscious and unconscious responses) prevented one or both of them from addressing the dispute head-on.

Because of the trigger event, they now consider themselves in a marital dispute and perhaps even a marital crisis. The entire family is instantly dropped into the state of uncertainty. They consult their friends and extended family, their clergy and lawyers, and depending on the culture, their godparents or even no one at all due to isolation or shame. They try some status quo testing: he sends flowers and chocolate; they talk on the phone; they have sex. They may attempt to reconcile and go on, thus trying to deny the existence of the conflicts and need to renegotiate their understandings.

If this status quo testing fails or neither is offering the signs of reconciliation, they must decide if they need intervention by legitimate coercive forces. They may file temporary separation, child support, restraining orders, or other forms of legal procedures, which attempt to create some order in the chaos and protect and provide for the children. At this time, the filing of certain papers triggers the noncoercive mediation system. Because many people in our society lack the financial means for legal recourse, they may not know of or be referred or mandated to family mediators until they scrape together the money to file for divorce, separation, or parenting-related legal proceedings.

By this time, their positions have hardened, and additional conflicts continue to accrue.

The family mediator provides a noncoercive process in an attempt to help both of them balance their power and renegotiate their interpersonal marital contract. If the mediation is unsuccessful, the court establishes a new balance of power between them regarding their finances and parenting. This may or may not be based on their true interests, since it is often a product of standardization rather than individually tailored to the unique capacities and credibility of each person. This new balance of power will last as long as they are able to comply or until external factors such as job changes, new partners, and relocation or changes in the ages and needs of the children change the expectations to the point that they can no longer tolerate it. If the parents are cooperative, they may be able to renegotiate their own new agreements and not go back to court for relief or changes. If they are not, the destructive aspects of the cycle continue, with more trigger events happening and more coercive sanctions being placed on the family.

If the judicial system is not accessible due to lack of money for filing or legal representation or mediation, the disputants are left to continue in a structure or situation of conflict or have continuing and repetitive trigger events until yet another balance point is established by the courts. This gives rise to the concern about the family's recidivism due to continuing unresolved conflicts, the need for "one family, one judge" unified court structures, and nonrepresentative advisers who educate families on their dispute resolution options before they file legal forms. All of the above can directly influence the effectiveness of mediation efforts.

Mediators as Part of the Conflict Cycle. Mediators are but one part of the larger social structures being accessed to deal with the family system in conflict. They are not responsible for the cyclical nature of conflict, but they may be able to help the family members achieve a new balance of power that will rest on their true interests, their true capabilities, and their actual credibility with each other. Over time, even the best-mediated agreement will no longer fit because things have changed. The family may be able to return to mediation efforts before another crisis, especially if mediation is offered as needed, not just at the point of divorce or separation, and if the family is aware of the cycle of conflict and their need to return when they first become aware of disrupted expectations. Such a return is seen not as a revolving door but as a step in the right direction of managing conflict appropriately for the future.

Conflict as a Cyclical Process

Another view of the cyclical nature of conflict is that offered by Kreisberg (1998): "A conflict emerges, escalates, de-escalates, terminates, and results in an outcome that becomes the basis for another conflict" (p. 25). In his view, a conflict can have intervention at any stage and at multiple stages of this cycle. When family members realize the bases for current or future conflict or the potential or actual disputes they have, they can intervene by engaging in open dialogue about those differences at that point, thus obviating the need for further escalation. These are the amicable divorces, the cooperative open adoptions, the families who openly discuss placement of elderly members. They have become aware of their potential bases for conflict and are renegotiating their understandings and agreements without having to escalate into ugly, vituperative disputes. When family mediators are accessed by families and systems at this point, they function more as a facilitative third party who guides the discussion and ensures that all possible points of view and all stakeholders are presented.

When family mediators are following this view of conflict and are intervening at this earliest level of manifestation of conflict, their role parallels that of a skilled facilitator. They share the three core values with facilitators: valid information, free and informed choice, and internal commitment to the choice for those making the decisions so that they take responsibility for implementing the decisions that are reached (Schwartz, 1994). Family mediators acting as facilitators of the small group of the family can intervene on the same five levels that Schwartz (1994) posits for the levels of intervention: the structural-functional, performance-goal, instrumental, interpersonal, and intrapersonal levels. This is consistent with the role of both problem solver and transformative mediator (Bush and Folger, 1994; Folger and Bush, 1996).

In Kreisberg's view, the more typical place in the cycle of conflict where intervention occurs is after the conflict has manifested, and is starting to escalate. This makes sense in families that will tolerate some level of conflict between members yet appeal to mediators and bring in other professionals such as attorneys and psychologists when they perceive that the conflict is escalating to the point that they can no longer predict or control the situation. Often family abuse continues for a long time and with increasing frequency and lethality, until it finally gets to a point where someone is willing to be the whistle-blower because it has "gone too far" or because other outside systems have become aware of it and have acted to protect the parties and deescalate the risks.

In Kreisberg's conflict cycle model, a conflict without intervention will ultimately deescalate, terminate, and leave the parties with the consequences of the conflict; intervention at the right time and in the right way can speed the process of deescalation. Some families with verbal and physical abuse resolve the conflicts by imploding and having family members drift apart or run away.

In healthier families, explosive conflicts about parenting or between parents and children due to developmental cycles, such as often happen with toddlers and teenagers, naturally drift away without intervention. The children grow up and change, or family members change their way of responding to the conflicts, often without intervention. The healing power of time and patience can sometimes create better circumstances, but not all family conflicts are resolved by letting them go.

When negative and conflictual patterns are entrenched, external parties such as therapists, mediators, courts, and others may be needed to intervene. The cases that need family mediation are referred because they have already declared themselves in dispute, filed legal actions with their positions, and may be increasing in their intensity of negative interactions. Because most family mediation is still initiated after or concurrently with legal involvement, mediators see a very skewed population of those who cannot simply let the conflict go or work it out themselves and need precise, helpful, and timely intervention to prevent reescalation.

Another time when family mediators can be brought into a case is when the conflict has had intervention by other social forces, such as child protective services. A new balance of power has been judicially or administratively determined and some deescalation has occurred, but the parties to the dispute have not yet given up the tension, retaliation, retribution, or emotional residue of the conflict. For family mediators, this can be a case where the judge has provided a ruling, yet refers or orders the case to mediation for working out of the specifics of parenting, reunification, adoption, or whatever else the situation is. Intervention by mediators at this phase of the conflict cycle takes a varied course, since the primary decisions are no longer the parties' to make.

Reconciliation After Conflict. Kreisberg believes that the stage of reconciliation after the official struggle is over needs more study, methods, and use of conflict management and mediation skills. In families, this is a time of reinventing self and repairing emotional and social damage. But some things can never be repaired, and some things must be accepted. This can be the breeding ground for continued vengeance, recrimination, shame, and blame, which can lead to the seemingly intractable repetitive conflicts or generational patterns.

Success as Equity and Stability. Kreisberg (1998) notes that the outcome and consequences of a conflict will be judged by all parties and those affected on two primary factors, equity and stability, and the effect these perceptions will have in the immediate and the long-term interactions. One of the consequences that is often an unintended outcome of family conflict is the willingness or unwillingness to use the same methodology for any continuing conflicts or even to acknowledge the conflicts or deal with them if they arise again. If one or both parties feel they have suffered injustices in the outcome or in the process, the continued feelings of resentment, disappointment, and unwillingness to re-engage may be predominant.

Conflict as Social Exchange

A third model for understanding family conflicts is social exchange theory. Based on economic theories, this concept proposes that conflicts in social groups happen when the outcome is not equal to the expectation or does not meet a standard of reciprocity and equality maintained by one or more of the parties. When the cost-benefit ratio does not equal the expectation, the perception is that an injustice has been done and an inequity remains, and the process or the outcome has not been fair. Parker (1991) has applied these constructs to the family mediation context specifically in terms of the communication and the power balancing during mediation.

Family relationships do have economic aspects, but unlike traditional economic theories based on a free market, some family members, such as children or dependents, are not free to withdraw at any time from their families as an investor can withdraw from an adverse stock market. Although we as a society have agreed that no-fault divorce allows marital partners to leave a marriage with a poor cost-benefit ratio, it is very difficult for children to leave parents or parents to abandon all their economic responsibilities to their children. Parents routinely minimize the cost side of parenting when they do not pay child support or effectively abandon their children through drug abuse, long work hours, and self-oriented activities, but then later do not get the social benefits of love, care, and concern as they age. "The conflict is especially intense when persons see themselves committed to a social relationship that is inequitable, for often one cannot easily leave such relationships" (Schellenberg, 1996, p. 74).

Family members such as adult children with differential responsibilities to an aging parent are not always free to end contact even if they feel that they are getting a bad deal by doing more than their fair share of the work or paying more than others to address the parent's needs. Children whose parents have been neglectful, abandoning, or unresponsive and irresponsible still love and try to please them, in complete denial of the "only work for gain" economic view. Even as they get less, they still give. Partners in unresponsive relationships continue way beyond when an economic partnership would declare bankruptcy. In this way, a strictly economic view of family relationships as tally sheets analogous to the capitalist market breaks down. Families and their conflicts are about more than the bottom line and an appropriate profit margin or ratio of gain to cost. Families and their conflicts have to do with intangibles that cannot be measured in strictly economic terms and will not respond solely to standard distributive negotiation techniques.

If the perception of inequality is one of the major sources of conflict, then one of the consequences of unresolved or inequitably resolved family conflict is the continuing internal dialogue about when and how to creatively cut off from those who have cheated or maintained the inequality. Certainly, a parent who does not believe she is being treated fairly by the other parent can use her power to make the deal worse for the other parent; she can withhold visitation or access to children, delay making payments, or procrastinate on decisions or implementation of mediated agreements regarding family members. She can become negatively reciprocal, thus starting the escalation cycle again.

The exchange theory does seem to explicate some of the bargaining that goes on in family mediation. The inequality in a situation of conflict or in a mediated agreement between parties who cannot stop the exchange can be perceived as a threat to the integrity of the person on the lower end of the exchange. The parent may perceive that she can go still lower in subsequent exchanges. Parents who "lost" the custody battle often negotiate fiercely with the other parent over the topics of hours on holidays and school breaks in order to even the overall cost-benefit ratio.

This brings us to the concept of determining the "good-enough" deal. If this parent can get a good-enough exchange on the parenting time for holidays and summers, she can often overlook and accept the loss of custody. Compensatory items for the "loser" in a win-lose situation can make a difference, and the attempt to make up for losses can go a long way in establishing appropriate negotiation between family members. Skilled negotiators who are essentially operating from an economic perspective often refocus on nonspecific compensation, unbundling issues, and reducing risks as a way to get an agreement that seems good enough (Lewicki, Saunders, and Minton, 2001). Family members, then, do social exchange as part of their mediation of family conflicts, and those conflicts can be reduced when all parties feel that the exchange is fair and equitable.

ANALYZING FAMILY CONFLICTS

Family mediators need to assess the family members and the conflict as part of their formulation of the case that will guide and direct the provision of mediation process (Lang and Taylor, 2000). One final way of looking at a family conflict is to use the five-part model articulated by Moore (1988), which is easily explainable to the participants and helps organize the information the clients are giving. In this model, each conflict situation may have within it some or all of the following general types of conflicts:

- Data conflicts, which are about information or lack of it
- Interest conflicts, which are about real or perceived competition for scarce resources and differences over what is important
- Relationship conflicts, caused by stereotyping, poor communication, or misperceptions
- Structural conflicts, which are due to unequal power and control built into the system
- Value conflicts, which are based on deeply held beliefs and goals

Most family conflicts have some part of the dispute that is associated with each of these categories. Almost all family conflicts have a component of values conflict about them. Although all types may be involved in a particular family conflict situation, the family members may prioritize each one differently or negotiate each one very differently. When the family mediator can help all members of the family understand the multiple parts of their conflict, they start to see the conflict differently. No longer can it be perceived as just one person's fault or responsibility.

In an example of a family reunification case, the primary conflict for the grandparent might be a values conflict between her and the adult child, while the primary conflict between the parents is an interest-based conflict. In the same case, the primary conflict for the placement worker from child protective services is about data concerning whether the abuse or neglect took place and is likely to continue.

It is imperative that family mediators understand and get information from all parties involved in the conflict in order to determine their views on what is in the picture for them. Since each has a different way of trying to resolve itself, a family mediator who is unaware of the values conflict between two parties or the structural conflict between the absent father and the absent mother in regard to the grandmother with temporary custody will miss important information that can help determine how to proceed with the mediation effort.

Intractable Family Conflicts

When there are no opportunities to provide exchange or there are continuing negative or unfair exchanges between family members, the patterns of interaction these encounters create can mimic the intractable conflicts of larger society, such as the tensions and continuing conflicts in the Middle East. In large societal conflicts that have been studied, this kind of intractable conflict seems to go through stages that include the following components:

1. A strong sense of threat to central commitments

2. The distortion of one another's positions because of the threat

3. Hardening of positions so that each side becomes convinced of some central assumptions that continue to fuel the conflict

4. The development of fixed patterns of response which assume the conflict is central and ongoing (Schellenberg, 1996, p. 76)

In working with family conflicts over the years, I have seen this perception of continued threat play an important part in the continuation of family conflicts. The injustices perceived, true or not, are carefully guarded and nurtured by one or both sides as the rationale for further retaliation and continued bases for conflict. This is often commingled with the internal working model of insecure attachment described in Chapter One, where the insecure person projects the negative expectation of distrust and scarcity onto others.

Together, these intrapersonal dynamics play out as repetitive cycles of familial conflict that also seem to become intractable. As we learn more about the reconciliation of large-scale social conflicts, it will be important to see if the techniques can be adapted to the smaller-scale conflicts within families. When family mediators are able to intervene on the deep patterns of interaction and injustice, it is more likely that the conflict will be able to stop the cycle and provide an opportunity for real reconciliation, not just temporary problem solving. Family conflicts in this way often need the emotional healing and transformative approach to get at, understand, and change the underlying dynamic.

The question becomes whether the situation of the dispute is intractable, as in inevitable aging or the inability of a problem to be solved in a preferred way, or whether what has been intractable is the way in which the dispute has been perceived due to triangulation, coalitions, and other family dynamics described in Chapter One. The sense of hopelessness perpetuated by the longevity of the active and increasing tension and conflict behavior is a common feature of these disputes. Family feuds are real and are attenuated by belief systems, cultural awareness, and personal resilience factors. Family therapists viewing these intractable conflicts seek to understand how maintaining the conflict serves the system. By redefining the needs and looking differently at the issues and the people, family members sometimes can change these deep and lasting perceptions that are fueling the conflict.

Family Crisis Versus Family Conflict

Cases that come to mediation while they are still in the phase of escalating conflict present the family mediator with a challenge, because the families are not only in conflict but also often in crisis in some way. The mediator must first work as a crisis intervention specialist, attempting to help the family members achieve security and protection and control anger behavior and violence that can maintain or exacerbate the initial conflict. Before starting to mediate the foundation of conflict, the family mediator often must

1. Assess past, present, and future danger to one or more of the parties

2. Get appropriate legal, social, financial, or medical intervention to reduce or prevent harm

3. Get one or more parties to problem-solve premediation issues that will stabilize the situation (through therapy or medical or legal intervention such as a restraining, antistalking, or status quo order)

A crisis intervention mode requires the family mediator to understand the cycle of family violence (discussed more in Chapter Five). Because some or all of the members of the family may be experiencing very different crises in addition to conflict, some assessment is fundamental. Mediators must first deescalate and help deal with any crises and then provide conflict management and resolution in mediation.

Because a crisis is by definition unpredictable, could not have been foreseen, and therefore cannot be totally planned for, it often puts the person into an emotional state of shock, unable to think adequately. When this happens, family mediators have an overriding duty to get clients in genuine crisis the help they need. A divorce, a termination of parental rights followed by an adoption action, a child being expelled from school, an out-of-home placement for a child, a mother who is going to a nursing home, a father who is dying and needs a decision about life support and heroic care: these situations may be both a conflict and a crisis for some or all of the family members. For example, if a birth mother suddenly is revoking permission for the family to adopt, this can be a crisis for both her and the prospective adoptive parents. Because they often come embedded in the context of preexisting situations of conflict, the crisis may not be the first thing the family mediator sees. It is often the family mediator's job to sort through the complexities of the facts to find which issues are truly crises and therefore need immediate attention and decision making.

Crises in family mediation can be financial, social, legal, emotional, medical, or physical in nature or overwhelming combinations of all of these. For example, a child who has run away but who has kept in touch and is willing to come to a parent-teen mediation session may sincerely want to solve the conflict with his parents and may set an appointment and show up. But when he arrives at the session, he displays a new set of dilemmas that must be dealt with as crises, such as no money, inadequate housing, or new health concerns such as human immunodeficiency virus (HIV) infection or bronchitis. An elderly parent whose medical condition has deteriorated so rapidly that family members must immediately find a care facility presents the family with a sudden crisis, which can affect them all financially as they pay the out-of pocket expenses, socially as they take time off from work and other activities to attend to it, and physically if the parent's house must be cleaned out and sold quickly because they need the money to care for the parent. Family mediators are often the first line of intervention for people whose conflict has escalated suddenly and violently into a new crisis and must now deal with all sorts of competing demands for their attention. Mobilizing family members by making assignments of tasks may be required.

This is a stronger, more evaluative and directive role than some family mediators are used to playing, but it is consistent with the role of a crisis intervenor who must often temporarily be highly assertive in order to get people in emotional shock moving toward the systems that can help them. Family mediators who are skilled at providing a calming influence but also practical information for the crisis are going to be most helpful. As family conflicts unfold, these crises might suddenly pop up in the middle of solid problem solving and transformative work or even at the end of a standard mediation case. A wise family mediator has emergency numbers for likely scenarios for families and can quickly facilitate these referrals from a place of personal knowledge and information.

Renegotiating Intimacy as Well as Power

Robert Emery (1994) has described the conflict of divorce as being about the need for former partners to redefine their roles as an intimate couple and renegotiate their role as parents. He describes the confusion that often exists for the divorcing couple as a slowly diminishing grief cycle of love, anger, and sadness in which the emotions that come out in the divorcing couple's behavior appear contradictory. One minute, they seem to hate each other; the next, they are depressed and inactive on their own behalf; then they are doing things that maintain levels of inappropriate involvement unexpected from people who are divorcing. Emery views divorcing partners as struggling to move away from the closeness and intimacy they had, which is a loss that triggers strong emotional responses. They are at the same time in competitive struggles to gain power and control over each other and the children in the divorce negotiation process and also trying to give up the struggle by letting go. The process of doing the former task can appear to be contradictory to the latter.

A great confusion ensues for the participants and the mediator about whether this is a power struggle or a struggle to maintain the former intimacy they had as marital partners. The dilemma is often between the polar ends of a continuum of connection and control: a family member who has too much connection lacks control, and if he or she has too much control over other family members, it may ruin the connection with those other members. Maintaining the conflict maintains at least some proximity and negative attachment and serves as the only substitute for the closeness that the former partners used to have.

In this way, conflict serves the paradoxical function of maintaining what at least one partner (the one who has been abandoned) would rather not lose. In the reverse logic of someone struggling with grief and loss, the negative intimacy gained is better than being done but completely ignored. "Thus, prolonged, seemingly irrational disputes between former partners may represent struggles about intimacy, not power, at least from the perspective of one of the partners" (Emery, 1994, p. 44). In this sense, the uncomfortable contact afforded by maintaining the conflict keeps the connection that serves the intimacy. Understanding this dynamic of conflict helps a family mediator perceive the meaningfulness of the conflict and the real nature of the struggle.

Divorce is not the only conflict situation in families where this intimacy and loss dynamic happens. I think it is safe to expand Emery's premise by applying it to other types of conflict in families, such as parent-teen troubles, conflicts between adult siblings, complicated out-of-home placements and reunification, and the terrible choices presented to family members during a relative's medical or health crisis. Disputants may frame the problem in terms of someone trying to have inappropriate power and control over them, with each of them feeling that the other is trying to gain the upper hand in standard negotiation procedure. The complaint and problem may really be that intimacy is going to be lost if the matter finally does get resolved. There is an inevitable loss and grief they are trying to suppress, and maintaining the conflict is assuaging this to some degree, at least as long as the conflict continues.

These seemingly interminable disputes in families are a way, albeit rather covert and destructive, to maintain the status quo. This is also supported by the legal-judicial process, which can often delay the resolution of a family conflict or require a level of intimacy that no longer fits the needs of the family as it is redefining itself. Family mediators working with any one of the range of family conflicts discussed in later chapters may find that when the usual techniques of negotiation do not work, this wave of cyclical grief and emotional resistance to letting go of the other is the dominant theme. If this is the case, the family mediator must help the family members recognize their needs to preserve some level of acceptable, more positive intimacy or accept the loss more fully and gracefully. Because family mediators cannot help what they do not recognize, it is very important that they reflect on whether this interactional pattern is happening.

REACTION TO CONFLICT: ANGER, INDIGNATION, AND AGGRESSION

Almost every disputant involved with a family mediation case comes to the mediation effort carrying some level of anger. This truism is unremarkable, except to say that the level involved in family-related conflicts is often much higher than those of commercial and other types of disputes being mediated. People's self-concept, self-worth, and personal integrity are riding on the outcome of these cases, not to mention their lifestyle, values, and deeply held beliefs. Family conflicts are some of the bitterest and most destructive disputes due to the self-involved nature of the conflict. Despite Fisher and Ury's motto (1991) of "separate the people from the problem" that has become the mantra of mediators, this advice is not always possible or even desirable in family mediation cases. This self-involvement means that the level of anger and frustration at barriers is also heightened, and family mediators often see seemingly irrational levels of anger toward issues that do not seem to warrant it. The level of anger is also related to common fight styles and strategies that turn up in family disputes, so it is helpful for family mediators to be able to distinguish the family rules and patterns of expression of the levels of anger within the family.

Anger is like a multiheaded gorgon guarding the path to resolution: until you can help the parties get past, you cannot find the treasure at the end of the journey. Slaying the dragon of anger (or at least finding ways to get past it unharmed) requires the family mediator to understand the different dimensions and responses to it. This section examines the features of the three most common types encountered in family mediation cases: simple anger, indignation, and hostility and aggressive behavior.

Simple Anger: The Continuum of Intensity and Control

Thinking of anger as a single thing is misleading. Anger is the natural emotional response people have to experiencing a barrier to their goal. It comes in many levels of intensity, from minor irritation to rage. Mild intensity levels allow people to respond through all faculties; they can discuss, think about solutions, and try to negotiate. As the intensity increases, though, it is inversely proportional to the ability to think rationally. A person who is fully enraged is not himself and not "in his right mind," for he has been highjacked by his own physiology. When heart and respiration go up in response to the perception of danger or threat, the person's thinking no longer resides in the upper cortex; instead, the autonomic nervous system takes over, and higher cortical functioning becomes subservient to the lower brain stem automatic functioning. This *fight-or-flight mechanism* is based on the survival instinct that tries to preserve the organism by preparing to run away from the danger or encounter it. This response pattern worked well in prehistoric times, but it does not do well in modern society.

John Gottman, a marriage and family therapist who uses empirical science methods, has done clinical studies of hundreds of couples and has determined that a pattern of high physiological arousal reduces a couple's chances to carry on meaningful discussion for solving family problems (Gottman, 1994, 1995; Gottman and Silver, 2000). This work has implications for family mediators, because family members can trigger each other's high physiological arousal state very easily, with the result that efforts to continue to mediate may need to be halted temporarily until the person is back to a more normal state. Once a person's arousal system is activated, it generally takes at least twenty minutes of reducing the stimuli from others and the distress-maintaining thoughts on the part of the person—both of which are creating the physiological arousal—in order for the person to return to normal higher cortical functioning, better thinking, and decreased anger and defensive responses.

A family member who has preexisting mental or emotional conditions, such as post-traumatic stress syndrome, or has been the victim of abuse and violence often experiences emotional flooding from past trauma or abuse. In those conditions (whether or not the person is on prescribed psychoactive medication or has other social or physiological stress factors), the person's ability to respond effectively to control responses is lowered. A mediation participant or family member may be unaware of the other person's intensity of emotional reaction and how this is affecting the other person during the session. Unless the family mediator has asked some background questions that might help determine the past factors for each participant, he or she also might be unaware of how the anger manifests and might be surprised when it seems to flare from nowhere.

In order to understand the level of intensity of anger, family mediators can have disputants declare their level of anger on a five-point scale, with 0 being none, 1 being irritated, and 5 being enraged. Because many people, especially men in our culture, experience anger as a unity—all-encompassing feeling—and are so used to it as their primary response to situations, this verbal labeling of the level of anger helps prevent distortion. It can be a relief to the angry client to realize that what he is experiencing is midrange or lower by his own self-report. Also, the mediator can ask the angry person to provide his level of control of the anger on the same scale. If there is high anger but also a high level of control, the situation is not as potentially dangerous as if it is mid- to lower-level anger with little control.

When people realize their anger is extremely high, they can then reflect on whether their emotional response to the situation is an overreaction or whether anyone else put in this situation would react with the same level of intensity. If it is an overreaction, it can help them realize that their anger response might be connected to something beyond the current situation. A family mediator skilled in directing a disputant's awareness to his or her own internal conflict can often help the angry one to find a more normative response or to review the confabulation of this issue with the past.

Acknowledging the legitimacy and level of the disputant's anger can do much to create conditions of acceptance. As Moore (1996) points out, structural conflicts, by definition and nature, would elicit a legitimate anger response of some level by anyone who inhabited that part of the structure, since the conflict, and therefore the emotional response, is built into the very structure of the system. The particular level of conflict experienced, however, will be entirely dependent on the past history of the person experiencing the structural conflict. By having the family mediator acknowledge the legitimacy and normalcy of the anger response (if not the level of anger), the angry person no longer needs to justify his response and can move away from the anger into more constructive directions.

Eliminating the barrier to the goal can reduce simple anger relatively quickly. Once the family mediator has helped the participants reestablish full personal control by deescalating and managing the process so that the anger event is controlled, the mediator can guide the discussion into problem solving, and the simple anger should melt away with the creation of acceptable alternatives. If the anger response does not stop after twenty minutes of no further stimulation by the other disputant, some other form of anger or other process is at work. For example, the person may be thinking of past injuries and situations or thinking distress-maintaining thoughts, even though the other disputant is not sending any messages that can be construed negatively. Getting the angry client to stop thinking in the old ways that restimulate the anger response is sometimes possible. When mediation efforts stretch into multiple sessions, as is common in family mediation cases, the anger reduction process is helped by the week-long gap between sessions, which provides time for deescalation and finding face-saving alternatives, as well as rethinking of positions, issues, and alternatives.

When anger of higher levels occurs during a session, the family mediator has a responsibility to monitor it to determine if the person is able to control his responses and continue mediating in the face of it. If the construction of the terms of the mediated agreement takes longer than twenty minutes, the family mediator should be able to see the results of anger reduction in the interaction between the disputants. If not, a strategic time-out or early cessation of the session may be required.

Indignation: Justice Concerns and Accountability

When someone has harmed you physically or mentally or has besmirched your reputation, self-concept, or status within a system, there is not only just simple anger at the event but also a perception of unfairness. One's dignity, integrity, and personhood have been questioned. Even when the problem has ostensibly been solved and all barriers surmounted, what rings in the ears of the one who believes (rightly or wrongly) that she has been harmed is the negative perception of self that has been uttered. Solving the problem will stop the conflict from escalating, but the loss of face and the lowering of self-perception involved in being connected to the conflict can continue indefinitely. This can make the emotional resolution of the conflict more difficult. Such emotional equity is as imperative as the actual specifics for completeness and harmony in the final outcome of mediation.

Retzinger and Scheff (2000) indicate that shame—the deep feeling that is generated when a person or his or her group has been the recipient of harm or dismissive, disrespectful treatment—is often intertwined with anger. The two together are the cause of mediation impasse and seemingly intractable, ongoing conflicts on both an interpersonal level and a larger-scale societal level. "In impasse, both shame and anger are hidden. In both cases, it is the hidden shame that does the damage, because it blocks the possibility of repair of damaged bonds" (Retzinger and Scheff, 2000, p. 76).

Indignation is the more assertive emotional reaction that happens when someone has been disregarded, and this can often be used to cover a deep shame as well as the anger. In fact, indignation might be said to be the flip side of shame—a face-saving reaction to having the deep feeling of lowered self-concept brought about by the attributions or implications of the other. Retzinger and Scheff note that it is the denial of the deep emotions and the alienation that brings that leads to intractable conflict; acknowledging the suffering and shame of self and others creates the conditions for resolution of the conflict. Until the emotional fact of the shame and indignation can be discussed, it remains functioning but unchangeable. When it can be acknowledged in a way that allows the person to maintain some dignity and provides face-saving, then the conflict can be dealt with directly because it no longer has the issue of shame and indignation covering it. Dealing with this issue then becomes the first task in unmasking the conflict prior to trying to resolve it.

In cases that involve indignity as well as simple anger, the one who feels controlled, harmed, or victimized is internally saying, "How dare you have treated me this way!" At the same moment, the one accused is thinking, "How dare you think I might have done this or had this intention!" Both the ostensible victimizer and the ostensible victim have the same theme of indignation, which neither overtly recognizes; yet both are responding from that same emotional reality.

This leitmotif of interactional injustice continues to play out in the dynamics between the parties until or unless they are able to discuss the theme openly and until some level of regret, remorse, or apology is offered or perceived. It is not good enough to solve the problem and create options and alternatives they select. The indignation will continue unless the amends are offered and the bond acknowledged and either repaired, restored, or officially broken in face-saving ways. It is the acknowledgment of the harm and the emotional impact it has had for the parties that recreates or reestablishes the bond between them that has been harmed. Retzinger and Scheff (2000, p. 81) have set out the necessary process and the appropriate intervention for family mediators in order to reduce shame and alienation while repairing the bond between the parties:

1. Acknowledge the source of the impasse or blockage.
2. Provide face-saving and respectful tactics that allow parties to find other positions.
3. Acknowledge the indignation and shame, as well as the level of bond between the parties.
4. Understand how the systems interact with each other.
5. Provide a secure base of exploration of the shame/alienation/indignation.

One method for reducing indignation is to provide this acknowledgment, and apology or sincere regret. Apology is different from forgiveness, which is not required in order to reduce indignation. When an apology is offered, it does not matter if it is accepted readily or completely or even at all. What is important is the statement showing accountability by the one who did the action. A helpful format for apology can be reduced to an anagram, FAIR:

Facts: A statement of the events, as the speaker knows them, without minimizing, blaming, denial, or other defenses

Awareness: A statement of the other's thoughts, feelings, and behavior as they have come to understand them now, without the thinking errors they had in the past or the emotional responses they had at the time

Impact: The consequences that have befallen them due to the event in terms of legal, social, financial, and emotional areas of life

Responsibility: A statement regarding the doer's accountability for both the past events and the specific behavior they will do or not do to prevent such an occurrence in the future

When an apology this detailed is offered, it is hard for the wounded party to remain recalcitrant and indignant. Having the other person intuit and empathize with the distress reduces shame. Mutual apology is often ideal, since each party carries a level of indignation left over from the past events.

When family mediators encourage and support this important emotional work to surface and have voice as part of the mediation effort, the results of mediated agreements can often last longer because the participants no longer have the need to keep vilifying the other. When their shame and indignation are reduced, they can make better agreements and are more willing to do so.

Hostility and Aggression: Beyond Thought

The topic of what causes a person to become hostile, aggressive, and even violent is of importance to many fields of endeavor and many disciplines, including sociologists, psychologists, justice professionals, and others who work with people in situations where conflict, social power, and accountability for behavior converge. In families, we know that family conflict can trigger severe reactions and can create the climate in which children learn about how adults use control, abuse, and violence. While family conflicts engender anger in almost all cases and indignation in most cases, there are a few cases where hostility and aggression are dominant themes in the interactions between family members or become an event of huge impact in the family mediator's office. It is important for the family mediator to have some theory base in order to understand this and then to make choices about how to deal with it.

Hostility as an Emotional Steady State. As I will use it here, the term *hostility* refers to an ongoing state of defense within the individual. It is not a casual remark or a feeling state, but rather an orientation to the world where the dominant theme is a negative expectation that becomes a self-fulfilling prophesy. People who are hostile anticipate that others are against them and therefore react to them in an angry way, leading to interchanges that are exactly what they believe would happen. Hostile people carry nonspecific anger with them like a protective shield. They believe that the best defense is a good offense, and they are often rude and offensive. They bring out the anger and indignation of most people they encounter, because they project it onto those they meet.

The meta-message that hostile people convey is, "I have been so harmed and insulted and have had no redress for my grievances or acknowledgment that they even exist that I don't have to respond to you in any way other than in anger. I will assume the worst and blame you before you have done anything." This has sometimes been called a *malignant victim stance,* because the hostile person feels victimized but then believes he is justified in harming others because of his injuries. Hostile people maintain this attitude and their own hostile behavior even when they are not being mistreated, and in fact cannot see when they are being treated positively. This can be very confusing to others who do not understand this dynamic. Kindness and reciprocity theory do not work with truly hostile people. They need to maintain their hostility as a justification for many other things in their lives and are not amenable to letting down this defense.

Hostility does not respond to the family mediator's usual skills and techniques of good problem solving, transformative approaches, emotional ventilation, or having someone frame an apology. A hostile person does not respond as most other people would to the bargaining during mediation. While people with simple anger can respond despite their anger and indignant people can leave their indignation behind if the injustice is addressed and an apology is offered, the truly hostile person cannot usually leave the hostility behind.

When we look at reciprocity theory or the theory of mutual influence, it describes how difficult it is for a person to remain unaffected by the positive behavior of another. Simple anger and injustice concerns often respond to the gentle influence of a positive person—either the mediator or the other disputant. By consistently being positive, maintaining pleasantness instead of being reactionary, and offering true remorse and apology, the family member may be able to reduce the anger and frustration and the other reactive behaviors of the other person. However, the usual prescription of "just be nice to them and they will stop being so angry" does not work with a truly hostile person. The hostile person remains hostile even in the face of contrition and apology, uninfluenced by the behaviors of others around them, because the hostility is an internal state, not a set of interactional dynamics. Hostile people do not respond reciprocally.

Reciprocity is "the process of behavioral adaptation where one party responds in a similar direction to another party's behaviors with behaviors of comparable functional values" (Folger, Poole, and Stutman, 2001, p. 103). People experiencing simple anger can start to be reciprocally influenced by the type of responses given back toward their anger. People expressing indignation will be slower to be affected by reciprocity, but may be able to become more reciprocal, especially when they receive acknowledgment of the grievance or injustice they suffered. Hostile people cannot respond despite our best efforts at reciprocity. They remain unmoved by the other's moves, as an unconscious, complex set of thoughts, feelings, and behaviors masks them.

Aggression as a Trait, Behavior, and Interaction. Aggression can be thought of as an individual trait or way of being for an individual and can be seen as the person's behavior. It can also be thought of as an interactional system of action and response. Psychologists have been looking at aggression as a behavioral manifestation of internal biological and physiological structures and processes. As a society, we often ask why one person becomes aggressive to the point of doing violent acts to strangers or even loved ones in their family. The answer for some researchers resides in human genetics, hormonal fluctuations, and other physical and biological features of that individual.

Recent brain and biological research is attempting to map and measure individuals and groups in terms of the physiology of aggressive and other behavior. The work of researchers such as Daniel Amen (1998), who has used new technology to show the areas of the brain affected during complex human behavior, promises important new discoveries about how to diagnose and correct problems that are truly physiological in nature yet show up in behavior and interaction with others, such as aggressive and impulsive behavior. In the next few years, we will likely see increasing sophistication of behavioral control due to increased sophistication in technology and medication. Family mediators may need to keep up with this field to understand the reactions and the drugs their clients are taking and to understand how these affect the interactions of their clients. A wise family mediator will take some continuing education credits in psychopharmacology in order to keep up with these new therapies and breakthroughs in medical science.

Amen's work indicates that brain scans of people who are violent and aggressive are significantly different from those who have never been violent. The major differences in their brain structure and function suggest that violent and aggressive people have the following tendencies:

- Decreased activity in the prefrontal cortices, leading to troubled thinking
- Increased cingulate activity, leading to getting stuck on thoughts or compulsiveness
- Increased or decreased activity in the left temporal lobe, leading to quick temper and anger outbursts

- Increased activity in the basal ganglia and/or limbic system, leading to anxiety and moodiness (Amen, 1998, p. 212)

Obviously, family mediators are seldom in a position to know the physiological facts of the people with whom they mediate unless that person volunteers diagnostic or physical information or one of the participants tells the mediator about a past history of behavior that might be indicative of such physical issues. We need not amateurishly try to diagnose a complex condition. Yet family mediators may need to understand which parts of human behavior are more likely to be able to change by volitional control and which ones are unlikely to do so, since the need for behavioral change is at the core of many of the mediated agreements of clients. This issue of what is changeable about a family member and what is not becomes important to the negotiation within the mediation.

This debate about whether behavior is created and controlled primarily by physical nature or social nurture is not an esoteric debate for family mediators, who are helping families who have the potential and often the past history of aggression and violence when they have conflicts. The dilemma this produces is that family mediators are using a logical and intuitive, sequential process that can be fully used only if the parties maintain their capacities to be logical, intuitive, and sequential. If disputants are being affected by their own biology such that they cannot maintain rational states and respond to the process, there is some question ethically about the advisability of family mediation.

Social Interactionist and Social Learning Theories. A way to understand the complex nature of aggression that is compatible with family mediation efforts is the social interactionist perspective; another is social learning theories of behavior. These theories do not undermine or dispute the new scientifically generated biological bases of people's behavior, but rather place emphasis on issues that family mediators can do something about. While family mediators can and should refer people to therapists and physicians if they need them, most of the time they will be working with clients who are caught in social dilemmas that have been created socially and will respond socially to the social interaction of mediation. These perspectives support and augment the family mediators' work and are useful theory bases to bring to the mediation process.

The social interactionist perspective of aggression rests on four major points of agreement (Felson and Tedeschi, 1993, pp. 1–2):

1. *Aggression is instrumental behavior:* it is voluntary and intentional, and it is a means to achieving values or goals, to influence others, establish and protect social identities, and achieve justice or retribution.

2. *Aggression is not uncontrolled inner forces,* libidinal energy, instincts, biological hardwiring through hormones, or other ideas that posit inner processes, but rather *a normal consequence of conflict in human interaction.*

3. *Aggression is perceived as being instigated and affected by situational and interpersonal factors,* so outcomes are not pre-determined but are dynamic and changeable, depending upon who is involved. You must look not only at the doer (actor), but also the antagonists and third parties to the aggression as well.

4. *Aggression often depends on the doer's (actor's) deep beliefs about justice,* equity, assignment of blame, and legitimacy of certain behaviors. In this way it is compatible with attribution theory and equity theory.

In this perspective, there is a differentiation between aggressive behavior that is dispute related compared to that which is more systemic and predatory in nature. In the former, the incidences of aggressive behavior develop out of a perceived grievance and injustice. The aggressive behavior is an attempt on the part of the doer to create some appropriate social control to deal with the perceived injustice. The reactor is attempting to right the wrong, and his social identities play a major role in his choice of behavior and escalation to aggressive behavior. The reactor believes he has provocation and that his role or status legitimizes the use of force.

The predatory type of aggression involves acts of exploitation and demonstration of power over others rather than as a response to injustice, and therefore does not have a precursor event. Reactive, dispute-related aggression is more often involved in family mediation cases, although occasionally a family mediation dispute involves a person who might be experiencing the predatory aggression and violence from another family member or an outside source.

An example will illustrate the concept of the social interactionist perspective on aggression. Parents often have the social role expectation that they are supposed to be in control of their minor children. A father taking on that belief could see his son's misbehavior as an injustice to him as the father ("he is not respecting my authority over him"). If the father has a deep belief that he has a mandate to use whatever force is necessary to control his child and that such force is legitimate, the father may behave aggressively toward his son (perhaps by spanking him) as part of an escalation of the conflict over regaining control and social justice. This retributive justice concept on the part of the father ("I have to punish him for the misbehavior") can lead to an escalating interactional spiral of negative behavior between the father and son. It can lead to mutual accusations and blaming on both sides, with both father and son believing themselves to be the injured party and becoming angry and indignant, and then sometimes stepping into aggressive behavior.

There are other choices that they can make when they become aware of the grievance each of them has: they can do nothing, exempt themselves or the other from blame (and thereby reduce anger), forgive the other, or negotiate about restitution or punishment. Which choice they will pick depends in large part on their beliefs about power and control, the preexisting father-child relationship, and their values about aggressive behavior, as well as about retributive versus restorative justice. This is why family mediators and other helping professionals cannot accurately predict which families or individuals will become aggressive during their conflicts.

Averill (1993) points to the uses of anger to legitimize aggressive behavior and notes that there is a difference between feeling angry and being angry. He identifies four propositions (pp. 172–173) that explain how anger serves this purpose:

1. *Anger helps legitimize aggression.* Because people think of it as an emotion or passion, they believe they cannot control their anger, and therefore cannot be held responsible for the consequences of their behavior when angry. Also, if they have anger, it involves someone being the instigator.

2. *Anger is identified (incorrectly) with feelings.* People equate feeling angry with being angry. Since people frequently behave differently dependent upon their feelings, this allows people to behave angrily and do behavior associated with anger.

3. *Angry feelings can be illusory.* If anger is unjustifiable, you can correct it by changing the false premises, but when it is illusory, it is the conscious awareness of being angry even though there is no objective reality that corresponds. In this way, a person can feel angry although their behavior does not show it.

4. *Anger is not an event, either psychological or physiological, that occurs within the mind (or body) of the individual.* Because of the interactional nature of anger, the origins and functions of anger are found in the social interaction between people, not in intrapsychic events within just one person.

The rules of appropriate expression of anger are culturally based norms that we develop in our homes, schools, and workplaces and are reflected in our laws. Because there are such social differences, we know that to some degree, the behavior associated with anger is socially learned rather than biologically determined. In our culture, the intent of harm or wrongdoing makes a big difference as to the legitimacy of the anger and the legitimacy of aggressive behavior toward the original error. Averill (1993, pp. 182–184) proposes, based on his research, that the following are hallmarks of our culture's rules about anger:

1. A person has the right (duty) to become angry at intentional wrongdoing or at intentional misdeeds if those misdeeds are correctable (for example, due to negligence, carelessness, or oversight).

2. Anger should be directed only at persons and, by extension, other entities (one's self, human institutions) that can be held responsible for their actions.

3. Anger should not be displaced on an innocent third party, nor should it be directed at the target for reasons other than the instigation.

4. The aim of anger should be to correct the situation, restore equity, and/or prevent recurrence, not to inflict injury or pain on the target or to achieve selfish ends through intimidation.

5. The angry response should be proportional to the instigation; that is, it should not exceed what is necessary to correct the situation, restore equity, or prevent the instigation from happening again.

6. Anger should follow closely the provocation and not endure longer than is needed to correct the situation (typically a few hours or days, at most).

7. Anger should involve commitment and resolve; that is, a person should not become angry unless appropriate follow-through is intended, circumstances permitting.

Under these typical social rules, families would not hold grudges or try for retribution and revenge, would not maintain anger past when it is useful to mobilize them to action, and would take no action that would be an overreaction. They would not become aggressive in their anger unless the situation called for it. Obviously, many families fall short of this list or hold very different values and tolerance for anger-related behavior. Averill's list may describe our ostensible collective social beliefs, but it does not accurately describe our social realities. Because we are a pluralistic society, not everyone grew up in the same anger culture that Averill is describing. It is important for family mediators to find out the family members' values and beliefs about anger as feeling and behavior and about their tolerance of aggressive behavior.

Like hostility, aggression is not usually amenable to reduction through reciprocity. A person who is acting aggressively is doing so by choice and out of deep-seated, but potentially changeable ideas, unlike someone who is hostile, who is doing the hostility without awareness or full choice. Neither hostility nor aggression will respond to the family mediator's usual set of behavioral responses, such as politeness, reminding the person of the rules, or even assertive or highly directive and controlling techniques. In fact, the more the mediator tries to demand control of the session, the more the aggressive behavior may increase in reaction to the perceived threat of the mediator. Family mediators need to understand these dynamics and make them part of their formulation of the people, the problem, and the processes that will work.

Anger and Aggression as Social Learning in the Family. It makes sense that since we learn the social rules about anger and aggression in our families, those who come from families where aggression was tolerated or expected tend to repeat the pattern when they become parents. This again points to the social and interactional nature of aggression as a means of conflict control and its escalation, while not detracting from any biological transmissions that may affect it. Daniel Goleman (1995), who has studied children, parents, and educational systems, has noted that children who are disciplined capriciously by their parents or experience aggression at home maintain higher levels of aggression toward their classmates. When the children were studied over their lifetime, their tendency to be more aggressive in their behavior continued over time:

> There is a lesson in how aggressiveness is passed from generation to generation to generation. Any inherited propensities aside, the troublemakers as grownups acted in a way that made family life a school for aggression. As children, the troublemakers had parents who disciplined them with arbitrary, relentless severity; as parents they repeated the pattern. [Goleman, 1995, p. 196]

Goleman's research leads him to conclude that aggression and lack of empathy for the other is one of the failures in emotional education. Families and schools responsible for teaching children about these feelings and behaviors can make the situation worse by being oblivious to the need to structure this learning socially or by teaching the wrong message about it. Patterns of aggression and lack of empathy tend to stay in families until there is a courageous act of change on the part of one or more members. Unless there is a clear message or requirement to change, the behavior tends to stay in effect. Preschoolers who hit and hurt others can be foreshadowing themselves as aggressive adults, who are more prone to depression and commit more aggressive crimes.

Goleman believes that instead of the physical brain shaping the social person, it may be that social interactions shape brain formation and function and serve as the mechanism for affective learning. He believes that brain functioning and neurochemistry are tied to the social interaction of individuals, giving hope to those who experience emotional abuse, trauma, and aggression. By training children and families to be more sensitive to emotional skills and growth and providing different models of conflict resolution, empathy, and other social skills, people will be able to break out of generational cycles and lead better lives. If people have better skills at being able to communicate their anger, indignation, and grievances, they may be able to short-circuit the aggression cycle and not be stuck in a style of interaction that gets them into trouble.

Family mediators can help family members voice their interpersonal griev-ances and keep their deep beliefs about right and wrong without having to resort to force, power-over tactics, and aggression that lead to damaging violence. They can adopt a theory of aggression that can be compatible with their model of mediation and effectively screen for family members who cannot handle the forum of mediation or control their aggressive behavior enough to benefit.

The Family Mediator's Role with Hostility and Aggression. Family mediators must have a view of hostility and aggression that is based on the newest research and is at least compatible with the basic presumptions of mediation. In some mediation approaches, such as the transformative, mediators are supposed to help the parties facilitate and discuss their feelings. (More discussion of these models of mediation follows in Chapter Three.) Expression of feeling is a vital part of the transformative approach: "In transformative practice, third parties view the expression of emotions—anger, hurt, frustration, and so on—as an inte-gral part of the conflict process. Intervenors therefore expect and allow the par-ties to express emotions, and they are prepared to work with these expressions of emotion as the conflict unfolds" (Folger and Bush, 1996, p. 271). A mediator following this approach would need to allow a hostile person to ventilate.

The problem is that this transformative prescription makes sense only with participants who have situational distress and simple anger or indignation, where ventilation of the feelings allows the material to become overt and there-fore able to be managed or resolved. It is the exact opposite in cases of hostil-ity and angry aggression or when disturbed behavior is biologically caused. In cases of aggression and hostility that involve deep brain structures and func-tions, the family mediator must not allow the expression of the hostility in ver-bal or physical aggression, posturing, threatening, stalking, and intimidation tactics, because ventilating violence and allowing aggression and anger expres-sion for hostile and aggressive people leads to more violence and aggression, not cessation of the behavior. This is why family mediators need a fairly sophis-ticated understanding of and screening mechanism for the differences between simple anger and indignation at injustice as opposed to aggression.

Family mediators can actually do harm if they have not correctly identified hostility or aggression. They need to know the features of hostility and aggres-sion, so they can provide the correct intervention, not follow simplistic pre-scriptions that work only for people in situational distress. People whose brains function differently cannot consciously will themselves to be different or to interact differently, and they cannot transform themselves quickly in mediation. People who are hostile are that way for a reason, and the defense mechanism of hostility is there because the person believes he needs to maintain that defense and to some degree it has been useful to him. Sometimes people who have hostility, aggressive behavior, or brain-functioning problems cannot effectively cope with a situation as stressful and complex as family dispute resolution and mediation without the help of specific prescribed drugs and talking therapies. Will the family mediator be able to make the decision as to who can benefit from further expression of anger and who cannot?

Although family mediators need not be medical or psychiatric practitioners, it certainly will be necessary for them to identify participants who are expressing the types of verbal and physical aggression and hostility that indicate longer-term, biologically connected problems; to make proper referrals for help; and to not foster unhelpful and potentially dangerous methods in mediation.

HOW FAMILIES FIGHT

Families and couples have different styles and methods for fighting. Since marital therapists see couples who are fighting, they have developed some ways of looking at the patterns of interaction that couples use. The first dimension to look at is whether the fighting is overt, open, and observable and people can talk about it, or whether it is covert, covered, and tucked away and people cannot acknowledge it. Overt fighting can frighten children and adults, but it can be more productive because it can be named and dealt with. Covert fighting requires that the couple or family start to identify their opposing tendencies as a precursor to resolution, and since they do not want to acknowledge these, the mediator must go back to a more facilitative role to help to make the conflict acceptable.

Styles of Reaction to Conflict

Each person has a general style of conflict response that will tend to function in family conflict and yet a person's style in the family may be very different compared to his or her conflict approach among strangers. Early studies of people's responses to conflict were divided into five categories, and a standardized test, the Thomas-Kilmann Conflict Mode Instrument (Thomas and Kilmann, 1974), was based on the level of self-assertion and cooperativeness they showed (Folger, Poole, and Stutman, 2001).

- The avoiding (flight) style, which is low on self-assertion but also uncooperative, because it does not allow parties to confront the conflict directly. The avoider can be perceived as not caring or being overly self-concerned and inattentive to the needs of the other.

- The accommodating (appeasement, soothing) style, which is highly cooperative but also low in self-assertion. It can be worrisome because the person gives in and becomes self-sacrificing and gives the other what he or she wants, but often feels resentful later or is perceived as being weak.

- The compromising style (horse trading, sharing), which is halfway cooperative and halfway self-assertive but can be too quick to make a deal and still not meet his or her own or the other person's needs.

- The competing (forcing, dominant) style, which is the most self-assertive and sees the conflict situation as a win-lose proposition, with a strong drive to be the winner. This style is not cooperative, because the competitor feels the imperative to win at all costs. This is often a style of people who have learned through personal experience that they "have to look out for number one." People who are always this way may be perceived as pushy, arrogant, or unbending.

- The collaborative (problem solving, integrative) style, which is also high in self-assertion but is also highly cooperative. The person sees it as a win-win situation and will stay at work until the needs of both or all parties are addressed. People using this style can be perceived as too demanding or long-winded, since they often need others to stay with the process long after the others are comfortable.

More recent work on conflict styles cited by Folger, Poole, and Stutman (2001, p. 221) uses these five basic categories but also looks at some other dimensions and levels:

- *Disclosiveness,* how much information people share with each other during the conflict

- *Empowerment,* how much power they keep for themselves and how much they let the other person share control or power in the conflict

- *Activeness,* how much the person is involved with the conflict

- *Flexibility,* how much range of movement in positions and options they are willing to give during the conflict

These rather static models do not actually describe what transpires in the development and resolution of conflict in a family. While a person may have a general orientation to conflict, the rules of the family may indicate that he must stay within a certain range in order to be perceived as being consistent in his role. For an example, if a woman who is generally competitive feels shame if she tries to compete with her partner or parent during a family conflict, she may also know that her competitive stance would be the best one for her interests but not for her role in the family.

Patterns of Conflict Interactions

The style of conflict reaction each person selects may have to adapt to the style of the other parties and may need to change during different phases of the family conflict resolution effort. For example, a divorcing spouse may need to be initially competitive to get the avoiding spouse to engage in the conflict regarding custody and access of the children, yet may want to become more collaborative or even compromising over the course of the mediation effort, especially around changing hardened positions or solitary options. Folger, Poole, and Stutman (2001) advise their readers to think about how effective and ethical their stance might be and to consider both the long-term consequences and the short-term gains, as well as the type of response they anticipate from the others in the struggle.

Marital Fight Patterns

Marital therapists have long found that couples who are experiencing the structure of conflict or a conflict situation (using Rummel's terminology) tend to form complex patterns of interaction that become almost second nature to them. Wile ([1981] 1993) has described these as three distinct patterns: the mutual withdrawal pattern, the mutual accusation or angry partners pattern, and the demanding-withdrawing pattern, where partners are polarized. It is not at all unusual for a particular couple or family to shift from one to another pattern in the course of communication, a day, or a week. Other couples pick one style and stick with it for all fights and conflicts.

No matter which style the couple has been using, according to Wile, there are three major interventions that must be done in sequence for all styles:

1. Clarify each partner's position to determine what the problem is for each of them.

2. Provide recognition that each partner is "in a difficult, no-win position and that it [is] understandable that each would be responding the way he or she [is]" (Wile, 1993, p. 158).

3. Help the parties construct a joint, mutual overview of the problem— what negotiators would call creating a single-text agenda.

Wile's approach is compatible with, as well as similar to, concepts from integrative bargaining and negotiation and the hallmarks of the transformative and problem-solving mediation models.

When the practitioner provides these three steps, the interventions are slightly different for each of the three basic couples conflict styles. In the withdrawal style, the practitioner has to be careful not to play into the disqualification and judgmentalism aimed from one partner to the other. Because partners stuck in this interactional style cannot legitimately express their complaints, they often feel cut off, isolated, and unable to talk about what is really bothering them for fear that the discussion will make it worse.

When the couple or family members can talk about the fact of the withdrawal and the fear rather than the specifics, then they can give each other permission to hold the hard discussion. This then promotes the opposite of their fear: a feeling of contact with the other and collaboration rather than distance in solving the problem. Getting the partners to describe the strategic withdrawal as a fact legitimizes it and allows that need to become part of the discussion and interaction. When the other party allows the withdrawal, it may no longer be necessary.

With overtly angry and fighting couples, family therapists and mediators may need to shift from "figure to ground," overlooking the angry confrontation in favor of finding the background of hurt, powerlessness, shame, and other swirling feelings. While early family therapists focused on teaching family members simple or complex rules and "fair fighting" techniques in order to have more tightly controlled, even scripted dialogue using patterns of communication that were taught, real couples express their anger in expressive, ungenteel ways and often reject or forget the rules in the heat of anger. Wile's approach is to help partners have the fight they need to have and to help them fight more openly and successfully, as well as recover from the fight. By helping parties sharpen their arguments, believe themselves, and gain more satisfaction from their fights, the need to fight will be reduced, and the recovery time and discussion about the fight will also reduce the acrimony.

Wile suggests having the couple fight but in new, more complete, and more effective ways that can help them bring justice and fairness that itself will lead to greater harmony. For couples who are vicious and unswerving in their anger, he recommends reflecting and acknowledging the hidden desperation they feel underneath the bluster. Facilitating the couple's anger will work only with socially constructed anger, not physiologically created anger or aggression.

For couples or families who are manifesting the third style of demanding-withdrawing or distancer-pursuer patterns of behavior, the cycle becomes one of a self-fulfilling trap. The more one tries to get away from the conflict, the more the other pursues, which forces the other to further distance, and so on. Lerner (1985) has described the "dance of anger" as a circular pattern of over- and underinvolvement, with the distancer-pursuer pattern being a very ancient "dance" that is often passed on and learned from one generation to another in families.

Wile (1993) approaches this demanding-withdrawing problem in the same three-step method used in the other patterns but also focuses on reducing blame and pointing out the hidden commonalities under their differences. There are often historical reversals of positions, which can indicate that each has had similar concerns. By being able to talk about the interaction they are having, they can change that very interaction.

Because the behaviors are interactional and behavioral in nature, these fight styles are amenable to change, and the interventions recommended fit with the role of the family mediator. One need not be a therapist in order to name the problem, help parties hold the hard discussion in more productive ways, and provide support for personal and interpersonal change in the family system. Whether the family mediator is transformative or problem solving, evaluative or facilitative, these awarenesses and techniques fit.

Family Interactional Fight Patterns

It is not just couples who fight in these distinct patterns. All family disputes are likely to fit these three styles that Wile articulated, and the interventions recommended are certainly within the range of family mediation practice, no matter what model or approach is used.

Some families recognize that they have a usual pattern of engagement of the conflict, roles they play during the conflict, and a preferred method of minimizing the conflict. For example, in a stepfamily, the biological mother may be aware that the worst fights in the family are usually triggered by her husband's commenting that her children are not doing their part of the house tasks; she then defends the children, which then leads to the children leaving and the mother and her husband continuing and expanding the argument and personalizing it to become threatening to their own couple relationship rather than staying with the parenting-related dispute. Some families find that their disputes always end up on the same topic or are handled the same way, with a walkout, an explosion, or an icy silence by the same person, no matter what the topic was. Deconstructing these fights gives the family mediator an idea of what the pattern is and which role each person has been assigned. Sometimes the child becomes the distracter by suddenly harming the other child to stop the negative interaction with the parents. With groups of adult siblings, the frustration of the old pattern is that the current situation seems to be replaying old patterns that were never successful. Hitting this wall of frustration when the family does the usual pattern is a wonderful moment for intervention in the family conflict if the family mediator is sensitive and aware of that critical time. When family mediators can intervene and reshape the pattern, it changes the process, which automatically changes the outcome.

The socially unacceptable and unhelpful construction of the family's fighting and conflict style can be changed by openly acknowledging the interaction, as well as the content. In this way, the mantra of the family mediator could be, "Process precedes content." Mediators of all types of disputes can benefit from focusing on the interaction of the parties. The most important interactional elements for a mediator to observe and intervene in include the following attributes of the disputants:

- Relationship
- Power and conflict orientation
- Communication
- Range of interaction

- Transparency
- Respectfulness
- Balance and neutrality
- The climate of the session
- The mediator's modeling of behavior (Lang and Taylor, 2000, pp. 158–159)

By helping the participants in family mediation understand their interactional style and by noticing which of these factors are affected when the family is in its typical interactive pattern, the family mediator can suggest some changes that will change the interactional quality. Looking at these interactional elements within Wile's three basic fight styles, the participants can hold an open discussion about how they fight, not what they fight about. Then they can make overt decisions about the style of interaction they will have during mediation, which prevents the covert, old pattern from reasserting itself. The family mediator can help them monitor the interaction and officiate to help them notice when they are not functioning in the new way but reverting to the old pattern, and can encourage them to continue in the stuck spots. When the family changes the way in which the dialogue is constructed and the roles they play, they are changing the pattern of fighting, and that will automatically change the outcome.

NEGOTIATION WITHIN MEDIATION

Family conflicts and disputes require family members either to negotiate together to solve the problem or to declare the problem impossible to resolve or manage. Because of the natural affinities and alliances that may be historical in families, the effort to negotiate the new condition is often hampered by incomplete negotiation, or not having the appropriate members of the family at part of the negotiation effort. Mediation of family disputes offers the family members new ways to negotiate among themselves to resolve or manage their dispute. Many family members are unsophisticated in the process of negotiating and must be shown how to do it. Others understand how to negotiate but find that the roles and rules of the family have usually interfered with their negotiation. Styles and communication efforts that have been successful in negotiations with strangers or work companions do not seem effective or seem totally inappropriate when negotiating with one's own mother, father, sibling, or child. The boundaries and double binds of the family interaction can prevent family members who are strong negotiators from doing their best in negotiating within their own family system.

Family mediators often need to be aware of the unique dynamics for negotiation that are taking place during the mediation process. Sometimes a family mediator called into the dispute is the only professional the family will see and thus the only one who can help realign the family relationships sufficiently to make the negotiative effort needed to resolve the conflict more effective. The way in which the family members are trying to negotiate with each other will be created by the perceptions they have of the appropriateness to be negotiating at all. The old family patterns and rules, which might have indicated, "Don't talk back to your mother!" may be inhibiting the need of a family member to hold a position against the preference of the mother in order to solve the problem. Families where there were implicit or explicit rules—for example, "Father knows best," or "You can't argue with your sister and still be one of us"—find themselves stuck in family conflicts. To negotiate places them in bad faith with their family members, but not to negotiate means that options that seem unwise or impractical may be selected in the problem solving without their input. They are in a lose-lose internal conflict as to whether they can and should be able to negotiate, let alone whether their negotiation with their family member is effective.

First families fight, then they try to negotiate, and when that does not seem to work, they call in family mediators either before or concurrently with when they resort to legal intervention and other coercive processes. This section on negotiation within a family and within the family mediation is included in this chapter's discussion of family conflict, because family members will be trying to bargain and negotiate with each other both before the family mediation commences and during it in order to try to solve the dispute. Direct negotiation among family members has often failed long before the mediator is called in, and the negotiative process that was used may have left some bitterness or feelings of vengeance for some or all of the family members. For these reasons, a brief review of negotiation and the communication in it needs to be included in this chapter on how families engage in disputes.

The family mediator needs to know what specifically was tried and the method of negotiation between family members prior to the mediation effort. Then the mediator will try to reengage the family members in direct negotiation during the mediation effort, as is true in all other mediation contexts.

Coaching Negotiation During Family Conflicts

The heart of all family mediation is direct, integrative negotiation between the participants. Some family mediation cases and situations include matters that lend themselves to traditional distributive negotiation techniques, such as disputes about family money during divorce, guardianship, child support arrearages, probate matters, and the use of medical insurance money. However, most negotiation in family mediation is based on the premises of integrative negotiation: that there need not be winners and losers, that there should not be bad deals, and that each person in the negotiation should be able to get some intangible needs met as well as a good-enough outcome. "In distributive bargaining, the goals of the parties are initially at odds—or at least appear that way to some or all of the parties. In contrast, in integrative negotiation the goals of the parties are not mutually exclusive. . . . The fundamental structure of an integrative negotiation situation is such that it allows both sides to achieve their objectives" (Lewicki, Saunders, and Minton, 2001, p. 89).

Most family conflicts are presented to the mediator as if they are distributive problems, whether they are or not. Divorcing parents present that they want "half the child's time"; a family facing placement of an elderly, disabled, or medically involved relative see the problem as limited options, scarce resources, and either-or choices between factions. Family disputes about placement of abused or neglected children are presented as if the child were an object to be divided among competing camps. The basic task of the family mediator is to move the perception of the participants from a distributive to an integrative perspective. Then the potential threat of loss is minimized, and more creative options that are not diametric opposites can come forward.

Measuring Family Communication for Negotiation

Because negotiation takes place in the dimension and medium of communication, it is important to focus on the communication style of the family. Olsen (1993) articulates the aspects of family communication, measured on three levels or six gradients that he recommends that clinicians rate when working with a family in order to come to a global family communication rating for the family:

- Listening skills of empathy and attentive listening
- Speaker's skills, of speaking for self rather than speaking for others
- The level of self-disclosure
- The clarity of the content of the message
- The level of continuity and tracking of a message in the course of communication
- The respect and regard for feelings and message of others (p. 137)

The mediator is inherently working with these factors for each family member as they begin to describe the conflict and their positions and interests. A family mediator who is able not only to listen to the overt content but also reflect on these levels of communication for the different family members can understand more about the family functioning. The communication level and patterns will either contribute positively to the negotiation and the perception of the parties who are negotiating or may be a hampering effect to the negotiation. If the latter, the family mediator may first need to help the family members change their communication methods in order to change the communication context in which the negotiation will take place. Suggested changes in the communication of some or all of the family members can lead to fewer problems in negotiation and may have to take precedence in the sequence of work with the family. Until most or all of the family members can achieve a sufficient level of listening, tracking, clarity, and not speaking for each other, it will be extremely difficult to negotiate anything among the members of the family.

Family mediators must often help unsophisticated or unpracticed negotiators learn what is effective and ineffective in their negotiation repertoire as the mediation process unfolds. Since negotiation is a specific form of communication, it can suffer from typical errors in the two parts of communication: sending messages and receiving them. The messages themselves can contain levels of meaning, including not only the stated content but the additional, sometimes unintended level of meaning that is sent or received, accurately or inaccurately. Lewicki, Saunders, and Minton (2001) have noted typical perceptual problems in communication that affect the negotiation noted: generalization, anticipation, stereotyping and halo effects, selective perceptions or filtering, and attribution or projection onto others. Each one of these may hamper the sender's or the receiver's capacity for communication; with many couples and families, these problems happen simultaneously.

Decoding Threats

Because the perception of threat is such an important emotional trigger for anger and other defensive responses, it is important that the communication be decoded to reduce unintentional or intentional threat. Because human communication comprises layers of meaning, some parties can take the following linguistic dimensions as indicators to be wary or can respond with defensive maneuvers to protect against a perceived threat or intimidation if they hear or see any of the following:

- Polarized language (black-white, good-bad)
- Verbal immediacy (urgency in voice)
- Psychological distancing (passive voice)
- Intensity of language (inflated adjectives)
- The level of diversity of lexicon and comfort with word usages (using more complex phrases and word choices)
- Power dimensions inherent in the style of expression

Persuasiveness of speech, use of metaphors, and other linguistic changes can be based not only on gender, culture, and context but also on subtle assertion of the former interactional system between the members of the family. By speaking with authority, a family member can subtly remind the other family members who historically has been "boss." The family mediator needs to listen carefully for the meta-message to determine whether the speaker is trying to change or maintain the status quo. Much of communication is what is not said directly or barely said.

Cognitive Biases That Clog Communication

In addition to these verbal communication factors, Lewicki, Saunders, and Minton (2001) indicate the typical cognitive biases that can create problems during negotiation. Beyond the sending-receiving process of communication, these are errors that have to do with the thinking-feeling-acting system of each individual who has received the communication. These cognitive biases are individual cognitive events but get played out in the interactional field among the participants. For example, if the family members have a cognitive belief system that tends to think in right-wrong, dichotomous, concrete ways, it may be difficult for them to overcome this bias of a zero-sum game. Similarly, if a family member always thinks of things out of a mind-set of deprivation and static, scarce resources, it may be difficult for that person to move mentally to the integrative bargaining mind-set that is more amenable to the mediation process.

Two other cognitive biases, ignoring of other people's cognition and reactive devaluation, are negative communication clogs that tend to be frequent in family negotiation. Family members can rule out a particular family member's opinions, interests, and needs simply because of who that member is. When they do this, they create an unconscious or willful blocking of the family member as an equal participant or important contributor to the mediation effort or the negotiated solution.

For example, parents stuck in custody or access battles can use this cognitive bias to reject out of hand the suggestions of the children (who are going to be directly affected by the outcome) simply because they *are* children; if the parent has a belief that "father knows best" or "moms always know their own children best," then the cognitive biases may show up in the way the parents negotiate. These failures to be aware of or to consider certain family members' input may be a factor of the former interactional system, where that person was usually or always left out of the decision making. Sometimes this is not as blatant as leaving the person out of the mediation effort or not responding to her or including her input. At times, this operates covertly, with the person being included ostensibly, yet never having her options, needs, or interests ultimately prevail.

Reactive devaluation is the process of not responding to the other party's concessions and movement in negotiation simply because it comes from them. Family members will simply not respond to any option, alternative, or suggestion made by a certain member of the family, not because the person is lacking standing as a decision maker but because of earlier problems and lack of trust.

Usually, there is a past history of minimizing that person. These credibility complaints are based on experience rather than on the merits of the current negotiation.

The neutral family mediator can often use the technique of neutralizing the statement or repackaging the option and reoffering the concessions for consideration. Because the mediator is a neutral party, the listener will not feel disregarded or discounted, as they might if the other family member tries to restate the option. Having the family mediator broker the offer may help the reactive family member hear those concessions more clearly.

The Double Bind of Family Negotiation

Negotiation in family mediation has all the usual pitfalls and problems of any negotiation, plus the added hazard of years of stuffed feelings, perceptions of the other, generalizations about other situations, and all the other history among the parties. It also maintains the dual demand: resolve the problem by *changing* things but also *do not change* the intrinsic quality of the family power structure and unwritten rules and roles. This dual demand of "negotiate for change but make no change" is frustrating for family members who can see that change must happen.

Getting rid of this dual demand must be the first item that is negotiated. If no change is possible or allowable by the family, no negotiation or mediation will be possible. The first negotiation in families must always be that the ones who are in charge of the family will allow change to happen.

FACE-SAVING IN FAMILY CONFLICT

When a father makes a mistake, does he apologize? When children make mistakes or misbehave, is it a negative reflection on the parents? If the family does not care for its elderly or medically troubled family member, has a member who is planning to use doctor-assisted suicide or use heroic means to maintain life, or has abuse or violence, is it considered a shame on the other members of the family? If a child is placed outside the family or sees her grandparent only once a year, is this an indication of a family rift? The answer to these questions, "It depends," indicates the complexity of the topic of generalizing about families. Each family might have a different response to these questions, based on their personal and collective culture.

The concept of face is each person's claim to be perceived as a certain kind of person. Maintaining face, or perceptions of self in context with the others one cares about, is a matter of perception of self and others. Threats to one's face lead to embarrassment, discomfort, shame, indignation, and other forms of anger. People lose face when their image or identity is challenged or ignored, and they immediately start to do defensive, face-saving behavior that attempts to rescue, repair, or restore their image.

Face is important in all cultures but different in each, socially defined and constructed, and subject to defacement, threat, and loss, the triggers of anger and conflict. Loss of face can bring feelings of deep shame and indignation, simple anger, and even a need for revenge and retribution. "Face is a psychological image that can be granted and lost and fought for and presented as a gift; it is the public self-image that every member of society wants to claim for himself or herself; it is a projected image of one's self in a relational context. Face is an identity defined conjointly by the participants in a setting" (Augsberger, 1992, p. 85). All family members have a certain level of face they attempt to maintain in their relationship and family, and conflicts can make all members of a family reconsider their image relative to the others.

Our image of self is not only in our own eyes but also in the eyes of others. This truism also relates to the family as a unit, embedded in the larger social structures. The answer to the questions posed earlier might be very different if viewed within the family unit and viewed outside it. The family members could perceive no shame among themselves, yet shame could be the response if the information is leaked to persons outside the family. The husband and wife could craft a solution that seemed to honor the interests of both of them, only to find that they receive intense threat to face when they try to explain their decisions to others in their family.

Face in High-Context and Low-Context Cultures

Cultures and smaller groups within large social cultures (such as families) can be classified into two basic orientations to their image or face. In high-context (Eastern) cultures, such as China, Korea, Japan, Mexico, and some Native American tribal nations, the larger group or system primarily determines face and identity, and the view of self is always in situational and relational terms. Who you are is to whom you belong: your status inside and outside the family, your family connections, and so on. These cultures rely on elaborate protocol, indirectness, and politeness systems in order to maintain harmony and face. Since these cultures have shared values of esteem for others' view of the self, issues of shame and honor and solidarity with the group identity are of highest importance.

In low-context (Western) cultures, such as the United States, Australia, and Germany, face is associated with an individualistic approach and is about self-esteem. Who you are is a core self, whom we expect to have be consistent with what we show to others. In these cultures, directness, honesty, and forthrightness are valued, and so the issues of face are about guilt, dignity, and pride. Privacy and autonomy are hallmarks of the low-context culture; maintaining connection and allowing elders and others in the community to provide influence are hallmarks of the high-context worldview.

In low-context cultures, like mainstream North American society, members of the culture who are in conflict tend to adapt to and adopt Fisher and Ury's four-part formulation (1991) of separating people from the problem, focusing on interests rather than positions, inventing options for mutual gain, and insisting on objective criteria, because these are culturally consistent concepts. However, people from high-context cultures view the people and the problem as inseparable and interrelated. "Thus the low-context cultures tend to view the world in analytic, linear, logical terms that allow them to be hard on problems but soft on people, focused on instrumental outcomes but easy on affective issues; while high-context cultures perceive the world in synthetic, spiral logic that links the conflict event and its impact, issue, actors, content, and context" (Augsberger, 1992, p. 91). People from low-context cultures view indirectness as cowardliness and weakness, whereas those from high-context cultures require indirectness as part of the forms of politeness required to maintain social face. This can lead to vastly different views of the meaning and appropriateness of open conflict and how to deal with it, especially within families, where the relational context is the highest.

Context Differences Within Families

Any family can have members who see the world from these very divergent views. Mothers can be very high context and relationally oriented, while fathers can be very low context and independently oriented. Children can be different from their parents because they have adapted to the mores of their own social group. Belonging to organizations, both positive ones like churches and negative groups like gangs, can also affect the individual's view of his or her own face-saving and face-maintenance needs and can put family members into internal conflict about which group norms to follow. Especially if there are issues of immigration, emigration, and acculturation from one larger social culture to another, these issues can play out in the dynamics of an extended family, across generations, or even between the primary members. Family members can either passively or actively accept divergent beliefs and may be in a double bind to maintain a level of face they no longer wish to hold.

Face-Saving During Mediation

Because maintenance of face depends on how we view ourselves and how others view us, loss of face requires us to deal with the fact that we will have lost more than just what was ostensibly at issue. For example, the parent who gives in and makes concessions to a child's wishes can perceive that she has lost face in the eyes of the child, the other parent, her other relatives, or outsiders such as the mediator or other professionals. In many family conflicts and disputes, the goal of maintaining face becomes just as or maybe more important than solving the problem. The parent believes he cannot allow the child to perceive him as weak or indecisive, yet may actually believe that the requested concession or option under consideration is the best negotiated agreement. Someone who perceives selecting a particular option as equal to losing face is likely not to select that option, because the greater good in that person's mind is maintaining face in the situation.

The family mediator must help this parent find a face-saving way to back down and change position without losing status or authority in her own eyes or in the eyes of her child. Similarly, an elderly family member must often lose some face in order to receive help and support, especially if that elder had maintained the strong low-context, individualistic worldview. Relying on anybody could be perceived by that elder as unacceptable, even when that person knows that it is necessary.

Face-saving problems can put even the most skilled negotiator and conscientious family member into an internal and interpersonal dilemma that must be recognized and resolved. As Folger, Poole, and Stutman (2001) describe, "Interaction usually cannot proceed without resolution of the 'face' problem and will be dominated by this problem until the speaker feels satisfied that enough has been done to establish the desired image" (p. 164). Family mediators must make negotiation in mediation acceptable by finding out the face requirements of all parties in the mediation effort. This is part of the assessment of the people and the problem that contributes to the formulation of the case by the mediator.

Folger, Poole, and Stutman (2001) also remind us that a perception of threat to a person's face changes the dynamics within a group. This fact could be extrapolated into the interactions within a family. When issues of loss of face emerge, the group can no longer maintain the social construction of being equal members. When conflict occurs in a group or family, typical responses include a perceptual shift away from the equality of members and group-centeredness to a more personalized, weighted, and individual-centered approach. This requires the family mediator to clarify the interests, options, and positions of each member rather than assume the continued adherence to a group mentality or subgroup configuration. For example, a husband and wife may disagree in major and minor ways regarding what is acceptable for their teenager, and the mediator should not assume that they are adhering to the groupthink of former family practices and values.

There is a tendency for members of a group to look for a prime cause, to blame and scapegoat others when conflicts occur, and to focus inappropriately on who started the conflict and defense of self rather than staying focused on problem solving. When members of groups and families allow for full exploration of each family member's point of reference, the interaction can become more genuine and productive. Letting each person within the membership of the family have his or her own voice can open up the conflict, even while it appears to be devastating the solidarity of the family identity.

These courageous acts of individual truth can help the family rebuild its identity later on a more realistic foundation. The family mediator can be instrumental in maintaining a mediative process that allows for honesty without retribution, genuineness despite the cost to the collective understanding, individual truth as the basis for collective truth within the family, and rebuilding face that has been damaged. Saving face of one or more members of the family should not become the primary task of the mediation process, and yet some face-saving may be required.

Ways of Saving Face

Folger, Poole, and Stutman (2001) identified three major forms of face-saving that emerge in groups, and these play out in family interactions also. One major form of face-saving is when the person who feels wounded conveys to the others that she believes she has been treated unfairly or has been intimidated. She will adamantly resist any attempt to negotiate or problem-solve until this injustice has been dealt with. These authors point to the fact that if the group (family) is able to help that member articulate the reasons and the basis for her feelings in healthy ways that do not prejudge others, then the accumulated effect on the group ultimately will be constructive. However, if the face-saving party is not able to back up her claims that she has been threatened or treated unfairly or if the feedback to other members of the group is ill timed or still a set of assumptions and attributions toward others, the cumulative effect on the group (family) will be to escalate the conflict. This escalation may not be amenable to mediation efforts and will ultimately become a destructive form of conflict.

Another form of face-saving is the unwillingness to back off from hardened positions. Because it takes more effort to explain why and how a person has changed his mind than to leave the earlier position in place, there can be a stultifying effect on the mediative effort. In families, this often turns into the face-saving maneuver by the ostensible leader of the family, which turns into a self-defeating holdout that actually loses him respect rather than maintains it as he had hoped. When he perceives that making change is a sign of weakness, he tends to hold steady even when he knows it is a losing cause.

Many parents in custody battles and entrenched family struggles are ironically trying the very method that will lose face, not save it. By not having capitulated, they believe they maintain their standing. I have heard parents in such struggles tell me that they cannot mediate to a conclusion that would actually serve their interests and the child's because they "never want their child to think they gave up." They will comply with a judge's order because they can maintain their own sense of face in the light of the legal imposition of the order that they had to obey. Resisting cooperative efforts and directly or indirectly choosing the coercive, top-down, power-over method typical of litigation and adjudication feels like face-saving for some people. Family mediators may undeservedly feel bad that a case went to court when face-saving was happening in this way.

The third major method of face-saving comes in the form of whitewashing and suppression of the conflict itself. If there is no problem, then no one needs to lose face over it. The alignment within the family to suppress or deny the conflict can actually feel good to members of the family who have not been included before, and the sense of providing a united front of resistance can be seductive for those who have felt out of touch. Whole extended families have been galvanized in the attempt to suppress conflict. The threat to face seems to be that they will be jeopardizing a good relationship if they acknowledge the conflict earlier and more directly, but again it works paradoxically to deepen the conflict.

In therapeutic circles, practitioners sometimes informally and irreverently refer to this as *ostrich behavior* on the part of the client, and *elephants in the room* that the family does not wish to or cannot acknowledge, or *sacred cows* that intrude on the situation but that the family cannot violate by reusing in more productive ways. Denying that the conflict exists is sometimes self-soothing behavior to minimize the anxiety that threats to face produce, and certainly the denial, minimizing, or suppression of conflicts within families rests on thinking errors and negative assumptions.

From a cognitive-behavioral point of view, the practitioner can help the party in a private face-saving way, such as caucus or individual session, to rethink her assumptions and understand the dynamics of conflict differently. This attitude or belief transformation about the constructive and destructive nature of conflict may have to take place before the problem can be acknowledged, let alone solved.

Responding to Face Needs During Mediation

Family mediators who are aware of face dimensions in the way the family presents (or does not present) the dilemma can help identify the face elements in the story as part of the narrative elements each member discusses. They can watch for the change of group dynamics from central to individual focus and help each party articulate his or her own truths. They can help all parties see the particular dilemma for each of the others, and ask, "What will happen to your family if we talk about the conflicts?" to get at dire predictions and cautionary tales that are affecting the family. If some or all members of the family are protecting their face, they may be able to acknowledge this fact, so preliminary discussions can include agreements about the maintenance of roles and respect as they define it.

Solving the problem but losing face and respect within the family will not feel like success, and most clients will resist the mediator if they sense that this outcome is likely. Family conflicts must be seen as integral to the self-concept and self-perception of everyone involved, even those who do not have an active decision-making role. When family mediators attend to face in the ways they set up the mediation and conduct the sessions and write up the mediated agreements, they will foster the longevity and durability of the agreement. In this way, face-saving becomes a crucial dimension for family mediation practice.

❧

The nature of family conflicts is similar to the way in which all other conflicts emerge, exist, and reconcile. Family mediators need to learn from other venues of alternative dispute resolution and mediation practice and the research that is going into the resolution of small social groups and workplace organizations that share many of the same features of families and into the idea of continued involvement past the resolution of the conflict. But what is unique about family conflict is the levels of past, present, and future the current situation brings. The parfait of conflict is very well layered with past interactions, family patterns, and the unique culture of the family.

The other issue so tied with family mediation cases is the high level of self-involvement and therefore the need to preserve the roles, patterns, status, and face within the family and without. Families are on a continuum from connection to control, and they want to find a mutually acceptable balance point for these two factors. Each individual within the family dispute needs to find a face-saving way to back out of untenable negotiative positions without losing their authority in the role within the family system.

Wise family mediators will have a clear understanding of what conflicts and reactions they can deal with and which ones they must let go to the next forum of coercive legal processes, as well as which reactions to conflict indicate they should monitor for safety and effectiveness. The next chapter explores the impact of finding a model or approach to mediation that will provide an organized and thoughtful way to intervene on the dynamics of family conflict.

CHAPTER THREE

Family Mediation Models and Approaches

Like all other applications of ADR and conflict resolution methodologies, family mediation has been quickly evolving in its depth, breadth, and understanding. This chapter provides an overview of the models and approaches being used in family mediation efforts. At this writing, there is a healthy plurality that demonstrates the interdisciplinary background and cross-training needed in this field.

Models and approaches in family mediation have grown historically by the efforts of singular trail-blazing individuals and have been promoted primarily from entrepreneurial efforts of individuals who own their models as copyrighted material with sole proprietary rights. There is often not full disclosure about the foundational concepts and theoretical orientation of the trainer or the model being used to train others. Sometimes this is because they are unique hybrids, generic catch-alls, or unorganized conglomerations that lack internal consistency and theoretical grounding. It is possible that a well-trained and competent family mediator will not be able to name the model or approach he or she is using. You may or may not find the training you had discussed here, or may realize that your training was a blend of several different models. You may need to find the kind of model you learned by comparing what you do to the descriptions of the models in this chapter.

Family mediation models and approaches must be informed by the theoretical bases of many disciplines and their effectiveness determined by quantitative research. This field has only recently had graduate-level programs where students can contribute to the knowledge and application in an organized academic way. Funding and academic support for well-designed research that could assist in the development of better practitioners and better system design is still sparse. Empirical studies that support or expand clinical judgment and intervention should be welcome additions, yet many practitioners of family mediation have little opportunity to review these different approaches and models or assess the effectiveness of any particular model for their unique setting and population. Information about effectiveness often has not been fully researched, and many training models are not used consistently by practitioners. Many mediation models, approaches, and materials have been developed as proprietary and copyrighted systems and have not yet been evaluated.

The newly formed Association for Conflict Resolution (ACR), which comprises the former Academy of Family Mediators (AFM) and the Society for Professionals in Dispute Resolution, is the second wave, or the next major evolution in the field, created from the original groundbreaking professional organizations that helped to pioneer and support many of these models and approaches. The hope is that this new organization will work collaboratively with higher education programs in conflict resolution and with ADR practitioners who are using and developing models to help further the field by testing hypotheses and empirically showing best practices. Another hope is that ACR will then require what we find to be the best practices to be part of the criteria for membership, for voluntary certification or licensure efforts it sponsors, or for standards of practice it promulgates.

Until there is a preponderance of evidence supporting a particular model or approach as the most efficacious or efficient, the field of family mediation should endeavor to support, elaborate, and understand all the various approaches. There is no single way to mediate, just as there is no single way of being or describing "the family." Nevertheless, there may be some models or methods that when looked at closely, reveal deep underlying assumptions or values that may or may not be consistent with a particular practitioner's own worldview, values, and intentions and abilities.

This chapter will help novice family mediators and practitioners from other disciplines such as law and education to understand and choose an internally consistent approach or model. It should also help seasoned family mediators review their past training and current choices of model, expand their understanding of other models they may wish to review again, and help them decide again if further personal development is necessary. By adopting the scientific attitude that mediation models and approaches can and should adapt to and evolve with new information, the field can continue to respond to the future while retaining its own unique characteristics.

MODELS AND APPROACHES: A DEFINITION

Models and approaches are not the same thing as styles, theory, training, skills and techniques, or methods of delivering interventions. Models are specific ways or methodologies for doing mediation that rest on two even more basic elements: the practitioner's central core beliefs and the practitioner's theoretical base, that is, the theories the mediator has adopted about abstract concepts, such as truth, fairness, and justice, that provide meaning and consistency. Unlike theories, which can be proved or disproved, models are organized collections of thoughts that guide and inform and usually summarize the practitioner's ideal or best practices. They explain how a practitioner should function. Each model is comprehensively organized in a definable way that makes it different from other models. Models tell us *why,* whereas methods, skills, and techniques tell us *how to.*

Taking an example from the field of medicine, allopathic medicine follows one model and methodology, while naturopathy, chiropractic, acupuncture, and holistic medicine are each a very different model of medical practice. Each one is based on a different set of beliefs and a different set of theories, and therefore each medical model operates very differently and has very different methods, skills, and interventions.

Lang and Taylor (2000) have this to say about models:

> Models represent appropriate, aspirational, or best practices; they include guidelines for implementing them. Most novice mediators learn a particular model and approach to mediation that encompasses guidelines, rules, procedures, and ways of understanding mediation practice. . . .
>
> Mediators who find their models inadequate to incomplete need to read more about other models and approaches, and to discuss the issue with other mediators to develop a more suitable and relevant model of practice. [p. 101]

Approaches, on the other hand, are general perspectives and prescriptive ways of looking at the work being done. They are not as specific, and it is therefore harder to measure whether a particular practitioner is functioning within that perspective. They often are more global and idealistic, and can be descriptive of several specific models simultaneously. A particular approach eventually may become solidified into a more comprehensive, named model of practice that embodies the principles in a more codified way.

This chapter explores the basic premises and models of family mediation that currently exist. Many of the models presented are fragmentary or partial, or have been developed as a trademark practice by a trainer or practitioner rather than as a demonstration of a model available for general use by any potential mediator. Sometimes practitioners who have been through a forty-hour basic family mediation training will not know what model or approach they actually learned. Although ACR has tried to help consumers and jurisdictions by creating standards for ACR-approved training, practitioners still need to understand the basic premises of justice, the role of the mediator, and the type of process that they are using and why. Family mediators can grow by understanding the range of current practice.

It is my belief that family mediators need to understand their own model fully before they can become artistic with it and realize that not all models fit all families and disputes or all practitioners. Practitioners need to evolve in their mediation approaches and refine and develop the models they are using to be better able to pass the information on to the next cohort of practitioners.

STAGE THEORY MODELS

A label of *stage theory model* can be applied to types of mediation in which the mediation process is perceived as following a generalized flow from beginning to end. These theories posit that most family mediation sessions or events have a common or usual beginning, middle, and end and that each of these holds specific tasks and processes that need to be accomplished during that period of time, because they are sequential building blocks for future parts of the process. Like a road map that shows the embarkation and destination points with general descriptors between, these stage models help give beginning mediators a sense of what is expected and also how to achieve some standard preset goals that contribute to the overarching mediation effort.

The following statement could articulate the basic belief system underneath all stage theories: *If the family mediator leads the participants through all the stages, without missing any, and if all the stages are done completely and correctly, then the participants will be successful in mediating an outcome. If any stage is missed, is not done completely enough, or is handled poorly by the mediator or the participants, then the likelihood of a successful completion is diminished.*

These stages are somewhat universal, descriptive of, and intrinsic to the mediation process itself. By knowing which stage the case is in, the mediator can effectively figure out where to go in leading the participants toward resolution. The assumption is that the mediator is the facilitator of these stages and acts as a leader and guide to the participants, ensuring that all tasks are done.

Stage theories were derived inductively and experientially. Practitioners who were being productive in family mediation tried to explain the processes they were doing to others by the inductive method, that is, by analyzing their successful cases and describing the patterns and the common features that had occurred. This de facto description of what they were doing then became prescriptive to other family mediators in subsequent training and writing.

Most of the stage model writers see the stages they describe as necessary, successive, and integrated. Although some of the writers indicate that there can be a return to earlier stages in a looping mechanism, the stage concept projects a linear movement from beginning to end. They believe that the stages follow a predictable course and that each stage is necessary for a complete family mediation.

Folberg and Taylor (1984) posited a seven-stage model of mediation:

1. Introduction—creating trust and structure

2. Fact finding and isolation of issues

3. Creation of options and alternatives

4. Negotiation and decision-making

5. Clarification and writing a plan

6. Legal review and processing

7. Implementation, review and revision [p. 32]

Some of these stages were done as part of the actual in-person mediation session, and some were completed by the participants subsequent to the actual mediation meetings. Still other stages were done by others outside of, and in addition to, the actual mediation effort. The first five stages are assumed to take place within the confines of the mediator's power and authority and with the mediator's presence during the session while acting as a neutral third party. The sixth stage was meant to be done by consultation and ratification of an advising attorney or judicial or authority figure. The final stage was seen as being done by the participants themselves, with the potential help of the mediator again in a truncated version of the first five stages if needed. This final stage hints at a circularity of process consistent with the Rummel conflict cycle concept described in Chapter Two. Folberg and Taylor view stage theory as universal to all mediation efforts.

Moore (1996) articulated a twelve-stage general process outline of how most mediation flows in terms of the tasks of the mediator and the movement of the case:

1. Establishing relationship with the disputing parties

2. Selecting a strategy to guide mediation

3. Collecting and analyzing background information

4. Designing a detailed plan for mediation

5. Building trust and cooperation

6. Beginning the mediation session

7. Defining issues and setting an agenda

8. Uncovering hidden interests of the disputing parties

9. Generating options for settlement

10. Assessing options for settlement

11. Final bargaining

12. Achieving formal settlement [pp. 66–67]

Christopher Moore's twelve stages assume that five stages take place prior to actual face-to-face mediation sessions, and seven active stages happen within the in-person mediation effort. The process does not propose a need to return to the mediation effort; it assumes that the conclusion will be a satisfactory and complete conflict resolution (rather than conflict management), and the conclusion will be effective over time. This model is silent about the need for further consultation and ratification by judicial systems after mediation efforts and any need for or modification by the participants after implementation.

Karl Slaikeu (1996, pp. 285–289) has reduced the stages to five key events that relate to how to sequence and conduct the in-person mediation event:

1. First contact with the participants

2. The opening meeting

3. The use of caucuses during the mediation session

4. The conduct of the joint/shuttle mediation sessions

5. Closure

This model assumes a single mediation event, or at least limited numbers of sessions, to accomplish these stages. Designed primarily for business applications rather than family disputes, it specifies the use of *caucus*—separate meetings with those on each side of the dispute—as a stage of the mediation process itself and does not speak to the need to revise or modify.

These three stage models of mediation are a general description and can be useful to family mediators as foundational concepts. The models will not, however, provide specific guidance about whether or when or how to switch from joint to separate sessions or how to deal with the nuances and dynamics of the family processes outlined in Chapter One. They are not, strictly speaking, family mediation models, because they are not limited to family mediation contexts; they can be applied to settings and dispute types other than family conflicts.

Just as a sturdy foundation is required to erect a strong physical edifice, foundational structures are required for creating any mental edifice. These stage theories are helpful as general descriptions and foundational understandings of the basic process that family mediators may tend to use. They give beginning family mediators a general description of the mediation process and provide generalized instructions on how to proceed. They describe the process from the perspective of the observer after the fact rather than from the perspective of the participant or the mediator during the mediation. They lack the specificity needed for step-by-step interaction and practice in family conflicts, and so are best used as they were meant to be used: as general descriptors and guidelines for the flow of any particular family mediation session.

John Haynes (1994) described a model of mediation that he believed is specific to family mediation efforts, designed from the practice of divorce mediation cases. He described the foundation of his family mediation practice as a constant cycling through five general stages:

1. Gathering data, during which the mediator verifies, displays, and shares the data

2. Defining the problem (from the data)

3. Developing options to solve the problem

4. Redefining positions from self-interest to mutual interests

5. Bargaining over the options to reach a mutual agreement [p. 7]

For each separate issue or set of complex decisions to be made as part of divorce or other family dispute, Haynes suggested that family mediators continue to cycle through these stages as many times as necessary until all decisions have been reached. Then the mediator writes a mediated agreement based on those decisions. Haynes illustrated this process for divorce mediation efforts, suggesting the topics, sequence, and negotiation that should take place for those issues. This stage model, designed specifically for and derived from his actual practice of divorce mediation, became a practical guide for mediators who wish to follow his lead. The basic assumption of all stage theories still shows through in his model: if the mediator follows these stages and discusses with the clients all the topics listed and then follows the repeating cycle of the five stages for each topic that needs an agreement, the outcome will be successful.

John Haynes demonstrated his model on videotape. The series of videotapes (AFM Video Series I; AFM Series II) shows Haynes mediating according to his looping stage model in different family problem types, including a divorce case, the placement of an elderly parent, and a parent-teen conflict (n.d. *a*, n.d. *b*). These tapes have served as one of the very few visual tools to show the differences among models in practice and can serve as a springboard for discussion and development during training of beginning and intermediate-level family mediators.

It has been announced at several recent professional conferences that stage theories are dead. To paraphrase the famous quote, rumors of this death have been greatly exaggerated. These stage models are the basic frame of practice for family mediators, as well as other applications of the mediation process, because they describe the general movement of the interaction through time and are consistent with general conflict cycle theories and actual practice. What they are not, and were never intended to be, is a set of expert rules, algorithms, or cookie-cutter patterns that will tell family mediators all they need to know. Family mediators following these stages may still not be successful, because they may not be responsive to the needs and dynamics of the families with whom they are working.

I propose that we think of stage theories as generalized descriptions of the general flow of a case through the mediation process. These are wonderful foundational concepts that support and describe the practice but certainly do not fully define it and cannot help a practitioner make the necessary choices during a family mediation process. In this regard, they are not full models of mediation, even if they are grounded on theories of human behavior, conflict theory, negotiation theory, and applied communication.

PROBLEM-SOLVING AND NEGOTIATIVE APPROACHES

Family mediation started with an orientation toward helping families who were stuck in power struggles and adversarial processes find a kinder and gentler, more efficacious and thrifty way of solving discrete problems of parenting, marital property, and support decisions during divorce than the traditional divorce litigation process. Problem solving embedded in the context of a third-party mediation process was the first wave of mediation practice, and many of the family mediation training models adapted the problem-solving process from community contexts.

Problem solving itself was perceived as an alternative to a retributive and distributive justice system, where people "placed claim and rights" to children as if they were chattel and had those rights distributed to them by the court during divorce. Early divorce mediators wanted to rectify this condition by providing conciliation and mediation services through the courts to determine the needs of children within the family in order to advise the parents and judge regarding the optimum custodial option for each family.

The Association of Family Conciliation Courts was developed by judges, lawyers, and social workers during the 1970s and early 1980s to help parties become less adversarial and work toward a more principled negotiation process during these heated disputes. Judges perceived rightly that they did not always understand the dynamics of a particular family, which affected their abilities to negotiate. By diverting cases to a trained mediator for problem-solving approaches, the mediator could help the family determine the issues and problems. Then the mediator could offer the parents information and education about how to make mutually acceptable choices more effectively rather than follow distributive or procedural justice approaches by going to court first.

Groundbreaking court systems, including the Los Angeles County Family Court, Hennepin County Family Court in Minnesota, and Clackamas County Family Court Services in Oregon, helped to develop these ADR services in ways that were loosely based on the problem-solving processes of brainstorming and complete option development, now applied to divorce decision making. It was believed that if the parents during a divorce action were given time away from the adversarial process of litigation and given appropriate information about children, divorce, and custodial options, the family itself would be able to resolve most of the disputes without having to do more than have final judicial review for the majority of divorces. Allowing the family the right to renegotiate its own new boundaries, rules, and patterns of parenting would reduce current and ongoing conflict and therefore reduce harm to the children who had become stuck in the middle of the controversy. The problem-solving/negotiative model still works well for the majority of cases referred to mandatory mediation, but its limitations have led to the development of newer models and approaches that include more of the family dynamics described in Chapters One and Two.

The problem-solving approach in its best form emphasized the development of multiple options and preserved the family's right to select the best option based on the standard of the best interest of the child. This concept of attaching paramount priority to decisions based on the needs and abilities of the children became a new judicial principle that tried to take the focus off the legal rights of the parents and put them onto the emotional and developmental needs of the children of the family, who were perceived as the most likely to be hurt by continuing legal and emotional struggle within the family. This move from a distributive, legal rights approach to more psychological health criteria was a major shift in the way courts, advising attorneys, social workers, and other therapists started to look at the decisions being made during divorce.

Influential to jurisdictions was the work by Goldstein, Freud, and Solnit (1973) and others who sought to integrate the understandings and knowledge from other fields such as psychology, social work, and child development into the legal process. To do this required more in-depth work with the family to determine what those needs were. Conciliators and then mediators in court-connected programs across the country provided the vital link between the legal and the mental health and psychology worlds, and the interdisciplinary movement led to increasing use of family mediators. Not only were early family mediators mediating between the members of divorcing families, they were also mediating between the courts and the family in a new form of child-centered advocacy by involving the entire family system. This need to help families self-determine the best options for their children and family structure was the major impetus to the development of family mediation as the preferred method for all divorce cases.

In the early days of the court-connected programs in the 1970s and 1980s, conciliators and mediators were provided to divorcing couples by the state at low or no cost to them to help prevent unnecessary divorce and to mediate the terms and conditions for children if divorce was the option. Mediators in these programs often served not only as classic problem-solving mediators but also as sources of information and education regarding the needs of children during and after divorce. They also served as therapeutic screeners to help families determine if their children's or their responses to the divorce required other therapy or intervention concurrently or prior to the legal divorce action in court.

Modes of Family Mediation Practice

Jane Becker-Haven's graduate work analyzing tapes of court-connected mediators in family court mediation sessions noted four distinct ways in which the mediators functioned. These modes of operation are as follows: rational-analytic, educative, therapeutic, and normative-evaluative. The *rational-analytic mode* corresponds to the usual concepts of problem-solving approaches, while the *educative mode* refers to the role of providing appropriate information about the issues being mediated. The *therapeutic mode* refers to eliciting feelings and dealing more directly with the family dynamics described in Chapter One. The dominant mode was the rational-analytic, problem-solving approach. In some jurisdictions, mediators and conciliators were given the power to subpoena the resistant or recalcitrant parent as part of the *normative-evaluative mode,* and some saw their role as being officers of the court who were combining mediation and arbitration and acting as spokespersons for the larger society or advocates for children caught in the middle of disputes.

For Folberg and Taylor (1984), who also saw the dynamics of the mediation process as following a problem-solving and rational decision-making process as well as stage theory, the problem-solving methods were derived from methods already developed in family therapy in the early 1980s as part of the McMaster Model of Family Functioning (Epstein, Bishop, and Baldwin, 1993). Family therapists at the time were also interested in the problem-solving methodology, since it fit well with the cognitive-behavioral approaches and the family contracting methodology they were using to get families to change. Because problem solving could be done by the family alone, early writers family-generated therapeutic differentiated problem solving from the mediation process, which by definition requires attendance and involvement of the third-party mediator. (See Wilmot and Hocker, 2001, for the format for a leaderless "family meeting" problem-solving process still in use and consistent with the aims of family therapists.) Mediation was therefore a more comprehensive process with problem solving inside of it, and the practice of family therapy and the practice of mediation both became very problem solving oriented, which made them somewhat hard to differentiate, despite the more expanded four functions of the mediation modes.

Hallmarks of the Problem-Solving Process

The belief of judges, court administrators, and even family mediators themselves in the early years of family mediation was that if families could have done a positive problem-solving process on their own, they would have, and they would not have filed contested divorce actions and modification. Therefore, mediators were needed to help divorcing parents become successful in problem solving by providing that problem-solving process in a better way. Parties to disputes who had filed contested proceedings with the court, and later all cases that involved children, were diverted to mediation services, based on the presumption that mediation processes could better help the family reduce conflicts and develop appropriate solutions to the problems they were experiencing by helping the family do this problem solving in a more effective way.

It became the mediator's job to lead the family through this problem-solving process in order to develop the options and alternatives prior to negotiation. Thus, the problem-solving process became perceived as a necessary part and the dominant mode and model of the larger mediation process.

Early family mediation problem-solving models (Taylor, 1981, 1988; Salius and Maruzo, 1988) emphasized the role of the family mediator in determining the issues and problems and then providing the logical problem-solving approach to solving or managing the dispute. Problem solving was the process of choice in the 1970s and 1980s, not just in conciliation courts and for mediators but also in therapeutic practices such as counseling, therapy, and social work because it fit well with the cognitive-behavioral approaches then being used in those fields.

According to Folger, Poole, and Stutman (2001), participants need the following beliefs and characteristics in order to problem-solve effectively in any context:

- Have a vested interest in the outcome.
- See collaboration as being helpful.
- Have faith that the parties involved can resolve the conflict by doing it.
- Actually find the true interests, not just make concessions to end the process.
- That both sides can be "right" simultaneously.
- Both sides can understand the other's perspectives, and will work to minimize barriers to working together, such as derision, defensiveness, and status differences.

As opposed to the other typical responses to conflict (such as avoidance, accommodation, compromise, or competition), problem solving or collaboration was perceived as being a higher, more principled response to conflict, and using a mediator was a way to help parties in dispute move to that more cooperative yet self-assertive place. It was believed that if mediators could get all disputants to focus on solving their common problems rather than trying to advocate for their own preferred solution or compete and defeat the others, then the mediation effort would go well, agreements would be negotiated, and outcomes would be more durable.

These assumptions about the problem-solving process may be true, but one or more members of a family in a dispute may exhibit none of the criteria necessary for effective problem solving due to other complex systems and personal issues. Also, problem-solving styles for dealing with internal family disputes may not be culturally consistent for particular social units (Folger, Poole, and Stutman, 2001). A family member may have no investment in losing face or being demoted to coequal status with the others. Family members may not be invested in solving the problem. Perhaps maintaining the conflict is somehow functional for them; they may gain secondary rewards from it or maintain their role within the family.

Family mediators will probably always find some distributive issues (money, objects, time, or resources that must be fairly apportioned) embedded in the disputes they mediate for families and therefore will always have to have a solid working knowledge of both distributive (win-lose, competitive) and integrative (win-win, collaborative) negotiation, as well as the basic problem-solving process in mediation. Excellent new books on negotiation, such as that by Lewicki, Saunders, and Minton (2001), thoroughly explain these distinctions between negotiative approaches.

At the heart of most successful mediation is some level of direct problem solving and negotiation between the participants. Family mediators will find that having a problem-solving model based only on distributive or integrative negotiation principles is often insufficient for the types of disputes and the complexity of the dynamics they will be mediating. As a model, problem-solving approaches based on negotiation make perfect sense for other applications, such as community-based and environmental issues, single-issue complaints, and disputes where the parties need and want identifiable outcomes or the problem seems clearly defined to all disputants. However, these models may lack the understanding of what is underneath the negotiation or recognize the family dynamics but have no method to deal with the dynamic that is creating or maintaining the conflict in family disputes.

Problem solving has been successful and useful in family mediation because families have real issues of allocation, distribution, and needs for certainty in their family disputes, especially in divorce, and so those hard issues can respond to a problem-solving approach. Certainly, divorce disputes require parents to determine custody, access, and other issues that can have only one option functioning at a time. Also, all families need to take unusable, frustrating complaint processes and turn them into effective decision-making processes that have knowable outcomes. At the heart of mediation still resides the need to clarify that which is not known. And yet family mediation requires practitioners to go beyond the dispute to understand the people and their system.

Problem-solving approaches emphasize both the definition of the problem and the selection of appropriate remedies for them, but family mediators are often mediating with families whose members all see the problem in different ways. Family mediators need models and approaches that are consistent with or have problem solving embedded within them, yet offer more understanding and help with the resistance to change that is often encountered in these situations. Therapeutic and transformative approaches, described later in this chapter, are additions to the basic model of problem solving that can help family ADR practitioners mobilize family members and the family system in different ways.

Limitations and New Paradigms

Sometimes in order to draw distinctions between an established paradigm and a new conceptualization, there is an initial definition by negation—that is, a disparaging of the former in order to present the need for the new. Many practitioners found this happening when Bush and Folger (1994) lambasted the problem-solving process because of its potential for undue influence to achieve results and demonstrate problems solved, whether they really were or not.

There is no need to vilify problem solving in order to extol the virtues of other more expansive models and approaches. It is not necessary for family mediators to choose arbitrarily between problem solving and other approaches. Instead, the wise family mediator should look for ways to integrate basic problem-solving and negotiative understandings with other approaches. There will be times in family mediation efforts when classic problem-solving, negotiative mediation, with its linear, methodical, rational, and conclusive decision making, will be the best process for the clients and the case.

However, most family mediators are now also training themselves in other models and approaches beyond a negotiative or problem-solving model so that they can more effectively deal with the family dynamics that can scuttle problem-solving efforts prematurely. Standard negotiation and problem solving is functional and foundational for family mediation, but it is not always sufficient for family mediation dynamics and disputes. Because many of the practitioners functioning today have been trained by problem-solving/negotiative mediators, it may be time to look at some newer, more systemic and dynamic models and approaches.

PROCEDURAL MODELS

Procedural models are similar in basic outlook to problem-solving and negotiative models, but add a dimension of following strict rules to create desired outcomes. These models propose that *if the family mediator and the participants follow all the procedures, then the outcome will be positive.* Like stage models and classic negotiation and problem-solving approaches, procedural models emphasize the dispute content and the prescriptive mediation process rather than the dynamics of the people or the systemic issues of the family context. Stage models give generalized statements that all mediation should follow and are sequenced in approach, and problem-solving approaches focus on the analysis of the dispute and a rational, linear process for examining the problem and the possible solutions and options through education, brainstorming, and finally negotiation on options. Procedural models require practitioners to work in a highly specific, organized, and sequential way, dealing with each case exactly according to the procedure, with little variation from case to case.

Traditional procedural justice requires participants to submit their issues and concerns to a set of processes that have been determined by society to be equal and therefore are assumed to provide fairness to everyone. Our judicial and legal system is based on these procedural assumptions and provide due process and equal protection of each side's interests by maintaining strict procedural safeguards. Courts provide due process in all civil and criminal proceedings, and citizens must assume that if the procedures have been scrupulously followed, the outcome will be fair. This is but one viewpoint of justice. (For an excellent discussion about the development of other forms of justice, such as restorative justice and interactive justice, see Bunker and Rubin, 1995.)

Because so many practitioners of family mediation come from the legal and judicial community and are steeped in procedural justice, many early models of family mediation continued these assumptions by outlining new family mediation procedures within this tradition. At first, the critique of family mediation was that mediators helped parties negotiate without these usual benefits of procedural justice and therefore mediators were "bargaining in the shadow of the law" (Minookin and Kornhauser, 1979). Those who were concerned thought that family mediators were in fact doing their clients a disservice, since they were not being provided the safeguards of procedural justice as they would be in the courts when they mediated an agreement and did their own "private ordering" and settlements without the benefit of case law and precedent.

Proponents of procedural models of mediation were attempting to bring the safeguards of procedural justice to the practice of mediation and thereby bring the practice of family mediation to a level of acceptance within the larger legal and justice communities. Instead, being outside standard procedural justice concepts and being truly an alternative resolution system, this was an attempt to make mediation acceptable by engaging in a different process although one based on similar concepts. As mediation processes of all types have been adopted as diversion programs for courts and as ADR has become now defined as appropriate for dispute resolution in combined courthouse programs, this issue of acceptance of mediation by the judicial community has largely evaporated, leaving the notion of procedural mediation processes.

Structured Mediation Model

One of the earliest articulators of a procedural model of family mediation for divorce cases was Coogler (1977, 1978, 1982), who developed the structured mediation model. Trained as an attorney and having undergone a divorce, Coogler realized that a better way could be developed for arriving at fair and workable divorce agreements by getting the parties to subscribe to a set of rules for fairness and for conducting the mediation session. Based on Morton Deutsch's concepts of the role of the third-party neutral as establishing norms for rational engagement and resolution, Coogler helped develop a set of rules that participants would have to embrace voluntarily prior to starting mediation efforts. In this model, participants found an alternative to the adversarial judicial system while still operating within procedural justice concepts. Because the practice was consistent with procedural justice concepts, it fit well with the existing judicial system. Participants could work collaboratively in mediation toward the mutual benefit rather than having to define each other as competitive adversaries, yet have the safeguards of an orderly, defined procedure to follow.

Because the mediation was done in a structured, procedurally fair way, the assumption was that the outcome would be more likely to be fair. The highly structured set of rules was based on prevailing principles of fairness, particular state statutes, and problem-prevention strategies, developed through Coogler's experience, to diminish dirty tricks, hidden agendas, and power ploys. "Coogler held that allowing the couple to resolve small pieces of the controversy helps the couple maintain their commitment to the process and provides continued success" (Grebe, 1988, p. 232).

At the conclusion of mediation, the mediator operating out of this structured mediation model would bring in an impartial advising attorney to advise both the mediator and the participants on the legal implications of the agreement they had just reached. The use of the advisory attorney was one of the more controversial features of this model (Grebe, 1988), because the attorney acted as a technical legal resource and advised the couple together and did not represent either party. At the time, this was a radical concept that was not taken lightly by the legal community; in fact, charges of unauthorized practice of law and other process concerns were voiced. Nevertheless, later acceptance that mediation was a legitimate and necessary part of the larger judicial structure and ADR movement helped make such mediation practices acceptable to the legal community.

Although the official structured mediation model that Coogler pioneered may not be operating in its original form at this time, it has been extremely influential. Basic mediation training now offered by jurisdictions and private trainers is often developed from or influenced by this model, and many trainers and systems have created trademarked and copyrighted variations that still rely on the basic assumptions of this model. Because it was developed specifically about divorce, it has not made the leap to the larger concept of applying mediation efforts to other family dilemmas and conflicts. Nevertheless, the underpinnings tend to continue in mediator development of other forms of family dispute resolution.

Hallmarks of Other Procedural Models

Many of the newer uses of mediation for family disputes are relying on models of mediation that were based on procedural assumptions and foundations. A particular family mediation model could be said to be procedural (although not necessarily part of the structured mediation tradition) if it has the following basic premises:

- The participants subscribe to a set of rules for mediation that will be fair in some external, objective sense and that follow a common format or process from case to case.

- This format generally follows standard procedural processes used in judicial procedure, such as equal time, equal processes, and scrupulous balancing of each participant's involvement.

- All parties adhere to these rules. Violations of them are quickly apparent and dealt with.

- By following the rules, the parties are operating in essential fairness and will accept the outcome as fair, thus reducing ongoing conflict.

A mediator operating from a procedural model would research the laws and develop objective rules that incorporate society's ideas of outcome fairness. That mediator would also develop rules of treatment during the session that require each person to follow the procedures to establish and maintain fairness during the session. There would be initial contracting by the participants, with the mediator requiring the participants to conform to these standards of fairness and rules and then a monitoring of their compliance during the mediation session. It would be assumed that the outcome of this fair process would be fair and should be upheld by each participant.

The problem-solving, logical, rule-based approach of procedural models does not work for all families and all family problems. Chaotically organized families would not necessarily be able to respond positively to procedural models initially, because they tend not to be able to maintain rule sets over time. The same is true when the family problem being mediated revolves around impulsive and egocentric behavior on the part of one or more members of the family. But if the family was able to complete the initial stages, the very nature of the step-by-step procedural methodology and model could help keep it on a consistent track.

A procedural model is more likely to work with families and disputes where all parties can agree to a common core of shared values and outcomes, such as, "We don't want to place Mother in a nursing home" or "We both agree that an out-of-home placement is best for this child." When the participants have enough personal resilience and calmness to work through a process that requires taking turns, subscribing to objective external standards, and obedience to a higher value of mutuality, collaboration, and fairness, then procedural models can work. If they lack these qualities or show impulsivity, lack of respect for rules and authority, and inability to follow logical sequences due to personal states such as attention deficit hyperactivity disorder, then the slow, methodical nature of the procedural process may be unusable and inappropriate.

Many practitioners have to develop their own model to fit a new and specialized application of family mediation, the needs of their jurisdiction or clientele, or because no specific training is available for them in the type of family dispute they wish to mediate. Because we are still creating the field, mediators need models of mediation that they can replicate for different problem types and different settings. Because models and the concepts on which they are based are transferable learning, they can serve as blueprints for the further development of family mediation. It is important that practitioners and those who are in charge of selecting or designing new uses for mediation within existing systems know what models they are using and why. Practitioners who feel confined by a procedural approach learned when they were trained might want to explore more facilitative and interactive models.

THERAPEUTIC MODELS

Therapeutic models of family mediation often bring the background and training of family therapy into the mediation, and the theories and practices of the clinical or therapeutic practice are adapted to the format required of family mediation, such as writing agreements at the end. Therapeutic models have a core belief that *the individual and the family unit must make a personal or system change before they can effectively make an enduring agreement.*

In the early days of family mediation, practitioners often came from other helping professions and brought their beliefs and theoretical perspectives with them. Because structural and strategic family therapy premises about ideas such as triangulation and coalitions, boundaries and secondary gains, and the structure and function of the dispute for different family members speak to the way in which the family is organized and behaves, these concepts were particularly helpful in organizing the family mediator's understanding of the people and the problem from that perspective. Thus, structural-functionalist therapists started becoming family mediators, as did Bowenian and strategic therapists. They simply added the problem-solving and negotiative understandings to their existing way of formulating the need for change. Therapeutic mediation approaches often seem to be blends of the basic conceptual framework of the therapy mode, with problem-solving mediation approaches blended in.

Early practitioners of family mediation often had to distinguish the differences in their practice between when they were mediating and when they were providing therapy. Early articles (for example, Kelly, 1983) tried to identify the differences between mediation efforts and traditional therapeutic models like psychotherapy, so that the field of mediation could grow from the same constructs but become a different practice. Understanding what was similar and what was different, practitioners could tell mediation clients and therapeutic organizations, licensing boards, and insurance companies when they were doing which function.

Therapeutic Family Mediation

One of the most fully articulated, comprehensive family mediation models is the therapeutic family mediation (TFM) model developed by Irving and Benjamin (1995). Based on over twenty years of clinical private practice, this model requires more time and investment than is typical within existing court-connected settings, since the average number of hours per case is sixteen to thirty-two, as compared to eight hours or less in most judicially based mediation services. Irving and Benjamin also indicate the limitations of the model and note that their high success statistics are based on the fact that their clientele "display fewer and less serious presenting problems and complaints" (p. 149) than is common in free, court-connected services. Based on these disclaimers, family mediators should consider carefully whether this model is appropriate for their setting and population. They may want to consider adopting this model for family mediation cases that present unusual challenges or may require more in-depth work because the more standard, briefer problem-solving/negotiative model is not working with a particular family. Although this may not be the first service delivery model that a mediator chooses for a specific case, it may, with some modifications, be the type of extended mediation process needed for intractable family conflicts even within existing court-connected programs and services.

TFM practice assumes that the practitioner has the necessary therapeutic background and training to help provide therapeutic assessment and intervention when needed. Unlike the other models already described, this one is based on the communication, structural, and strategic models developed in family therapy rather than the negotiative and problem-solving models alone. It assumes certain basic foundations from those therapeutic theoretical approaches.

This foundation leads to a working premise that the family in conflict is an ecosystem that must be dealt with systemically rather than from a rights or a negotiative perspective. Mediators using this model believe that families display dysfunctional behavior on a continuum and that mediators must always be on guard against being co-opted or included inappropriately in the system, which would destroy their neutrality and effectiveness. Mediators further believe that unless they are effective in changing the behaviors within the family system that are unhelpful to the mediation effort, their efforts are likely to fail. Therefore, the model is based on a personal and systems change perspective rather than a procedural justice perspective.

The TFM model requires providing mediation service in four distinct phases:

1. Assessment (screening by level of readiness)
2. Premediative phase (counseling and therapy)
3. Negotiative phase (in-person joint mediation)
4. Follow-up process (six weeks after mediation)

The first two phases of assessment and premediation counseling and the final phase are not typically found in most court-connected mediation programs or even in most private practice settings.

The first phase, assessment, is a screening process that sorts the participants into one of three categories:

Level 1: Those for whom mediation is contraindicated

Level 2: Those who are ready to enter the negotiation phase of mediation immediately

Level 3: Those who would likely benefit from premediation counseling or therapeutic intervention, then reassessment for readiness for the negotiation phase

Assessment of the parties in this model includes at least the following seven major categories:

Postdivorce spousal functioning, including communication, level and type of conflict, violence, trustworthiness, usual behavioral patterns and flexibility, the attachment, divorce readiness, and the plan for their separate futures

Parental functioning, including ability and functioning, involvement, changes since separation, attributes of the children, the children's reaction and how they were told, and the level of closeness and attachment between children and each parent

Resources, including stress levels, coping, and financial, social, and emotional resources

Ethnicity, including the cultural values and beliefs, immigration and acculturation history, and language fluency

Interpersonal context, including new partners, support networks, and institutional involvement

Court involvement, including how long the court has been involved, whether the parties are legally represented, and how adversarial the legal involvement has become

Marital status, including whether this is a first or subsequent cohabitation or marriage, prior separation experiences, and any hidden agendas or assumptions

Twenty percent of the couples presenting for divorce services were screened into the Level 1 (contraindicated) group, based on a number of factors—for example,

- Overwhelming, intense stress
- Obsessive preoccupation with the spouse who was initiating the change or dispute
- Intense anger, rage or uncontrolled conflict
- Involvement of others, or enmeshment within the family dynamic
- Current or on-going family violence
- Severe cognitive dysfunction by one or both the spouses (Irving and Benjamin, 1995, p. 172)

One of the reasons that the outcome agreement rate is 70 percent in this model is that it screens out the most difficult 20 percent of cases. This is something that public mediation services cannot do, so they naturally show a lower rate of outcome success. The Level 1 criteria that are used to screen out cases denote the exact cases that often need help the most, require the most adaptations and specialized services, and are the most challenging population for whom to design appropriate family mediation services.

Level 2 participants showed many of the same characteristics as Level 1, but in a significantly lesser degree, and so were evaluated as capable of functioning adequately in the negotiative phase. Level 2 participants start in that phase without additional premediation individual sessions. Most mediators would see these as the typical cases they work with: some problems and other issues but sufficient emotional and negotiative skill and motivation to do the standard problem-solving, negotiative processes of mediation efforts.

Benjamin and Irving report that approximately 30 percent of the cases presenting for services were functioning at Level 3 and so qualified for premediation services. The TFM model provides several individual sessions for each spouse in this level of functioning in order to assess, support, and develop each person's ability in the following areas:

- Accept the reality of the source of the dispute (the ending of the marriage)
- Make a commitment to the mediation process as opposed to adversarial approaches
- Develop information for informed decisions during the negotiative phase
- Provide specific support and training on how to become better at communication and negotiation during the session
- Ensure safety to protect against threats, intimidation, or violence
- Reduce the intense dysfunction of the person, the spousal system, or the parent-child system
- Reduce blocks in the family's relationship to outside systems, such as relatives, lawyers, and other social and judicial agencies

Once these concerns are sufficiently resolved so that mediation efforts can be effective, the premediation phase is concluded and the third, or negotiative, phase of the mediation process starts. Based on the principled negotiation literature that emphasizes mutuality rather than adversarial process, the mediator helps the parties make the complex decisions regarding the structure and function of the new postdivorce family system. The authors point to the use of positional bargaining occasionally for specific issues. This model allows participants to use brief time-outs to regain emotional control and also provides the premature ending of any particular session to have participants work out their plans separately as their preferred options and alternatives prior to the next session.

Although they generally follow the same procedures outlined in other models for this negotiative phase, Benjamin and Irving highlight their use of reframing techniques and finding superordinate, mutualized goals to keep the process moving in a positive direction. However, if these are not sufficient, then a temporary time-out can be called while one or both return to the earlier individualized therapeutic approach of premediation to deal with the relational issues before resuming the negotiative process.

The authors describe the process as a series of systemic feedback loops or variations on the pattern based on specific issues. Those who need different levels of therapeutic involvement can get them in this model, since they can enter at different points based on the assessed need and capacity of the disputants. The need for a highly variable process reflects the systemic rather than generic view of families.

Assuming the negotiative phase was successful or that the return to the second phase of individual therapeutic sessions was sufficient to get the process to actual agreements, the mediator then provides a written agreement and automatically sets up the fourth and final phase of mediation: the follow-up process. This usually happens six weeks after successful negotiation; there can also be periodic checkups or on an as-needed basis. The goal of this phase is monitoring the family functioning to prevent dysfunction and to reinforce the negotiated agreement without damaging repetitive cycles of litigation and legal modification efforts.

Although this model refers out to traditional adversarial process any cases that appear unlikely to benefit, it has the advantage of being able to be customized to the parties and their situation. Its hallmarks are its built-in perspective that each family, despite the similarity of the dispute, has different needs. It attends to this by designing the system as it evolves and by adding the important first phase of comprehensive assessment of the clients as well as the dispute, along with a secondary phase of individual work with each person separately in order to help prepare everyone for the actual mediation negotiations. The practitioners are not limited by their model, but instead provide therapeutic functions concurrently with or prior to the problem-solving negotiation phase to preempt problems and coach the clients to become more effective decision makers.

About their model, Irving and Benjamin (1995) conclude,

> Any inflexible model of mediation practice will fail with some proportion of these couples simply because something other than negotiation must happen before they are ready to negotiate. Therapeutic family mediation, by its emphasis on an ecosystem sensitivity and understanding of client couples and their social contexts, seeks to establish the optimum fit between the need of client couples and the mediation techniques available to assist them in reaching an amicable and durable agreement. [p. 197]

The TFM model's limited utility in current court-connected centers and settings, its inability to deal with the lower-functioning 20 percent of families who need mediation services, and the expense of the multiple sessions leave this model as perhaps the most fully articulated but least likely to be adopted by jurisdictions and private practitioners entering the field at this time.

Perhaps new approaches could be developed within the same constructs for those who are inappropriate for this model, and funding sources and judicial systems would see the importance of therapeutic intervention. If this happened, the TFM model could become used more extensively, even in court-based mediation programs, as well as adapted to other family problems besides divorce and separation. Those needing premediation therapeutic intervention could receive what they need as long as they need it to help make mediation successful.

Intensive work with the 20 percent of cases screened out of this model could also make this model adaptable by jurisdictions and practitioners. Because it is so fully articulated, this is a model appropriate for research and replication. It fits with the new judicial principles of "one judge, one family" and the concept of multidisciplinary partnerships and building a spectrum of continuity of care in service delivery systems recommended by knowledgeable sources (Johnston and Roseby, 1997).

Strategic, Structural/Functional, and Bowenian Models

In the formative stages of family mediation perspectives, family mediators tried to include family therapy perspectives in order to understand families and help them restructure themselves. Brown and Samis (1986), Gadlin and Ouellette (1986), and others applied these perspectives to family dispute resolution to ground mediation practice in these family therapy theories and practices.

A basic tenet in strategic family therapy is that the therapist must help the family redefine and reframe the problem so it can be solved, or find a solvable problem that the family was ignoring. Strategic family therapists use physical and behavioral symptoms as symbolic representations of the problem, and find that the attempted solution to "the problem" often becomes the real problem to be dealt with in therapy. Another hallmark of strategic therapy is the active stance of the therapist, who often uses highly directive techniques, such as paradoxical injunctions or directives, to get the family to change the problematic family structure or pattern. Applied to family mediation, these therapy models would require the mediator to become highly directive in moving the participants toward change by making them change how they interact. Amundson and Fong (1986) integrated John Haynes's mediation work with the structural/ strategic concepts of reframing, directives, and use of rituals to break patterns and create new structures within the family.

Peter Maida (1986) articulated the Bowenian concepts of fusion and differentiation as useful for family mediators working with separating couples. Wayne Regina (2000) continues the tradition of discussing Bowenian family therapy constructs for family mediators. The longevity of these constructs speaks well for their usefulness and the universality they still hold for practitioners working with families who are in conflict and crisis. The wise family mediator will become familiar with these models of therapy and mediation because they still speak to the nature and change process of families.

Many of the Bowenian understandings about families were included in Chapter One, since they inform so many practitioners. Those who have come from therapy backgrounds will no doubt have had some exposure to these concepts, but those who have come to family mediation from law, business, or other professions may not have the grounding in this theory that would be helpful to practice. It is beyond the scope of this chapter to articulate the theory and practice of Bowen systems theory fully, and readers are urged to do more reading on these constructs. Of particular note to family mediators are the concepts of levels of differentiation, the differences between the intellectual and the emotional systems, and the way this theory posits that families make change.

Family therapists following the Bowenian method would routinely allow for some individual time or caucus, partly because it provides an opportunity to see if the participant has the capacity to differentiate himself from the others in conflict. A family mediator using the Bowen systems theory perspective might find that caucusing needs to be used with caution because it leaves the mediator vulnerable to triangulation and at the same time requires a high level of differentiation for the person in the caucus. The same is true for the issue of whether to use a co-mediator. The decision would be made from the Bowen systems theory model based on the co-mediator's ability to defuse the triangulation and the participants' level of differentiation rather than just on efficacy, preference, or money. Many other choices a family mediator might make during the mediation process could be informed by the Bowenian perspective.

Bowen systems theory and Bowenian-informed family therapy is now considered a classic approach in the field of marriage and family therapy. Family mediators should be familiar with the constructs, even if the model of mediation they practice did not directly develop from these therapeutic understandings.

Another therapeutic mediation approach, hybridized from the structural family therapy literature, is that articulated by Donald Saposnek (1998). Saposnek takes the foundational concepts from strategic family therapy and applies them to the mediation context of family disputes about custody and access for divorcing families.

Larry Fong, who collaborated extensively with John Haynes to develop the underpinnings of family mediation, considers his family mediation model to follow directly from the systemic family therapy perspectives and literature created by the Milan group, a small band of practicing therapists who have influenced the development of family therapy. Fong's early article with Jon Amundson (Amundson and Fong, 1986) pointed out that Haynes's pattern and recommendations for family mediation had theoretical underpinnings that were consistent with the strategic family therapy perspective. They noted that when couples in divorce mediation were being asked to do negotiation on budgets, the process required by the mediator (John Haynes) was similar to the strategic therapy perspective of creating a therapeutic double bind, where old nested patterns in the relationship reemerge. The promotion of empowerment and individuality of the individual by ending established patterned behavior is one of the basic tenets of the strategic and structural family therapy movement. Those therapy models also emphasize the therapist's use of techniques of reframing and positive connotation, therapeutic directives, and creation of rituals that address the systemic patterns to bring about change. Amundson and Fong (1986) point out that "the entire Haynes model of mediation and its directives may be seen as a protracted and extensive therapeutic ritual aimed at evoking a perspective useful in the ongoing management of separation as a product of divorce" (p. 73).

Larry Fong, Donald Saposnek, and others continue to refine the mediation process by applying these family perspectives. This crossover knowledge and theoretical base shows why family mediation is truly an interdisciplinary practice and must remain open to constructs, theory, and research from other therapeutic and family-serving fields.

Impasse-Directed Mediation

Another theoretically grounded therapeutic mediation model is impasse-directed mediation, which was developed and articulated by Janet Johnston (Johnston and Roseby, 1997). This model is aimed at divorce and separation cases where high conflict and domestic violence has created emotional harm for children. These are cases where the parents' conflict and interpersonal dynamics are so pervasive and destructive that they either cannot be brought to standard mediation or fail in the attempt. This inability to come to resolution of the dispute through standard mediation or litigation creates ongoing legal recidivism in the form of successive and contentious litigation, modification, and evaluation processes, which in themselves are harmful to children and further enmesh them in the conflict dynamics.

Based on earlier work by Johnston and others who wished to create a more therapeutic mediation process that would more effectively reduce harm to children caught in the crossfire of unremitting conflict, this model starts from a research-proven assumption that parents who are experiencing and are themselves stuck in these escalating cycles of conflict have diminished ability to meet their children's needs and buffer them from the harm (Johnston and Campbell, 1988). These parents tend to compromise their parenting choices and practices by not dealing with underlying personal problems that may be fueling the conflict or by being so distracted by the conflict that they can no longer see what is in the best interests of their children. The goal of this model is to educate parents about their children's needs and provide direct therapy with the parents and children in order to help them cope better and manage their family conflicts and dynamics.

The impasse-directed mediation model assumes that impasses or continuing conflicts in families happen on three levels: the internal dynamics of each individual, the interaction between the disputants, and the external dynamics between the members of the conflict and the larger social network. Any particular impasse may have one or all of these levels—for example,

- Internal: Divorce as loss, triggering personal attachment or loss issues
- Interactional: Idealized images and shattered dreams; traumatic separations and negative images of divorce
- External: Extended family involvement, or "tribal warfare"; pathologizing labels by evaluators and court personnel

As initially designed, impasse-directed mediation is a fusion of direct therapy and mediation, and in many ways is similar to Irving and Benjamin's TFM model, except that it works with the very cases that TFM excludes. Impasse-directed mediation comes in two forms: individual, in which a single family is seen for sequential therapy and mediation sessions, or group, in which five to eight families are provided a series of twenty-five to thirty-five multihour sessions. Cases are directed to attend by court referral, but the impasse-directed mediation, in both forms, is provided as a private service outside the court setting. In both the individual and group formats, the four-part process is the same.

First is an assessment phase of six to eight hours in which the children are observed, parents are observed interacting with the children, and these clinical observations are added to a detailed, standardized assessment process, which includes a history of

- The dispute
- The parents' personal development
- The marriage or relationship, and its breakdown
- The developmental stages of the children
- The impasse or conflict and its effect on the children

The outcome of the first phase is formulation of an intervention plan, which is agreed on by all the service providers to the family in a strategy conference.

From there the model moves to a pre-negotiation counseling phase, in which each parent is seen separately as a therapy intervention rather than a mediation. In the group mode, these separate sessions are held as separate groups for parents and for children, and two counselor-mediators run the adult groups, while a different counselor-mediator runs the children's groups. During this phase, the practitioner acts as a therapist, selecting the most efficacious persons or subsystems to provide intervention. These interventions range from asking questions to working with the new partner or extended family members, or even direct advocacy to get the child what is needed, such as additional therapy or a change in schedule. At the same time, the practitioner of this model is working to educate the parents and provide direct feedback and communication based on what is being seen in and said by the children, which lends urgency and credibility to the interventions with the parents. Significant others such as new partners are included as needed, as well as collaboration with other service providers.

If the hardened positions of the parents are still not being affected, the practitioner switches to more of a reality-testing approach, where the likely scenarios if they remain recalcitrant when they go to court are played out in detail. Offering this reality check is not the same as giving legal advice but instead focuses on the response and potential for harm to the children. The second phase is the longest, and it can extend as long as the families need it to, which often leads to twelve to sixteen hours of direct intervention.

The third phase of this model is negotiation or conflict resolution, in which the typical problem-solving and negotiative mediation process in joint session (unless violence precludes this) is used, but focused on the dynamics that have created the impasse as already identified in earlier phases. When there are concerns about safety, shuttle mediation is used. This tends to be a brief phase of one or two sessions, with the goal of making agreements that do not exacerbate the emotional dynamics of the impasse.

The fourth phase calls for final implementation. A concluding session helps each parent clarify the agreements and necessary tasks; referrals to other resources such as therapy or court services are made; and the counselor-mediator remains on call for emergency consultation or mini-mediation sessions. There are six-month and two-year follow-ups to determine the durability of the agreements and any changes in the needs of the children.

While this model fits the criteria for short-term therapy, it was perceived as too long for court-connected or publicly funded programs, so a modified version, called the brief impasse consultation model, was developed. It shortened the assessment phase to just an interview with each parent plus either collateral contacts about the child or an interview or observation of the child. A feedback session strategically represents the child's dilemma and needs to the parents; then there is a redirecting session, in which the parents agree on the procedure they will use to resolve the impasse and meet the child's needs. The parents are then referred to community services, which monitor and support implementation of the agreement.

Quantitative research conducted on this model shows that the families for whom it is most effective are those in which the parents "are vulnerable to loss and rejection, those who have experienced traumatic or ambivalent separations, and those who are enmeshed in 'tribal warfare' within the larger social network. The approach may also be beneficial where children are showing symptoms of distress or are at high risk because the parents are too preoccupied with the fight to focus on their needs." (Johnston and Roseby, 1997, p. 238). Johnston and her colleagues caution that this model, as extensively therapeutic as it is, cannot work well with parents who have severe personality disorders; there is some question as to whether such mental conditions are strong indicators of inappropriateness for any model of mediation. (See Chapter Five for more discussion of mental health issues in mediation.) This model also is not recommended by its creators when there is a pending investigation of severe domestic violence, when there has been parental abuse of children, or when other extremes of family dysfunction are present. The research also shows that this model is most effective when used along with legal restraints and sanctions, such as restraining orders, supervised visitations, and other court interventions, early in the case.

TRANSFORMATIVE APPROACHES

In the 1980s and early 1990s, mediators realized that there were many limitations to the models they were using, particularly the procedural and problem-solving approaches. Larry Fong (1992) asked mediators to examine the paradigms they were using, the deep beliefs under the models, and the techniques they were using.

Bush and Folger assaulted the old paradigm with their important new paradigm shift in their controversial book, *The Promise of Mediation: Responding to Conflict Through Empowerment and Recognition* (1994). They described an approach to mediation that focused on transforming people by promoting the deeper human values and needs for recognition and empowerment rather than keeping the focus of mediation on the dispute and the problems to be solved sequentially and logically or on outcome documents, mediated plan, and not going to court. Suddenly, the focus of family mediation was on changing the people rather than changing the dispute. The need to solve problems and come up with written agreements through direct negotiation was subsumed by the need to transform clients. Family mediators who subscribed to this model saw themselves as changers of attitudes and not just behaviors, transformers of people rather than problems. Problem solving was painted in sinister terms in this book, and family mediators operating out of the old problem-solving models were perceived as becoming unduly influencing toward their clients. What mediators were supposed to be doing and why suddenly seemed to change, and trainers and trainees now described themselves as transformative.

The concept of problem solving became a problem to solve with the development of transformative mediation approaches. The fact that family mediators had been helping participants define the issues and then push toward resolution and agreement became a grave concern because it allowed the mediator too much room for meddling, pressuring, and manipulating the process so as to achieve an outcome that would not last because it was not based on the true interests or abilities of the parties. As Bush and Folger (1994, p. 75) put it, "The problem is not with individual mediators but with the approach as a whole."

Transformative mediation was a concept that seemed intuitively right to many practicing family mediators, because they had experienced the limitations of the stage theories, procedural, and standard problem-solving/negotiative approaches for some mediation sessions or with some or even many families. Their existing models did not explain why they did not work some of the time or with some of the cases. It seemed obvious that the disputants own the dispute, and that to change the dispute, one would have to change the people. This change from getting behavioral agreements to changing disputants' attitudes and self was a huge paradigm shift that rocked the mediators and brought a firestorm of controversy, self-examination, and review of models.

While many practitioners became enamoured of the transformative approach in concept when it was introduced in 1994, it took several more years before mediators had a real sense of how to practice family mediation using these constructs and the transformative mediation model.

Hallmarks of Transformative Process

The following ten concepts that Folger and Bush (1996, pp. 263–278) articulated may not constitute a fully formed model of practice but nevertheless serve as guidance on how to do mediation from the transformative perspective.

1. "The opening statement says it all": Describing the mediator's role and objectives in terms based on empowerment and recognition

2. "It's ultimately the parties' choice": Leaving responsibility for outcomes with the parties

3. "The parties know best": Consciously refusing to be judgmental about the parties' views and decisions

4. "The parties have what it takes": Taking an optimistic view of parties' competence and motives

5. "There are facts in the feelings": Allowing and being responsive to parties' expression of emotions

6. "Clarity emerges from confusion": Allowing for and exploring parties' uncertainty

7. "The action is 'in the room'": Remaining focused on the here and now of the conflict interaction

8. "Discussing the past has value to the present": Being responsive to parties' statements about past events

9. "Conflict can be a long-term affair": Viewing an intervention as one point in a larger sequence of conflict interaction

10. "Small steps count": Feeling a sense of success when empowerment and recognition occur, even in small degrees

These ten statements sum up the philosophy of the transformative approach and also show the change of this approach from classic problem solving, which put the responsibility for the process and the outcome more on the skill of the mediator than the ability of the participants. Very different from procedural models that require strict rules and lockstep uniformity, this model posits a flow and interaction in the session that is both unpredictable and only generally controlled by the mediator and is self-led by the participants.

In this respect, transformative mediation practice embodies the deep democracy and faith in the power of the participants to determine a unique process that is consistent with their true interests. This approach emphasizes the freedom of the participants to determine their own process, to be full co-constructionists in their own drama. It allows, even demands, that family mediators be free of confining, preconceived notions of what is important, how to proceed, and the trappings of procedural justice.

Doing Family Mediation Transformatively

Family mediators who want to adopt the premises of this approach have only the ten principles to guide their practice of providing empowerment and recognition. At this point, there are no videotapes that show a family mediator who identifies with this model; indeed, the approach itself is antithetical to scripts, rules, or prescriptive manuals. Because it is interactive and based not on procedure but on appropriate response, this approach cannot be taught in a methodical way. When programs and researchers have tried to quantify the definitions and practices, the differences between problem-solving and transformative mediation practice have had to become more solid. How then can family mediation practitioners adopt this approach and integrate it with their own model of practice? How can we know when a practitioner is doing the transformative mediation approach within some reasonable standards for its practice?

Sally Ganong Pope (1996), an established family mediation practitioner and past president of the AFM, describes how these principles helped her change her practice from a more standard problem-solving approach to one where she "invited fortuitous events" of empowerment and recognition to flourish more. She rethought her mediation practice and tried to include the participants more fully in the setup and function of the mediation session. Instead of providing a process to the family where they were passive recipient of her services, she now offers opportunities for clients to participate in the work they came to do. Family mediators who have been practicing from more negotiative and directive, outcome-based, problem-solving, or procedural models will find this a refreshing reminder that even highly competent mediators may need to add dimensions to their practice as it evolves.

One of the critiques of this approach is that it cannot be quantified and delivered as a training commodity or as an expectation in court-connected settings. Although a family mediator might try to have clients provide each other recognition and empowerment as a prescriptive solution, and while novice mediators arrive out of their initial forty-hour training describing themselves as transformative in approach, this concept is hampered by several factors. One is that we do not have a video library of practitioners who are using this approach, so new and experienced mediators alike have no way to see for themselves how transformative concepts are translated into interactions during a typical mediation session. At some point, researchers may be able to help the field refine the definitions and functions of this approach and then be able to measure whether a particular practitioner is within a standard deviation curve. Another inhibitor of this approach is that by its very nature, it cannot replicate itself. Doing a transformative approach the same way each time would be the exact opposite of the nature of the approach, so practitioners have difficulty in extrapolating and learning from each case to the next how to perfect this approach.

In order to research the effectiveness of this approach, the definitions and actual functions of transformative process will have to be more defined and quantifiably measurable. We can hope that this approach will continue to evolve and that practitioners who ascribe to it will help others to understand its scope and practice.

NARRATIVE MEDIATION MODELS

Developed out of narrative therapy, narrative mediation maintains a different worldview and requires a paradigm shift for mediators. Like transformative mediation models, narrative mediation attempts to bring about change, not just agreements. But unlike the former, narrative mediation is predicated on philosophical perspectives that require practitioners to view the conflict from a stance very different from most conflict resolution perspectives.

The premise of this model is that the mediator is not an expert who will do something *to* the participants, but rather that the mediator will do something *with* the participants: co-create a new story of how they can be without the conflict. The mediator is invited into the story they are telling themselves about the conflict, helps them see what about it they want to change, and then helps them engage in dialogue about what it would be like between them in an alternative to conflict. Then the participants make the choice to change toward that new story and make sets of agreements from it.

In narrative mediation, the major task of the mediator is to help the participants articulate and engage in dialogue first about their story of their conflict and then to deconstruct that story and replace it with a newly co-constructed story that embodies hopefulness, cooperation, and peace. Winslade and Monk (2000) differentiate their approach by delineating the following hallmarks:

- The privileging of stories and meanings over facts
- The hearing of people's stories of conflict as they are produced in discourse

- The clear separation of conflict-saturated stories from stories of respect, cooperation, understanding, and peace

- The use of externalizing conversations to help disputants extract themselves from problem stories that have held them in thrall

- The creation of a relational context of change as a primary task of mediation in preference to the pursuit of an agreed-upon solution

- The selection of alternative stories for development as pathways out of disputes [p. 250]

Phases of Narrative Practice

Narrative mediation passes through three major phases:

1. Engaging the participants

2. Revealing and deconstructing the conflict-saturated story

3. Creating the new alternative story that reduces or changes the conflict

Narrative mediation assumes that the mediator is going to take an active role in all three of these elements and that the role of the mediator is to help the participants move through these phases if possible.

The philosophical underpinnings of narrative practice come from a postmodern perspective; there is no objective reality, only subjective multiple realities that we create separately and together from our language. In this view, people and the world are multiple identities, and conflict is the interaction of these different views or stories or meanings acting on each other. In postmodern thought, all persons, including the mediator, are part of the larger society's dominant discourse. These shared constructions of reality or taken-for-granted assumptions dominate people's own view of what is possible, likely, and meaningful.

By creating open space and dialogue with each other, the narrative process allows the participants to co-construct a new reality that is their own, and this is the desire to have unique outcomes, or a story different from the dominant story or conflict picture. The narrative process helps the disputants hold on to hope that they can bring about a unique outcome and then it actively constructs the agreements and responsibilities so that they can tell a different story.

For example, the dominant discourse is that a divorce will be ugly, aggressive and competitive, harmful to children, and emotionally and financially harmful to the spouses and that mothers should have primary child care responsibilities. People expect that will be true and start to construct a conflict-saturated story about their own marriage and divorce. Those automatic assumptions that are fueling the conflict can be discussed, and a unique outcome can be constructed that does not follow the predicted disaster. It will take the couple's full cooperation and desire to create that alternative story rather than to slip back into the conflict story.

In order to engage, the mediator must build trust, rapport, mutual respect, and true willingness to be part of the conflict and part of the new order. Unlike problem solving, where the mediator is often trying to become a disinterested third party, the mediator is in the thick of it in this model. The stance of the mediator is not a detached expert imposing information or directives on the participants or a scrupulously neutral facilitator, but rather an actively curious coequal person who sometimes acts deliberately ignorant to encourage the dialogue.

The narrative mediator invites the telling of the stories and then helps the participants hold an externalizing conversation, where they objectify the problem and place it outside themselves, as if it were a separate entity. The narrative mediator then maps the effect of the problem on the participants and the participants on the problem, not just as a listing of facts but in the way they make meaning of it. By naming the problem and reflecting out loud on how the problem has historically affected each of them and how each of them has affected the problem, they are better able to understand how they have contributed to the creation of the conflict. In this way, the basic premise of this approach is that *the people are not the problem; the problem is the problem.*

All the participants in the mediation and the mediator together then start to deconstruct the problem story, and watch for the small signs of hopefulness and strength that can lead to the creation of the alternative story. The participants are then invited to reflect on whether they really want the conflict story or an alternative. If it is the latter, then they work on creating it by answering more reflective questions about how it could be. Because the participants are so steeped in the conflict story, they often hearken back to it; when this happens, the mediator doggedly returns to the possibility of an alternative, keeping hope alive until the participants become more invested in it.

Reflective Questions and Writing Memos

In narrative mediation, the mediator's major activity and technique is to ask reflective questions that allow the participants opportunities to do these processes. They do not power-balance in the traditional sense of shutting one party down or speaking for another. Mediators in this approach are deeply respectful of each person's voice. They actively engage the topics of entitlement and try not to become unwitting spokespersons for the dominant worldview. In this regard, narrative mediation as an approach is highly invested in the concept of client self-determination and requires the mediator to be congruent to these concepts in practice.

Because narrative mediators focus so heavily on understanding and giving voice to each person's story, as well as creating the necessary trust and rapport, they encourage the use of individual time with each participant prior to the joint session or within the joint session context. By allowing this process, the mediator is able to allow more complete stories that are less vulnerable to alternative interpretations (Winslade and Cotter, 1997).

Narrative mediators write down the outcome agreements and also function as a process recorder for the ongoing changes in the dialogue and story. Narrative mediators write memos that hold in place the changes and intentions of the participants to gain momentum for the alternative story while it is being created. Because words and stories hold so much importance in this model, this activity is seen as vital to ensuring movement toward the development of the alternative.

Because narrative mediation requires the practitioner to introject the philosophical base and the active, reflective process, it is not a model that can be ransacked for techniques without damaging the intent and process it requires. The practitioner needs to accept the premises fully in order to do the practice of narrative mediation adequately. Speaking about narrative therapy, Monk (1997, p. 2) states, "The co-creative practices of narrative therapy require a particular ability on the part of the therapist to see the client as a partner with local expertise," and he sees it more as a way of being rather than as a specific practice.

Adapting the Narrative Model to Mediation Practice

The narrative model fits well with family mediation because it acknowledges the systemic nature of the couple or family as co-creators and it provides for a multiplicity of perspective. It may not be the most easily accessible model for family mediators who have been operating from a problem-solving/negotiative perspective, because the foundational view is vastly different about the role and function of the helper. Family mediators who wish to adopt this model should receive training and feedback on their narrative mediation practice rather than assume that they are practicing this model simply by asking reflective questions.

Narrative therapy and narrative mediation are relatively new models that fit intuitively for many practitioners, but they are models that have not yet been studied analytically for their success in creating not only satisfaction but also durable agreements, when compared to other models. Future research may show the efficacy and desirability of these respectful and thoughtful approaches. Like all other processes that have grounding in philosophical positions and ways of being, the validity and usefulness of these models rest on those foundations. These models may be best for cultures that are not so imbued with the scientific worldview and not so used to professionals' acting as experts in order to gain credibility and authority with them. They may also be ideal models and processes for family disputes that are primarily relational rather than distributive. As models, their beliefs and their practice are well integrated.

INTERACTIVE APPROACHES

Lang and Taylor (2000) are part of the paradigm shift from more directive and negotiative procedural or problem-solving approaches to the more interactional, transformative, and unique approaches to the mediational process. They promote the imperative that family mediators must understand their own model and approaches, or constellation of theory, and that they should bring that understanding to mediation.

They propose that each mediator is constantly assessing the interaction, overtly or covertly, and creating a formulation of the people, the problem in dispute, and the mediation or ADR process to use in order to help the participants in the best way. This is further informed by the mediator's background of theory—whether from law, business, and distributive negotiation or from therapeutic and human service perspectives. Although Lang and Taylor would not dispute the ten hallmarks of the transformative approach, they also would not prescriptively set about to provide a transformation of people. Instead, they offer an approach that is constantly monitoring and assessing the interaction between the mediator and the participants and between the participants themselves.

Although they agree that the mediator has a major responsibility for the balance and neutrality of the process in general, the climate during the mediation session, and modeling of appropriate negotiative and communication methods, they see that the mediator is only one person in a newly formed and unique interactive system of three or more people. By having the mediator become more aware through reflection during the session and after, the interaction of the multiparty interactional system can be changed. The mediator is urged to become more self-aware and bring up the awareness of the interactional process during the mediation session.

In this approach, the mediator is trying to become more aware of the following primary interactional elements during and after the sessions.

Relationships: How formal or distant and how connected are they, and what level of relationship are they likely to have after the mediation?

Orientation to power and conflict: Are they competitive or avoidant, do they understand their own forms of power over each other, and do they use them well?

Communication: Do they have a consistent theme, how do they address each other, and how do blocks to their communication happen and resolve?

Range of interaction: Are they free to express themselves or constricted, and are they able to honor each other's boundaries?

Transparency: How open and honest are they? How much is covert? How forced or natural do they seem to each other?

Respectfulness: Are they able to express genuine empathy and provide the empowerment and recognition for themselves and others, or are they caught in defensiveness and disregard?

Interactive approaches always include the use of the material generated during the session, since that holds the key to understanding what the nature of the dispute is and how to help change the interaction into more positive forms. How the session unfolds forms a microcosm of how it has been for the family members outside the session. Each moment and interaction by the participants holds the clues to how the interaction is either helping to resolve or manage the conflict, or is stopping the participants from effective interaction that could help lead to positive outcomes.

One fundamental belief of practice in this interactive approach is that *there are no positive outcomes if the interactional process is negative.* What must be changed first is the way the participants interact during the session rather than transforming the people themselves, as in the TFM or the transformational approach.

The other basic belief of interactional approaches is that if the parties change the way they interact to a more positive, open, and complete dialogue, then the change of interaction will allow for a better likelihood of finding a way out of the conflict situation. Interactional mediators transform not the people but the way the people interact, so that they can then change their thoughts, feelings, and behavior, which will change the way they interact with each other. In this view, mediators will always change the interpersonal dynamics, no matter what they do or do not do as interventions, because the mediator is now a new entity in the interactional field who changes the interaction just by being there.

It is still incumbent on mediators to choose the best intervention based on their model and theoretical understandings and on their sense of what is happening during the interaction. In all events, the outcome will have been different because of the intervention or lack of it by the mediator. This approach allows mediators to use the knowledge and skill they bring and is inclusive of the other models of mediation practice as long as the intervention selected seems to fit with the formulation. Whenever there is a mismatch between the interaction and the intervention, the participants can change either side of the equation.

Haynes and Haynes (1989) speak to this constantly fluid type of interactive model:

> There is no one set of "cookbook" strategies that work with every situation; rather, I determine each strategy according to the nature of the issues and the nature of the behavioral conflicts. In some cases, I am controlling, keeping the couple on task and permitting few distractions. At other times, I am more flexible, allowing the couple to deal with the issue in the way that makes them comfortable. With some couples, I am strategic and do not say what I am doing.

With others, I carefully explain each of my interventions. Sometimes I am an educator, at other times I am a reality tester, and in a few cases I tell people what to do. [pp. 18–19]

The family mediator's choice of what to do depends on his formulation or hypothesis of the case, what his model of mediation tells him, and his sense of the appropriate interactive sequence for what is going on in the room at that moment. Family mediators who select an interactional approach to their work need a level of basic competence and skill in one or more of the other more unified and prescriptive models in order to have a basis for making these judgments.

Interactive models are best learned and used when the practitioner has an active, in-session supervisor or colleague or the capacity to videotape and play back sessions. These allow a feedback loop to help the practitioner reflect on the interventions after the session, so that the reflection and intervention during the session can become more responsive and attuned. The more the practitioner can see the critical moments for intervention and apply appropriate theory and skill to those moments, the more competent he can become. A practitioner who subscribed to the transformative approach could search for critical moments of interaction when recognition, empowerment, and the other hallmarks of that approach could be actualized and supported by intervention. Someone operating from a more problem-solving or negotiative approach could also become more aware and interventionist at those critical moments in interaction that would support direct negotiation and expansion of options by the disputants.

In this way, the mediator who is practicing from an interactional perspective does not need to give up his former models; rather, by paying more attention to the interaction, he will become more skilled in providing the intervention that is recommended by his model. Interactional approaches augment but do not replace the other models and approaches; a family mediator needs a base model of practice in order to use the interactive approach.

NEUTRALITY CONCEPTS ACROSS MODELS

Because different models and approaches propose very different roles for family mediators, the level of directiveness, activity, intervention, and neutrality of the mediator will vary considerably in the literature and in actual practice. Cohen, Dattner, and Luxenburg (1999) point out that the issue of "how neutral is neutrality" is particularly poignant for the family mediator, since there are often competing ethical stances and standards, depending on whether the mediator is practicing from the negotiative problem-solving approach or a more therapeutic or interactional way. Although family mediators are supposed to function as neutral third parties, they often see the plight of the unrepresented third parties, the children, as needing advocacy and feel compelled ethically to intervene to protect and support the children's interests separate from the parents' view.

I recently proposed that the dilemma of neutrality for family mediators comes from the tension between two very different histories and concepts of neutrality (Taylor, 1997). One side of this continuum is the scrupulous or strict neutrality stance; in this role, the mediator essentially says, "I just provide the opportunity; they are responsible for the outcome." This view of neutrality comes from early ethics and standards of practice in the field that were developed from the more negotiative, problem-solving, and procedural perspectives. The other end of the continuum is the more liberal interpretation of neutrality; this expanded concept is represented by the concept of the mediator as not automatically biased or unduly influencing during the mediation. This concept has developed from human services and the models of mediation practice that allow and encourage an expanded view of the role of the mediator as educative, therapeutic, and normative-evaluative as well as rational. Obviously, the model of mediation practice a practitioner selects will determine where along this continuum that practitioner's neutrality will stand.

Additional factors that affect neutrality in action in a session is how interventionist a family mediator becomes. This also will depend on which model of mediation the mediator is using. Family mediators who are using procedural, structured, or problem-solving models are usually strongly interventionist and directive, since they see it as their role to move the participants to the solution, keep them on track, direct the conversation, and define the topics and options on behalf of the mediation effort and toward an outcome that supports settlement. Family mediators using models and approaches that are more client centered and client directed, such as the therapeutic, transformative, narrative, and interactive approaches, are less likely to intervene or will intervene and direct the process but not redirect to create a specific end product. They may provide advocacy for unrepresented parties directly or indirectly through pointed questions for the participants.

When it comes to the issue of power balancing between the participants in a dispute, an active process that can certainly affect the participants' perception of the mediator's neutrality, we have an odd merging of models. (See Haynes, 1988, for a complete discussion of power balancing for family mediators.) Transformative mediators might well try power-balancing techniques, which offer opportunities to provide participants with the empowerment they need. Yet it could also be that the empowerment would have to come from the participants, not the mediator, in order to be truly out of the transformative model, since all interactions in the session are based on the premises of the clients, not the mediator, knowing best. Those practicing from the problem-solving and negotiative models do power balancing with impunity, while those following the

TFM model might also power-balance by using individual therapeutic sessions as needed to provide opportunities for personal transformation.

The practice of family mediation needs more clarity in the basic concepts of neutrality and levels of intervention within a session. To talk of these concepts as if they were outside the models is unhelpful, since each of the models has a view of how to be neutral and interventionist. We can hope the field will do more empirical research and provide more modeling through videotape and supervision that will enable us to understand these concepts in relationship to the different models of practice.

ECLECTICISM, INTEGRATION, AND PERSONALIZING MODELS

Many family mediators have created personalized models from their exposure to different trainers, models, and approaches or based on the practicality of their setting and experiences in working in court-connected mediation services, private practice, or as the attorney mediator who does the family mediation cases in a firm. Personalization of learning is an important stage in professional development, and family mediators need to adopt an organized approach to their work at least initially, so that their interventions and service delivery are consistent, practical, and effective.

There should be a correspondence between what a family mediator tells the disputants about how she practices and what actually occurs during the session. Mixing and matching, picking up techniques from other practitioners, and sharing tools of the trade are often the substance of training and workshops, but such technique shopping can create strange and even hazardous, slipshod approaches that have little internal consistency or provide professional integrity. Unfortunately, even our professional societies have promoted this "cut and paste" approach to family mediation by sponsoring conference workshops and brown-bag lunches that ask the attendees to share a technique that worked for them, forgetting that the technique is meaningless without the models and theories under it and that the same technique used on a different family structure or dynamic might not work so well or even be harmful to the family. We do need to learn from each other, but not in this way.

Experienced mediators may need to expand from a limiting beginning model to develop and respond more consistently with their personal and professional values and beliefs. Between maintaining a unique practice as a solo endeavor and giving it away piece by piece lies enough room for personal growth and development, for becoming artistic in one's approach. Practitioners need to see their career and their models as evolving along with their level of professional development (Lang and Taylor, 2000).

Because problem-solving and transformative approaches start from different justice principles and move toward different end points, they were originally conceived by Bush and Folger and others as essentially mutually exclusive. But is this true? Must family mediators pick between these, or can they use both?

In an attempt to differentiate the two approaches to find out how transformative versus problem-solving the volunteer mediators in a community-based program were and what difference the model made to the outcome, Martin (2000) outlined the differences between problem-solving and transformative approaches in order to operationalize the definitions for research. He looked at features of the two models, such as the assumptions about and response to conflict, the goal to which the mediator works and the role and action they take, and the general focus of the mediation process. Although Bush and Folger had indicated that the two models are mutually exclusive and antithetical, Martin's direct field research found a different result. Even volunteers who had not studied transformative approaches used both problem-solving and transformative interventions and actions within sessions. "This flexibility, which included moving from problem-solving to transformative, seemed more prominent in the more experienced mediators" (Martin, 2000, p. 43). The interactive approaches are not antithetical to other models and perspectives, and in fact they require a base model of problem-solving and negotiation. Thus, there *is* a way to blend the usefulness of each as part of the greater mediation process.

In counselor and therapy training schools, students study a variety of methodologies and are encouraged to start with one integrated, comprehensive model of practice. Then, in long-term professional development and through continuing education, therapists are encouraged to develop their own approach. Some practices in that field depend entirely on the personal charisma and marketing ability of the developer, whereas other practices are classic and remain unchanged over time, proven effective not only in clinical practice but by empirical testing.

It is possible to hold to a basic model of mediation, yet be open to other ways of seeing the case. I follow an interactive model that has roots in problem solving, and yet I understand and try to incorporate the benefits of therapeutic and narrative mediation during practice. I usually start with an interactive, problem-solving/negotiative approach and switch models if there is evidence that the model I am using does not fit the people or the problem. I sometimes review the case from a transformative or therapeutic lens after the session, even if I stayed in the interactive or problem-solving model during the session. Many of my colleagues use different models, and when we discuss cases as part of an ongoing monthly peer review process, the different models show up in their response to the case presentation. This sharing has enriched my view of cases by looking through different lenses, without necessarily having to change my own model, and often it gives me needed insight on how to work differently.

As family mediators become more sophisticated by experience and training, they will be able to add more complexity to their model of practice to explain and inform their work. Continuing education in this field should be seen as a need to grow in depth and breadth of theory and ability to know and apply different models as needed for a particular set of dynamics within a family. Instead of just counting seat hours to meet statutory or professional requirements, or attending conferences to gain hours, the real goal of continuing education is to develop models and theory, not just facts. We continue to need more research that helps answer hard questions as to whether certain models of mediation bring about more healing of family systems, more durable agreements, or better outcomes for the entire family affected by the dispute, so that mediation models are tested to determine whether they are based on preference or principles that last.

✂

In this chapter, we have reviewed the major models of family mediation and have put the models into several large categories based on their underlying assumptions and background theoretical underpinnings. Few of these mediation models and approaches are stand-alone, complete theoretical models that fully explain why as well as how. Because of the need to convey a lot of practical information about the content of the mediation, mediation books and articles have tended to be collections of facts more than integrative models grounded on empirically proven realities. Some approaches are great ideas that but leave the family mediator without enough instruction or theory to make intelligent guesses in difficult cases.

Family mediators will be seeing a greater push on the national and local levels to unify service delivery, provide consistency, and develop models and methods that respond better to diverse populations and specialized applications. I hope the field will be able to keep its diversity of approaches while maintaining its basic integrity of process. I also hope we will expand and refine good practices until they evolve into newer, more effective methods that can be passed to the next group of practitioners.

Wise family mediators should adapt what has been learned in other professions to the practice of family mediation and adapt and change a basic model only when there is strong evidence from research, clinical practice, or direct personal experience that it no longer fits the practitioner or the participants. Starting with an integrated, comprehensive model that gives direction is best, and then adapting that model through research and clinical practice with feedback from supervision and direct observation is the best next step. Finally, articulating new models and approaches through the literature serves the entire field.

Family mediators can allow eclecticism personally and professionally when the blending augments and provides a better blend. By sharing what, why, and how we are doing family mediation practice, the field can evolve. Part of being a mediator is the recognition of the truth inherent in opposites and the desire to reconcile without negating either side. Contained in the dichotomies within our field (problem-solving versus transformative, facilitative versus evaluative, procedural versus interactive, mandatory versus voluntary) is a range of truths within which the field will operate. How family mediators handle the issue of inclusivity of approach while still maintaining adequacy of standards of practice will be the challenge of the second wave of family mediation practice.

Imperfect and incomplete as they are, it is better to have some model than none at all. New family mediators need to find one, and practicing family mediators need to reassess theirs.

CHAPTER FOUR

Family Mediation Skills and Techniques

F amily mediators do not just use a set of skills and techniques like tools; rather, they select a method of intervention within the practice of mediation that is consistent with their own understanding of families and their own model of mediation. Selecting techniques or skills without having an organizing principle about why or how or when to use it can be irresponsible and even harmful. Mediators can have working knowledge of and skills from several different approaches and make a selection that matches best with clients' needs and expectations, as well as the requirements of the setting. Mediators can grow and change and can maintain multiple approaches as long as they do not mix techniques randomly.

For this chapter to be useful, readers must have made some discoveries about their own conceptual frameworks and must initially be operating out of at least one organized, integrated model or approach; otherwise, the chapter will be descriptive without adding guidance.

This chapter describes typical topics and practice issues for family mediators, no matter which model or approach they are using. The discussion points out the discrepancies among models, where there is room for professional discretion, or where the models describe the issues and topics very differently. By knowing that these issues and processes are likely to surface, no matter which model the mediator is using, readers can think ahead and select an orientation that will be internally consistent and helpful in practice.

CASE ASSESSMENT AND FORMULATION

Every mediator, formally or informally, makes some assumptions or assessment about the people, the problems, and the process that will work the best for that case. Depending on the mediator's training and theory base, this will be either a formalized part of the process or a covert and cursory look. I urge practitioners to use a comprehensive and organized method of assessing each case by moving from the more general to the very personal, like concentric rings. In the outer rings are the basic facts, in the middle ring is the relationship dynamics, and in the central ring is each person.

Mediators who are following a stage theory model or doing classic problem solving or a negotiative approach may do no assessment at all, in the belief that the past is less important than the future and that the issues will surface as negotiations begin. In fact, if Kreisberg (1998) and Rummel (1991) are accurate in their analysis of how conflict emerges and if Moore (1996) is correct in stating that different kinds of conflict function and resolve differently, then having some sense of the history of a particular conflict and its precursors would be very helpful, no matter what kind of mediation model is used. Even if the assessment is limited to conflict-related discussion and does not involve internal personal understandings, some knowledge of the history of the conflict and positions already taken could help the mediator from these perspectives.

If the mediator is following the narrative approach, this process of understanding the people and their dilemma will not be seen as an objective organized assessment, but rather will come in the form of listening carefully to the participants' narratives and understanding each participant's view through the narrative. In this approach, the mediator will not try to tell the participants what their problem is or analyze it but will listen to the meta-message of the story to determine if it is the dominant discourse or conflict-saturated story or part of a new alternative that may help that person think about the conflict differently. A mediator who is following the transformative approach will be determining which people need more personal empowerment and recognition as part of the less formal assessment. In some therapeutic approaches, such as the TFM model, the self-report and interviewing are very organized and comprehensive. It will cover the personal and social history of the participants, based on the concept that the more comprehensive the assessment of the parties is, the more likely it is that the therapeutic mediator can help identify what specifically needs to change.

Assessing the Family System

Families are complex in structure and membership as well as in interactional dynamics. Even a case that seems simple may be covering a fact or event in the past that is important to understanding the interaction and reaction of the disputants. No matter which model of mediation is being used, a wise family mediator makes a detailed map of the family before deciding the exact plan for mediation. This could not hurt, and it may help. Social workers and therapeutic family mediators often construct a formal genogram—a pictorial representation of important life events like births, deaths, and illnesses, ethnicity, and important relationship issues such as alliances, conflicts, and support across three generations of the family (McGoldrick and Gerson, 1985; McGoldrick, Gerson, and Schellenberg, 1999). Computer programs that generate the physical map of the family based on the standardized notation developed through years of practice are now available. Practitioners who want a quick reference of the parties and their households but do not want to learn these standardized notations may find the computer programs helpful.

Appendix A contains a simplified format called a household map that I developed in a county family court mediation service specializing in divorce, where time was short and families were often complex. By using this standardizing form as a tool for mapping families and current and historical households, mediators can quickly see past and current relationships and fluctuating households. Mediators complete this form by filling in the names and ages of the family members who are identified as being in dispute and then drawing lines around households to indicate current parties who are living together, starting with the parties who present themselves for mediation services, then working outward to other past and potential future relationships. When couples have multiple children with different parents, adding units where appropriate can modify the basic form. The form also has spaces for outside agencies and others who are influencing the dispute or its resolution, such as child protective services or court-appointed special advocates.

Mediators need not take the time to learn complex notation or use any special form in order to do this background information gathering and mapping of the family and the parties. The simplest way is to start at the center of a legal-sized pad with the names of the disputants, figure out their relationships to each other, and work outward from there. A mediator can include important auxiliary relationships, such as therapists, advocates, and attorneys. Having a visual quick reference to the people, their historical and current relationships, and the family units and expectations is helpful in interpreting and understanding the data generated in the course of the mediation effort.

However a family mediator does this task, it is important that it be done within the first telephone contact or first visit. To neglect this may lead to problems later, when someone suddenly "remembers" that a child died in someone else's care, a relative has been convicted of sexual crimes, there are other children not being discussed for whom the parent has legal or financial responsibility, or there are outside agencies or persons who are still affecting the situation. If mediators do not ask, the client might not tell important information; if the mediator does ask and explains why this information might be relevant to the current dispute, the participants are more likely to provide good and complete information that can lead to better-quality and more complete agreements and understandings.

The belief that practitioners who are trying to help distressed couples and families should first assess the current functioning is a concept supported by Karpel (1994) and other couples counselors and therapists. A family mediator could assess a family mediation case based on Karpel's evaluation criteria of couples presenting for couples therapy, modified below to relate to mediation.

Facts

- Are the parties married or cohabiting, and are all the members of the household on the map or genogram?
- Have they been speaking to each other? If not, what was the quality of the last interaction, and when was that?
- Who contacted whom about getting mediation started, and who is paying for it?
- How long have they been together? How rich was their former relationship before the dispute?
- What external stressors have they been dealing with separately and together?
- What are their financial arrangements with each other?

Characteristics of the Individuals

- Are there chronic, acute, or historical emotional or behavioral problems for any of the family members (those mediating or those who will be affected by the mediation)?
- What phase of the life cycle and family life are each of them in?
- How committed to each other and other members of the family are they?

Relational Context of the Dispute

- How do attachment and autonomy play out between them?
- How functional is their communication?
- Are there power differences due to gender, age, or other factors?
- What other systems are affecting the dispute or family?
- How much credibility do they have with each other regarding trustworthiness and fairness?
- What protective or systemic function might be served by maintaining the problem or dispute?

Readiness for Intervention

- Have they used mediation efforts before, and do they understand exactly what mediation is?

- How much rapport does the mediator have with each person?

- Are they ready to do face-to-face mediation, or do they need some other service or help before that?

Determining Preexisting Conditions and Readiness

In looking at the people involved in the dispute, the first question a practitioner should consider is, "Are these people experiencing distress due to the dispute, or did they have preexisting personal or social problems before the dispute developed?" For practitioners who do not have clinical diagnostic skills or who resent having to label their clients with psychological or mental health terminology, the basic issue here is whether the person has all his faculties available to help him during this dispute event or whether, due to preexisting conditions, his resilience or personal skills have been compromised before the attempt to resolve the dispute. For example, in a family reunification case, the emotional and mental status of the parent and any partners is critical to understanding whether they are ready to have the child placed back in the home. In elder care situations, the behavioral status of not only the elder but also the caregivers may be part of the issue. Situational distress can create behavior that can look similar to acute, historic, or chronic problems.

If the perception of the family is that the current dispute is part of the typical pattern of interaction or just a repetition of former negative behavior or emotional problems by one or more of the participants, the mediator's response will be very different than if the perception is that this is a temporary aberration in an otherwise emotionally and mentally stable individual. Temporary emotional distress of one or more of the participants might be a reason to slow the mediation process down long enough for the participant to get emotional support or stability. For example, if a parent is just starting drug or alcohol treatment, her responsiveness to making good long-term decisions in family mediation efforts may still be affected by her substance use. Waiting to do the face-to-face mediation session later could give the parent a chance to prepare better. Readiness to mediate in joint session is part of the initial assessment, or joint family construction, that family mediators need to understand.

Assessment is often done without formalized procedures or lists of questions; the mediator fits what the participants are saying as answers to the questions. A mediator following the narrative approach will listen for the story each person tells and then help each one "re-story" the dilemma. The mediator will help the participants objectify or personify the problem by holding the externalizing conversation. These questions can spark other questions, and interactive mediators who believe in transparent processes will share with the participants whatever they learn by listening, asking, and even verifying information with others (assuming a signed release of information by the clients to allow them to do this). Because any agreement will rely on the credibility, interests, and capabilities of all the participants, the question of each person's current and future status is critical to achieving a positive agreement. By whatever means the mediator prefers, knowing the personal and social reality each person is experiencing is the adventure and challenge in family mediation.

Evaluating the Problems to Be Solved

In the process of finding out each person's perspective, the definition of the issues and problems may change. Redefinition of the issues and concerns can become more inclusive and therefore more complex. Like all other single-text negotiation efforts, these disparate views need to be surfaced and a single new synthesis developed from all the participants. Many writers in the field of mediation refer to reframing as a technique to help change the narrative and attitude.

For example, in a family reunification case, the problem may change from a dichotomous single-option dispute that could be summarized as

- To reunify the child with her mother or have the child remain in foster care

to a dilemma with many options that must include several complex sets of conditionals:

- *If* the mother is able to complete drug and alcohol treatment successfully, *and* if the grandparents are willing to house the child temporarily, then what should be the level of involvement of the parents and grandparents during the treatment episode, in the first six months after care, and from then on?

The definition of the problem changes from a simple, binary choice to a very fluid, conditional set of possibilities. If grandparents are not included in the mediation effort, their valuable though limited role cannot be adequately discussed. In keeping with the systems theories discussed in earlier chapters, family mediators who find ways to include all members of the system are more likely to find other resources and options, as well as learn the other complexities.

Usually, the problem that is brought to family mediation is not the problem as all the participants define it. It is the tip of the iceberg and has often been distorted or changed by the legal or social institutions that have come into contact with the family. A mother's drug and alcohol use that has led to neglect of a child and an out-of-home placement with involvement by child protective services and the court has been socially defined as a crime and an emergency. When this case comes to the family mediator, it is important for him to find the different perspectives from family, therapists, and social workers. Each of them needs to comment on the nature of the parental bond, the availability of the grandparents, and the mother's motivation to change in order to get a complete picture of the dilemma for the parent and for the child.

Because children whose parents have had multiple relationships belong to several family groupings simultaneously, it is important to find similarities and discrepancies among these groups regarding the nature of the problem. In a blended family with a parent-child dispute, the new stepparent might identify the problem in the following way: "This kid has never had any discipline, and I am just trying to set things right." The mother will define the problem differently: "My child can't get along with my new husband, and he's trying to make me choose between them." The biological father might have this to say about the situation: "The stepparent is alcoholic and abusive, and my daughter is just trying to survive in bad circumstances." And the child's school counselor has defined the problem in yet another way: "This child has severe emotional problems that need family counseling, but the family refuses to get help." These are very different views of what "the problem" is. If this were a multiple choice test, the right answer would be that "all of the above" are a part of the problem.

Obviously, the family mediator must avoid the role of evaluator of the family. Not all mediators operating from all the models and approaches described in Chapter Three would ask the family for permission to get additional input from other parties or involve the biological father in the current three-party dispute. And yet if the mediator's role is defined as helping this three-person system function more effectively within the larger family and social sphere in which it functions, then getting additional information to augment the problem definition makes sense. How can a mediator help the family put together a puzzle without all the pieces?

It is always important to differentiate between the primary disputants and those who are connected but only secondarily. In this situation, the stepfather has no legal parenting rights or responsibilities, but is doing the parenting job and therefore is a primary participant in the dispute and should be in the mediation. If the mother and biological father are coequal joint legal custodians, then the father should be considered a primary participant in the mediation effort (but not in the dispute), even if the stepparent and mother do not want him involved. His input could become vital to any outcome agreement regarding the child, and as a legal co-custodian, he should become aware of the situation and active in finding a solution. Many mediators might miss this important distinction and mediate only between the stepfather and child or among the mother, daughter, and stepparent rather than finding some way to involve the biological father.

This brings us to a critical point: mediators are the ones who must sort through the information and decide the groupings and sequence of the mediation effort by using these expanded views of the problem definition. This is a problem of how this threesome gets along, but it is also a problem of how the co-custodians function (or do not) to protect the child. By expanding the vision of the definition of the dispute and orchestrating the mediation effort in ways that honor the different subgroups and larger systems, the mediator can help the family see the larger picture. If the mediator has assessed the family members and indicated the desire to define the problem differently, then the clients could decide whether they agree to work this way.

Assessment, however it is done and no matter how extensive or informal it is, will change the way in which the family members are defining the dispute and the dilemma for each of them. By defining the problem differently and allowing the family time to accept the larger view of the problem, the mediator has changed the problem and offered help in a new way. When the problem has been clarified, expanded, and accepted by all members, the mediator can use her chosen model to provide change, solve the problem, or help change the people so they can solve the dilemma for each of them and thereby manage or resolve the problem.

SHAPING CLIENT SESSIONS FOR EFFECTIVENESS

Unlike community-based mediation efforts, in which the mediator expects to conduct a single, effective session to resolve all issues in one sitting, or public policy mediations, in which caucusing and table sessions can last years, most family mediation takes place over a series of sessions that may span a few days to a few weeks. Very few family mediations can begin and end in a single joint session, although many family mediations end abruptly in the middle of a sequence or a particular session because one or more of the participants feels that it is unsuccessful or unsafe. Each session is a microcosm of the larger effort: each session has a beginning, a middle stage, and an end. At any point, one or more of the participants may refuse to participate further. Most family mediators, no matter what their model, know that they are responsible for maintaining a safe, adequate process. When a session ends abruptly, mediators need to view this as participants' exercising their rights to opt out, but the mediator also needs to monitor what happened in the sequence and process of the session that made it untenable for one or more of the participants.

Time and Structure of Sessions

Most family mediators find that the classic "fifty-minute hour" of individual therapy is too short to allow both (or multiple) participants to express the problems, search for options, and start the selection process, let alone do the personal transformation, therapeutic interventions, or changes in interaction that may be wanted or needed. The first fifteen minutes or so of each session is used for repositioning each participant in relation to each other, a recap of the past session and any homework or new information, and review of any significant changes between sessions. The final fifteen minutes must be devoted to closure behaviors, to assigning tasks and instructing participants how to get ready for the next session. If a mediator holds a ninety-minute session, then there is effectively only one hour for that session's agenda, plus beginning and ending the session. Most family mediators find this to be the minimum time they need, and for many, this feels very rushed.

Family mediation sessions that last too long see gains reduced as the participants lapse into old unproductive behavioral patterns or become weary. Since most people's attention span is twenty minutes without some sort of break, an appointment time of ninety minutes gives the mediator the first ten minutes or so to help participants feel comfortable in the room and review the previous session or the initial understandings about mediation. The session then moves into three twenty-minute intervals, with twenty minutes left to summarize progress, make suggestions for the next session and set the appointment, and then get the clients out of the office.

If appointments are scheduled every two hours but last ninety minutes each, mediators have time to refresh themselves emotionally and physically between and before the next case. Because so much is going on, many family mediators find this work to be simultaneously emotionally draining and exhilarating. Whether the family mediator is working in private practice or public service, professionals working with family disputes must pace themselves and meet their own needs in order to be fully available for their clients. However the family mediator schedules cases, a break needs to be scheduled to allow the mediator and the family time to recoup, rethink, and restore themselves. Marathon mediations often produce false agreements and are artificially intense, which can lead to decisions that are broken immediately because they were not carefully considered.

Conducting three different mediation sessions in one day is a lot, and mediators must practice good self-care to guard against burnout and vicarious traumatization from the levels of hostility, the descriptions of abuse, and actively modulating the often vicious emotional dynamics during the interaction. To guard against creating mediation mills where cases are ground out without regard to the needs of clients to reflect and be clear, family mediators must help service delivery systems plan adequate pacing and spacing of cases. Just as managed care has required therapists to quantify their therapeutic planning in short-term modules of service, family mediators need to determine a sequence and pace that fits the clients and their own needs, not just the expediency or efficiency of the system.

Family mediators should think about their series of mediation sessions as a working contractual plan that can be changed by mutual agreement. They have professional standards that require them to educate the clients as to their best guess about how many sessions, in what sequence and frequency, will be needed. This should be discussed as part of the initial contracting for mediation. If mediation is being paid for by a third party or a governmental system, the participants need to know what they are entitled to and the outside limits of the service.

A Mediation Plan for Sequential Sessions

The first one or two sessions need to be about developing some level of rapport, trust, and understanding of the participants and some understanding of the mediation problem or dispute as they have defined it. These first sessions form the beginning assessment phase. The clients are deciding whether there is a match between their hopes for mediation and the reality they are experiencing. They are deciding whether to commit fully to the process. The largest task of this phase is not only to gain the assessment but also to get enough compliance and suspension of negative behaviors to enable whatever model the mediator is using.

The next two to three sessions are usually the middle phases where direct expression of feelings, communication between the participants, and bargaining must start. Without some indication of compliance and cooperation, the participants will lose faith in the process or the practitioner. During these sessions, mediators will be helping the participants re-story and rewrite the problem, provide recognition and empowerment, and start looking for areas that require classic problem solving and outcomes that are behavioral or functional in nature. They are helping the participants reshape the meaning of the dilemma and realize that there is hope for doing things differently that will bring at least relief to the most important concerns, if not complete revision or change.

During this second phase, all participants have to wend their way between acceptance of what is not able to change and making plans to change what is possible to change. During this phase, the transformative and narrative work must usually be done to enable the options for change to be developed. Some level of ownership of the problem and of the need for change must happen. The participants must acknowledge and take responsibility for the current situation. There needs to be a move away from blame, guilt, and finger-pointing toward a more self-oriented acceptance of each person's role, function, and contribution to the dilemmas. Participants need to show some willingness to take personal responsibility to change what is theirs to do and contribute to a better situation for everyone involved in the dilemma, not just themselves. Until this happens, any agreements will be incomplete and often perceived as lacking credibility. In the most simplistic terms, each person must state to the others' satisfaction, "I did it [or didn't do it], and I truly regret it." Offering apology often happens during this part of the mediation effort, either in formalized, ritual ways or informally.

Sometimes just hearing the participant accept his or her own level of involvement and responsibility for the dilemma is sufficient, without the apology.

In the final phase of mediation, the participants move to resolution: the statements of what they will or will not do to improve the situation, reduce the dilemma, solve the problem, or develop the alternative narrative of hope. They have stated to each other what they did and did not do, may have expressed some level of regret, and have provided the others some acknowledgment of the dilemma they have co-created. Now they must move to the third step, stating their willingness to take personal responsibility and make personal change. By this time, they often have agreed in principle but are still working on the final details, or they have learned what they can and will mediate and where they are unwilling to make any changes, concessions, or negotiation and where they need external coercive forces to tell them what to do. They are moving to the more active stance of translating responsibility into behaviors that will make the dilemma better.

In this third phase of mediation, the participants want and need reassurance that the work they have done so far is important and necessary and will produce something of value and that the other people have accepted responsibility and the need for change. In a transformative approach, the final sessions are about trying to problem-solve again, having been transformed by the earlier discussion and process. From a narrative perspective, this phase is about actively co-creating the new strength-based story that changes the separate and negative narratives they had been operating from. From an interactional perspective, this phase is characterized by positively changed interaction that then can lead to changed conditions and specific agreements. If the mediator has been operating from a procedural or problem-solving/negotiative approach, there is usually a push in this phase to clarify the exact agreements, changes, and responsibilities for change.

Family problems and dilemmas did not develop overnight, and they need adequate time to allow everyone to reconceptualize and transform their relationship to the issues. Family mediators have to help families plan mediation that is long enough to allow these important personal and social processes to emerge. Family mediators should also be contracting for their services based on some realistic estimate of the usual time and money involved in a case.

Two to three sessions of ninety minutes each for complete divorce decision making may be realistic, but if the clients have less time due to court standards or payment regulations, it is important to let them know how much time they do have. In some jurisdictions, public sector family mediators have eight to ten hours of prepaid or allocated time for each case; in other jurisdictions, money and time are scarce, and the effective time is one to three hours. In the private sector, families may need more time but be unwilling or unable to pay for what they actually need. Contracting for a realistic time and sequence is important to counteract unrealistic expectations.

Parent-teen mediation sessions are often set up more like community mediation, with a single three-hour session but sometimes a second session if all agree to it. Bringing disparate family members together for elder care placement decisions may also have to be managed as a single long mediation session when all the members can converge, after conducting some of the important fact gathering and personal transformational work through telephone calls and separate sessions prior to the in-person joint meeting. If sessions are long or there are transportation issues or other reasons that the mediation effort must be concluded in one day, it is imperative that the family members be given adequate breaks to relax and time to consult with advocates and advising experts and attorneys. This time is also important for family mediators, who must maintain their own strength and stamina and who need time off from the interaction to reflect on what has transpired and what needs to happen next. Pushing people beyond their physical endurance or emotional control is counterproductive.

Whatever is decided about the best way to conduct the sessions, standards promulgated by all the major professional mediation societies indicate a need for at least a verbal understanding, and preferably a written contract, that outlines the expected sequence of sessions and duration of each session, with the option for adding time. Like all other professionals, family mediators need to give clients accurate disclosure about how many sessions there will be and what needs to be done in mediation. Each mediator should provide that to the clients and ensure that this full disclosure has happened within the first phase of mediation. If expectations change, mediators must inform the clients about the need for additional sessions or costs.

Single-Session Mandates

Despite the mediator's realistic expectations of how many sessions are needed for a particular type of family mediation, some clients announce their willingness to contract for only a single session. Often this is a statement of lack of knowledge or trust in the other participants or the mediator, and is offered as a challenge or a way of masking a feeling of powerlessness in the dispute. It is true that some positives can be gained from single mediation sessions that do not come to completeness. Talmon (1990) wrote eloquently about how to make even single therapeutic encounters productive, and the analogy to mediation seems to hold true. Sometimes just the act of recognizing the need for even a single mediation session is a great leap forward. Sometimes the act of describing the dispute and receiving some validation and support during a single session will be sufficient to help reluctant clients agree to more mediation or will pave the way for less acrimonious encounters in subsequent dispute resolution processes.

Mediators have an obligation to be realistic with their clients regarding how far a single-session mandate will take them in resolving the issues they have presented. If the mediator cares more about the success of the mediation than the participants do, there is a power imbalance; the mediator will be doing too much work and allowing the participants to ride the mediator's motivation rather than the other way around.

Marking Headway

It is always good practice to remind participants of where they are in the mediation sequence. If they contracted for several sessions, the mediator should foreshadow the ending of the process when the family arrives at the halfway mark. This brings a realization of the limits of time and money, and this fact can sharpen the discussion and focus the participants on the agreements and the areas still not decided. Mediators operating in an interactive and reflective manner can reflect the changes of perspective, the personal changes, and the changes in the dialogue during the session. If there are new barriers to agreement or new topics or perspectives that have surfaced, the mediator can help integrate these or record them so that the participants can refocus on the areas that are being most useful. The participants themselves can help determine what is productive.

Something productive should be happening in each session. What that is may be different for each family member and may be defined differently by mediators practicing from different models. It may include facilitation of each member's thoughts and feelings, or recognition and empowerment, or better listening and comprehension of each other's dilemma through the use of narrative, or the development of trust and empathy, or even developing classic problem-solving options and direct bargaining that is leading to agreement. Sometimes just the act of being able to talk about the dilemma is productive, because it makes overt what was covert before. If someone other than the mediator can point to effectiveness and progress, the session will more likely be perceived by all as worth the effort. If there is not a sense of progress, this situation serves as a perfect opportunity for the mediator to ask for feedback about what could make things better. The mediator can share his own perception of what has happened and invite the participants to share theirs as part of the closure of each session. Establishing this as a norm can help clients who are reluctant to complain to voice their concerns in a positive way.

Closure

The final part of a mediation effort is the effort to codify what has been promised, what each person or entity has chosen to do or not do, and how these agreements are a positive step toward collaborative effort at reducing the dilemma for one or all the parties. Because family processes tend to be ambiguous and amorphous, they are hard to describe. Participants know that something has changed and yet find it hard to know how to describe those changes. When the family mediator takes on the role of family recorder and tries to help participants create their own collective memory, he is doing the standard scrivener function of classic problem-solving mediation but in a new way. He is asking the family members to use their own words to describe the changes, not just as solid behavioral agreements, but as understandings of the changes the family has made in understanding, attitudes, and awareness.

Family mediators try to record not only the behavioral agreements, but also the personal changes and processes that the family has come to understand that speak to the new personal and social awareness the family has created in mediation. These may not be translatable into subsequent legal documents, because they are agreements about recognition and empowerment and about changes in dynamic family processes, not legal rights and responsibilities.

For example, in a parent-teen dispute where the dilemma centered on the teenager's low grades, the family mediator would record this "hard" agreement: "Tommy will show his homework to his parents after dinner, and if it is completed correctly, he will be able to play his music in his room from 7 to 9 P.M." The family mediator would also record the "soft" agreements and understandings of the family members to help them remember their new processes: "Both parents understand the importance to Tommy of keeping up with the music his group of friends listens to, and Tommy acknowledges and shares his parents' concern about maintaining adequate attention to his math and English homework."

Family mediators trained in classic negotiation and problem solving and those who are used to writing only legal documents may find it difficult to write these softer attitudinal changes, and yet the family mediator is recording the changes in perception and process within the family. Including family members' attempts and intentions can go a long way in memorializing the result of reconstruction of their family relationships, which is the primary business they came to do.

MEDIATING WITH MULTIPLE FAMILY MEMBERS

When family mediators are working with complex, intergenerational problems or multiple stakeholders, the sheer numbers of people and the logistics of sessions become more cumbersome. One approach, similar to multiparty mediation efforts in complex public policy disputes, is to get another mediator to help function as a team. The team then splits up the tasks, holds planning meetings between sessions, and maximizes the time in mediation sessions by having done lots of in-person smaller group contacts or caucuses prior to the larger group session. This team approach works only if members of the team have similar theoretical approaches and clinical impressions, or if they have worked often and well enough together for effective functioning. Because of the additional time and cost, even complex family cases are not always able to function in this team approach even when it would be easier and desirable.

If there is a mediator team for the case, then the team can distribute the tasks of the mediation between the team members for best time management and in keeping with the relationship each team member is able to develop with the family members. For example, in parent-teen mediation cases, one model has a teenage mediator as part of the team, so that the teenage disputant does not feel co-opted or overwhelmed by adults. The teenage mediator helps speak for the teenage disputant and can provide role modeling and facilitation of communication for the adults. The automatic affiliation and communication of the teenagers (often referred to as "joining" in family therapy) helps the mediation team work more effectively for both the parent and the teenage disputant.

When family mediation services are built from preexisting ADR and community-based programs, the concept of a team of one paid professional staff person and one volunteer community member may be adopted. Because of the personal nature of family disputes, this model is not always beneficial; the family in dispute may not be comfortable being self-revealing no matter how well trained and discrete the community volunteer is.

Another advantage of team mediation is the help the team members can give each other in tracking the interactions, sharing perceptions and information, and relieving each other during long marathon sessions in the tasks of active facilitator of the session. Some of the typical role divisions are one as active facilitator and one as notetaker, or the assignment of one mediator to relate to one participant and the other mediator to the other, based on factors of personality match, gender, race, profession of origin, or ability of the mediator to withstand certain defensive or offensive behaviors or communication styles of the client. In some jurisdictions, court-connected mediators may opt to work as a team if there is an unusual feature about the case that could benefit from this special adaptation. Having two in the room reduces risk to the mediator and provides additional safety for the other disputant if one of the clients becomes disruptive, intimidating, or out of control. Some mediators in private practice team up on particularly complex or difficult cases for these reasons.

Another reason to consider team mediation approaches is for the advancement of the field and the training of the next wave of mediators. Although reading about family mediation and being mentally prepared for the job comes through classes and workshops, the way most mediators learn to mediate is by watching and working with a skilled practitioner. We could hope that future training programs for family mediators would institutionalize this internship-mentoring process as the counseling, social work, and other helping professions have done. For all these reasons, team mediation in family mediation cases still remains a viable option and a helpful resource to new and experienced mediators, and family mediators are encouraged to try it occasionally as part of their own professional growth and development.

CAUCUSING

Many family mediators allow themselves opportunities to use caucus or hold individual sessions with only one person or one faction within the dispute. The term *caucus* comes from the problem-solving/negotiative approach, and many mediators who have moved away from this model have also moved away from the use of separate time during a joint mediation, based on their systemic view of the family. The use of separate solo time with each participant between or within a joint mediation session is therefore controversial and should be based on a deep and consistent model or perspective rather than on utilitarian concerns.

When a mediator's model is consistent with the use of caucus, which I call solo time in this chapter, there is a set of reasons when and how the time should be considered. Mediators who allow or even require separate sessions with the primary participants (or with affected secondary parties like children) do so out of a belief that is useful for one or more reasons.

Using Solo Time for Face-Saving

When participants know that they need to move away from a hardened position or need to change their approach to the other person, solo time gives them an opportunity to describe the dilemma. They can use that time off from the interaction with the other family members to talk to the mediator without fear of repercussions and to strategize and discover what would be the alternative without being committed to the change prematurely or further embarrassed by the dilemma. It also gives time away from the others to develop a new image or persona that they are not yet comfortable in showing to the other members of the family.

For example, if a father had always had a belief that the man was the "king of the castle" and yet realized that he needed to act in a less domineering way in order to solve the dispute, he may need some opportunities to practice this new way of being before he returns to the joint session to concede or reduce his resistance to an idea. This solo time allows him to think about the personal transformation and its consequences before he announces it. It provides some time to coalesce the personal change and may also help to strengthen his resolve to make this change.

Emotional Respite and Reducing Diffuse Physiological Arousal

Many participants in family mediation have determined to themselves that they will not become emotional during the mediation, and yet they find themselves struggling for emotional control. They need a few minutes to weep silently or regain their composure by talking to the mediator without the other participants watching. Also, some participants are aware of how emotionally triggering the other person is for them. They have learned or been forced to use and need a five- to twenty-minute time-out or cooldown if they have been emotionally triggered by the verbal or nonverbal behavior of the others. Children are taught this in school, and families often practice this, yet mediators forget to allow this process in their urgency to solve the problem or to follow their mediation model's prescription of allowing only joint sessions.

When diffuse physiological arousal has set in, the person's pulse is over 100 beats a minute, and the person is unable to access his own best thinking, because his brain and its higher cortical functioning have been "highjacked." He is functioning out of other parts of his brain, including the lower brain stem, which then takes over to produce an autonomic response, and he does not have access to his full range of cognition. He is actually incapable of doing the logic that is inherent in the problem-solving/negotiative approach until his arousal has been reduced.

Using some solo time to deescalate an angry or scared participant is necessary if mediators are to maintain mediation sessions as safe opportunities for empowerment. Taking the escalated person into solo time provides the short-term intervention to help prevent further stimulation and escalation; it provides the escalated person an opportunity to ventilate safely without ruining his bargaining position and gives him an opportunity to rethink how to come back to the session. The mediator can then talk with the nonescalated person about how it feels when the other person "goes off," how she is coping, whether she sees her own triggering behaviors, and whether she can change the way in which she reacts when these situations occur. Lots of good learning happens for each participant, and they can then return to the joint session in a new interactional frame. This option gives the mediator a vital management and intervention opportunity.

Strategizing with Participants

Mediators can serve the client as a reality-based sounding board and a friendly coach. They can help a participant who is sorting through options or trying to find a more advantageous way of relating to the other participant. From a narrative perspective, allowing some solo time gives the participant an opportunity to develop the externalizing conversation and practice the new narrative. From an interactive perspective, it allows the mediator to work with each person specifically rather than in the shared construction of the interaction.

Confronting Clients

When a participant is using intimidation tactics, is saying two different and mutually exclusive things, or is so off-putting and offensive to the other participants or the mediator that the mediation effort is jeopardized, the mediator can use solo time to confront the participant with this behavior comfortably. Meeting with the participant privately reduces the risk of further embarrassment to the client, which might create further defensiveness. If part of the mediator's role according to the model in use is being a monitor of the process, the solo session allows the mediator to change the interaction by bringing the awareness only to the one who is doing the behavior. If there is a process difficulty that is directly attributable to the behavior or attitude of only one participant, the mediator can use this solo time to bring it to the participant's awareness to see if the person is willing and able to make personal change.

Resolving Power Struggles Between Client and Mediator

Occasionally, participants perceive the mediator as a member of a disliked class of people—perhaps as an agent of "the system" or "the government"—and a family member will be openly or covertly aggressive or demeaning toward the mediator. Sometimes this is displacement of anger and frustration with the other participant, or it can be characteristic of a long-term hostility the family member maintains with everyone.

When mediators become aware of tension and power struggles or discounting by a client, solo time allows them to explore this territory, express their own needs and limits, and do so without changing the power balance between the participants. It gives the participant a chance to reflect on this before it is brought to the awareness of all and gives the mediator an opportunity to reconfirm the rules and limits without shaming or blaming the client. It can be a strong intervention that foreshadows either the right relationship and process during mediation efforts or ending the mediation effort. It provides some modeling of appropriate boundary setting without tipping the negotiative process between the participants.

Depending on her model of practice, the mediator might try to bring up the topic in a therapeutic way, asking the person if he is aware of the tension and requesting information in order to understand the meaning of it. A mediator who comes from a procedural or problem-solving perspective might remind the participant of the rules or review the prior written agreements as a behavioral contract that the family member is violating. As with all other things, the model of mediation will determine why a mediator might do this intervention and how to do it if is done.

Pretesting an Option Prior to Joint Session

In the problem-solving/negotiative approach, some participants need to take a few minutes and think about consequences before they are ready to make concessions or agreements. They may want to test the water by proposing a new concept in solo time with the mediator, literally hearing themselves think out loud, before they offer it as a realistic option. Also, the mediator may have thought of an option or perspective that may be helpful but contrary to earlier positions. These possibilities can be talked about in solo time with no prejudice.

From the narrative perspective, this might be seen as a way and time to hold a private view of the future, to have the externalized conversation about an idealized future before sharing it with other members, because it may or may not be shared by the other family members. When done in solo time, this allows the one stating it to erase the screen and project several possibilities before sharing any of them.

Exploring Sudden Shifts

If a mediator is operating interactively and notices that a participant who had been strongly holding out just conceded a point, the mediator may want to call for some solo time to find out why the participant has suddenly reversed his position. Was the sudden concession out of fear of retribution, a sudden fatigue factor, a perception of unfairness and impossibility, or is it a true and well-considered change of stance? Solo time allows for this exploration and prevents participants from suddenly making drastic changes that could be devastating to their own perspective and place within the family.

If the mediator is operating therapeutically, a noticeable change of tactic in the joint session may be something the therapeutic mediator wants to reinforce or prevent. It can indicate a return to earlier negative personal patterns, systems requirements forcing a family member back to a former role, or a courageous choice for change that needs to be rewarded and acknowledged. Discussion about the meaning of the change is important from this perspective.

Assessing Control, Abuse, Violence, or Threat

We know that victims of abuse and violence are unwilling to name the abuse in front of the abuser, and yet will talk openly to the mediator when given an appropriate, safe time and place. With more than 65 percent of all divorce cases having had some level of abuse, violence, or threat and with elder and child abuse in many families, most family mediators carve out at least some solo time for each participant in order to offer this opportunity for revealing the abuse, threat, or intimidation. (Chapter Five provides an expanded discussion on this important topic.)

Issues in Conducting Solo Time

The mediator must be sensitive to several additional issues when using the technique of solo time for participants in a mediation.

Balancing Between Participants. When mediators allow themselves the use of caucus or solo time with each client, it is important to balance the equation between them and hold some solo time with the other participants. Starting with the participant who is in turmoil or appears to have more of an agenda and then balancing the procedural fairness by also seeing the other person is the usual method. Even if there is no particular agenda for one of the participants, asking for that person's perception of how the mediation is going can contribute to rapport and understanding and provide that client with a private forum to uncover concerns about the mediation process or the family system.

Reporting to Others. A mediator who is using solo time needs to be extremely clear regarding the use of any information derived from the solo session during the joint time. Confidentiality should not be pledged, because solo time is the most likely opportunity for child and elder abuse or major concerns about violence to be revealed, and the mediator may be ethically and legally required to report to outside sources what is revealed. Because these reporting requirements transcend any private mediation agreements or state, national, and professional rules regarding the confidentiality of mediation efforts, the use of solo time during family mediation becomes one of the hardest issues. Often, it feels like an ethical minefield, since there are ethical and legal issues no matter which way the mediator chooses. See Chapter Six for an expanded discussion on confidentiality and reporting requirements.

Discussing Solo Time in Joint Session. Another issue in the use of solo time with participants is what the mediator tells to everyone about the session. The family mediator must remain above suspicion about inappropriate alignment with one participant against the other or colluding against an option or person.

To reduce suspicion and facilitate movement from the solo time, it is best to rehearse with the solo participant what will be said in joint session. If there are misunderstandings about what must or cannot be said, this gives the mediator time to educate the participant still in solo time. If there is sufficient trust, the mediator may be able to describe generally what topics were discussed, then cue the participants to bring forward their own ideas, needs, and concerns that were voiced during the solo time. In this way, the important material that is relevant to the joint discussion can come out by the choice of the participant.

Reasons for Not Using Solo Time

Many highly regarded family mediators, including John Haynes, have stead-fastly held to a standard that anything that is done in family mediation must be done in joint session. This principled stance includes the important perspectives of systems thinking and narrative therapy, that reality is co-created and that the problems have been created by the family system and therefore must be solved by the system, not individuals acting separately. Also, some Bowen-influenced mediators might not want to use solo time because it could create unhealthy perceptions of triangulation.

Many other highly principled family mediators differ. Especially given the potential for emotional and physical harm if there is hidden intimidation, retri-bution, or threat that is not uncovered or when the teachable moment of ther-apeutic importance happens that could allow the individual the perfect opportunity for transformation or personal growth, a solid case can be made for the use of solo time.

I have mediated with and without use of solo time, and I have been per-suaded not only by information but also by experience that holding a five- to ten-minute caucus or solo time with each participant at the beginning, to allow for domestic violence and abuse screening, has never hurt and usually helps. I sometimes have used solo time within a session to do many of the tasks already noted.

I cannot say that the reverse is true. I believe that when I did not use solo time, I actually did harm to some clients by not having a way for participants to share concerns about violence and intimidation. My lack of awareness lead to a continuation of that pattern during the mediation, which I believe was a harmful revictimization that I inadvertently allowed. Similarly, I have experi-enced problems with rapport, process, and uncovered material when I have not had some solo time with participants. I believe that the use of caucus or solo time is a necessary and important part of ensuring fairness and safety and that the skilled use of it, consistent with the models of mediation, contributes to pro-ductivity, despite its risks and difficulties.

Due to the prevalence of domestic violence and intimidation issues in fam-ily mediation, I believe the pain is well worth the gain, and fits with an ethical approach to family dispute resolution. Mediators should not use their model to blind them to this need to have some brief time alone prior to or as part of each joint session. If we do not ask, they may not tell or show and will be operating from that fear dynamic. More will be said in Chapter Five about the issue of domestic violence and in Chapter Six about the family mediator's ethical respon-sibilities.

POWER BALANCING

Power has been defined by many writers, and perhaps the most elegant definition is from Bertrand Russell, who declared in 1938, "Power may be defined as the production of intended effects" (Russell, [1938] 1992, p. 19). Spouses who are divorcing soon find out that they do not have the power to stop the divorce, but they do have the power to make it miserable, and children find they do not have the power to get their parents back together. Although the family may want the right option for an aging parent and are working to keep the elder at home, they may not have the power to produce the intended effect due to financial or medical reality.

John Kenneth Galbraith (1992) notes that power comes in three forms:

- *Condign power,* which wins submission by inflicting or threatening appropriately adverse consequences, such as punishment or losses
- *Compensatory power,* which wins submission by offering an affirmative reward, such as money, discounts, or other benefits
- *Conditioned power,* which wins submission by changing beliefs or persuasion—for example, through advertising, slogans, or societal pressure

Families usually use a unique blend and pattern of these three to produce their intended effects. Divorcing spouses may start with offers and bribery as part of their compensatory power, then threaten condign power moves when the conditioned power of the family rules and roles no longer works. Parents are certainly familiar with the situation of a minor out of control, where compensatory power of new stereos and cars has not been sufficient and the family has resorted to condign methods, such as sending the youth off to a distant relative.

No matter how we define it, some level of power is happening between family members before they enter mediation for a dispute, and some method of power is functioning during the mediation effort. In order to know whether the family needs the mediator to balance their power, first the system of power within the family needs to be evaluated and understood.

The Two Paradigms of Power

To understand how the family system reacts to power in general gives the family mediator an idea of whether there are power dynamics that need to be addressed as part of the mediation effort. There is one model of power that requires dominance and submission: the *power-over* paradigm. The other more collaborative partnership model can be called the *power-with* paradigm. Families usually have one basic orientation and paradigm they use in regard to their power dynamics, although individual members of the family may be in the opposite paradigm and in open or covert opposition to the dominant power theme in the family.

Family mediators who operate from a perspective of problem-solving/negotiation and procedural methods tend to resonate with the need for power balancing during family mediation more than those who operate from a narrative or transformative perspective. Power balancing assumes a very directive role of the mediator to maintain an equality that is posited as necessary for mediation. One of the critiques of family mediation by feminists and others is that because the construction of modern society is inherently unequal, this disequality walks into the mediator's office and can be consciously or unconsciously perpetuated by the family mediator. Power balancing is seen as the remedy to this disequality.

French and Raven (1959) have noted five basic forms of social power:

- *Information power,* based on who has and can use the data
- *Referent power,* which is the influence exerted by a reference group of people with whom one identifies and maintains affiliation
- *Legitimate power,* which is the power inherent in a role or position within society
- *Expert power,* which is the influence exerted by increased knowledge and ability
- *Coercive or reward power,* which is the capacity to provide incentives and punishments to obtain the desired effect

Haynes (1988) notes that the balance of power within a couple or family is multiple and fluid. Each person has a particular set of power bases within the confines of the relationship, and this may or may not relate to the person's exterior power outside the family. For example, the high-powered corporate executive may have lots of power in his company, but little information or referent power or expertise over his own spouse or teenager or elderly parent, even though he has some level of coercive power available through the family finances and legitimate power as the father.

Haynes notes that with the power system of a family, there is reciprocity: the person who appears to have the power automatically confers a compensatory power to the other. For example, if a mother has the power of the purse by having the information and expertise for keeping the family checkbook and savings accounts in order, the father has been given the compensatory power to remain ignorant of the state of the family finances and not worry about it.

Spouses and family members trade their power, or come to terms with the particular power currency each of them has. In this way, Galbraith and others see power as a fluid medium like cash currency, which can be gained, bargained for, or stolen and can be transferred from one party to another but seldom leaves each person totally bankrupt.

The Power of Passivity

Most people, even those who feel victimized or left out, have some power currency. Haynes points to the power of passivity, that is, the power to make oneself a social load. When people have been trained within the family to be passive and helpless, it has served someone else's interest (the dominator or provider), but it has also served the passive person's need to be taken care of. The literature of substance abuse calls this *codependency,* acknowledging that there is a reciprocal payoff in being used in these ways. This echoes the important early research of learned helplessness identified by Seligman (1975).

One of the benefits of mediation is the opportunity to change these dynamics through active power balancing by the mediator and participants. When the passive or subordinate spouse or family member stands up for himself or herself during a mediation session, the power balance is altered irrevocably. The participants can no longer pretend that the person is incapable of such action.

Problems with Power

Many family disputes are based on perceptions by one or more members of the family that the power currencies have been unfairly stolen, distributed, or used. They are often complaints that their actual sources of power are not being recognized or empowered in the former family structure, or that the legitimate power bestowed on them by virtue of their role is not being wisely managed, and someone with more expertise needs to do the tasks.

Sometimes the power problem in family systems is that condign power is being used when compensatory or conditioned power should be used. In order to do appropriate power balancing at all, the first task of the family mediator is to understand the forms of power, the type of power that has historically been used within the family, and what the current power dilemma is for each member.

The task of power balancing for the mediator, then, is to identify not only who has what specific overt power but also who has what type of compensatory power and the reciprocal influence each person's power has with and for the other. Because the format and process of mediation prevents the usual power trades between spouses, new forms of power may come out during the mediation process. An adult sibling may have to use conditioned power instead of condign or compensatory power to get the aging parent to accept the need to move. Child protective services may have to stop trying to use condign power with the neglectful parent and start using incentives that are real for that person.

Changing the Power Paradigm

Instead of power-over tactics of domination and submission, a parent enmeshed in a parent-teen dispute may have to try a new paradigm of power, power-with, where the parent and the child provide each other recognition empowerment of each other's power sources and work as a team to enhance rather than to dominate. This often requires the personal transformation of several members of the family, who must change their relationship to power use within the family and therefore change the relationship they have with each other.

Power balancing can be approached using all of the models and approaches within family mediation. If a mediator is problem-solving/negotiative, the power balancing will tend to be consistent with that approach and require the mediator to become the power broker. In this model, the mediator actively levels the playing field by controlling information, ruling items off the table, and managing any overt power tactics by the one who is perceived as power-up (dominant, or having more power over the other). The mediator becomes the monitor and broker.

In the transformative and therapeutic models of mediation, the mediator power-balances by creating the conditions for the family members themselves to reposition their power relative to each other. Rather than the mediator's doing something "to" the family, in these models the individuals themselves have personal breakthroughs that enable them to change the power hierarchy or style within the family. Instead of accepting the father's automatic right to make independent decisions regarding money or children, his wife stands up for her right to be a coequal decision maker. The mediator operating out of these models allows but does not take over the job of brokering power. Instead, she supports and encourages the changing of power currencies and styles by the participants, as part of the transformative and therapeutic advances, rather than imposes them on the participants.

The focus difference in power balancing is important. In classic problem-solving/negotiative mediation models, mediators are responsible for power balancing as an active process they do to the clients. In transformative and therapeutic and narrative mediation approaches, mediators create the conditions that allow and encourage such changes, but they do not do the power balancing; either the participants do, or they are not yet ready to change. In all events, family mediators must be astute in their understanding of the nature of their role and function regarding power balancing during mediation.

NEUTRALITY AND CLIENT SELF-DETERMINATION

Family mediators find the topic of neutrality difficult to discuss because there is not yet consensus about the models of mediation. Since the model of mediation that a practitioner uses determines how active she will be, how directive, and what type and level of intervention she will use and how, the model has a direct bearing on how neutral the mediator really is.

A basic requirement of any ADR process is that it be provided in a fair and equitable way, without bias or prejudice. Mediation has been offered to the public for family disputes as a neutral process, and by definition, mediators are third-party neutrals, but the question becomes, "How neutral is neutral in family mediation?" This becomes less clear as mediators feel a need to bring into consideration the effect of decisions on underrepresented third parties, such as children during a divorce struggle. The more the mediator feels like an advocate for the disputants themselves, a power broker for society or the court who needs to set the case or the family straight, or a representative of larger society who is trying to inculcate community or moral values, the less the mediator can genuinely function as a neutral. A mediator with an agenda is a pitiable creature, since neither the dual demands of the social agenda nor the requirement to maintain neutrality can be fully expressed. Mediators cannot express their opinion to try to influence the outcome of the mediation effort in the way they think it should go. This is very different from the role of legal advocate, who is supposed to advise clients as to the best course of action. For family mediators who have come to this work from a legal background of taking responsibility for the direction and outcome of a case, this demand not to decide is very hard to maintain and will force them to operate out of completely different models of neutrality than they had been using as a legal adviser or counselor. Therapy-based family mediators also struggle, especially if they were trained to intervene actively on behalf of their client.

Because some family mediators in the public and private sectors have been mandated to act in the three different roles of advocate, power broker, and agent of larger societal values, this issue always comes up. How unbiased and neutral can a family mediator be when a person sees the role as being a healer of the family? How much self-determination for the participants is there really when governmental structures mandate cases to mediation based on case types and expect instant outcomes in single sessions? How realistic is it to believe that family mediators leave their cultural, gender, and other biases aside when they are working with families? To answer these questions, family mediators must look at the job description, the model of mediation they aspire to, and their own personal orientation to their work, as well as the models they follow.

Impartiality and Equidistance

Rifkin, Millen, and Cobb (1991) point to the paradox of the mediation condition: mediators tell themselves that they are neutral, unbiased, and impartial, yet empirical evidence shows that they are not functioning that way. In fact, mediators operate by directly changing the discourse that the participants are having, and such changes are in fact nonneutral behavior by the mediator.

Rifkin, Millen, and Cobb define *neutrality* as having two elements: the concept of impartiality (the mediator does not have any vested feelings, values or agendas) and the concept of equidistance (the ability of the mediator to help all sides of the dispute to express their views equally without suppression). A neutral mediator is supposed to maintain a disinterested stance relative to the outcome of mediation and an equal stance relative to each person's perspectives.

By ruling things in and out of mediation, by being the "communication cop" who allows or disallows the participants to discuss certain topics or discuss them in certain ways, many mediators are no longer truly neutral according to the definition of Rifkin, Millen, and Cobb. Family mediators can violate the equidistance concept when they do not allow one participant to dominate the conversation.

The remedy these authors suggest for the paradox is to allow the parties to tell their story in their own way; by allowing full and open narrative by each side, the mediator maintains neutrality in both aspects of impartiality and equidistance. But consider the situation in which a family mediator allows the family tyrant to rule in the mediation office; the mediator may be acting neutrally under this definition, but may also be losing the trust and regard of the other participant.

I have outlined several of the reasons that family mediators have more difficulty with the issue of neutrality than labor mediators, community mediators, and others who are doing more classic problem-solving/negotiation forms of mediation (Taylor, 1997). Family mediators are always dealing with participants' emotions, thoughts, attitudes, and values, and not just concrete, external items or entities that can be bargained or negotiated. We are helping family systems, and we are helping families bargain and solve intangible and emotional issues of face and self-concept. While classic problem-solving/negotiation mediation efforts in other types of disputes focus only on the behavior that must change for each side of the dispute and try to secure concise behavioral agreement, the focus of much family mediation effort is on internal, attitudinal, and personal change. Participants in family mediation often are not just bargaining; they are making their own values and creating personal and social change. It is hard to remain neutral in the face of these issues, because as helping professionals, we often have a clear view of what we believe to be helpful and harmful with regard to these items.

From Strict Neutrality to Expanded Neutrality

It may be more helpful for mediators to think of neutrality on a continuum or scale, from one extreme of strict neutrality, characterized by directing the process rather than the individuals, to the other extreme of expanded neutrality, which would allow the mediator to intervene and refocus the mediation on personal or social change. Mediators may be able to place themselves along this continuum for certain types of issues during a family mediation process instead of having to choose between two dichotomous views of neutral or non-neutral.

Some models of mediation lend themselves to a usual position on this continuum. Mediators who are operating from the narrative, therapeutic, or transformative perspectives necessarily have to be closer to the expanded concept of neutrality, because they are active interventionists who are using their considerable influence to affect the process and the people directly. They do not maintain strict impartiality or equidistance, because they treat each person as an individual who may need particular interventions.

Classic problem-solving/negotiative mediation and procedural methods are much closer to the strict neutrality concepts, because the nature of the procedure automatically disallows the mediator from actively providing undue influence to the people, the process, or the outcome. Mediators from other dispute types who are familiar with the constraints of strict neutrality are often shocked by how loose the family mediator becomes when working from an expanded neutrality perspective. Lawyers who are cross-training as family mediators or mediators who have mediated in other types of disputes may find this expanded neutrality disconcerting and uncomfortable.

Because family mediators in most models allow themselves to provide the participants information and education on topics under discussion and deal with emotions in active ways, they are already adding on two other modes of mediation than labor and commercial mediators usually use. Instead of staying in the logical, rational/analytic, sequenced problem-solving mode, a majority of family mediators actively deal with the internal issues, not just the objectified, external problem. Some family mediators also allow themselves to move occasionally to the normative-evaluative mode, where they actually tell the participants what they can or cannot do. Whenever that is happening, the mediator is shedding neutrality in that moment in service of what she thinks might be a greater good to prevent harm or act as a representative of larger society. In this mode, family mediators truly may be violating their neutrality.

Family mediators cannot help but influence their clients just by being there, and depending on the model they use, they may believe they are mandated to do direct influence to create personal and interpersonal change. Family mediators are actively trying to do positive persuasion without leaving the participants out of the process.

The task of remaining neutral means not unduly influencing the participants in ways that they are not willing to be influenced. Even expanded neutrality concepts draw the clear bright line at coercion, intimidation, manipulation, and other power-over tactics by the mediator that reinforce that the mediator must be obeyed or that the participant must submit to the intervention. At the base, the participants must always remain in charge of change, free of even well-meant persuasive or intimidating actions or interventions by the mediator.

If the mediator is transformative or therapeutic in orientation but the client is not interested in being transformed, the duty of the mediator always is to our highest ethical stance: let the clients be self-determining. Some family members do not want the family mediator to balance their power with others in the family structure or to create better family systems, and they narrowly define the family dispute in order not to deal with these aspects of the family. They want a problem solved, not a new paradigm or a newly transformed way of being. They want help with the manifest conflict, not change with the underlying dynamics of their familial relationships. If the mediator's model requires them to investigate and make changes, the clients may feel disregarded, not helped, and even violated when the mediator does not listen to this. The fine balancing point is exploring these issues while still letting the family members themselves decide whether they want to go in that direction.

Family mediators of any model must adhere to the basic concept of neutrality: families and individuals are always the ones who must choose not only the outcome and solution, but also the process they are willing to follow to achieve that outcome. This discussion is not just an esoteric dialogue among practitioners but a very real issue in each family mediation session. If one participant believes the mediator is not working for and with them, is not respecting their needs, or is doing interventions that limit the participants' equality, that participant may believe that the mediator is biased in favor of or against them. A power struggle for control of the session, a cancellation of the mediation effort by family members who do not show up, or nonpayment may be the reaction of the clients to heavy-handed or insensitive mediator practice. Maintaining active neutrality is a practical issue; without it, family mediators will not be successful, and the family mediation process and profession may suffer.

Family mediators always need to provide trustworthiness, unbiased treatment, and participant self-determination in all aspects of mediation. They must work equally hard, although in slightly different ways, for all their participants simultaneously. This total respect and proper interaction creates active neutrality of either the strict or expanded kind. All participants always need to know on a deep level that they are not judged, disrespected, discounted, or unattended to, and that the family mediator does not play favorites, create unhealthy alignments, or stifle client expression, while at the same time is able to maintain a safe and open environment for everyone. Neutrality is not the absence of the negative condition but the active presence of equality of treatment by the family mediator for everyone present, no matter what model the mediator is using.

TRANSFORMING IMPASSES

When a family mediation case has been moving through the process well but suddenly seems to come to a screeching halt on some point, what does this mean? Is this a sign of failure for the mediator? What can the family mediator do to restart the process and get the mediation effort to be productive again? Since the success rate for outcome agreements for family mediation can vary widely from program to program, mediator to mediator, getting the session unstuck is an important skill that can affect not only the particular case but the continuation of funding for mediation.

The very way the mediator thinks about this topic will be dependent on how he sees his role as mediator. Is he there to "get agreements," so anytime no agreement results, the mediation is a failure? Is his job to provide the participants with a forum for stating their views, listening to each other, and seeing if they can collaborate? This is a very different view of the role of the mediator, the hallmarks of success, and the way to deal with nonagreements during mediation.

The term *impasse,* like *caucus,* comes directly from the negotiation literature and inherently holds some implications. It implies that two opposing and equal forces have come together to rebalance their power and have not been able to declare a clear victor. It can mean that in a dominant-subordinate power paradigm, no one is being declared the winner, which is distressing because the system is set up to demand the win-lose condition. The fact that no one is clearly achieving his or her aims and taking the power position in the situation may in some cases be a victory in itself. When the dominating mother cannot bully the children into submission or if the manipulative and intimidating father has not had the other family members give up to get it over with and the situation is at stalemate, it might be a indication to check the power dynamics to determine if they must continue to find a competitive solution instead of a collaborative one they could all agree to. It also implies that this is a permanent stalemate; there are no other moves on the chessboard of the competitive situation. These are the classic problem-solving/negotiative explanations for this condition.

Impasse as Boundary Marker

If a family mediator were to think differently about this from a different model that looks at systemic functioning, an alternate view is that the dispute is not stuck in a hopeless impasse, but that the family is in the process of forming new boundaries or that neither participant wishes to or is able to breach the former rules. They have learned the limits of their ability to compromise, make concessions, or make change. Where they are now is not stranded, but rather it is their particular *angle of repose,* the term used for a stabilization point in shifting sand. They do not need to move in a cooperative direction any more, because they are where they need to be relative to each other. An outside coercive or manipulative force may be able to force this to change; for example, the court could impose legal sanctions and decisions on the parties to get them to change. They are communicating to each other that they will go no further on their own motivation without some form of external influence. Their stalled condition may mean that this is as far as they are willing to go in their ability or willingness to change and be cooperative. It is a marker not of failure but forward progress. From this viewpoint, impasses systemically show the boundaries and the range of motion each person has. This is a vastly different, more client self-determined and positive view of a phenomenon that has always been seen as a failure and problem. The question then becomes, "Where is this particular case stuck, and why?" Only after there is a premise should the family mediator then look to his or her model to answer the subsequent question: "What, if anything, should I do about it as the mediator?" Perhaps there is nothing to do, except to acknowledge that this is as far as they can go in their own negotiation without externally imposed answers.

Problem-Solving Answers to Impasse

Moore (1988) outlines the typical types of conflicts embedded in the larger divorce or family dispute and suggests that the effort to remove the impasses and barriers to agreement needs to be based on the specific causes in that case. The doctor must analyze the illness before making a specific selection and intervention with a remedy, and the remedy for one problem will not necessarily work for the others. Moore provides specific remedies to typical data, structural, interest, values, and relationship conflicts in divorce cases, and his suggestions are accurate and helpful. I have referred to his work many times when the focus of the mediation has been problem solving and negotiation and the participant's bargaining has slowed or stopped.

For data conflicts that get stuck in impasse, Moore (1988) recommends the same remedies that a mediator would use in any mediation: agree on what data need to be collected and the criteria to evaluate these data, and then seek a third opinion. For interest-based conflicts, he recommends searching for the true or mutual interests, expanding options by creative brainstorming, and finding integrative solutions. For structural conflicts that rest on power and external factors, he suggests changing the time constraints by making agreements for smaller bits of time, reallocating ownership and use of resources, changing the actual physical environment, and modifying the usual means of influence. For value-related interventions, he suggests creating spheres of influence where each person's value can have priority and making it acceptable to disagree without a need to change to a unitary value. In relationship-based impasses, he suggests controlling the expression of the emotions or alternately promoting the exploration of feelings by legitimizing them, clarifying each participant's perceptions and interpretations, and blocking the repetitive negative behaviors that are reactions to the perceived problem.

If the family mediator were to use the alternative explanation that the stuck spot is meaningful and not necessarily a problem but a definition, and did not necessarily require intervention by the mediator (or even the participants), what would that mediator do? If success in family mediation is about more than coming to a set of behavioral agreements that can be turned over to attorneys to be subsumed into legal orders of the court, then could this impasse be a signal that the participants are done with mediation? Could the softer success criteria of being heard and being empowered to say no be acknowledged? In order to answer this, mediators must know what levels of success they are trying to promote.

Success Criteria as Keys to Impasse

Success in family mediation lies in two different sets of criteria:

The Outcome Success

- Have the participants been able to define the problem in a way that supported mediation efforts?
- Are there full or partial agreements that can be written into a mediated plan for submission to attorneys, courts, or other agencies?
- Do the participants know what their next legal and social steps are?

The Process Success

- Do the participants feel that they were allowed full expression and were heard by the others?
- Does each participant feel that he or she was afforded equality of treatment by the mediator and the other participant?
- Have all of the participants gained knowledge and understanding about their particular dispute or dilemma and their position relative to each other?

If the reason for the impasse or blockage is due to the mediator's model not allowing the participant a real opportunity to say what he or she needed to say, or if the mediator allowed the mediation session to bully, victimize, or stifle one or more of the participants, then the impasse or blockage might have been created by the mediator, not the participants. In the medical world, a cure that creates its own set of problems is called iatrogenic. In family mediation, if mediators do not understand the meaning of the impasse or do the wrong thing when one happens, it may make the situation worse and become an iatrogenic intervention.

Dialogue for Clarity

A mediator working from the narrative, transformative, interactive, or thera-peutic models rather than the problem-solving/negotiative or procedural could stop to ask the participants if they notice the stuck spot. He or she would use that moment to ask what meaning the participants attribute to it, what each of them wants and is able to do about it, and whether they see it as a permanent fatal flaw or just the furthest they can go at this time. The mediator could allow true client self-determination by raising this to the clients' awareness and mak-ing them choose what to do. They could remind the participants of what they had been successful in doing in the process and what agreements, if any, they had reached before the impasse or stuck spot was encountered. A mediator operating out of the neutrality concept of impartiality might not impose some intervention, because that would be the mediator's having an agenda for the clients that they do not have for themselves.

Impasses and stuck spots in mediation require family mediators to question their own assumptions, models, and behavior. It requires them to listen again to their requirements about neutrality and not be more invested in the outcome than the clients are. What causes and what helps when impasses occur is a huge topic that mediators need to reflect on each time it happens and is useful grist for the supervisory or consultation mill. They can serve as those critical moments described by Lang and Taylor (2000) that create growth and change for the practitioner as well as the client.

Impasses are meaningful not only for the participants but also for the medi-ator. If several cases in a row seem to hit the wall and seize up into an impasse very quickly or right at the end of the session, it may be an indicator that the mediator is insensitive to his or her pace, that the underlying issues and family systems dynamics have not fully been dealt with, and or that the mediator is trying to use a model of mediation that does not give everyone a chance to say all that needs to be said.

Just as families form patterns, mediators do too. Mediators may want to keep a log or journal of important events that lead up to impasses in their cases to help look for patterns that could indicate a need for growth or change in the model or method the practitioner uses. Perhaps the best way to think of impasses and blockages in family mediation is as opportunities for mediators to challenge themselves and the clients to greater understanding.

❧

Family mediators have spent a lot of time considering the topics covered in this chapter: how to evaluate the people and the problem to determine if they are ready to mediate, how to set up mediation sessions for best effectiveness, how to understand power and the mediator's task of power balancing, and how to deal with impasses during mediation efforts. They discuss how to maintain neutrality in the face of a desire to intervene with negative dynamics and how to be effective without overstepping their role.

Because so many of these topics depend on a mediator's point of view, which is in turn determined by the selected mediator model, this discussion seems generalized almost to the point of unhelpfulness. You might be thinking, "Why don't you just tell me what to do and not do about caucus and impasse and power balancing and neutrality?" Certainly all mediators received from their initial trainers and educators some expert rules, some clear delineation, some prescriptions and caveats of how to avoid impasse, and what to do when there is one, and how to deal with power. These are useful starting points for deeper thinking and were specific to the model the trainer was promoting.

But mediators may disagree on these topics, because the skills and techniques of family mediation flow from the assumptions and premises of the model. This book is not trying to promote one model over another, one view as better or more effective, because we do not have the level of research that we could use to demonstrate that one is far more effective than another. Rather, this book is meant to be a compendium of the different thoughts currently in use by family mediators that may be helpful to practitioners. Chapters Three and Four are a companion set; the one relies on the other. They are both about the way in which family mediators look at their work and typical topics we struggle with. If reading about different views of the same old topic have whetted your need to know more about that view, these chapters have been successful.

Having looked at current thoughts about the people in family disputes, about how the disputes manifest and change, and the lenses that family mediators use to look at them, it is now time to examine in Part Two some of the dynamics of practice in family dispute resolution of all kinds.

PART TWO

FAMILY MEDIATION PROCESSES

CHAPTER FIVE

Special Case Issues

Family mediators often deal with difficult cases that have significant features requiring specialized consideration or a different awareness and process. Some of the most challenging people and problems are what this chapter will cover. In most of these, family mediators need additional training and knowledge to ensure that they continue in ethical practice consistent with constantly updating standards. These cases are not only emotionally draining and mentally challenging, they are like an obstacle course through a landmine field: perilous, hazardous, and potentially devastating to mediator and participants. In these cases, the first ethical dictum of "do no harm" to them becomes foremost, but mediators must also prevent them from harming each other or the mediator.

Using narrative therapy concepts, these special case dynamics become "the problem," and if we were to hold an externalizing conversation with ourselves, we would find that the problem is often lack of information, lack of experience, or lack of opportunities to reflect. Something is lacking, and that is the externalized problem for the mediator. The conflict-saturated story we tell ourselves is that these cases are too difficult, too threatening, and too complex for our process. As practitioners, we need to believe and have hope that there can be an alternative story we can tell about these cases, that not all of them are condemned to failure and continuing problems, that hope exists for them and for us as the practitioners working with them.

This chapter explores some of the parameters of typical problematic cases that may require different techniques, processes, or models in order to be successful. All cases should be special, but these tax the mediator's wisdom, centeredness, and knowledge. Family mediation is not for the faint of heart. By reframing these cases as exciting challenges, opportunities for change, and places where we must firmly place boundaries and make appropriate adaptations, they lose their malevolence. The people in these cases, as in all other cases, are just people, struggling with harder issues and dynamics than most others do. Maintaining empathy and respect for their struggle while applying firm standards and ethical walls will still be the best way to start.

CONTROL, ABUSE, AND VIOLENCE

When one participant in mediation has done or is intentionally doing harm to the other, it brings into question the essential ethics of allowing client autonomy and self-direction against the principles of doing no harm. Advocates for battered women have found that family mediators in the past have been unaware, insensitive, or inconsistent in their approach to this issue. Although professional organizations such as AFM have created task forces and developed positions on this topic (see Appendix B), the task of creating a single standard for how to deal with domestic violence was never ratified by the board due to valid concerns raised by groups representing public and private mediation contexts. What a private mediator who mediates at the pleasure of the clients may do can be very different from what a public sector mediator does because he or she serves at the pleasure of the court, the agency, or the community.

The incidence of domestic violence in all its forms is huge in our country and becomes one of the larger reasons that couples and families part. Because it affects not only the adults in the couples relationship but also the parenting plans that are appropriate for the children, this topic is of vital importance to family mediators. It is also involved in cases that are not divorce, custody, or parenting related, because control, abuse, and violence within families are often an unspoken theme in other types of family disputes, such as placement and care of elders, family reunification after child abuse, and parent-teen mediation.

According to the study of five different sites across the country done by Pearson (1997), at least half and up to 80 percent or more of all cases that come to these mediation services have some level of domestic violence. This means a majority of a mediator's cases will be in this category and the mediator will have to deal with this issue in some way. A family mediator needs a solid grounding in this topic and should receive ongoing, in-depth training and personal consultation with an experienced family mediator.

Because the definitions can vary and change the meaning and perspective on this topic, here I use the term *abuse* to mean unwanted, harmful, and intentional behavior, including verbal, physical, emotional, sexual, and psychological behavior and harm. *Domestic violence* will be used as the term to indicate overcontrolling, abusive, or violent behavior or threats of violence to people who are part of the family. It includes spousal abuse, child abuse, and elder abuse, each of which may have separate statutes and legal definitions within each state. In addition to parents, children, and spouses, in the inclusive definition used here, it can encompass other family members and persons who are related or connected, former cohabitants and partners, and their children.

Problems with Power and Control in Relationships

Domestic violence is primarily a problem with power and control in relationships, where one person feels entitled to dominate another who is supposed to submit, in a power-over rather than a power-with partnership. People use power and control tactics, threats and fear, and the various forms of abuse and violent behavior to try to establish or maintain dominance over others. They do this when they feel out of control or have lowered power and are attempting to gain more personal power and control over the other person or the situation. A domestically violent person often has deep beliefs of entitlement and duty to do the abusive or violent behavior, or at least has been raised with or taken on a core belief that this behavior is acceptable.

The most common emotional triggers, which combine with the person's socialization and deep beliefs, happen when the person is feeling one or more of the following feelings:

- Isolation, being left out, or rejected
- Anger and fear, plus other negative feelings such as embarrassment, sadness, or hurt
- Challenge, or threat of any kind, coming toward self or other people or things the person cares about
- Loss of people, things, possibilities, or qualities such as face or status
- Lowered self-esteem, ridicule from external sources, or a personal view of the self as unworthy, shameful, or guilty

Under this definition, domestic violence is a range of controlling and abusive behaviors designed to help the person regain control. It is not just a problem with getting angry that can be dealt with by providing the abuser with anger management classes or biofeedback techniques to reduce stress before harming others. Far more systemic and pervasive, it is about the reflexive system of self and others and requires changing not just behavior but beliefs and values in order to change the problem for the abuser.

Underneath the behavior of abuse is usually a belief system that allows the abuser to feel justified or entitled to do the abuse to others. Abuse is not on or off in a binary way, but rather manifests along a continuum or range from mild to severe. Abuse is either covert, unacknowledged, and hidden or overt, where the abuser is admitting to or even proud of the abuse. Abuse comes in many forms but usually falls into one or more of the following major categories, each of which can be seen as a range or continuum of behaviors and patterns.

- Overly controlling behavior—not allowing others the usual freedoms, such as telephone calls and visiting friends; acting jealous
- Verbal abuse—constant put-downs, name calling, and use of demeaning terms; lowering someone's self-esteem and confidence
- Emotional abuse—intentionally trying to hurt another's feelings to get the person to feel shame, hurt, embarrassment, and other difficult feelings
- Psychological abuse—intentionally trying to confuse or convince
- Physical abuse—along a continuum from shoves and hitting to battering and use of weapons
- Sexual abuse—forcing unwanted acts, underage involvement, or marital rape
- Educational abuse—using information to mislead, control, or put down
- Financial abuse—using money or lack of it to control another, bribery and reward, withholding financial information

Patterns of Domestic Violence

Early work in the field of family mediation and domestic violence often emphasized the cyclical nature of spousal abuse as a singular pattern, with males responding out of a wheel of violence where there was a distinct buildup of tension, then a violent action or set of actions, which reduced tension and created a honeymoon phase where abuser and abused felt closer and intimate, only to restart the cycle. This cycle was originally described by Lenore Walker and other researchers (Sonkin, Martin, and Walker, 1985) at the Domestic Violence Abuse Project of Minneapolis, Minnesota, in the mid-1980s and is the basis of the Duluth model, which has been used by many women's advocacy and shelter programs to explain the cyclical nature of spousal abuse.

When they view this pattern as the sole descriptor of domestic violence, many victims and abusers alike do not admit to the existence of domestic violence in their household, because the levels and patterns of abuse they have experienced with each other do not fit this model. It simply does not describe their reality, so they can easily minimize, deny, or otherwise defend against the label instead of admitting and dealing with the abuse that is in fact happening. The Los Angeles County Family Court training tape *Mediation: The Crucial Difference*, made in the 1990s for mediators, accurately and vividly describes domestic violence from that singular approach to the topic. While helping to alert court-connected mediators to the need for screening for domestic violence in family mediation cases, this single model approach leaves out many other issues of power and control that may be happening within the family relationships.

More recent large-scale research and continuing clinical insight and intervention as reported by Johnston and Roseby (1997) have led to a newer understanding that domestic violence and the control-abuse-violence continuum is not just one thing. Instead of only one pattern, domestic violence seems to occur in several different patterns, each with its own set of initiations, manifestations, and consequences for children and adults stuck in the pattern.

Ongoing or episodic male battering. This cyclical pattern often starts during courtship or pregnancy, where the intolerable tension, supported by male entitlement, chauvinism, or social and cultural beliefs, is released by doing violent actions, often to life-threatening levels.

Female-initiated violence. Frustration at her partner's passiveness leads to increasing levels of verbal, emotional, and physical violence.

Male-controlling interactive violence. Arguments get out of control, with a spiraling need for both partners to gain domination and power over the other. Usually no more force is used than is needed to gain the upper hand. This tends to be a repetitive pattern that can increase in frequency and severity over time and is often linked to substance use or sexual excitement. It may be culturally supported.

Separation-engendered and postdivorce trauma. Uncharacteristic acts of violence happen when a partner is faced with the situational distress of abandonment or threat of loss of the relationship, property, or children. This nonrepetitive violence often starts right at the point of announcement of leaving and may continue during and after the divorce as new situations retrigger rage and resentment. This can significantly reduce already eroded trust.

Psychotic and paranoid reactions. A very small percentage of domestic violence cases involve mental or physical illness, severe drug- or alcohol-induced toxicity, or delusional or distorted thinking, which leads to sudden and unpredictable violence of all levels, often escalating to lethality. Helpers of the victims can also be targeted.

The family mediator should identify the pattern of violence that is happening and try to get some information regarding the range of threat, abuse, and violence for both direct victims and indirect victims, who are often children and dependent elderly. Indirect victimization, or having violent acts done in front of children, can be so damaging that in many states acts of violence done in front of children are felonies. Janet Johnston and Vivienne Roseby (1997) have explored how the five patterns of direct and indirect violence in the preceding list affect children of different ages of development. They describe how therapists and helping systems can attempt to mitigate some of the damage to children who are caught in families experiencing these patterns and other power and control dynamics like parental alienation by crafting more appropriate parenting plans that acknowledge the existence of the abuse and protect children better.

Because abuse and violence are so common in domestic relations cases of all kinds, there has been a continuing effort by many groups to find appropriate safeguards, adequate screening methods, and procedures that reduce further harm to victims. Local, state, and national organizations for women's issues, domestic violence coalitions and shelter programs, domestic violence councils, judges and state justice institutes, the American Bar Association (ABA), and private researchers have been working over the past two decades to develop an understanding of and procedures designed to help provide mediation services when appropriate, yet screen out cases that should not come through the usual mediation process due to concerns about increased harm.

In the 1980s, many family mediators were concerned about this issue, and the Academy of Family Mediators created the Task Force on Spousal and Child Abuse. That group issued a report that was last revised in 1995 (see Appendix B). Although it was never adopted as AFM policy, it remains a helpful document in considering whether the controlling, abusive, or violent behavior is sufficient to call into question the appropriateness of mediation. It also gives family mediators some practical suggestions of what to do if abuse or violence is part of the history or current conduct between the mediation participants. It outlines the ethical duty of family mediators to screen for abuse and violence and recommends excellent adaptations for procedures to mitigate safety concerns if the mediation is to proceed.

The Need for Screening

Family mediators are not the only group interested in or concerned about best practices in dealing with domestic violence and abuse in family-related cases. In 1991, the National Council of Juvenile and Family Court Judges in association with others developed the Model Code on Domestic and Family Violence, which they hoped could serve as a national model legislation from which state legislators could develop substantially similar state statutes to protect victims and prevent future violence. In that document they outlined that family mediators have an affirmative duty to screen for domestic violence and to make decisions regarding the appropriateness of mediation and the inclusion of specific adaptations, such as advocates or alternative procedures, for victims. They also emphasized the need for specific education in domestic violence for court-connected mediators.

Girdner (1990), who published one of the early triage screening methodologies, along with other knowledgeable family mediators, collaborated with the Academy of Family Mediators, the ABA Center on Children and the Law, and the State Justice Institute to develop and refine the screening of cases for appropriateness for mediation. They developed, provided, and evaluated a curriculum for judges, attorneys, and court-connected mediators to provide the necessary training to meet the Model Code (State Justice Institute Curriculum, 1997). The curriculum pointed out that the existence of some level of physical violence in a family mediation case was too broad a measure of whether it was appropriate to mediate that case. The premise of the curriculum is that an effective screening tool or methodology needs to ask questions and make determinations of appropriate accommodations not just about physical abuse. Screening and decisions about appropriateness for mediation or the need to modify the process also need to look at past and current threats, fear of harm by or to family members as retribution, and whether the abuse or violence that has already taken place is in one of the established patterns.

Girdner created four major categories to help court-connected mediators screen cases effectively. Two of those categories are for cases that involve actual violence or fear of violence, and two are for cases with no actual violence or fear identified through the interviewing and screening process.

Category A (Always). The screening procedures indicate no actual violence, no threat or fear, and no overcontrolling behavior, with relatively equal power between the participants. Proceeding with standard mediation processes makes sense.

Category B (Be Careful). There has been no violence, fear, or threat, but power imbalances between the participants could affect their ability to mediate fairly or safely. The mediator needs to determine the level of this imbalance and consider the different options for dealing with the variations. If there is a high level of coercion and control, the mediator should disallow mediation. If those concerns could be addressed by using special accommodations, the mediator could put conditions on the mediation effort and continue while monitoring carefully.

Category C (Conditional). The screening shows past violence, fear, or threats. Even if the abused party wishes to mediate, the mediator has to decide whether to allow mediation to continue with special conditions. Perhaps some external conditions, such as safety planning, need to be met, with an offer to reconsider mediation after specific controls are in place. If the participants are unwilling or unable to put these conditions into effect, the mediator should disallow mediation at that time.

Category D (Don't!). This category is reserved for cases where there has been violence, fear, or threats, and the abused person does not want to mediate. Clearly, this case should not be mediated and participants should be given safety planning help.

Many good assessment tools and resources for screening policies and procedures currently exist in different jurisdictions. Lane County, Oregon, created a specialized publication that has been instructive to many jurisdictions, and Family Court Service mediators in Alameda County, California, use a standardized checklist that reminds the mediator what to ask and quantifies the level of concern. Private sector mediators working independent of the court might want to find out what procedures their local jurisdiction is using and at least follow those same procedures in their private practice. Because private mediators can select not to take cases, some set a boundary that routinely excludes any cases that would bring up these issues, a position that court-connected family mediators cannot take.

Screening Effectively

Part of the recommended interviewing and assessment process involves having sufficient time alone with each participant and an adequate idea of what constitutes abuse and violence. Most reports and recommendations on this topic reconfirm that this separate time and solo screening is the basis for getting accurate enough information to be able to make a considered judgment. Mediators should have the opportunity to interview each participant separately not only at the beginning of the mediation but also at any time later if there are concerns about intimidation, fear of retribution, or other changes in the client that might be indications of threat, fear, or abuse and violence.

Private and public sector mediators can have access to public records of past abuse, restraining orders, and other related criminal charges such as stalking and harassment by checking with the records departments of their local jurisdictions. In many court-connected mediation programs, requiring a solo session prior to the start of any joint mediation session has become policy when the potential mediation client is asked if there has been any violence or if any restraining orders have been issued in the last year and the answer is affirmative. Many jurisdictions have access to computerized judicial information systems that make this easier, but building in a double check is important for private mediators too. The question about restraining and no-contact orders needs to be asked routinely during intake in all cases, not just when there is self-reporting or concern by the client. Offering or requiring separate first sessions reduces the likelihood that the two will collude to suppress the information. Separate sessions will also provide the mediator an opportunity to hear each person's view about past control, abuse, or violent episodes without further fear of retaliation or inhibition of the other.

Mediators should believe clients when they allege violence and abuse, but because there is such a tendency to hide, minimize, or selectively forget that events have occurred, checking the judicial record can ensure that the screening was thorough enough to prevent purposeful or inadvertent suppression of important events or information. When intake procedures allow for solo sessions and a further checking of the court records, the mediator is working with two hands: self-report and verification.

During the solo session, the mediator who is assessing for domestic violence and abuse should ask questions that will develop specific information about the past, present, and potential future abuse in the following categories:

- Severity
- Frequency of occurrences
- Lethality of the violence and access to weapons
- Levels of contact between the abuser and the abused
- The (potential) victim's willingness to flee and access to alternative living situations and shelters
- Safety plans and physical security within the environment
- Whether law enforcement has been drawn into the situation and whether there is a family abuse prevention restraining order, a domestic relations restraining order proximate to the legal filing, an order of no contact, or a status quo order to protect children
- Whether there have been additional crimes and victimization, such as stalking or harassment, in addition to the direct abuse event

In addition to these more data-oriented questions about their past and present violence events, I want to know more about how each participant interprets and makes meaning of these events, what they think and feel about them, and also what I think and feel about these. I ask questions and listen not only for what they both agree on, but also what they do not say. I ask myself the following questions before I make a decision about whether a case with abuse in its past or present is appropriate for mediation.

- What level of correspondence do the potential participants have between their stories? What are the discrepancies? Is someone exaggerating, minimizing, or denying? Are they both leaving out the same things, indicating collusion or coercion?
- How much does each person recognize his or her own part and accept some level of accountability for the abuse or loss of control, even if it was responsive rather than initiatory?

- How personally resilient is each person? Does he or she need some help and support from therapists, advocates, or others to be able to make courageous acts of change with the other person? Is each person emotionally and cognitively ready to do this?

- How much have they made others, such as a child, witnesses and indirect victims of this abuse and violence?

- In what way is this pattern of abuse or violence unusual or characteristic? Has this abuse become part of the folklore or expectation of the family as normative behavior?

- How do I feel about the abuser and the abused now that I know the story of the violence? Am I uneasy around, unable to empathize with, even scared of this person? Do I need to do something to protect myself as the mediator from this person's abusive or vindictive behavior?

- Will I be able to recognize and control any loss of control or triggers the participants might have during mediation?

- Am I really ready to mediate this?

Ending Mediation Without Harm

If the mediator decides not to mediate based on the screening process, the next hurdle is to relay this information to the parties and their attorneys in such a way that the refusal to mediate will not increase the likelihood of harm. Obviously, if this is a first revelation of covert abuse and violence, the abused person is going to be worried about the possible effects to him or her, and if the abuser is sitting in the next room waiting for a joint session to begin, the mediator has a delicate and potentially dangerous situation to deal with. The mediator needs to get the abused party to safety, end the mediation at least temporarily if not permanently, and state the conditions under which the mediation could take place, all without demeaning or upsetting the other party, ruining the mediator's impartiality and neutrality, and further angering the abuser and endangering everyone else. It is important to think through what to do in this situation and have office staff know what to do that would be helpful. To prevent this difficult situation, some mediators do the screening over the telephone or in person prior to any joint sessions.

Responding to the Challenge of Violence

So where does this leave the family mediator who wants to work fairly with families where abuse and violence have taken place? Marthaler (1989) pointed out that public sector jurisdictions need to mediate the parenting agreements even when there has been abuse, because the mediator is far more likely to be able to help the family craft an agreement that is adequate for protection of children, but that more highly conflicted cases need more time. These cases present many issues.

Yellott (1990) called for sufficient cooperation within jurisdictions among law enforcement, the bench and bar, women's shelters and advocates, and mediators to advise and refer abusive cases appropriately. Especially given the more recent development of screening and the need for referral options and safety planning, that call still needs to be remembered. A relatively recent large-scale study of over two hundred court services (Thoennes, Salem, and Pearson, 1995) found that although 80 percent of the agencies are screening for abuse and violence, 40 percent were not doing this by using private sessions or caucus, and very few cases were being excluded from the usual mediation processes by the mediators, nor were victims dropping out of mediation when solo sessions were made a voluntary choice, even though there is no disincentive to use solo time.

The obvious need is to provide adequate screening and special accommodations and adaptations for the most severely troubled cases, but also to build into the mediator's process with clients the types of procedures that will allow full disclosure and subsequent decisions regarding the appropriateness of mediation efforts. Most models of mediation have stated ways they encourage mediators to assess for abuse and violence, and even indicate usual procedures in order to do this assessment consistent with the model. Erickson and Erickson (1988) described a spousal abuse case for which they were able to do complete divorce decision making by relying primarily on relatively minimal open-ended questions. Robert Benjamin (1991) also described ways in which mediation could be successful in cases that had child sexual abuse in the picture.

In the therapeutic family mediation model, Irving and Benjamin (1995) note the importance of screening for violence and include it as one of the categories of postdivorce spousal functioning they assess routinely for each case. They use this and ongoing conflict severity as part of the cutoff criteria to contraindicate the use of mediation, and see cases involving current and ongoing family violence and child abuse as part of the 20 percent of cases that they do not mediate.

Other models specify what they will do if the case is suitable for mediation. Accommodations to maintain safety when there has been abuse or violence are a common option offered when participants fit the criteria of those who can benefit from mediation. Winslade and Monk (2000) acknowledge this issue and concern not only about actual violence but also about the deeply held beliefs of entitlement and culturally supported paternalism and domination expectations by class, race, and gender that might serve to hold the abuse as normative, reasonable, and immutable.

They suggest that the mediator use narrative constructs to facilitate an "externalizing conversation" about the violence, threat, and fear, while also offering accommodations to safety—for example,

- Safer seating arrangements
- Immediately identifying threatening or abusive statements
- Negotiating a safety contract in force during mediation efforts
- Using intermediary processes while keeping the parties in separate rooms
- Having an advocate or other support person for safety

Appendix C presents the Control, Abuse, and Domestic Violence Screener, an organizer tool I developed, which tries to bring together all the information presented here. It starts with a modification of Linda Girdner's decision tree approach, to establish exactly why a case is not going to be accepted for mediation or which special adaptations of the process will be used or which specific conditions must be met before mediation efforts can commence. Its goal is to help the family mediator sort through the patterns and elements that made up the decision to continue, to modify or require conditions, or to refuse to mediate.

The topic of domestic violence and mediation has had major evolution and change over the years, as research, practice, and awareness have converged through interdisciplinary dialogue to provide necessary safeguards to ensure a safe, fair process. Even if the incidence of abuse or domestic violence decreases, this topic will remain a crucial one for mediators, because the population that mediators serve tends to have patterns of abuse and violence that create or compound the conflicts they seek to mediate.

While private mediators can attempt to screen such cases out of their private practice, public sector mediators must deliver appropriate services to all, while providing other more protected options to those who should not mediate. The family mediator's job is to help discern and decide, based on the best information and most ethical and reasonable procedures currently available. Wise family mediators will continue to educate themselves and their clients, promote better processes in their own mediation practice, and encourage the field to continue to monitor and refine standards and behavior.

MENTAL HEALTH CONCERNS

Another strong reason that divorcing partners and families may have continuing conflicts with each other is that a member of the couple or family has a mental illness. These long-lasting or acute mental and emotional problems often lead to erratic, irresponsible, or unacceptable behavior, which can lead to divorce, family conflicts, and ongoing disputes about the placement and parenting of children. Entire extended families have become polarized or incapacitated by the intensity of behavior and threat to self and others that these conditions can sometimes place on the couple or the family unit, and family secrets, covert process, and myths about the nature of the person's capacity now and in the future may abound.

Because the term *mental illness* presupposes a medical model and all that goes with it, such as labeling and diagnosing and a sense of finality and permanency, it may be more useful for family mediators to focus less on the labels and more on how the mental and emotional conditions affect the person during the mediation effort and after. Having family disputes that contain issues concerning mental health and emotional steadiness can tax the limits of mediation, especially in the light of concerns about autonomy, fairness, and self-determination, as well as the relative power stance of each participant toward the mentally ill or upset person. Family mediators are often confronted with conflicts that are harbingers and hallmarks of particular kinds of mental health distress. A family mediator who has enough training and background in understanding the most usual ones that may present for mediation is often the first one to help the family acknowledge and deal effectively with the problem.

Unfortunately, despite tell-all television programs and talk shows that openly discuss many mental health problems that in the past were hidden and considered shameful, the dominant discourse or stereotyping beliefs even today are that people who are suffering from undiagnosed or untreated or unmanaged mental illness are "crazy," likely to be violent, a danger to themselves and others, and unproductive citizens who cannot handle themselves, let alone make decisions collaboratively or handle child-rearing responsibilities as parents should. They are often perceived as deviant and abnormal and as hopeless causes who cannot (or resistantly will not) change or be able to care for themselves or others.

Concerns About Power When Mediating Mental Health Issues

Another dominant theme is that mentally ill people are powerless. Those labeled with psychiatric terminology and diagnosed as belonging to a group of people called something often lose some, if not all, personal liberty, fun, companionship, belonging, and affection from others, as well as self-worth. They are often not personally or socially powerful enough to stop this from happening. Many mentally ill people are powerless due to the actual illness or symptoms and behavioral problems they are experiencing. Others become more powerless due to having been labeled and subjected to the scorn and derision of partners, employers, and friends, as well as the often unintentional negative effects of the institutions that have been designed to help them.

Some people introject these labels and responses and become even more emotionally fragile, discouraged, or angry and upset. Mediators can unconsciously slide into these negative response patterns and unwittingly join with other members of the family to maintain the distorted and negative perception or trigger the negative response. Suzanne Retzinger (1990) describes this situation:

> Stereotyped imagery of the mentally ill can create bias by assuming fundamental difference, violence, or incompetence. . . . The mediator can be perceived as hostile if his or her manner seems accusatory or interrogatory. . . . Diagnosis is not an appropriate task for the mediator and can make it more difficult for the mediator to stay out of the family system, as well as the larger system of stereotyped beliefs that may contribute to the problem. [p. 154]

Because of these problems, mediators must be careful not to jump to automatic conclusions or stereotypical responses but must instead be sensitive to the automatic power differentials. If the mediator's model allows for active power balancing, it may be severely needed in these cases, since the mentally ill person starts in a lowered power status compared to the others. If it does not, the mentally ill person may find that mediation does not have enough safeguards of his or her equality and can actually be harmful.

Diagnostic Labels Versus Functional Behavior

Some family mediators have tried to cope with their own dilemma of dealing with mental illness by gaining more information and education regarding the typical diagnostic labels and hallmarks of common conditions. Generally information cannot hurt, but it sometimes can in these situations if attorneys and others without substantial training in making inferential and differential diagnoses become armchair diagnosticians of their clients.

Nevertheless, some information may be helpful in understanding what the participants in mediation are telling about themselves when they offer the mediator their diagnosis within the first five minutes of the encounter. Feinberg and Greene (1997) provide good information on this topic and warn against substituting sloppy lay terminology for pseudo-psychological jargon without a deeper understanding. They suggest that family mediators from all backgrounds may be able to differentiate among the three major categories used by clinicians:

> *Major mental illnesses,* which describe a number of conditions that usually fall into one or both of two subcategories, cognitive (thought) disorders and major affective (emotional) disorders. These can range from schizophrenia to manic-depression (bipolar) conditions.

> *Adjustment reactions,* which are characterized by exaggerated responses to situational distress, which can be serious and prolonged, such as may happen with separation, divorce, and loss of children and home.

> *Personality disorders,* which are long-standing and durable problems in clients' way of relating to the world that negatively affect all aspects of their lives, including their relationships and work. People with these problems can be very distrustful and hard to deal with and often are involved in repetitive litigation.

The Dynamics of Depression

A common mental health issue that presents itself in family mediation is depression. Participants who are depressed will not always be able to negotiate and track information effectively, to parent their children in the same way as the other parent or as they did in the past, or to react to the mediation setting in the best way. Because women suffer far more frequently from depression than men do, it is important to observe and ask some questions during the individual time or first session to help gauge whether depression is an issue. Information now abounds on the Internet about depression, and clients can self-assess with a few simple questions whether their depression needs some attention by a professional beyond the family mediator.

While many divorcing or conflicted family members are situationally depressed due to the very real losses and changes that are taking place, some will be so depressed that their condition can lead to harm to themselves or others left in their care. Because depression and suicide are linked, the ethics of doing no harm leads the wise family mediator to ensure that anything that looks like depression has been checked out with someone who knows and can do something for the client, such as ongoing talking therapy and medication. Because it can take time before the depressed person is emotionally strong enough to handle the quantity and importance of the decisions that may be at stake in the conflict being mediated, mediators may have to ask for a brief moratorium on the mediation until the person is ready. This can be phrased in such a way that the other participant does not feel stalled or placated, although he or she may respond to such delays with insensitivity and frustration. It is the mediator's responsibility to not allow intimidation or coercion, so the mediator must not allow a depressed party to participate if the depressed or mentally ill person is not ready. The mediator must often hold this line with clients and attorneys who want a quick resolution in mediation to speed up the legal process.

It is important to remember that whereas a participant with a major mental illness may have been prescribed medication, persons with personality disorders often self-medicate with illegal substances. Substance abuse can mask the signs of mental illness, make the behaviors worse, or be a co-occurring disorder along with the mental illness. The best dictum here is, *when in doubt, make a referral to someone who knows,* or even require release of information from the prescriber as a requirement before beginning mediation efforts, especially if there is questionable history or behavior that has been observed or described in the first or preliminary sessions.

Family mediators cannot always know that their clients are having problems or had them in the past, and many people are put on antidepressant and antianxiety and social anxiety drugs for even minor situational distress. It is always wise to ask the questions about medications, as well as street drug usage, and to corroborate from the Internet or *Physician's Desk Reference* what condition the medication is for after asking the client.

Determining Appropriateness for Mediation

The first task in any case involving actual or suspected mental health involvement is to determine the suitability for the mediation to start in the first place or continue after this issue and information arise. This can be handled in a similar manner to the special condition of domestic violence and abuse: by determining the reality of the problem from self-reports and then determining how it affects the participant's ability to maintain herself in the process without harm, undue stress, or prejudice by observation and monitoring of the process. Getting verification through signed releases also helps bring the other professionals in on the decision about whether the client is ready to mediate and, as a professional courtesy, can alert them to the fact that the symptoms may get worse with the stress of beginning mediation. Forewarned, the mediator and the other professionals can seek to help the client maintain balance and know when the mediation is unproductive.

The second most important point in working with cases involving mental illness is for the family mediator to recognize that the behavior of people with mental illness can cause the mediation effort to seem more laborious, difficult, or even untenable to everyone involved. These cases, if started, are far more likely to end without completion or in ways that feel unsatisfactory to the participants or the mediator. People with mental and emotional problems must be fully accepted for who and what they are; they are not readily amenable to quick change and can tax the patience and resolve of the mediator. They can suddenly become vicious verbally toward the mediator who is diligently trying to work with the problems or vindictively calling into question the competency of the mediator. These cases can be marked by what in therapy is often called *parallel process,* which means that the helper unconsciously starts acting in the same way as the problem behavior of the clients. These cases call on our own emotional strength and boundaries to maintain ourselves while in the maelstrom of the case interaction.

Just as the existence of domestic violence or substance abuse requires family mediators to reflect on their assumptions and assessment, these mental health concerns or personal conditions of a participant force the mediator to monitor and evaluate constantly, always determining if the context of mediation is appropriate for the mentally ill participant and the others. The mediator needs to reflect on these questions:

- Can this person track the often complex cognitive and logical factual development and data in the mediation session, or are internal events (thoughts, feelings, physical sensations) so distracting that he or she cannot follow?

- Is this person automatically counted out by the other members of the family? Is she already discounted before she has even had a chance to represent her view, her needs, and her actual capacities? Is she starting mediation efforts with a power shortage?

- Is there a functional concern about the mental illness that could be talked about in behavioral terms rather than as a result of the person's illness?

- How capable is she of making enlightened, autonomous decisions during the mediation, and does she need an advocate or adviser to support her?

- In what specific behavioral ways does everyone, including the mentally ill person, believe that the condition is or could affect the situation?

- Is the mentally ill person stabilized on medication, responsible about taking it, and capable of affording it so she can maintain herself this way?

- Will the stress of mediation add to the distress, and is now the best time for her to be tackling problems?

- Is she working regularly with a therapist, or just being dispensed psychoactive medications? Is she willing to sign a release-of-information form to allow the family mediator to ask the therapist's or physician's opinion about her readiness and capacity to mediate (and not about her diagnosis)?

- Does someone in the family system have a vested interest in keeping this person "sick" or not having her use her full capacities?

Assuming that all these factors can be successfully dealt with, the family mediator and the other participants in the mediation effort have to deal with the issue of the mental illness or concern not only in terms of the mediation process but also in the substantive negotiations and content. Depression may lift and anxiety reactions may calm, but the parties must make contingency plans for what happens if the troubled person stops taking medication, needs to go back to the hospital for treatment, or cannot become stabilized or reliable enough to do what she is pledging in the agreements. Mediated agreements need to be fashioned with these contingency plans in order to be complete. For example, if a mother had her child placed out of the home while she was untreated for manic-depression, she may need to have two plans: one for when is taking her medication, and another if she loses her health insurance benefits and can no longer afford to buy the medication or goes off it and symptoms return.

There is still a stigma attached to having mental health problems, and the very real problems of keeping this population on needed medications due to changes in residence and finances and society's changes in insurance coverage and benefits, social programs, and deinstitutionalization. Because of this, some of the people who need help the most are likely to have periods of stability followed by fluctuations and increasing functional and behavioral and relationship problems.

Developing Accommodations

Children can be frightened by these suddenly changing events and behavior, and supervised visitation programs may be the best option for access, at least until the parent complies with therapy and medication routines and has become stabilized enough to take on more responsibility. Some parents will never be able to function in regular visitation or parenting plans and will always need a buffering party, such as a grandparent, social worker, therapist, or friend in attendance during contact. This can be a hard realization for the other parent or family members. Sometimes parents who are struggling to find answers to the dilemma will frame agreements about contact with caregivers to verify therapy, medication, or stability.

Some child development specialists like Hodges (1991) recommend limited contact between the mentally ill parent and children with adequate safety precautions to prevent the child from idealizing the mentally ill parent or vilifying the protective parent for preventing contact. Johnston and Roseby (1997) describe the intent and delivery of supervised visitation programs and other innovative programs designed to provide safe contact that provide children regularity and predictability to foster attachment, while providing regularity of access by establishing the visiting habit for the parent who has had child support payment or other problems that have interfered with access to the child.

REPORTING CHILD ABUSE AND NEGLECT

Family mediators may be the first ones who hear reports of child abuse and so must be ready to deal with it for their participants in mediation and with the child protective systems to which they must report. Although we pledge our clients confidentiality, family mediators are not exempt from the duty to report past or present harm to children, elders, and the participants. Child abuse allegations can be some of the hardest issues to deal with because there are two pressing concerns. Not only is there concern about the use of those allegations for strategic bad-faith bargaining and gaining of domination in a competitive legal setting, there is also genuine concern for the child and worry that whatever the mediator does may make the situation worse.

The Mediator's Decisions and Role

Most family mediators try to exclude cases where child abuse is a stated part of the conflict or the abuse is current or pervasive, on the basis that the case is inappropriate for mediation. In fact, these cases often do not mediate well because the dynamics of the family are chaotic, enmeshed, or distant to such an extreme that collaborative efforts are not likely to succeed. The usual mediation effort is often not recommended or sufficient for these cases:

> Moreover, it has been argued that mediation is inappropriate for many dysfunctional families with histories of chronic litigation, severe domestic violence, or allegations of child abuse and molestation. . . . Poor mediation outcomes are generally predicted for parents who have rigid, highly divergent perceptions of their children's needs, which they tend to confuse with their own needs, and who harbor a pervasive distrust of each other's capacity to provide a secure environment. [Johnston and Roseby, 1997, p. 231]

Irving and Benjamin (1995) rule out any cases with child abuse when they do extensive screening prior to providing their therapeutic family mediation model. Most family mediators, no matter what their model, hesitate to embark on a regular mediation process with these cases because of the risk of inadvertent continuation of harm to children and the lack of the parents' ability to arrive at consensual agreements in standard mediation processes.

The usual response of the judicial system is to send cases with child abuse first through child protective services (CPS) and later to use custody evaluation processes rather than mediation. Evaluation processes provide credible, admissible evidence to override parental rights and give the court the rationale necessary to provide CPS temporary custody. Then the CPS worker or the court can be authorized to make safe, out-of-home placements and other related parenting decisions in place of the abusing parent. (Chapter Twelve examines some of the new uses and hybrids of mediation process that are being used in these contexts of child protection and family reunification cases.)

Robert Benjamin (1991) points out that the family mediator is one of a number of professionals who intervene in the family system when accusations have been made. It is important that the mediator not act in ways that empower and offer as many choices as possible to the participants.

Benjamin recommends individual sessions, with the mediator keeping each party informed about the content of any meetings that he or she did not attend, in order to minimize distrust. He also indicates using shorter, more frequent sessions with crisply outlined goals and objectives, which allow for the incremental changes in self-perception, attitude, and position between them, as well as reducing hardened beliefs and strong defensive stances by creating cognitive dissonance and developing discrepancies in order to bring about the internal change necessary to create movement.

In working with these child sexual abuse accusation cases, Benjamin points to the importance of reducing the labeling, jargon, and imposition of pathologizing or medicalizing paradigms of the situation, while maintaining the power hierarchy of the family by involving the parents. He suggests that rather than allowing the professionals to run the family, the family members themselves should be put back into the roles of protector and decision maker as much as possible. "The mediator needs to avoid slipping into being perceived by the parties as merely the instrument of the professional, the court, or the other party" (Benjamin, 1991, p. 238). Although he acknowledges that many mediators will not mediate these cases to prevent ethical or safety problems, he also points out that mediation with sufficient safeguards can provide a more open forum where the family is empowered to renegotiate and repair the damage of the abuse and the subsequent trauma of the imposition of helpers and systems who have often made the situation more traumatic. He points out that even small agreements the family has made willingly can reduce further trauma to the children and be more durable, helping to prevent or mitigate damage or some future conflict.

When Allegations Are Made During Session

No matter how carefully a family mediator screens for abuse and even if the mediator has made a decision to divert cases with child abuse to other processes or systems, there are still times when the abuse will occur during the course of an otherwise regular mediation case or the participants to the mediation did not fully reveal the past or current abuse. Family mediators may be faced with difficult process and reporting dilemmas, even in cases they would not have guessed. For example, parent-teen mediation cases, grandparent rights, and other types of family conflicts that tend to come to mediation services may have child abuse revealed as part of the case.

When child abuse allegations or revelations surface as part of the mediation effort, it is important for the family mediator to have had a prior discussion with the participants about how these allegations will be handled. The mediator should have told the family at the outset of mediation the exceptions to confidentiality and the fact that the mediator is a mandatory reporter. If this has been done, then the need to report will not come as a total shock to the participants. The revelation of child abuse is a meaningful event, and the participant who reveals it wants it to go forward.

Although family mediators are mandatory reporters, they are not investigators or CPS workers. They should try to get enough information to make a cogent report but should not become interrogators, evaluators, or investigators. They have a duty to prevent harm to the former and potential future targets of the abuse but do not act as a legal advocate for the children, the protective parent or person, or anyone else. All persons in our society have a duty to report child abuse, yet this duty is not the same as becoming the children's direct advocate during the mediation session. Mediators must always advocate safe and ethical mediation practice for everyone.

The mediator must report the allegation of abuse without knowing if it is true or if the revelation is accurate. The mediator must also determine what meaning the existence of abuse has for the abilities of the parties to continue mediation. To allow oneself to be diverted or biased against one or more of the participants seriously hampers the mediator's ability to function for the participants. These situations are full of ethical dilemmas, and the mediator needs to go through the process outlined in this book to determine the ethical choices and standard-of-practice requirements of mediators (and their profession of origin). These situations can leave the mediator feeling vulnerable, confused, and worried.

When the revelation of abuse comes during a joint session, the issue is not just how and when to report, but also how to maintain the balance of power and integrity of the mediation process in the room without having tension escalate to the point that a participant walks out. Discovering discrepancies in the accusatory story can often be helpful, and the mediator may assist in redefining terms and dispelling myths about the nature of abuse and neglect and the need for those who know about it to report.

It is a good assumption that the mediation participant has revealed it in the joint session exactly because it is a safe forum in which to accuse directly and ask for refutation and information, or to find out additional information that will either confirm or deny. Both accuser and accused sometimes have mistaken ideas of what constitutes child abuse. Mediators who are familiar with the statutes can educate all of them. When the family mediator names the events or behavior as abuse, it legitimizes the concern and need for action, prevents minimization, and supports the social values that have been put into law. It can also polarize, enrage, and threaten the accused party and make that person more resistant and forewarned.

Uncovering the abuse in joint session does not determine what should happen next, and the mediator is not the person who should determine that next step. Rather, the authorized societal agents (child protective services, law enforcement and the judiciary) need to become involved in order to deal with the situation.

Some Important Reminders

A mediator should never allow an accusation of abuse that fits the legal definitions to be bargained away or ignored or to continue mediation as if it were not there. Joint session revelations allow the mediator to say these things directly to the participants and allow the parties to do what they need to do within the limits of safety and balanced process. The accuser needs to take personal accountability and responsibility for pursuing the accusation, and the accused needs to know how to pursue his or her own legal rights and responsibilities given the accusation.

The mediator needs to manage the session, help all participants know where they currently stand, educate the parties about the other institutions that will now be involved, make the report, and shut down the mediation effort until the authorized agencies can investigate and determine the next steps or outcome.

It is inappropriate for mediators to be mediating terms and conditions of parenting or family conflicts if there are immediate safety and security concerns for the child, or if there is an open abuse investigation pending or could be one soon because of the newly revealed accusation. This is true if for no other reason than the fact that the other institutions will decide who is the decision maker. The parents in this situation often lose their autonomy and rights to determine the decisions for the child. If the child becomes a ward of the state or is put in temporary foster care, the parents or other family members may not be the ones who currently or ultimately will have the decision-making capacity.

It is better to find out who has legal decision-making authority before mediating decisions between parties who may no longer have the authority. If the social worker on behalf of the CPS now has the final decision about custody, placement of the child, or the legal timelines are already in place, the mediator may have the wrong parties involved.

If the revelation of child abuse comes out in solo session or caucus or as part of solo preliminary session, the joint mediation effort should be put on hold. Solo session revelation can allow the family mediator to call the protective service agency or reporting agency and observe the accusing person make the direct report to the appropriate agency, thus ensuring that the person with the most knowledge of the event is directly reporting to the correct entity. If there is current danger, CPS should be alerted to this fact.

The direct report of the accusing party does not relieve the family mediator of making a report. Family mediators who believe they must report should start the conversation, then hand the telephone to the revealing person. When it is safe to do so, the family mediator also needs to acknowledge to the accused person (or his or her representing attorney if the situation is unsafe) that this action was taken by the mediator due to legal requirements. This prevents the reporting of the abuse from appearing to be an unholy alliance with one person or a conspiracy to withhold information from the other participant of the mediation.

Revelation During Caucus or Solo Session

If the revelation happens as part of a solo session embedded in the context of a joint appointment and the accused person, aware or unaware of the revelation, is in the mediator's waiting room, then the dilemma for the family mediator becomes how to get the revealing party out of the office safely, educate the other party to the issue, and shut down the joint mediation session safely. This must be done in ways that will not endanger the revealing party or collude with that person to disempower or discount the needs of the accused person to know what everyone else seems to know. In this way, a family mediator still attempts to retain balanced and impartial mediation process, even in the light of these troubling circumstances. This situation is perhaps the hardest ethical and practice issue a mediator will encounter and requires prethinking, supervision and support, and adequate safety and mediational practices to prevent harm to children and parents.

Mediators need to be aware that any report to authorities may engender rage and retaliatory action toward the revealer, the child, or the mediator. They must be prepared to assume responsibility when the other party finds out that a report of the accusation has been made. Stopping the mediation as inappropriate without any explanation can frustrate and enrage the accused party and seriously jeopardize the mediator's ability to work with both parties again after the investigation is over. There is no one way in which the telling of the accused should be done, and each way poses some risks. Family mediators need to find the safest way for a particular case and may need guidance from others in order to determine this.

Assessing Safety

The first task in any revelation of child abuse is to assess the current and future safety of the child and revealing person and to help CPS to secure the child's safety in whatever way is necessary. Adaptations of the same categories used in assessing domestic violence and spouse abuse, such as the past history and current realities of proximity, severity, frequency, and pattern of abuse, can help the mediator prethink the information needed from the revealing party.

Some mediators may want to create and use a form similar to the Control, Abuse, and Violence Screener (see Appendix C) that has been modified to the concerns that are revealed about child abuse. Using those same categories of lethality, proximity, pattern type of abuse, and other criteria can serve as mental markers of whether the danger level is so high that immediacy of protection becomes urgent and requires major intervention for protection. It may help guide the decision that all that is needed now is just awareness of the risk potential and reporting of the past abuse.

Reporting Abuse

In most states, even past child abuse that no longer holds current urgency or current threat must be reported, although sometimes the agencies want it reported by a different method, such as on paper rather than as a telephone call to the abuse-reporting hot line. This is to ensure that perpetrators of abuse do not have current access to children. It can help accumulate evidence necessary for the protective agency and the judicial system to act. Family mediators need to check the laws and requirements of their jurisdiction and discuss with other practicing family mediators the precautions and procedures they use to deal with this intense ethical concern.

If there was past abuse but there appears from adequate screening and interviewing (and verification with the protective services that no current action is being investigated) that there is no current danger, threat, or protection issue, the mediator may want to proceed carefully with the case. The questions then become the following:

- Will the mediator know if the situation changes and endangerment or abuse is happening again?
- Does the mediator still have sufficient empathy and rapport with the participants to continue mediating on their behalf without prejudice, bias, or favoritism?
- Will continued mediation actually do harm, because it helps the parties deny the reality or escape the consequences of the past abuse?

The dynamics in families where child abuse has occurred are often unhealthy or dysfunctional, and even persons who know the abuse is wrong and want to stop it often feel unable to stand up to the abuser, hold to appropriate behavioral boundaries, and be actively protective of their children. If the family mediator believes the parent is currently unable or not ready to make courageous acts of change for the family or take responsibility in keeping children safe, he or she may not want to mediate the case. If the parent who should be protecting the children or who should become an active, protective, adequate parent or partner cannot do so, then the context of mediation may not be the proper forum for these participants, even if they want to continue.

If the mediator has a model of mediation, such as the therapeutic, transformative, narrative, or interactional models, that allows direct intervention and work to empower and strengthen the resolve and action of the persons who need to do the protecting, then the family mediator may serve as the catalyst for change of the family system and its members. This support and empowerment may be sufficient to allow the continuation of the mediation effort without continued fear of harm. Otherwise, the family mediator should end the mediation effort and try to secure appropriate evaluative and other supportive services, such as court-appointed special advocates, friends of the court, special master's programs, and other innovative adaptations along a continuum of services as noted by Johnston and Roseby (1997). Another avenue is innovative hybrid mediation-counseling programs described by Barsky (1995) to provide care for these cases rather than allowing them to mediate in the usual ways.

Cases that involve past, current, or potential future abuse are among the hardest for mediators to deal with ethically and show in what way mediators bargain in the shadow of the law, being fully aware of where those shadows fall. Family mediators need to review all standards of practice, codes of ethics, and policies and procedures of their setting. They need to keep up with this topic by reading professional journals—such as *Family and Conciliation Courts Review, Conflict Resolution Quarterly* (formerly *Mediation Quarterly*), and journals from other therapeutic fields that deal with abuse issues—as well as by attending specialized training to learn how best to handle child abuse cases in family mediation.

FRAMING AGREEMENTS FOR SPECIAL ISSUES CASES

Mediators working with any of the special issues highlighted in this chapter should focus on adapting not only the content but also the process of mediation they use. Direct confrontation of the issue, whether it is a parent's substance use or mental health problem, is usually unproductive and can lead to the negative confrontational spiral that can ruin a mediator's neutrality and effectiveness with the client. Mediators need to practice what I call "coming in the back door," or accepting the problem as a fact and reducing the shame, threat, and defensiveness of the identified problem person, while also trying to help build agreements that will substantially reduce risk of harm to children and the clients by focusing on the substantive issues. Although many parents will not admit directly to a substance abuse problem, they will make appropriate agreements that will protect their children from being subjected to it as long as their problem is not overtly named.

Focusing on Functioning, Not the Label

When the mediator helps focus on the practical issues that the protective parent is worried about, it helps diffuse the problem. The mediator can help the parents or family members refocus on specific content issues, such as who will provide substitute care when the problem is happening and how the parent will maintain the children's health and safety. Other issues are who cannot be present or what will or will not transpire during their parenting time and who and how transportation can be done safely. For example, parents who are struggling with substance abuse can make specific agreements that if the protective parent is worried about the condition of the using parent, all adults will agree not to transport the children until they are proved clean and sober after calling the police to do a breathalyzer test. A parent who is worried about the other parent's maintaining mental health medications could request that that person agree to sign releases about verifying attendance at therapy with the prescribing professional prior to release of the child to that parent's care. When direct abuse has happened, parents could agree on terms of access or placement back in the home only after completion of specific abuse control programs or diversion programs.

It is important for the family mediator to ensure that the discussion about these special issues does not become demeaning or disenfranchising to the person with the active problem and that the systemic nature of the problem (the codependency of the one who enables the irresponsibility of the other) is discussed. It is important to legitimize the debate in terms of the actual functionality of each person, not the diagnosis or the problem label. In this way, the problem needs to be reframed or externalized in ways that focus on how the problem affects the parents' abilities to function, not whether they fit the label of alcoholic, addict, or mentally ill.

Agreements between participants in mediation with these special issues need to include very clear descriptions of behaviors that will be the criteria for revision or change. Addicts and alcoholics, mentally ill persons, and abusive parents and partners many times do change through treatment and become ready and able to take back their full levels of responsibilities without severe limitations. Based on the belief of growth and optimism, they can determine the behavioral hallmarks of the parent who is ready to resume parenting duties. The participants can negotiate these issues, and the negotiation in itself becomes the standard for growth and hope.

Writing Up Agreements

Because mediated agreements as outcome documents of the session are not subject to strict confidentiality and may be released to attorneys and others or become the basis of legal public records, it is important for family mediators to be careful of the way in which they write up agreements in these special issues cases. They should not use labels in mediated agreements, but rather define the problem in functional behavioral terms. Instead of writing, "Because of John's alcoholism, Mary will have to transport," the wording could be, "Both parents agree not to transport the children when intoxicated." There is no reason to point fingers in the final write-up, and yet some rationale for any strict limitations or unusual agreements need to be in the document to serve as a basis for the agreement. The same is true of contingency clauses. Do not collude to keep family secrets hidden, but do not blatantly highlight them.

Because mediators in these cases are trying to solve specific concerns and problems in the sets of agreements, they often forget to help the participants enumerate the hallmarks of success or the strengths that each parent brings despite the specific concern. For example, if a mother has excellent bonding and attachment with her children but has been clinically depressed lately, some acknowledgment of the bonding that exists reminds everyone of the goal for the family. Many mediators start their process with having the participants outline the superordinate goals, such as maintaining stability and continuity and rebuilding active parenting. How will they know when they have gotten to where they want to go? Mediators can help the clients be specific about these factors or elements of health.

Because many of the special issues cases described here require the strongest levels of interference on parental rights and the most severe limitation on their access through supervised visitation, at least temporarily, family mediators need to be familiar with these options and local providers. When making referrals and writing agreements for special issues cases that are using supervised visitation (or out-of-home placement), mediators need to bring up not only the logistics of who is capable and available to act as a strong supervisor but also how long the supervision will last and the criteria for lifting this sanction.

Basing Parenting Plans on Special Conditions

Parents with any of these special case issues will likely need very different and much more limited parenting opportunities, at least temporarily, in order to maintain safety and security for the children. The Parenting Plan Rationale (adapted from Taylor and Goldberg, 1998) in Appendix D was created to help court-connected mediators and their clients more easily use recent information about the three major factors that should be considered when making parenting plans: the child's age and developmental capacities, the level of attachment between the parent and child, and the skills and circumstances of the parent.

This chapter has reviewed the issues and concerns of family disputes that involve the outer edges of individual or family functioning. Because of the systemic nature of the family, the issue is not to label or pin the problem on the person who is identified with the issue but rather to see how to screen out cases that should not mediate from those that can and how to make adaptations in the process the mediator provides. It is a starter set of information but should not be where the practitioner ends the search for understanding the people, the problems, and the processes that fit them. Because cases with these hard dynamics often test the mediator's limits and ethics, the next chapter focuses on the standards and ethics and the confidentiality requirements for family mediators.

CHAPTER SIX

Ethics and Standards, Confidentiality and Privilege

Family mediators need to understand the basic tenets of ethical practice to wend their way through the thicket of standards of practice that have been developed over the years. They need to understand the concept of confidentiality and privileged communication so that they can interpret what is acceptable and what is not when asked by clients and associates. They also need to understand some of the exceptional cases with their special dynamics and needs for reporting to other services and agencies while preserving the necessary privacy under the standards.

As this text goes to press, there is not a nationally uniform mediation law that interprets this for all mediators in all states in the same way, so each family mediator has to research and develop a specialized and personalized understanding of these issues for his or her own state and circumstances. This chapter is not intended to supplant this necessary inquiry, but to set out the complexities and issues that mediators need to research and develop for themselves. Soon a uniform national law may be ratified and passed, or state laws and professional organizations and licensing or certification requirements will be changing the requirements and expectations.

This chapter, which is an overview of the topic, may be old news before it can be read because of the potential for the adoption of some uniform laws, but it can still be helpful to mediators in organizing their approach to the topic. Banding together into regional and statewide organizations helps family mediators stay on top of the constant changes in the area of legalities and standards.

ETHICS AND STANDARDS

Although the four general ethical principles that guide and inform professional practice remain sturdy and immutable, the standards of practice for all mediators, and family mediators in particular, are constantly being rewritten and refined by national and international professional organizations and other professionals, such as social workers and lawyers, in order to differentiate the unique role of mediation for their members. Legislatures and judicial systems have created a bewildering array of laws, local court rules, and procedures, which means that there is not yet a single statement about whether mediators have privileged communication or what the limits of confidentiality are. Let us take each of these separately to define the impact of each for family mediators.

Key Principles

Ethics are the general principles by which we do our work, and family mediators are bound by ethical principles similar to those of other helping professionals. Although the specific standards may change between professions and roles, the ethical principles remain fairly constant. All ethical principles are supposed to be in full force at all times if the process and the product are to be deemed ethical. The five basic ethical principles articulated by applied ethicists across disciplines (McDonald, 2001) should also be embraced in the field of mediation.

- *Do no harm*—do not allow intimidation, overcontrolling behavior, or verbal, mental, or physical abuse before, during, or after mediation.

- *Try to do good*—use standards and best practices to promote the goals of the mediation effort; allow free exchange of ideas with clients about what this would be.

- *Be fair and promote justice*—treat clients without prejudice or discrimination; try to maintain balance and respect toward them; do not allow bias or personal values to interfere with the process; maintain impartiality and appropriate neutrality.

- *Client self-determination*—allow full disclosure; empower clients to make their own choices free of undue influence from others; protect their right to choose despite a mandatory setting; ensure the right to opt out of mediation without sanction; make sure that the decisions are voluntary and uncoerced.

- *Fidelity to promises*—do what you said you would do contractually and interpersonally.

Of these five principles, the one that has been held as the highest for the field of mediation is the concept of client self-determination. This is the ethical requirement that creates the uniqueness of mediation, as opposed to arbitration, litigation, or adjudication processes, where clients do not make their own decisions. Evaluators, adjudicators, and arbitrators try to do no harm, do good, provide fairness and justice, and follow their contracts, but they do not allow the clients to decide for themselves the outcome of the process.

Sarah Grebe (1992) has outlined the philosophical and ethical base of mediation and points to the fact that all professions must adhere to basic values and constructs about ethics. She points out that autonomy of action is the primary principle of ethics and the fundamental concept that must be present in mediation, similar to the client self-determination requirement of the ethics principles. She points out that the concept of autonomy includes at least the following concepts:

- Freedom from coercive restraint
- Freedom to choose
- Informed and reasoned choice
- Choice based on the recognition of moral values

The particular issues and concerns for mediators who have backgrounds in the helping professions of therapy, counseling, social work, and other fields have often centered on the shared value system of these professions. Ann Milne (1988) describes not only the history of the development of standards but also the internal conflict some mental health professionals may feel as they enter into the mediation practice: "The desire to support, protect, and advocate for an individual is a recognizable value for a mental health professional but may be in conflict with the value of best interests of all family members, as practiced by the mediator" (p. 386). Human service workers have a usual role of active interventionist—a helper who takes on certain responsibilities for the clients— and that active advocate role may contradict the more balanced and impartial role of mediator.

Standards for Attorneys and Social Workers

Thomas Bishop (1988) described the development of standards for attorneys who wanted to function as mediators and the necessary components and need to define and standardize the definitions of mediation and the scope of practice. Linda Silberman (1988) also discussed the concerns of attorneys who are functioning as mediators as the struggle to determine the differences between the ethical requirements of attorneys and those of mediators. An attorney functioning as a mediator relies on both sets of standards and codes of ethics. It would be unethical for an attorney to mediate without having explained to participants at the outset of mediation the difference in function between mediator and attorney. Bishop also pointed out that in order to meet the attorney-mediator's ethics, the standards had to involve disclosures necessary to clarify the process for clients, including such items as the following:

- Differences between mediation and other processes.
- Costs and payment methods that are ethical. Outcome-based contingency fees are not ethical in mediation, but may be ethical and even standard in legal representation.
- Responsibilities of clients to be active full participants (as opposed to having the lawyer do things for them as their legal agent).
- The right to opt out of mediation (similar to attorneys, who must end their legal representation in specific ways).
- The role and function of the mediator and the specific methodology he or she will use (not usually included in attorney-client discussion).
- The confidentiality and privacy of information in mediation (a very different set of rules from legal advocacy and privileged communication as a representing attorney).
- The impartiality and unbiased condition of the mediator. Here the mediator will be working for both parties, which is ethically prohibited for attorneys.
- Any conflicts of interest (prior function as an attorney for one of the participants or other relationships).
- The need for full disclosure of all relevant information by the participants to each other to ensure fairness. (If the person were acting as an attorney, such information could be shared only with the represented client, not both parties).

By defining these as disclosures, the attorney who is functioning as a mediator is not only stating the differences between the role of mediator with participants; the attorney is also reminding himself or herself how different the roles, rules, and requirements are for mediators. This is an ethical reminder that what is ethical behavior for an attorney may not be ethical for a mediator. Attorneys, who can be disbarred for unethical practice, have historically been quite concerned about the ethics of their role as mediator and the necessity that they not practice law, however ethical, when mediating.

Social workers, in like fashion, have tried to differentiate the practice of standard social work from the requirements of the mediation process, which does not allow them to advocate on behalf of their client, which would be standard ethical practice in social work. Like attorneys, social workers and other mental health professionals working as family mediators do not want to do an unauthorized practice of law, nor do they want to violate the ethics of their primary profession. Social workers, realizing that there are some disparities in ethics and standards from their usual role and procedures, developed the specialized Standards of Practice for Social Work Mediators as early as 1987, when the National Association for Social Work first promoted the minimum requirements for professional competence and practice as a social worker–mediator.

Ethics for Different Models and Approaches

In their best forms and provided as intended, all of the models discussed in this book promote the five ethical principles and the clients' autonomy and right to choose at least the outcome. Some models emphasize the client self-determination principle not just in the outcome but also in the way in which the process is provided.

Some models of mediation, like the procedural approaches, give great lip-service to client self-determination yet do not allow the participants any leeway in how the mediation will be run, what to talk about, or how to frame their concerns in terms of the process of the mediation itself. The client has no self-determination other than to comply with the process as outlined and offered by the mediator or opt out. In other mediation approaches, especially the narrative, transformative, and interactive, the clients themselves shape the way in which the mediation process proceeds, and client self-determination is a part of every aspect of the process being provided. Clients are asked, not told, what to do, given choices, and required to make decisions about the process as well as the content of the discussion.

Resolving Ethical Dilemmas

Ethical dilemma results for a mediator when by responding to and honoring one of these principles, the mediator seems prevented from holding to another principle simultaneously. For example, if participants in mediation are proposing an option or agreeing to something that the mediator believes could be harmful to themselves or others, the two principles of client self-determination and harm reduction collide. The mediator needs to know that they are in an ethical choice, not just a matter of personal predilection or procedural problem.

Using the ethical worksheet developed by Bivins (2000) and the sequence suggested by McDonald (2001), a mediator caught in an ethical dilemma can follow this sequence for dealing with the ethical concerns:

1. Identify which principles are in conflict in this situation.

2. Identify the behaviors you would do if you were honoring each one separately and not having the dilemma.

3. Determine likely steps and outcomes, for the clients and for you, of each of these courses of action.

4. Note your inclination and dislike for each choice, and determine the reasons: Is it personal, professional, or lack of information or support?

5. Consult with someone knowledgeable—a supervisor or consultant, another experienced family mediator or colleague, or a legal adviser— to get a second opinion.

6. Check the current ethics, standards, and laws—not just for your own profession of origin but also the local and national mediation organizations.

7. Consult yourself again. How will you react if what you choose creates further harm, gets you in trouble, or even jeopardizes your practice?

8. Make a choice, document it, and pursue it with alacrity, while remaining open to other possibilities that may present themselves.

9. Keep going through this sequence even after the dilemma is done, for best personal learning and growth.

10. Share what you have learned with other mediators. Discuss your concern with others, try to prevent other occurrences of the same dilemma for you and other mediators, and share the experience with ethics bodies of professional societies so they can provide opinions and guidance for problem prevention.

Common ethical dilemmas for family mediators include switching roles when working with the same clients, such as when a therapist changes roles to be a family mediator for one or more of the clients previously counseled, or switching back to therapist or attorney after being the mediator. To solve these dilemmas, family mediators often look to their professional bodies and standards of practice promoted by professions or imposed by state statute. These vary considerably, so careful study is required. Wise family mediators stay up-to-date on these in order to be prepared for any dilemma that arises.

Evolving Standards

Standards of practice could be defined as "a reasonable effort" or as "what the majority of other family mediators might do in the same circumstances." It can be also be defined as "within the range of acceptability," given that the practice of family mediation is widely variant based on very different models and paradigms. Standards of practice can be written as aspirational, as in the best practices or idealized ways of functioning, or they can be written as minimum requirements, below which the mediator is doing unacceptable practice. Several sets of standards written in the past twenty years have had very short global statements that are the actual standards, followed by commentary explaining the full impact and the controversy or range of practice of the standard, as well as the allowable or notable exceptions. This provides a compromise that acknowledges the practice differences of mediators using different styles or working with different types of disputes. These standards have been extremely hard to develop, not only because of the variance in practice but also because of the vested interest of some groups in maintaining the broadest possible statements to reduce liability concerns.

No matter what the background is of a particular practitioner, when that person is functioning as a family mediator, he or she may be held to standards of family mediation practice that he or she has not specifically adopted or ascribed to. This is a daunting thought. The standards for family mediation are there, and practitioners' behavior can and will be held to those standards.

Standards are not just esoteric discussions, but practical boundaries that will be enforced. They serve as definitions of adequate and inappropriate practice. When professions license or certify, they usually require their members to adopt their standards. Because most family mediators in most states are not yet licensed or certified, family mediators often have a hard time finding and determining which standards they must recognize and follow. Once a family mediator joins a professional organization, he or she has some guidance regarding standards.

Since 1982, interested groups such as the Association of Family Conciliation Courts, the American Bar Association's Family Law section, and many other state and national groups interested in family mediation have been collaborating in order to provide more consistent, concise, and coordinated model standards for attorneys, court mediators, and others working with divorce mediation and other family disputes. Each of these groups had separate, constantly changing standards, which sometimes conflicted or left important issues unaddressed. In 1996, the Family Law section of the American Bar Association realized that its 1984 model standards needed updating, so participants in a series of conferences and a symposium drafted documents that went through multiple review processes with many interested groups. The result has been the development and adoption by the convening organizations of the August 2000 version of the *Model Standards of Practice for Family and Divorce Mediation* (Association of Family Conciliation Courts, 2000).

This document differentiates between the "may" language of conditional choices in the realm of professional judgment and model or style preferences and differences, and the "should" of highly desirable, preferred, and assumed behavior that mediators must use most of the time and deviate from only with strong rationale. It also uses occasional "shall" language, which indicates standards that family mediators must be held to without the discretion to vary from them.

While the new *Model Standards* were intended to delineate a range of acceptable behavior by family mediators, not to be legal rules that would carry penalties or criteria used to measure liability, they will become the de facto foundation of adequate mediation practice and so become like the Constitution in relation to our state laws—all other standards must conform with it or be judged as beyond the boundaries of acceptable practice.

Standards I and II speak to the nature of the relationship the mediator and the family should have: the highest principle of client self-determination is again upheld, and the family mediator is required to have knowledge of family law, child development, domestic violence, child abuse, cultural issues, and the impact of conflict on parents and children, and to share that training and expertise with the family. Standards III and IV speak to the special case issues noted in Chapter Five. Under the new *Model Standards,* mediators have an absolute obligation both to end the mediation process if they believe the participant is unable or unwilling to participate, and to maintain impartiality in dealing with the case. Screening of cases for these conditions thus becomes imperative for those following these standards. Standard V requires disclosure and specific behavior regarding fees, and Standard VI requires family mediators to educate families while it specifically enjoins them from providing therapy or legal advice.

Standard VII requires complete discussion of the extent of confidentiality, specifically as it applies to communication during solo sessions or caucuses, or when there is threat of harm to self or others. Standard VIII again exhorts the family mediator to educate parents about children's capacities and needs, participation of children during mediation, and referral resources. Standard IX requires mediators to report abuse or neglect and to assess the need to terminate mediation if there are allegations of such issues. Standard X requires specialized screening and accommodations for families in which domestic violence or any form of control, intimidation, or threat exists. Standard XI spells out the requirements for family mediators to end cases in situations of threat of kidnapping, impairment by drugs or alcohol, unconscionable agreements, or coopting of the mediation process. Standards XII and XIII require truth in advertising and continuing professional development and training in cultural sensitivity.

Family mediators should review the *Model Standards* in light of their own practice type and model to ensure that they are substantially in compliance, and they should remain connected to state and national organizations that will keep them posted on the continuing evolution of standards that affect standard mediators. The new *Model Standards* describe good practice, if not best practice, for mediators. Revision of the *Model Standards* is an attempt to guide family mediators, inform participants of what to expect, and promote public confidence in the use of mediation by ensuring reasonable standards for practitioners. Although there are other statutory and organizational standards that a family mediator may choose to follow, this document will likely become the primary one adopted and used by the majority of family mediators, since it brings together the best minds and the two primary forces shaping our field: the legal world (including the ADR community) and the helping professions.

It is likely that the field of family mediation will continue to move in the direction of creating standardized testing, voluntary or mandatory certification or licensure, and competency-based training and approval standards of practice that are based on actual ranges of behaviors of practicing mediators, in addition to these voluntary standards. As this happens, practice will become truly more standard, and practitioners will need to conform to the new standards or risk censure. The field will still have to deal with the multiplicity of models and practices outlined in this book. Just as there is no single way to mediate, our standards must maintain our high ethical imperatives and yet be appropriately flexible to allow for diversity of model and approach.

Common Ethical Concerns for Mediators

Although the standards of practice change and proliferate, the common ethical dilemmas that affect mediators tend to stay fairly similar over time. Following is a list of common ethical or standards issues that family mediators should research, based on their unique pattern of professional background, state or national rules, and current professional organizations.

- *Can I switch roles?* This is an important ethical and practice issue for therapists, attorneys, and others who are adding family mediation practice to an existing private practice of something other than mediation. Dworkin, Jacob, and Scott (1991) point out that historically the field of family mediation has promulgated various ethics statements and standards from different professional organizations regarding this dilemma, and those standards show a wide range of answers—everything from prohibition to allowance for specific conditions. At this writing, our new combined professional organization, the Association for Conflict Resolution, will no doubt have to revise the current standards of the organization for mediation practice, which should provide guidance regarding this question.

In the meantime, mediators should ask themselves these questions:

- How could it help or hinder any of the participants if I switch roles?
- Will I have a tendency to use my prior knowledge in ways that could help, or will it tempt me to overstep my boundary as a family mediator?
- Have I fully disclosed to participants my former role, and do they have any concerns about my impartiality, neutrality, objectivity, or involvement?
- Are they all comfortable with my switching roles?

- Why should I maintain a connection with them rather than refer?
- Is this about my needs or theirs?

- *How does my profession of origin (attorney, social worker, therapist, or other discipline) affect my requirements as a mediator?* First, most licensed professionals want to maintain their credibility and license in the original field in which they have their licensure, certification, or listing, as well as function ethically within family mediation. How to do this without leaving one or the other behind used to be a vivid debate and has created polarization within the mediation field, with mediators referring to themselves in hyphenated terms, such as *attorney-mediator* or *nonattorney-mediator.*

Many mediators who were not legally trained have been concerned that there will be a closing of the door, a legal bias, or even a requirement. This is not idle speculation or paranoid concern. As of 1999, at least nine states plus one province in Canada had enacted local laws that require either a law degree or a substantial number of years of study in order to be considered qualified to be a civil mediator. Since family law is part of civil law, this could affect many family mediators who want to mediate all types of family issues that could be litigated. It is comforting to see that the ADR section of the American Bar Association does not believe that this should be the case, as evidenced in its recent adoption of the following statement:

> The Section of Dispute Resolution has noted that many court connected ADR programs and other dispute resolution programs have restricted participation to neutrals who are lawyers. The section believes that the eligibility criteria for dispute resolution programs should permit all individuals who have the appropriate training and qualifications to serve as neutrals, regardless of whether they are lawyers. [American Bar Association Section of Dispute Resolution, 1999]

Fortunately, over time, some answers have come to us from the other professions when they have considered their usual role and compared it to the role and function of a mediator.

An attorney who is functioning as a mediator *is not* functioning as an attorney or legal advocate and is not legally representing anyone. Because the roles and rules are so very different for being a mediator and being a legal advocate or counselor at law, the ABA has tried to provide attorneys who are acting as mediators with a set of rules and standards in addition to those they have from mediation organizations (ABA Family Law Task Force, 1997; ABA Family Law Section, 1986).

The field of social work has seen that social workers who are functioning as mediators are doing a process that is different enough from the usual practice of social work that it needs to be designated as a separate role. The national body has promulgated several sets of standards for their members who are performing different functions or working in specialized contexts, including mediation. A social worker who is functioning as a mediator is still doing social work but is termed a *social work mediator.* Social work mediators have standards for functioning in this way that are different from the usual social work case management standards. The complete Standards of Practice for Social Work Mediators is now available on-line and should be reviewed often by social workers who are functioning as family mediators (National Association of Social Workers, 1987).

A counselor or therapist may or may not be doing counseling or therapy when functioning as a mediator, depending on the definitions of their state or national licensure or certification and the codes of ethics of their professional affiliations, the definition of their counseling or therapy model, *and* their specific family mediation model and practice.

Although the American Association for Marriage and Family Therapists (AAMFT) does not specifically create a specialized role for a therapist functioning as a mediator, many of the ethical statements in its current and future Code of Ethics (both available on-line at the organization's Web site) could be instructive for family mediators, even if they do not belong to the organization.

This still begs the question, which must be answered personally for each therapist or counselor functioning as a mediation practitioner. For example, a cognitive-behavioral counselor or therapist may well be doing cognitive-behavioral counseling as part of her family mediation practice if she is using a therapeutic mediation model, but if she is using a procedural mediation model, then her role as mediator is substantially different. Conversely, therapists who are doing mediation from a variation on the therapeutic family mediation model may well have considerable correspondence between what they do as a mediator and their usual therapy role.

Counselors and therapists should check with their licensing bodies and professional organizations, along with their insurance carrier if it is connected to their profession of origin, to determine if their mediation practices fit the description of scope of practice and legal descriptions of their licensure or certification. Often it will not match in significant ways, which could create insurance coverage problems and ethical dilemmas about full disclosure. Similarly, school counselors must make a personal inventory of the definitions, requirements, and similarity of approach they have with their role as family mediator.

• *Can I blend my roles and offer what I know from my other professional practice?* This question again gets at the boundaries between the practice of mediation and the practice of other roles and functions. The biggest worries are whether a mediator is acting outside the role by giving legal advice as opposed to providing legal information as a mediator. Similarly, the issue is whether the mediator is providing therapy or therapeutic mediation. The question of unauthorized practice of law has haunted many attorneys as they themselves ventured into family mediation, and those who came from legal or judicial backgrounds often became overly concerned and refused to educate their clients appropriately about legal information in ways that might be helpful and within the role of mediator. Similarly, nonattorney mediators feared that giving information was the same as legal advice, which it is not. Therapists who were not following a particular mediation model were often tempted to go into areas of emotional questioning and support that was not productive toward the joint mediation effort, or they found themselves trying to be the mediator and someone's informal therapist during the session, skewing their neutrality.

The simplest answer to this question is that you can, will, and even must bring what you know into the room and use it ethically in the service of the clients' goals and the practice of mediation. An attorney need not erase all legal knowledge in order to mediate, but must refrain from providing legal advising or advocacy on behalf of either of the mediation clients, while still educating if that is relevant and within the model of practice. A therapist or social worker or counselor may still understand the generational patterns, the transference issues, the emotional issues, and the social disenfranchisement without necessarily bringing them into the dialogue or interaction and without distracting the process of mediation being used by exploring it to the detriment of the mediation effort. So the answer is to bring your knowledge and expertise in, but use it only if it fits the mediation process the clients and you have agreed on and the usual approach within your model.

• *Can I provide two different services simultaneously or sequentially?* Almost unanimously, ethics and standards of most professions protect clients against dual relationships, that is, when the professional has more than one role at one time with the client. Dual relationships can be an ethical minefield where the clients' personal boundaries can be easily broken. The quick answer to the question is to avoid all dual relationships and multitasking. Be one thing at a time to your clients.

As to the sequence of roles, it may not be advisable to start as one role and change (from therapist to mediator, from mediator to attorney) to another, even when there are safeguards to these role changes. It is far better to play only one role. This may not be possible for those mediating in small towns or rural jurisdictions, where they must serve in sequential roles because there is no one else to refer to. If you decide to take this risk, make sure you separate the roles by having separate contracts signed for the different services before starting them and give full disclosure of the rules and role differences and the differences in confidentiality and release of information.

Some Safe Assumptions

The safest assumption to make is that if you are doing family mediation, your first responsibility is to the ethics and standards of mediation in general, and family mediation in particular, as those become more refined and codified as differentiated from other mediation venues. Second, you should consult with the definitions of scope of practice of your profession of origin to see if there is any crossover or discrepancy of definition, practice, or ethics or standards. Third, you should be aware of those dilemmas before they present themselves in a case by mentally role-playing situations in which your requirements will conflict. In other words, as problem prevention, provide yourself an imaginary ethical dilemma and try to solve it by using the steps set out in this chapter—before you have a real dilemma.

Fourth, remember that if you said you were a family mediator and have contracted in verbal or, preferably, written form to provide family mediation services, then that is your clients' view of your role and function. That document should have offered your clients the current family mediation requirements about disclosure at the beginning of mediation. It should have had at least some professional disclosure about your background training and a lot about your model or approach to family mediation, and it should identify the standards of practice and the definition of scope of practice that you are using and adhere to. The clients should be alerted to any issues or concerns you have about multiple or conflicting standards, as part of your requirement for ethical practice and their right to full disclosure in any profession.

CONFIDENTIALITY AND PRIVILEGED COMMUNICATION

It is obvious to most family mediators that they need to protect the privacy of the communications within the mediation session, but when an attorney representing one of the participants calls, can the mediator talk with him or her? What can the mediator not talk about? If the judge or other referring agent wants to know if the case has gotten started or how far along it is, can the mediator provide this information? Can a mediator be forced to testify in court regarding issues discussed or not discussed in mediation?

Jay Folberg (1988) describes confidentiality as "the reasonable expectation that information, documents, and opinions that are exchanged in a professional setting will not be shared with others. . . . An expectation of confidentiality may exist because of the private nature of the family dispute being mediated, an express or implied contract of confidentiality, professional ethics and standards, or the wording of a statute" (p. 320). Family mediators need to protect client confidentiality for all four reasons. Clients also have this responsibility: they should pledge confidentiality to themselves and hold each other accountable for any breaches. However, because we cannot control the behavior of clients, the discussion examines only the mediator's responsibility.

Exceptions to Confidentiality

Ethical principles require a family mediator to review and perhaps release otherwise confidential material in the following situations:

- Reporting child abuse and elder abuse
- Immediate threat of harm to self or others
- Medical emergencies
- Providing information to other agencies or professionals working with one or more of the participants
- Discussing the case with interns, supervisors, and other staff members who have a need to know
- Allowing case information to be used in scientific research or reporting requirements
- If the client sues the mediator for malpractice

Immediate threat to a participant or to the mediator allows the mediator and the client a reason to break confidentiality and get the help they need. Clients can threaten harm to property, which usually does not constitute bodily harm to others. It is good to remind clients that to engage in that behavior puts them in jeopardy of committing a crime, for which there are consequences. If the threat to property could affect someone else's safety (for example, loosening the brakes in a car so the person will have an accident), then it is a threat to the intended victim. A threat is equal to the action and should be treated the same as an action, because no one can know if another person will carry out the threat. Even trained professionals who are experts cannot always predict who is likely to carry out their threats.

Threats of suicide and other self-harm also fall into this exception and should be dealt with expeditiously, with (anti)suicide contracting and help from other professionals who are specialists in this area. Family mediators should not rule out the possibility that someday they may be in a room alone with someone who has not only the intention but also the capacity. Family mediators who do not work in secure settings need to prethink their responses in this situation. Taking a course on personal self-defense, harm reduction, and diversion of physical threat can help a family mediator feel better prepared should this situation arise.

Responding to Threats of Harm

Any threat of harm requires two sets of responses: one to report the information to law enforcement and other authorities to prevent the action from taking place if possible and the other to attempt to warn the intended victim. A landmark case in California (*Tarasoff* v. *Board of Regents*, 1976) has been responsible for changes in most standards of practice and recommended practices to require this additional set of responses.

If the disclosure happens during the joint mediation effort, family mediators need to have procedures in place to keep or get the clients to safety. Having procedures that have been practiced with the office staff and having emergency contact numbers or codes readily available is an important part of ensuring the safety and security of all concerned. Family mediators need to address this topic in their actual setting.

Notifying the intended victim poses logistical problems if the mediator does not have adequate contact information for the client, if the client is a minor, or if the mediator cannot readily locate the intended target of the violence from the contact information. In this situation, turning the information over to the law enforcement agency responsible might be the only avenue for the mediator, but it does not relieve the mediator of responsibility. Diligence in pursuit of this is required ethically as an emergency situation. The difficulty is not to overreact and overrelease information or to create further harm in the way in which the process is carried out. A wise family mediator should review procedures with other family mediators, attend workshops on this topic, and make personal choices regarding these ends.

Medical emergencies run into the same logistics problems. Having drill and practice simulating someone with a medical emergency in the office will quell everyone's anxiety and identify important information about what is missing in the procedures. For confidentiality reasons, it is important not to release any information that is not necessary or asked for as a need-to-know by the emergency providers. Once emergency providers are in charge, the mediator's responsibility to provide information diminishes but may not end if such information is needed for the person's immediate care.

Professional Protocols

Most family mediators have standard release-of-information forms that participants sign to authorize release of information to other helping professionals or agencies. Some family mediators in private practice require such releases as part of the contractual understanding in order to mediate. They make a pro forma contact to other concurrent services to ensure that the others agree that the participant is ready and able to manage the stress of mediation. (See Chapter Five's section, "Mental Health Concerns," for more information.)

If the mediator will be discussing the case with interns, supervisors, or other colleagues, that should be acknowledged in the contractual understandings at the beginning of mediation or a separate acknowledgment and release should be signed. Mediators who are being administratively supervised as an employee of a system but whose supervisor does not understand or is not qualified to advise on the mediation effort itself should resist releasing confidential case information to that supervisor. In this situation, they should present the administrative supervisor with standards-of-practice concerns they have, in order to get a qualified supervisor to provide actual case supervision, in which case client information may be released in order to obtain supervision.

In group practices and mediation services, it is important not to use identifying information when discussing mediation techniques and concerns in group supervision, informal discussion, and peer review sessions. Many mediators adopt a style of discussing their cases over lunch or in other open settings, sometimes with little regard for their tone or attitude. This work is demanding, and sometimes mediators who gather together tell war stories or gossip about clients inappropriately, breaching their confidentiality duty. Although release of tension may be personally helpful, mediators should never do it to the detriment of their client's confidentiality, and any such breach should be confronted and even reported to an overseeing supervisor, the ethics board of a professional society, or the licensing or certifying board of the practitioner's profession of origin (until mediators have their own licensing process).

This same attitude of respectful release should be the stance with research and reporting requirements. Any well-done research should protect client confidentiality in the way in which it is being conducted, or else the researchers should obtain signed permission directly from the client if the information they need is confidential. Researchers who observe, write notes, make videotapes, or review records should sign confidentiality agreements with the agency or mediator, as well as with the clients.

A mediator who is sued for malpractice may produce notes to defend against the suit, which would necessarily reveal some confidential information. Because this is always a possibility, family mediators are urged to make notes that conform to professional standards and that will indicate what they did during a session. Notes should be minimal, but enough to help jog the memory, and should never include disparaging remarks, labeling, or inappropriate use of quasi-psychological terms.

Whenever an exception to confidentiality has occurred, it is imperative that the mediator document it adequately in the case notes, to state clearly what made her think such a breach was necessary and what she did to fulfill her responsibilities. The specific threat that was made and the information that was subsequently released should be fully documented in the case notes and should probably be filed as an incident report in case an accusation of inappropriate release ever arises. Direct quotations, the names and numbers of parties contacted as part of the release, and information given out and taken in by the mediator, the other participants, and the client in question should all be listed.

Privileged Communication

Privileged communication, a concept created by statute, refers to the ability of the court to compel the release of confidential information. Someone who has privileged communication cannot be compelled to testify. Although many professionals have quite a bit of protection against revealing confidential information, they are not technically privileged communicators, because they can be compelled in certain situations. Currently, attorneys, doctors, and priests unambiguously have privileged communication; ministers and rabbis, therapists, counselors, social workers, and family mediators usually do not. Changes are taking place even in formerly sacrosanct privileged relationships, requiring even priests to report child abuse not divulged in the confessional and limiting attorney-client privilege.

> It should also be noted that the privilege against courtroom disclosure belongs to the client and not to the professional provider. The client may waive the privilege. In other words, if the client of a lawyer or therapist chooses to have the information made available in a court proceeding—or most accurately, does not object to testimony about the information—the lawyer or therapist cannot invoke the privilege. [Folberg, 1988, p. 326]

In the early years of family mediation, many mediators tried to prevent problems by including clauses in their contracts with clients that they hoped would in effect provide them a type of privileged communication, but these were not enforceable. They only set an expectation of resistance by the mediator if called to testify. Mediators felt that they needed stronger protection against revealing information in court.

The Uniform Mediation Act

Because there is an abiding social value in maintaining the privacy of mediation efforts to encourage the use of mediation, many states created statutes about confidentiality in mediation in general, or specific to family mediation or court-connected mediation, that gave the mediator, as well as the client, the privilege. Because each of these state statutes is very different, it left mediation as a profession without a single answer to the question of whether family mediators have privileged communication with their clients. Courts, seeing this dilemma, attempted to curb testimony by mediators by creating supplemental local court rules and other policies and procedures that gave a clear message to attorneys not to attempt subpoena or seek testimony of mediators. While this created some support, the field of mediation continues to have concerns about this issue and needs a larger answer to solve the dilemma.

Currently, there are efforts by the ABA Section of Dispute Resolution, along with the National Conference of Commissioners on Uniform State Laws, to create a national Uniform Mediation Act (American Bar Association, 2001). In the August 2000 draft, Section 7 would clearly grant mediators privileged communication, separate from the parties to the mediation. Under that draft, the mediator's privilege could be waived, and the exceptions to privilege would be clearly listed. Those exceptions would significantly modify the ones listed earlier, and because all state laws would eventually have to conform to this if passed, it would become an important document solidifying mediators' rights and responsibilities.

Because mediators function in such vastly different areas of practice, the Uniform Mediation Act is an attempt to create appropriate exceptions for widely diverse uses, such as in juvenile courts and in adult felony situations when conducting victim-offender and restorative justice mediation. In certain settings and contexts such as public policy disputes, because of sunshine laws that require proceedings to be open to the public scrutiny, there needs to be specialized consideration of confidentiality and privilege. To be truly uniform and encompassing, the rules of confidentiality and privilege must be broad enough to cover all contingencies yet specific enough for states to use as a basis when redrafting their own statutes so as to not conflict. Greg Firestone and Dennis Sharp (2001) have reviewed the Uniform Mediation Act on behalf of the Association for Conflict Resolution and have found some issues in regard to confidentiality that might be of concern to those working in child protection mediation cases. Further discussion of their concerns and the Uniform Mediation Act can be found in Chapter Twelve.

The wise family mediator will stay aware of the potential changes in the Uniform Mediation Act and other state statutes and national efforts by affiliating with professional organizations that will influence the direction of the changes and distribute this information to practicing mediators.

Family mediators need to keep current with the changing scope of their practice and the constantly changing standards that reflect good practice and define what is unacceptable. These are complex, because of differences in practitioners' profession of origin, differences in state law, and the changing professional societies that collate and promote standards. There is still a need to band together with other local and national bodies to make sure that mediators have adequate guidance that gives the same protection to clients and mediators no matter where they live.

❧

Remaining ethical is vital to maintaining the integrity of mediation as a field of practice and as a defined service to people in crisis and conflict. The next chapter explores the information and standards for working with an increasingly diverse population, where the family's culture may be unknown or even in conflict with the presumptions of mediation.

CHAPTER SEVEN

Cultural Issues in Family Mediation

Culture, as used here, is a mental, emotional, physical, and spiritual lens through which we understand and interpret our own world and which co-creates our world and identity. In the broadest sense of the word, we are all members in good standing of several different cultures simultaneously. We simultaneously belong to (or are at odds with) different groups that we have chosen to belong to and groups to which we could be assigned by certain attributes.

The values, status, and outlook of those different groups help to create our worldview. Starting from birth through all the years of our development, we learn and create our personal identity by belonging to or being ascribed to groups and identifying with the ways and beliefs of these groups or reacting in opposition to them. Culture, then, is how the individual interacts and co-creates the social systems and the social systems interact and co-create the individual in order to produce an identity that is fluid and changeable. Culture is the outward and observable manifestations of individuals with some aspects that have become a shared identity.

Usual ways of thinking about a person's culture stem from the most obvious observable aspects of the person and move to the inner self. The usual categories of belonging or attribution are about gender, race, and age. Others looking at or interacting with the individual will likely have some preconceived notions about the person based on these factors, and those may be true or false assumptions. Short of very dramatic new technological interventions, most people can do little to change these factors about themselves, although they can be very different from the normative expectations for those classifications.

Another major category of attribution has to do with social and economic status, national origin, and disabilities. There are also factors of personal and group culture that we rarely can change. Another of these somewhat variable categories of culture is our chosen or imposed religion. Most of these aspects of personal attributes are part of the antidiscrimination laws and protected classes of people in the United States. People in our society are not to be judged by or denied rights or opportunities by others because of these factors. And yet these factors are real and do indicate differences that are noticeable and meaningful. Family mediators should not discriminate against their clients, but also should not be blind to the real differences between people of different ages, sexes, and racial or ethnic backgrounds.

There are observable or ascribable categories that we tend to think of first in the formulation of a person's identity and culture, such as his or her race, gender and sexual orientation, national origin, educational level, religion, and work or other activity. Adults are part of a culture of their families, their school and educational system, their socioeconomic class, their corporate or workplace culture, their disability group if they have one, and their activities. They define themselves by these features, and not to notice or bar discussion about how these things affect the person would be to discount important information about the individual. Children experience their own developing personal identity and family culture, and also their parents' separate cultures from the extended family, as well as their school cultures, which are often quite different.

Over a lifetime, people experience multiple identities as they change affiliations, acquire new affiliations, and make changes and choices. Some people are born or become bicultural, or multicultural, fully participating in two or more cultures. For example, a person born without hearing may be raised in the deaf culture. Later in life, with new technologies, that person may become able to hear and therefore relate to the hearing community, becoming bicultural in the process. Similarly, a person raised in a highly religious family may experience extreme distress with family members who become involved in the criminal culture or the culture of drug and alcohol abuse, which carry different values, ways, and status.

To illustrate this point, let's focus on a person who has a child outside marriage. That person not only belongs to the classification and culture of parenthood, but may also be ascribed by others to a classification of unwed mother, teen mom, or welfare mother, depending on the circumstances. But what if this person is male? Will he be labeled and thought of as an unwed father, a teen dad, or a welfare father? These attributions, whether meant as descriptive or pejorative, can throw the person into a culture that he or she may or may not have personally accepted. The attributions and assumptions of others about the meaning of a person's multiple cultural identity may or may not be true, or more likely may be true to some degree and not to some degree on a continuum. Cultural identity is not just about fitting people into categories, but about their degree of acceptance of the usual worldview and behaviors of that group.

Sociology, social and individual psychology, cultural anthropology, and new materials on specific cultural awareness plus many other fields all have important information about the development, maintenance, and effects of loss and change of culture on the individual and the larger social groups we all belong to.

The purpose of this chapter is not to summarize this vast literature base, but to remind family mediators that they are working with people and families who have complex combinations and histories of identity and culture. They cannot and should not be categorized into neat boxes or made inflexible by categorization. Mediators should not make assumptions about the cultural identities of their clients based on external factors, since attributions can be wrong and do not show the depth of affiliation even when they are right. Family mediators need to remember that we all carry the multiple layers of culture that we have learned and adopted or rejected.

FAMILY CULTURE

Each person is raised in at least one culture: the culture of his or her family. Families have different focuses, both positive and negative—for example, fun, education, religion, sports, crime, or abuse. These central identity features are important to understand because they become the means by which a unique family social identity is maintained. However, this is modified by the reality that in the United States, many children have more than one family during their growing-up years. Approximately 75 percent of American children will not live in a unitary family during their entire childhood; they will have more than one family of origin. Each one of these family or live-together household groups becomes a culture in itself, because of its unique norms, status, values, attitudes, behaviors, and patterns and the people who inhabit them. Each household may be characterized by the multiple focuses they create, such as a certain religion combined with physical abuse or a child focus plus a certain racial or ethnic identity.

It used to be that parents had lots of children, but now, due to more frequent divorce and changing patterns of cohabitation, children have many "parents," some of whom are active and involved with them and others who are benign babysitters, uninterested parts of the environment, or even actively abusive or neglectful. A household map (see Appendix A) or genogram can help to identify the various characters and successions, but it may not tell all about the reality of the culture in each grouping.

Approximately one-third of all births in the United States are to women who are unmarried; in some places, the majority of births are to women who are still teenagers themselves. Within a short span of years, the culture of covert shame and stigma of the unwed mother has changed to a culture in which teenage pregnancy and single motherhood are no longer seen as problematic by a sizable percentage of the population. It also means that the cultural context of parenting has become subsumed into the larger youth culture. Many teenagers have now placed parenthood inside their own teen or street culture rather than the more traditional view of parenthood as requiring the parents to submit to the mainstream expectations of family life and maturity. When and how does a pregnant teenager or the other biological parent become acknowledged and responsible as a full-fledged parent? Our larger American culture has very ambivalent answers, depending on factors of class, race, and ethnicity, and each family experiencing this issue may have a different answer.

In addition to the changes of culture that a changing home situation can mean, the majority of parents with preschool-age children work outside the home and leave their children with others while they do so. This means that children at a very young age are experiencing other cultures, such as the worldview and habits of babysitters, child care institutions, and home care situations into which they may be placed. It is not unusual for even a young child to have as many as five different caregivers and environments to deal with in a week and to have very rapid turnover and changes that can affect their ability and desire to attach to others. In cases of very young children about whom important decisions, such as custody, physical placement and residence, and temporary or permanent access or adoption, are being made, it is especially important that the mediator get the parties to tell each other about the reality of those household cultures so that good decisions can be made in mediation.

Gender and Sexual Identity

Gender and sexual identity or orientation is also part of each person's personal identity, as well as the social identity ascribed by family members and other systems. The culture of gender and orientation certainly plays a major role in the mediation of many family-related disputes but is often covert. Who does what in the family, based on their gender and the unwritten expectations placed on them by the larger society, are important dynamics that function during the particular dispute and that may or may not be consistent with the culture of the family.

There are many such gender issues: the claim of a first-born son, the naming of a child after a relative, the expectations for behavior that each family member holds for each other because of gender rather than personal attribute, the religious upbringing, and the exposure (or lack of it) to certain types of mainstream or minority practices. Issues of gender and entitlement lie at the heart of many family disputes about children and parents, and these often stem from or relate to the larger societal disputes about the roles of women and men and the issue of sexual identity and orientation as it affects child rearing.

Each person brings to mediation a view of his or her own meaning and role as a member of the culture of his or her gender and sexual orientation. The family mediator must find out exactly how that identity affects the issues at stake in the mediation. To forget or ignore gender as a primary source of personal identity with meaning within the family identity would be to bypass a topic of huge importance in understanding the special dialogue and structure of the particular family in mediation about a particular dispute. As Ellman and Taggart (1993) point out, gender differences are the result of social construction and learning as well as biology; expectations for family roles have been evolving and incorporate views of self, power dimensions, and major changes in how family life is lived, so they have profound effects on the family systems we mediate.

Class and Racial Identity

It has been said that in the United States, people will talk openly and endlessly about their sexuality, religion, and money, but class and race are the two topics we do not dare discuss. Yet class and race can be at the heart of the dispute within a family. Because these issues are covert and not part of the dominant discourse, they are sometimes hard to bring up, and yet they may be fueling the conflict.

Lack of resources in a society that values and requires consumerism of its citizens to keep the economy stable throws a family into a financial class that may not fit with the family's former values; such is the case for women and children after divorce and for those who have encountered systemic discrimination due to race or intergenerational poverty. Poverty and economic deprivation can become a culture in themselves—a culture that can be socially learned and transmitted, passed from one generation to another when the possibility of change is minimal because of the larger economic and social conditions. This complex interplay of societal discrimination due to race, class, and poverty can lead to racial stereotyping on the part of both mediators and clients and can only be addressed when society stops blaming the victims and provides empowerment through change in helping systems such as family mediators, courts, and other societal institutions (Boyd-Franklin, 1993).

Consider a parental access case involving two parents who had recently emigrated from a country in the Balkans. The mother was offended that the father was so emotionally loose that he would tell their twelve-year-old daughter about his sexual affairs with other women, and he hung a huge bullwhip on the wall above his place in the dining room where they ate. She was not offended for the reasons that an American-born wife might be. From her unique cultural lens, she saw her husband's behaviors not as abusive, or indicating undiagnosed mental illness, or poor role modeling and parenting, or male cultural entitlements. Instead, she saw them as what she called "lower-class behavior." She felt that his behavior demeaned her and her daughter in terms of their status as educated upper-class people and lowered the class standing of their entire nuclear family in their own eyes.

When Mediator Culture Clashes with Family Culture

A recent concern of many mediators is that the very foundations of problem-solving/negotiative mediation are not culturally consistent for sizable percentages of the population they serve. Having people come to agencies or offices to sit in small rooms and talk in logical, problem-solving ways with a third party paid to be there seems inconsistent with the "rough justice" or privacy needs of many people's lives and cultural expectations. When the family that is a social minority finds no representative of their minority group among their choices of practitioners to provide mediation services, what message do they get, and what meaning do they make of this fact?

Mediators themselves might find a disconnection between who they are culturally and what is expected of them in mediation. Practitioners of family mediation who are of an ethnicity, race, or culture other than the predominantly white and middle to upper class are themselves underrepresented in our court services and mediation programs, as with the justice systems they serve. The rigorous training and requirements necessary for what has been declared necessary for family mediation professionalization makes becoming a mediator less culturally consistent for many persons who could provide direct help and support for minority populations.

The majority of family mediators are not bicultural or bilingual, and they come to the field with their own professional cultures that can be very biased or rigid in perspective. This can have a chilling effect on the use of mediation for populations within American society in which the professional paradigm is not predominant or the medical, psychological, or scientific method is not accepted as valid or important. Family mediators carry with them into the room their own unique mix of self, family, and professional cultural expectations and worldview, and they must be culturally aware enough to know what that is and how it might affect their participants and processes.

ASSESSMENT OF CULTURAL FACTORS

In perhaps the most thorough exploration of this topic in the family mediation literature base, Irving and Benjamin (1995) summarize the recent tidal wave of information to find the features within each particular sociocultural, ethnic, or racial group that most relate to this issue of family identity and patterns that can be cross-compared. They list six such factors that should be taken into consideration when analyzing, understanding, or working with a family's identity. Together, these factors form a pattern of interaction that can be observed and handled across families of different cultural backgrounds. Irving and Benjamin (1995) indicate issues and concerns to discuss and potential discrepancies with the mediator's model and process:

- Modal social class, based on education and income level. This affects the family's resources and opportunities for basic needs and aspirational wants.

- Definition of the family, based on the cultural expectations of who is in and who is out of the socially constructed family expectations.

- Life cycle, based on the stage of development that the family as a whole is experiencing, such as "newly formed couple," or the phase of development of the individuals, such as "young adult." This designation influences and sets the expectations for the behavior of each participant in the different stages.

- Marital relations, based on the cultural expectations of how husband and wife can and should relate, and the acceptable range of variation, regarding their power and decision-making dimensions, the relationship of the marriage to the parent-child responsibilities, and the requirement for commitment to each other under circumstances such as problems and other affiliations.

- Parent-child relations, based on the level of autonomy and deference required between parents and their children, the basic system as democratic or despotic, and the gender differentiation of authority, obedience, and duty.

- Perspectives on treatment, based on how culturally consistent it is to have the mediator function as expert, decision maker, helper, or analyst and how open the family should and can be regarding the full dimensions of the problem or its solution.

Missing from this schema are other important cultural factors that a family mediator may want to ask about or understand for the family they are working with—for example,

- The relationship to time orientation, where certain cultures have different understandings of the meaning of timeliness and duration of a problem. Does their lateness for an appointment mean a lack of interest, or is it an expression of their culture, where things happen as they do and being late is acceptable?

- The urge for social or economic mobility, which can lead to stronger bargaining, hardened positions, or a refusal to consider options. Are the participants bargaining from hopes to gain or not to fall back in economic class?

- Hierarchy within the family, both between the generations and interpersonally within the generations. Is the paternal grandmother the real head of the family, or is it the father or the mother who must be listened to and obeyed?

- Common emotional and psychological states, which are not personal pathology but culturally acceptable and predictable behavior and feelings. For example, in Mexican families, those who believe they have been touched by a folk illness such as the evil eye may exhibit symptoms that could appear to be a diagnosable mental health condition to those from a Western medical model of mental health.

- Language capacity—that is, their ability to understand the social and interpersonal discussion and context of mediation efforts with nuances of meaning that convey more than the basics. This is one of the issues in having an interpreter.

- Culturally consistent responses to stress—that is, what people are allowed or expected to do in their culture when experiencing distress. Some cultures have elaborate grief patterns that mimic mental breakdown.

- Communication patterns or requirements, such as directness, the use of intermediaries, the lack of voice, speaking for the entire family unit, or taboo topics within the culture. Asian cultures often have very different communication issues from Western cultures.

- Migration and acculturation issues, or the level at which this process has affected each member of the family. Do they all want to acculturate?

- Dimensions of face, such as typical insults to face, face-saving behaviors, and face-maintenance strategies. This factor is usually associated with high-context cultures.

- Understandings of pain and suffering and mental and emotional illness. In some cultures, stress and problems are more or less manifested as somatic complaints and symptoms; in others, a person who is "crazy" has heightened or lowered status and expectations for his behavior.

- The relationship to problems and self-efficacy, such as beliefs that make certain conditions intolerable or unchangeable by people because they believe it was willed by God and therefore unchangeable.

Taylor and Sanchez (1991) point out that understanding a particular family's culture requires the mediator to understand the dominant cultural themes and values of the ethnic culture from which they came, so that the family and the mediator can understand how close the particular family remains to the expectation of that theme. The task of the culturally conversant family mediator is to understand some of the dominant themes in order to ask the right questions of the particular family.

Cultural Entitlement Beliefs

Winslade and Monk (2000) speak extensively about the personal, family, and societal expectations that people can hold for each other and their family mediators based on their concept of personal or social entitlement. Within each culture they inhabit, a person may experience more or less entitlement, based on race, gender, age, sexual orientation, disability, class and affluence, and religious affiliation. In this way, a teenage bisexual boy may be disenfranchised and have little sense of entitlement within his family of origin or the larger social community, but may have a large sense of entitlement and voice within his particular criminally oriented peer group in his school. Winslade and Monk speak directly to the need for mediators in family mediation cases not to fall into the trap of maintaining the patriarchal gender-based entitlement system, or the age or racial entitlement systems, even if they may be reflective of the traditional or common relationship pattern. They caution mediators to be careful to allow all participants their own level of empowerment to ensure truly open discussion without automatic cultural assumptions.

Naming these factors of cultural awareness and competency means that family mediators have to ask themselves some important questions about their starting assumptions about people, their problems, and the processes that they are offering. Are minority families such as African American, Orthodox Jewish, Mexican, or Salvadoran families so very different that mediators should adapt the process or the expectations for them? Are there certain issues that seem to be of concern more often in cases where the participants are newly assimilated or not yet part of the dominant media-induced culture? Are cultural awareness and sensitivity sufficient, or should family mediators who are not of the same cultural identity consider referring the case to someone who is of the same gender or racial, ethnic, social, or cultural background? Is that even possible, given the need for mediation services, the number of cases, and the paucity of mediators from different backgrounds?

Cultural Differences in Interactional Patterns

Two concerns are whether nonmembers of an ethnic or cultural group can effectively understand and work with those of another ethnic or cultural group and whether they bring their own ethnocentric ideas and practices into play, preventing genuine communication. In order to measure this, studies would have to look at least at the levels of the following factors for each group.

- Confrontation
- Emotional expression
- Public versus private behavior
- Self-disclosure
- Conflict approach or avoidance

Using these categories, Asian, Hispanic and Latino, and African cultures could be said to be on one end of each continuum, and current American culture, influenced greatly by European cultures, would be on the other end.

Recent research by Goldstein (1998) developing and using those categories in studying a community mediation center has indicated that there were not significant differences in outcome in mediation cases in which an Asian American mediator rather than a European American mediator was used. Goldstein's conclusion points to the fact that the culture of the mediation process is itself a microculture into which practitioners subsume their other cultural affiliations. The model or type of mediation process used may be a far more determining factor than the practitioner's personal and primary cultural affiliation and background. The logical conclusion we can draw from this is that if mediators have adaptations within their models and methods that allow them to be more responsive and match the cultural expectations and rules of the clients, then it should not prevent them from practicing effectively if they are not of the same ethnic, racial, or cultural background as the clients. We can mediate with others unlike ourslves.

The task of the family mediator regarding culture is to determine in exactly what way the multiple cultures of the people involved are affecting their view of the dispute, the possibilities for problem solving and transformation, and the choices and changes they may make. Family mediators need not be specialists in diversity issues, but they should have undergone extensive enough diversity training to create the habit of wondering, if not fully knowing, about cultures. The more that mediators listen to their clients and ask questions, the more that they can be open to holding the hard discussions about diversity issues as part of the mediation effort. By suspending their own paradigms and processes, mediators can be more open to the ways of knowing and being that are part of the people they are attempting to help.

This chapter is a start toward acknowledgment that culture in its broadest sense is what is in conflict in family mediation cases. It is a brief step toward what should be the wise family mediator's lifelong path of self-exploration and self-education about diversity, identity, and cultural aspects of society.

IDENTITY, ADAPTATION, AND ASSIMILATION

Self-identity is created in families, and identity of families is created in larger groups, such as neighborhoods, cities and regions, nations, and time periods. When a family has moved recently or even generations ago, that sense of identity of self and family can be altered. The family that has moved, immigrated, or emigrated has found itself in a different context and terrain, and even when this has happened as a choice, it can have effects on the reactions of the family members. When an entire family uproots and moves to a new country or a new situation, not all members of the family assimilate at the same rate. One of the most important things to find out from families that have migrated is what level of acceptance they feel they have toward and from the dominant culture.

Children who arrive at a new country or language or culture before the age of twelve can usually assimilate faster and more easily than those who came after that age. Fluency for those age twelve and under is likely, and true biculturalism is usually higher, since there is a desire to fit into the new culture and be accepted. Older adults, who often have fewer socializing contacts with others and institutions such as schools, often grieve the loss of a way of life, their former status, and their vital social support system, and they often attempt to re-create something similar in the new place. This juxtaposition between the young pursuing the new culture and the older members trying desperately to preserve the old ways can lead to increased tension and intrafamily generational conflicts. Within one generation, the original language spoken in the home may change to the new, leaving the older members even further isolated.

When a family has migrated to escape a trauma, such as war, famine, political strife, religious persecution, or natural disaster, the family itself as a system and many, if not all, of the members may still be in shock, mourning, and grief, with the additional burden of recovery this brings. In migrant or migrated families, it is important to find out how resilient each member is and whether there is a need for additional referral to other services. Helping systems are often hard to understand and interpret, and the family often uses its youngest or most fluent members to find resources. This can place a terrible burden on the younger members, who become the interpreters, resource scouts, and brokers between the family and the outside systems.

Misunderstanding the Basis for Dispute

Families that are culturally different may find that they are involved in conflicts that they do not understand. Sometimes these are created when the family tries to maintain solidarity against the rules or mores of the new culture or institutions. These become classic identity conflicts, the struggle of "us against them," and while it may be perceived that way, the task of the family mediator engaged in helping the family and the institutions is to find ways to move beyond the us-versus-them mentality to a more cooperative stance.

Identity-Based Conflicts in Families

Families that feel embattled against larger systems can demonstrate the characteristics of what have been called identity-based conflicts, with multidimensional psychological and historical issues that perpetuate the us-versus-them mentality. Rothman (1997) has worked with identity-based conflicts in organizations and larger social groups, where factions can keep identity-based issues as intractable problems. He describes identity-based conflicts as essentially different from resource-related problems and interest-based conflicts; identity-based conflicts usually have interest or resource issues, but the reverse is not always true. "Conflicts that start primarily as interest-based, when ignored or poorly handled may evolve into identity conflicts; the longer a conflict continues, the more people connect their dignity and prestige with the dispute. Conversely, identity conflicts addressed as if they were primarily about resources may grow from bad to worse" (pp. 11–12).

This process of evolution of perspective can also happen in families where the culture of the family seems opposed to the culture of the larger world that the family members encounter. The parent-teen dispute then becomes not just a conflict about how the parent and teenager relate but about the culturally determined dignity and prestige of the parent as a person worthy of respect despite the lower status of immigrant or corresponding lowered social standing than in the former country or area. The identified conflict between a family member and an outside entity can become the focal point for internal and intergenerational conflicts about fears of assimilation and loss.

Assessment of Cultural Transition

Landau (1982) identified some of the factors that a helper working with families in cultural transition needs to ask about and understand from the family members' perspectives:

- The reason for the migration, which can affect the dissonance between expectation and reality
- The availability of support systems within the new community
- The stage and structure and healthiness or dysfunctionality of the migrating family
- The degree of harmony between the former and the new social culture
- The adjustment potential and rate for each family member

Landau recommends a complete mapping of the generational family in the light of the transition and the provision of services that will train selected members of the family to function as the link, the coach, or the therapist for the others. The link person becomes the one who interprets the problems based on an understanding of the old and new cultures and helps interpret the new demands in culturally consistent ways. In a similar way, Taylor and Sanchez (1991) recommend finding a bicultural or culturally acceptable person (such as the priest or the godparent in Hispanic families) to become the co-mediator of the case, lending their credibility and understanding to the process. This is one simple adaptation that family mediators can do without extensive structural change of their service delivery. Lee (1982) also recommends for Chinese families finding interpreters or helpers who understand the particular strains of immigration and acculturation, are familiar with the services needed, and do not create hierarchical problems or loss of face by being inappropriate due to closeness, age, or gender.

When there have been recent transitions in culture, inclusion of new members in the family, or changes in location and family structure due to immigration, it is important to review all the factors of culture listed at the start of this chapter. The mediator should help the family members develop and voice their own understanding of the usual dimensions of what a healthy, functioning family would be like in the former culture and the new culture to determine the discrepancies, rather than have the family mediator's cultural view determine this. Finding out what is considered "good enough" means that the family must define that condition based on past and current realities and cultural norms.

Family mediators who are attempting to work with families who have experienced such disruptions need to be able to separate out the practical and resource-based issues from the cultural dilemmas for the family and provide mediation in a setting and using a method that will be respectful and interested in preserving the most important concepts and ways for the family. Immigration is a continuing large phenomenon in the border states with Mexico and along the West Coast, but also affects mediators in other areas of the country where minority ethnic populations have settled in order to secure jobs, such as the industrial Midwest and the Eastern seaboard. Family mediators everywhere must be ready to deal with the issues of immigration, acculturation, and cultural difference.

Mixed Cultures Within a Family Unit

Another area for further exploration is in culturally mixed marriages and families, where the basic assumptions of marriage, family, children, and change are not always the same. Bicultural families experience the same culture shock, discrimination, and alienation as do those who migrate or immigrate permanently, and they need to develop a new blended family identity and culture. They can have as many or more contradictory beliefs and be in denial that there are differences between them that stem from cultural issues. In family mediation, this can put the least acculturated member of the family at an automatic disadvantage unless the mediator acknowledges the issue and tries to start from the need of the family to determine the new family understandings.

I worked with a family where the mother was of lower socioeconomic white culture and the father was a recent immigrant from Mexico. He was from a middle- to upper-class family, but his lack of knowledge of English limited his job options. Although the father was a hard worker, the mother had major negative stereotypes about all Mexicans. The father was upset that she would not tend the child and expected him to do tasks like changing diapers, which was not culturally consistent for him; he had been raised with maids and a strong separation between women's and men's tasks. The custodial dispute was not just gender, not just class, and not just miscommunication. They had very different assumptions about the role and meaning of parenthood from their own culture of origin and were having constant disputes in their mixed cultural family.

THE MEDIATOR'S CULTURAL PERSPECTIVES

Perhaps the best way for mediators to approach the topic of culture and identity as it relates to family mediation efforts is to realize the limits of their own information and comfort with other cultures and minority populations and to ask themselves and clients the following questions:

- In what way do the clients identify with their ostensible minority community or culture, and how do they describe and see themselves culturally?

- Do they believe themselves to be bicultural, able to navigate in the mainstream and their heritage or alternative culture at the same time?

- What is their usual personal response to conflict, and do they see this shaped by their culture? Might someone else misinterpret their response?

- In what way is their culture influencing their perception of the conflict?

- How do they culturally perceive the role of the mediator and the mediation effort? Are there automatic barriers or concerns due to cultural differences, and do they believe that these can be surmounted?

- Do any of the basic premises of mediation (equality in the room; fairness and neutrality; self-determination; and problem-solving, transformation, or narrative approaches) seem foreign or imposed by the mediator rather than something that the client wants and understands?

- How much do the clients really trust the mediator and the process? Are they just complying with a requirement?

- Are there any special cultural themes (such as saving face, maintaining correctness, or being self-reliant) that are imperative to preserve as part of the mediation effort?

- Are there some assumptions or ways of mediation that they cannot and will not tolerate? What adaptations do they express that they need?

- Do they need someone with more understanding or a more nuanced perception of their culture to be present or involved periodically in some way in order to create optimal conditions and to be able to express themselves fully?

- How will they describe this experience to other members of their culture? Would they recommend mediation to others?

When family mediators ask themselves and their clients these questions and respond appropriately to the answers, they are doing the best they can to be culturally sensitive and responsive, a positive goal for a family mediator. As mediators build understanding of and adaptations for special populations with whom they work and these become known and standardized, the field will be more culturally competent.

AFRICAN AMERICAN FAMILIES IN MEDIATION

African Americans are underrepresented as practitioners in the field of family mediation, in the evolving literature in the ADR world, and as participants in family mediation, although they are disproportionately involved in the criminal justice system. There are complex social reasons for this fact. Hairston (1999) points out that although there is an awakening in our literature and professional societies that has promoted more cultural awareness and differentiation in the provision of family mediation, there have been few, if any, articles in journals that reflect the specific differences and needs of this population. The invisibility of this population even as smaller minority groups are highlighted, Hairston notes, indicates the way in which vast cultural forces marginalize and maintain this population as part of the underclass.

While not underestimating this reality, there is an alternative way of viewing this situation. Because of the historical forces of slavery, emancipation, and institutionalized barriers to the means of social elevation (such as capital, education, and social support), African Americans and other people who identify with black American culture have created very different social and familial systems to deal with problems and conflicts. They tend not to seek out professional services of any kind, preferring to handle issues and concerns within their own circle of family, friends, and friendly institutions such as churches. Because the social conventions and culture of family are different, legal and quasi-legal services like mediation are often suspect or unneeded. If a family has formed and lived together without the legal intervention of the state-imposed rules of a license to marry, it often reformulates internally without officially granted permission from a court or intervention by a mediator to part company and find appropriate care for children. Mediation services are redundant and extraneous if the family is taking care of itself within its own culturally acceptable guidelines of fairness and expectation.

Another reason this population is underrepresented and sometimes resistant to family mediation efforts is that it is embedded in systems and services that are devised by and run by the dominant white culture and therefore perceived as potentially discriminatory and intrusive. "The intake process may increase suspicion and resistance because African Americans generally place high value on privacy, because it is one of the few societal assets over which they have control" (Hairston, 1999, pp. 364–365). Hairston believes that court-ordered mediation services that do not seem to meet a felt need for services on the part of the family serve to reinforce the perception of interference and the negative power-over stance of the dominant culture toward the black family and its members. From personal and community experiences, the members of black families of lower socioeconomic level may experience the mediation effort of helping the family as one more of a series of demeaning, biased forms of discrimination against them personally and their culture.

Hairston points out that many models of mediation are not culturally consistent for African American families. Mediation requires sitting around a table in an unfamiliar setting, having their dialogue controlled and censored, and with an unrealistic expectation of creating rapport and trust between the family and the representative of the oppressive social system. This still echoes the oppressive paradigm. It is very easy to see that mediation is white America's process, on white Americans' terms, and imposed on African Americans rather than allowed or offered. This is the "white box" experience that Taylor and Sanchez (1991) describe as limiting and inhibiting to truly culturally sensitive and well-designed mediation services for many minority populations. The way in which family mediation is triggered and provided and the expectations for behavior of the participants are out of sync with the cultural imperatives of this population.

Similarly, Irving and Benjamin (1995) indicate that their review of the literature shows a very different family system structure for African American and Caribbean black families in Canada than that found in many white families.

As generalities, they found that African American families are more often in working-class or lower economic levels; try to maintain multigenerational, inclusive, informal kinship systems; tend to be mother centered with role flexibility between the husband and wife or unmarried partners; and have authoritarian parenting styles that allow and support physical punishment. Given the high level of teenage pregnancy, incarceration of males and absentee fathers, solo working mothers reliant on child care, substance abuse, poverty, domestic violence, random violence, lack of safety in poorer neighborhoods, and other social problems, the measures of a good-enough family structure may need to be different for this population.

Pinderhughes (1982) points to the adaptability of the African American family structure as its strength, given the victimization and oppression they have encountered historically and currently. Like all other family systems, the African American family needs to provide enough but not too much structure, nurturing, and stimulation for their members. Like all other families, the more the African American family is isolated from support systems by geography, lack of resources, or other factors, the more stress the family experiences. Because the African American family has usually looked to resources within itself for financial, emotional, and parenting support, full assessment of informal friends and supports becomes crucial when evaluating options.

These issues are the same for families of any race or ethnicity, so trying to understand which issues are primarily class and economic, compared to which ones are unique to the racial and ethnic makeup of the family, is difficult. When members of this group become part of the upwardly mobile corporate culture that demands huge time commitments and geographical relocations, they have lost access to the extended kinship system and therefore some of what has historically helped African American families cope.

Middle-class black American families tend to be structured and act much more like other middle-class American families of any and every racial and ethnic background, because they have subsumed their unique racial and ethnic identity into the class cultural expectation. Family mediators still need to understand the barriers and opportunities for each family they work with without making false racially stereotyping assumptions.

Power Dynamics and Emotional Expression

In my practice, I have noticed some differences in the interactional dynamics of black families in mediation compared to families of the dominant culture: two are a heightened resistance to mediation initially and a difference in how power is manifested within couples and families and also with the mediator. Many black family members seem to have learned a dominant-subordinate, power-over paradigm and accepted it as normative within families rather than holding a belief in a power-with paradigm of equality. Family members expect to be either the one telling others what to do or the one being told what to do, and this attitude toward power limits their initial response to mediation, where no one is the boss. This power dynamic may cause mediation to become part of the power struggle between family members; it may cause the family to opt out of mediation in false compliance; or it may cause overt noncompliance on the part of the family. In the mediation session, a mediator may experience a process parallel to the dynamics within the family, where someone is placed in the role of boss and the only options are to resist or comply, or the passive-aggressive stance of seeming compliance but no follow-through. African American men tend to show response patterns of accommodation and avoidance, quick compromise, or outright competition, depending on their socialization in different parts of the country, at different time periods, and the level of threat and violence within their family and community. Since each of these response patterns is learned and based on survival strategies that work better given certain life circumstances, younger black men seem to have a different response pattern than older black men. The mediator may be able to determine the client's response pattern from information received without a formal assessment tool like the Thomas-Kilmann test. The response to power and conflict may determine the family member's response to the mediation effort, especially if the mediator is a member of the dominant culture.

Another difference in working with African American families is the level and style of expression of emotionality between the participants. Frequency and intensity of feeling and its expression are culturally consistent, whereas they are often not part of the culture of mediation the practitioner has learned, especially if the mediator practices from a procedural or problem-solving model. Mediators who sit passively in their chair and never raise their voice because they are following the politeness rules of the dominant white culture and the mediation model they were taught may find that they have lost the respect and cooperation of the African American client, who needs to see responsiveness, power, and control in order to respect and trust the mediator.

Similarly, family mediators who try to control the conversation too tightly, use professional language, or insist on requiring their clients to speak without profanity or in stilted "I statements" will lose the reality of the interaction by overcontrolling it. If they require the African American client to do it their way rather than understanding and allowing a more realistic and natural expression by the client, they will lose rapport and cooperation.

Understanding and allowing people their own unique language and style is respectful and necessary in order to understand them. Family mediators can and must draw the line at intimidation, threat, and fear in the room, no matter who is the client. Mediators who are not used to black American colloquial speech and nonverbal communication may need to find members of the community to act as social interpreters. When working with a family situation where the culture is truly different, it is always wise to hire someone who understands it. A family mediator who is not familiar with the usual language and culture of African American clients should consider having a co-mediator available who is bicultural or at least knowledgeable about the issues in the African American community.

The higher the socioeconomic aspirations and actualities of the family are, the fewer adaptations the family mediator needs to make since there is closer conformity to the social conventions of the dominant culture. The lower economically the family is, the more the reality-based problems of scarce resources, hardened rage, and powerlessness and incapacity dominate the discussion and become the context and content of the discussion.

Black Fatherhood

Black identity is a socially learned combination of self and social expectations and role models or culturally acceptable roles or images, as is any racial or ethnic identity. Cross and Fhagen-Smith (1996) discuss the development of black racial identity patterns as a dynamically changing set of choices made over the life span. Black childhood and fatherhood has often been complicated by inadequate or absent role models and lack of financial capacity, so those who have an interest in being active and involved fathers may need help to develop their capacity in ways that are not demeaning (Hutchinson, 1992).

The standard suggestions or options for solving family disputes by referring out to parenting classes or therapy may not work for black fathers because of cultural dynamics. Changing deep beliefs may be necessary for the family in order to prevent conflict. Redefining or reconfirming the importance of the role of the father may be necessary, as it is with families from other cultural groups. Attaching the struggling family to a healthier role model father or family within the community may provide a more culturally consistent support than suggesting or requiring parenting classes or therapy.

Biracial Couples

Partners in mixed or biracial couples often do not have a unified view of the expectations they have of each other and can often misinterpret the culturally appropriate behavior of one partner as abusive or neglectful from their own cultural perspectives. Like all other couples or families that incorporate two very different cultures, there are usually tensions that are culturally created, and it is very easy for the couple or family members to mistakenly attribute cultural issues to the personality or character of the other in negative ways. These are areas that a family mediator might explore prior to any standard problem-solving approach or before assuming a need for personal transformation. Recognition and empowerment of the cultural as well as personal issues help everyone deal differently with the disputes and the differences of perception.

Reflecting on African American Families

There is so little research or specific information about the unique qualities of African American families in family mediation cases that to say more than this seems to be overreaching. There is a thick and rich body of literature in the counseling and therapy fields about African American families that family mediators should review. Mediators can continue to integrate the information available from other reputable fields such as therapy and social work, and they should more adequately assess the methods and impact of family mediation with members of the African American community themselves to develop more culturally sensitive and appropriate models, methods, and services.

A culturally sensitive family mediator might want to reflect on the following questions before, during, and after a mediation with a family that has African American members.

- What are my cultural myths about and relationship to members of this community? How much do I really know about current realities of this culture?

- Due to differences in nonverbal interaction, time differences, and style, do I think that I can relate to these clients as well as I do to others? What are my feelings and thoughts when I notice differences?

- Are there structural barriers to this family's using my mediation services?

- Is this family more a part of the mainstream middle class, or do its members identify more with their cultural heritage? Are they carrying a lot of concern about my ability to relate to them or my position within the dominant power structure?

- Am I treating this case differently because of their identity, their family structure and values, or other cultural issues? Should I do so? If so, how? With whom can I consult to discuss this issue?

Case Example: Hairbrushes and Grandmothers

In a custody case between unmarried parents, the father was a young white man about to be married to his white fiancée, while the mother was black, attending college, and working part-time while taking care of the two-year-old who was the source of the controversy. Dad's parents had never accepted the grandchild as theirs and felt that the mother had tried to entrap the young man with the pregnancy, while the mother's side of the family saw the father as irresponsible and uncaring, but readily accepted the two-year-old into their family.

Miscommunications happened that led the father to accuse the mother of abusing the child, but all turned out to be false and based on cultural differences in child-rearing practices. Mother used a hairbrush to make the child sit still while doing her hair in cornrows, a long and uncomfortable process for the squirmy child, who had told her father that her mother had hit her. The mother was hurt by the allegations but found it hard to tell him that her mother had done her hair the same way.

Moreover, to the father, the care of the child by the grandmother instead of the mother seemed negligent, while to the mother, the grandparental care of her child was well within and even better than her own childhood experience. Racially carried but socially learned differences in expectations about child care fueled this conflict, but it was difficult to discuss until the mediator brought up the topic, which allowed the parents to discuss their cultural assumptions openly.

HISPANIC CULTURAL THEMES

The first cultural awareness that is necessary for working with this population is to realize that the culture and experience of Spanish-speaking people is not a unitary one. The terms *Hispanic* and *Latino* are therefore meaningless labels without a further understanding of the ethnic and national history and the family's unique story of their background and acculturation:

> The experience of a person from El Salvador who has come to this country seeking political asylum is vastly different from the migrant farm worker from Mexico or the person from Puerto Rico or Cuba, or the person from a Spanish family which migrated to this country in the 1880s, yet all are linked by the variations of Spanish language, just as Americans, from the Bronx to New Orleans to Los Angeles, all ostensibly speak the same language. Cultural diversity within this minority population makes it as hard to speak with any authority about "all Hispanics" as it is to speak about "all Whites." [Taylor and Sanchez, 1991, p. 118]

Because of the colonization and imposition of the Spanish dominant culture and religion onto indigenous people, there are many similarities among Hispanic and Latino families that are based on that culture. However, the indigenous people had their own culture and religion, parts of which remain a blend of cultures for many families. Migrant families from Mexico may have been from those indigenous Indian cultures and are illiterate in Spanish as well as English. Problems ensue if the mediator does not ask enough questions about or makes assumptions about the language spoken at home, the level of literacy and fluency in the assumed language, the class level in the country of origin, and the level of acculturation. "Unless we have a true understanding of the cultural background and worldview of the participants, as well as the realities they face, we will be ineffective in creating outcomes that are culturally consistent and able to withstand the economic and social pressures that will be placed on them" (Taylor and Sanchez, 1991, p. 119).

The Latino and Hispanic culture tends to be far more high context than mainstream contemporary American culture, and so the values of cooperation, sharing, deference to age, authority, and wisdom from the past are strong. Dominant cultural themes among traditional and less acculturated Latino and Hispanic families are a relaxed time awareness, loyalty bonds to the family under all circumstances, inclusivity of the family, and the need to preserve honor and loyalty by correct behavior.

Several cultural themes seem to emerge from the literature and experience with families from this culture. First, the family is defined very openly and laterally, with grandparents as high authority and godparents as active parts of the extended family. Parental authority is extremely valued, and adults belong to and relate to their families of origin. Elderly and ill members are taken care of by the family rather than using external resources. Family rituals and celebrations, often centered on Catholic beliefs such as baptism, confirmation, the *Quinceñera* celebration or coming-out party for fifteen-year-old girls, and marriage, require the active involvement of the godparents, who have a special relationship of trust and responsibility to the family and the godchild (Eason, 1998). It is not at all unusual for family members to have to leave jobs, partners, and their current family obligations in order to return to the original family area for such family celebrations and duties, even when such leaving will bring negative consequences.

Respect, Warmth, and Indirectness

The concept of respect (*respeto*) of all people is magnified when looking at the elderly or those who are in hierarchically higher positions. Another cultural feature is the concept of personal warmth and knowledge (*personalismo*), which requires sharing some personal uniqueness or sense of individuality and inner emotional quality in order to understand, trust, and cooperate with someone. Hispanic and Latino clients need transparency and a sense of joining and acceptance in order to understand the people with whom they are dealing before they feel ready to share. Professional degrees or the professional style expected in white culture, without personal and genuine warmth and caring, will not suffice. Hispanic and Latino clients would first want to hear about the mediator's family and activities in order to get this personal warmth and rapport, rather than jump into the usual procedures or problem solving.

The value of politeness and congeniality *(simpatia)* means avoiding direct confrontation, aggressiveness or harsh assertiveness, and anything that could be construed as criticism. "The cultural script also requires that the Hispanic listener appear to agree with a message even though he/she has no intention of following the advice or did not understand it" (Eason, 1998, p. 36). This is supported by two other cultural themes: control of aggressive and sexual impulses (*controlarse)* and the need for avoidance and indirect mechanisms to heal problems *(indirectas)*, which allows other parties to intervene (Irving, Benjamin, and San-Pedro, 1999).

Because Latinos may have their pride and dignity harmed but must not show lack of control, they often will not directly challenge or contradict the speaker. False agreements and incomplete change may be likely unless the agreements in mediation truly come from the parties themselves rather than from the mediator. This culturally supported avoidance of conflict may make it difficult to have parties generate their own options or assert themselves or contradict each other in the negotiation phase of mediation. Mediators may need to use more individual sessions or intermediation techniques to avoid the direct confrontations that are culturally unacceptable. Family mediators may need to observe and perhaps change their ways of relating and style to respond to the cultural expectations and needs in order to build the working relationship that will foster good mediation efforts.

Irving and Benjamin (1995) point to another difference with this population: the changes in the typical life cycle. Children have an extended childhood but shortened adolescence, a prolonged courtship with a brief couple stage, an elongated middle age, and a shortened old age. Boys are expected to show their manhood and virility by sexual conquests and staying tough with their male friends *(machismo)*, and girls are expected to show modesty and submissiveness and maintain their virginity *(marianismo)*, leading to a double standard and gender inequality. Because early childbearing is acceptable and educational expectations for girls are usually lower than for boys and because marriage and family for young people are expected, this population has difficulty in pursuing higher education and employment advancements in the mainstream American culture.

The husband-wife dynamic tends to be more authoritarian, with the man being dominant and the wife subordinate in more traditional, less acculturated families. As they become part of mainstream American culture, Latina women push for more gender equality and hold more liberal ideas, including considering divorce under some circumstances. Division of labor in traditional Hispanic and Latino households is clearly along gender lines, yet the reality of modern economic life is that it takes two salaries to maintain a family, and many Latinas must balance their traditional family responsibilities with a new economic one. Because so many Hispanic and Latino families are in the working-class or lower economic rungs, the realities of life are hard. Those in this population often bring problems of poverty, economic scarcity, and discrimination as the backdrop to their problems.

In traditional Hispanic and Latino families, parent-child relationships are also different. Children clearly must obey their parents, and parents do not try to become friends or equals. Mothers are supposed to be self-sacrificing, and children often are nurtured in ways that would seem overly involved or even enmeshed in other cultures. Because strict gender differentiation is a strong cultural priority, children often completely rebel against the oppressive rules. Parents, especially fathers, become stuck in rigid positions with little room to move, while mothers can become intercessors and form coalitions and alliances to enable children to get around the father's rule setting. In such family situations, it is important to find a face-saving way for the father to stay in control as the head of the family while working for reasonable changes that will be more tolerable for the more Americanized child.

One important pattern is when the family, or more often the man, is a migrant worker who is gone for long periods of time and sends money home to his multiple dependents. Because the culture is so involved in the extended family, being away from wife, mother, and family can be extremely hard on the man, who not only has the rigors of hard, dirty, and dangerous work, but few of the basic comforts that family contacts bring. Loneliness brings a great risk to the man that he may fall into snares of alcohol and drug abuse, crime, and sexual and physical abuse by others. If the man brings his family along, they are subjected to often overwhelming issues of unmet needs, health and environmental concerns, lack of stability, and loss of the support system of the extended family. Isolation can lead to families that break apart without benefit of support services.

After a Hispanic or Latino man has risked border problems and trauma, found employment, brought the family to a location or found a partner to start a family with, and established residence in a place, the issues of discrimination and assimilation become important in understanding the context of the family and the conflicts they are experiencing. Although Hispanic and Latino populations are the fastest-increasing populations in the United States today, they represent a very small percentage of those receiving family mediation services, because of barriers such as night work or nonstandard work hours, lack of child care, and unwelcoming attitudes in the community. Along with these barriers come concerns about immigration status and work permits. Fear that they might jeopardize their economic or legal situation and general misunderstanding of the alternative dispute resolution and standard legal system can stop these families from accessing services, even when the barriers are reduced.

Adaptations for Mediating with Hispanic Families

Recent research from a court-connected mediation program that surveyed forty programs nationwide tried to find the answers to whether there were particular methods that family mediators were using with or would recommend for Latino and Hispanic families (Gooden and Galvan, 1998). They reported the following results:

- *Administrative and policy:* Translate all documents used, hire bilingual and bicultural mediators and staff, hire interpreters, build extra time into the sessions, use co-mediators, and research the local population to understand them.

- *Premediation strategies:* Hold an orientation with information about children and domestic violence issues, use formal language constructions, and start sessions with a brief conversation off the topic (*platica*) to establish trust and comfort.

- *During mediation:* Meet with participants separately and allow feelings to emerge, emphasize connection and rapport, learn levels of vulnerability, assess acculturation, acknowledge differences between the mediator and client cultures, uphold the primary value of respect, interview children only after getting permission, use liberal amounts of storytelling, and caucus and use outside support services, such as the church or the godparents.

Taylor and Sanchez (1991) recommended outreach to this population by finding appropriate people within the Hispanic and Latino community to train as informal or co-mediators. Training priests and other spiritual leaders, elders of the community, and godparents as informal community-based mediators or as go-betweens and bringing in entire extended families when there is a family-related dispute can serve these families better than the standard model of mediation, which requires a professional atmosphere of confidentiality and only the biological parents in the room.

Irving, Benjamin, and San-Pedro (1999) suggest that practicing mediation in a more culturally acceptable way, with personal involvement and warmth, patience and a slower and more tolerant pace, a more accepting atmosphere, the offer of home-based programs, and respect for the values of the culture will help mediators work better with this population. More extensive assessment of the kinship, residence, and history of the family may be needed to understand their concerns and fears. Having acceptable helpers who have bilingual and bicultural capacity, with firsthand knowledge of the nonverbal communication and the resources available, will help. Understanding the family mediator's assumptions and biases will always be a first step. The second might be to cultivate friends and develop information about the specific Hispanic and Latino community needs and resources in the mediator's area.

The wise family mediator may want to reflect on these questions while working with a family of Hispanic or Latino background.

- How familiar am I with the Hispanic and Latino community? How comfortable am I in working with this case? What are my concerns?

- How might the members of this community perceive me based on my gender, age, background, professionalism, and style?

- Do my mediation services have built-in structural barriers to this family, such as lack of access to public transportation, no child care, or daytime hours only?

- Would I feel comfortable having an interpreter? Can I get one, or should they bring someone? Could that person maintain necessary social boundaries?

- Am I treating this case differently because of their level of acculturation, their family structure and values, or other cultural issues? Should I? If so, how? With whom can I consult to discuss this?

Case Example: A Wedding in Mexico

Francisco had come across the border with his eldest brother when he was sixteen to find a better life and to earn money to send to their struggling large family. When he first arrived in Oregon he stayed illegally with others from his town in a migrant camp. One night he met a woman, Valerie, at a bar. He was shy, but she encouraged him to become her lover, and soon she was pregnant. Francisco was appalled and delighted, but he could not afford to set up the kind of household she and the baby deserved, even though he and his brother had moved out of the camp and into a shabby, small house. If they had been in Mexico, the young couple would have lived in Francisco's mother's home. Francisco was smart and diligent, and he had realized that he needed to get his citizenship and an education in order to progress. He also realized that his increasing bilingual fluency was a job asset. He had determined that he would study to become a medical practitioner of some sort. He offered to have Valerie and the baby live with his brother and him in their house, but she declined and said she wanted to live with her mother. He wanted to claim the child, and he wrote to his mother about little girl's arrival. Valerie was content to live independently, receive some economic help now and then, and generally act as if he were not the father. Their relationship ended ambiguously but without incident.

Within three years, Francisco had worked his way into legitimate INS status, was taking citizenship classes and local community college courses, and had a good reputation at the local community welcoming center that provided services to new migrant families. The social workers there felt he was a positive influence on other families and were strongly encouraging him to continue his education, helping him find grants and services. His brother had saved enough money to return home to marry the fiancée he had left, and Francisco himself had a new girlfriend, Amy, an Anglo woman with a seven-year-old child from a former marriage, Becky. Amy stood to inherit her parents' land and home, and Francisco was now living with her. Francisco had been caring for his daughter, Angela, every weekend for two and a half years, while Valerie struggled from one job and relationship to another. Angela had a bedroom in the shared home and got along well with Becky and Amy, although Amy felt the child often seemed ravenously hungry and a bit developmentally delayed; Angela was still in diapers at three and a half, and often grunted rather than used words until better communication was required by the weekend family.

Everything was going well enough until Francisco asked Valerie in June for permission to take Angela to his brother's wedding in Mexico, planned for mid-October. Francisco could finally afford the fare, and his mother longed to see the child; since Francisco's mother was experiencing health problems, this was a good opportunity. Valerie stalled and balked for months. When Francisco finally got fed up and demanded an answer in late August so that he could buy the ticket before the rates got too high, Valerie said Angela was not his child, hung up on him, stopped bringing Angela for weekends, and filed a temporary order of custody with the court, alleging that she feared that he would not return the child to her. Francisco was beside himself; not only was he confused and angry about the situation and missing his daughter, but the status quo order made the possibility of attending the wedding with Angela less likely the longer it continued. Francisco was fearful that no matter what he did, he would not be powerful enough to regain ongoing contact with his child. With or without her, he had to attend the wedding as best man; it was assumed by his family that he would be there, and the ticket was already paid for. He did not have the money to pay an attorney to sue for sole custody and fight an extended custody battle that might have to include allegations of neglect. At that point, the conflict was referred to the mediation program within his local church community, where a trained mediator co-mediated with the local priest, who had great credibility with the Hispanic community.

Tracing Valerie was the hardest part of the mediation effort; she was not a member of the faith community, had moved several times, and wouldn't return Francisco's calls, but finally she did talk with the mediator from the community program in a solo phone conversation. From Valerie's perspective, everything looked very different. She was not sure that Francisco was the biological dad, since she had been addicted to drugs and had had other lovers besides him. She was not worried about his care of Angela but had heard horror stories from a friend whose child had never returned to her. Valerie was working part-time, was in drug rehab and on probation, and had gone to the local family court facilitator's office, where she had learned how to file the status quo order. The facilitator's office had recommended mediation, determination of Angela's paternity, and filing of child support obligations if Francisco was proven to be Angela's father. Valerie had balked at pursuing these processes, simply because she couldn't afford further time off work or more emotional hassle. It had been highly inconvenient for her to not have Angela go with her father on the last few weekends, since she didn't have reliable child care and worked some weekend times. Valerie decided that it was a good idea to meet with Francisco in mediation, and she agreed to allow the priest to co-mediate. A mediation session was set up immediately, and at that mediation, which took place at the community center in a very informal, living-room setting, Valerie and Francisco were encouraged to tell each other the difficulties the conflict had made in their lives, and the reaction that Angela had been having to missing Francisco and her other family members. The mediation team encouraged them to show pictures and have pride in the child, and to speak in a very open way, so that it was culturally consistent for Francisco and demonstrated *personalismo* and the values of high-context culture. The first agreement reached was allowing the weekend care by Francisco to resume, because everyone, especially the child, benefited.

The second issue framed by the co-mediation team was Angela's attendance at the wedding. Francisco was able to tell Valerie how excited Angela was to be the youngest child, to be part of the ceremony, and to wear a fancy dress and special shoes, and also that he had no intention of kidnapping Angela or staying in Mexico himself, since his new life in America was so good. He wanted Angela to know her Mexican heritage and at least meet her grandmother, who should have been a bigger part of her life, in his view. Francisco shared that his struggle was to attain a good life for himself and his children, and that even if the paternity test proved he was not Angela's biological father, he wanted to be able to adopt her so that he could continue to take care of her.

Valerie was able to tell of her fears of kidnapping and loss, and how important having her daughter was to her motivation for her own recovery process. She had gone through hard times, but Angela made it all worthwhile, and she was very afraid that if anything happened to Angela, she would also lose her sobriety. She was afraid to acknowledge how little she had been able to do for her daughter so far, for fear that it could be used against her to take the child away from her. She acknowledged that the concern about paternity had been suddenly trumped up to discourage Francisco more than to deal with a mere possibility. She didn't really think there was another father, and she wanted the new start that included her taking better care of Angela, so she needed reassurance that Francisco would not try for sole legal custody or prevent her from taking better care of Angela. Both Valerie and Francisco were able to reassure each other that they wanted to solve the dilemmas socially and amicably, and not involve the legal system that both feared would make the situation worse.

After having the informal talks and receiving heartfelt reassurances against their fears, Francisco and Valerie were able to negotiate an agreement, complete with contact people in Mexico who would assure Valerie of a safe trip and good care. The priest offered to call the local Mexican diocese to explain the circumstances and further ensure the safety and return of Angela when the weeklong festivities were done. Provided with these reassurances, Valerie agreed to the Mexican wedding plans and to modify the status quo order and sign notarized statements to allow Francisco to convey Angela across the border, if Francisco would agree to not file suit for sole legal custody at that time. Francisco wanted agreement that his name would be on Angela's birth certificate, that the issue of paternity would be dropped, and that they would return after the wedding to mediate a more formal parenting plan that would outline the terms of his parenting and potential additional trips to Mexico, so that disputes like this would never happen again. The mediation team reminded Valerie and Francisco of the child support issue, and both acknowledged that they needed to follow the rules and pay according to the formal system.

Angela attended the wedding and returned from the trip, and life continued on a new, more formal ground for both sides of the family. The case demonstrated themes of attending to cultural issues by working through established authority figures such as priests, honoring family obligations, and using informal conflict resolution methods rather than resorting to legal processes.

ASIAN PERSPECTIVES

Americans with Asian heritage are widely diverse, and generalizations about a unitary Asian culture should be taken as they are meant: general descriptors of cultural values and patterns that may be truer if the family is less acculturated or assimilated into mainstream American culture. As Irving and Benjamin (1995) note, included in this overly broad category tend to be those cultures that are now part of nations as widely diverse as China and Taiwan, Japan, and Korea, along with India and Pakistan, the smaller Southeast Asian countries of Indochina (Burma), Vietnam, Thailand, Laos and Cambodia, and the Philippines. Because these countries have had extensive histories involving multiple cultures and ethnicities, occupations or colonization, and the major religions of Buddhism, Shintoism, Confucianism, Hinduism, and animism, this category is so broad as to seem almost meaningless unless looked at in the broadest themes of Eastern culture compared to the more Eurocentric, Judeo-Christian cultures referred to as Western.

The history of immigration of people from these areas to the North American continent has undergone separate waves and cycles, often brought about by economics of cheap labor, war and subsequent guilt and reparations to a few, and the American hegemony. Chinese laborers, like the African slaves before them, were brought to do backbreaking work. They built the transcontinental railway, dams, and other infrastructure of the developing nation at a time when men, not machines, were the needed but expendable source of power. This led to a social condition, not unlike that of current Hispanic and Latino migrant workers, of camps and city clusters of solitary men who sent resources to dependents in the home country. Eventually, when they could afford it, had gathered the necessary permissions, and arranged for the transportation, they sent for their families.

Because of the cultural norm of communal extended family involvement in their primary culture and the language and cultural barriers to integrating into mainstream Western culture, Japanese and Chinese communities formed support groups, economic opportunities, and harmonious interrelations through intermarriage and business association, providing their members opportunities to develop an economic and social system parallel to the mainstream. Over time and acculturation and with the acquisition of language and education, many families have been able to overcome the original stereotyping and prejudice and enter the mainstream of economic and cultural life. In fact, this acculturation has been so rapid within families that many second-, third-, and fourth-generation members have completely lost the former language, creating hardships between generations who cannot directly communicate their cultural expectations.

Cultural Support for Faster Adaptation

The triple factors of language proficiency, business or technological skill, and family values and social environments that promote hard work, education, and achievement are related to the rise of many members of Asian populations. New immigrants, who may lack language proficiency or other skills, often start in the lowest-paid jobs with long hours, and the family adapts to this condition. Because of the informal networks that foster economic opportunity and self-sufficiency that have evolved in Asian communities over the years, recent immigrants from Asia can often proceed up the economic ladder faster than those from other populations.

In recent years, immigrants from these populations have been from educated, upper-economic levels in their home country and have brought an influx of human and economic capital with them. In the high-tech and computer industries, it is not at all uncommon to find a high percentage of the workforce in upper-level jobs from these cultures, particularly East Indian, Japanese, Chinese, and Korean. Because these families have invested a lot in the education process, their economic and social expectations for themselves may be more consistent with mainstream America and the transition much easier.

Traditional Family Structure

In traditional families from these cultures, the structure of the family is hierarchical, and each member owes reciprocal duties to each other that must be honored. Rank and status within the family and between families and others are often more rigid than flexible, and inclusion comes at the price of maintenance of these obligations and responsibilities to maintain status and convention.

These cultures prefer harmony in interaction to open conflict or self-assertion, and they view competition or struggle within families as exceptional, uncomfortable, and problematic.

Diane LaResche (1992) looked at the differences between the standard problem-solving/negotiative style of community-based mediation and the Korean American harmony restoration process and found a very different set of starting assumptions and process dynamics. In the Korean American process, the sequence started by getting an honored and respected person of the community to review with the participants an external standard of appropriate relationships and proper conduct. This foundation then allowed the participants to contemplate and plan, using a go-between who could openly offer solutions, which then created mutual understandings that would meet the overt goal of restoring harmony.

Cultural Themes of Duty, Face, and Obedience

Cultural themes of family honor and shame, duty and obedience, and the authority of elders over others are dominant. Because these values and themes were consonant with the English and European class system and ideals brought and maintained by many of the middle- and upper-level ruling forces in America, and with the current middle-class economic requirements of hard work, deferred gratification, upward mobility, and care of family problems within the family, these populations have found more acceptance than others within the dominant culture.

Although fathers in these cultures can be placed in the role of the strict disciplinarian with the final word, mothers are allowed to show affection openly; children are to show respect and obedience to the adults who surround them and to work on behalf of the family as a whole. In many of these cultures, sons are more highly valued and more highly pushed to achieve; women are meant to be the nurturers of the husband and children and intercessors on their behalf, providing the children their primary attachment figure. After the father, the oldest son becomes the ruler of the family, but this is modified by the role of the devoted mother, whose reward for all her care is to influence the son but indirectly. "The influence of the wife and mother is more covert, through her ability to influence primary male figures, as contrasted to the overt authority influence of males" (Shon and Ja, 1982, p. 212).

Gender and Indirectness

This cultural insistence on indirectness by females may make the process of mediation with more traditional and less acculturated families from these backgrounds much more difficult to ensure fairness and equality for women. This indirect style of influence rather than direct power and the communication style of indirect and ambiguous communication to avoid direct confrontation or disharmony are very different from mainstream American culture, where most women feel empowered to express themselves, make their own choices, and hold independent or interdependent power.

Communication within the Asian system is as much about what is not said as what is said. These cultures also see time as polychronic and issues as multiple and interconnected rather than as separate and unconnected. Many Asian cultures do not require completion of one task before going on to another in a linear, sequential way, as is familiar with mainstream American negotiation and mediation models. To hold Asian families to a rigid time schedule, to push for answers prematurely, or to complete one item as if it were discrete and separate from the others is not culturally consistent. Wong (1995) suggests that a lack of nonverbal communication can be mistaken for lack of interest, when it is more appropriate culturally to allow silence for introspection and consideration of ideas.

Because of the culturally and religiously supported belief in nonaction in Zen Buddhist thought and the teachings of Confucianism and because of the potential problems for creating disharmony and upsetting the thick layer of familial ties and rules by exacerbating a problem or conflict, families from these cultures may tend to minimize, deny, or be inactive in the face of problems that would send other families to help sooner. Divorce, parent-teen problems, and placements of elders away from home might tend to be viewed as bringing shame on the family, and so the culturally consistent response would be to avoid the conflict or accommodate others rather than a more appropriate compromise or open competition or conflict.

Collaboration, because it promotes win-win solutions and harmony, is a preferred process. "Asian conflict negotiation is rooted in traditional norms and values. As a result, a mediator can feel confident that a fair agreement is made, but without examining the degree of cultural influences, may equate passive compliance with affirmative acceptance" (Wong, 1995, p. 118). Family mediators working with this population may need to do more questioning of participants in solo caucus to determine if they are accepting and acquiescing or making an active choice they are willing to put into practice.

Barriers to Services

Asian American clients, like their Hispanic and Latino and black counterparts, can find barriers to accessing mediation services: the hours available, lack of child care, and lack of interpreters or bilingual and bicultural mediators. If they are working in a family business or in a low-paying job with long hours, they may not be able to come during standard court hours. They may have a double dose of difficulty because of their own cultural requirements not to acknowledge problems, not to take problems that could bring shame outside the family, and not to follow any directives other than those given by the elders or designated male within the family. A crucial factor in providing mediation services to any family from this cultural background is to find out what response the elder males have to using mediation. Joining or gaining acceptance of the service with them may make it more likely that mediation will be used.

Also, because families are so used to being told what to do within the family and by others within their neighborhood or community, they are often not used to the role of the mediator as a neutral facilitator and may keep asking questions and expecting the mediator to function as an expert who should tell them what to do. The strict neutral role or the narrative approach, with its insistence on projecting the problem as an external reality, may not fit well with this population; mediators may have to modify their style and stance relative to each person. A younger female mediator may not be able to instill confidence in the family unless her level of professional credentialing is such that she becomes an expert in the eyes of the men as well as the women.

Adaptations for Mediating with Asian Families

Similar recommendations can be made for this hugely diverse cultural grouping: identifying members of the community who are already accorded high stature, respect, and authority may be the best ones to talk to first, even before contacting the primary parties, to find out how the community would view the involvement of the identified disputants. Trying to have recognized high-status intermediaries present, such as the paternal grandfather or grandmother, to act as co-mediators who do the active advice giving that may be required can honor the embedded quality of the conflict within the existing power and hierarchy of the family structure. Wong (1995) suggests the use of premediation sessions to reduce shame, the use of co-mediation teams, and a procedural or more directive, unambiguous process that asserts the mediator's power and authority and formality of process.

A wise family mediator working with a family that belongs to an Asian population may want to reflect on some of these questions:

- How long are the historical roots of this family in Western cultures of any kind, and what is their language capacity? Do I need an interpreter, and do I have access to one who would be acceptable to this family?

- Is this family struggling financially, or are they involved in other immigration or political struggles that created personal or family trauma?

- How much does this family accept the notion of the mediator as a guide rather than as an expert? Do they understand and want the process I will provide?

- Are there additional factors such as my gender that make it harder or easier for some members of this family to talk with me?

- Am I treating this case differently because of the level of acculturation, family structure and values, or other cultural issues? Should I? If so, how? With whom can I consult to discuss this?

Case Example: A Trip to China

This mediation case came to a court-connected domestic relations mediation service. It was presented as a divorce dispute, but it also illustrated the need to reframe the presenting problem in light of cultural dynamics and the hidden conflict involving cultural themes. The couple was middle-aged, and both partners were of Chinese descent. The husband had emigrated from China when he was twelve and had never returned, even when his mother died, because of scarce financial resources and obligations to his business and family in America. The business had grown more lucrative, and the husband's recent health problems were the basis for his increasing interest in returning to China to visit his mother's grave. He bought two round-trip tickets, thinking that this could be the trip of a lifetime for him and his wife. What a shock it was when his wife, who was third-generation Chinese, did not object to his going but did not want to spend the money and had no interest in going with him. In anger, he offered her ticket to his niece. The niece was delighted, and the husband was satisfied to have someone to travel with. But to his wife, it was the worst insult imaginable, and she put her foot down again, stating that if he went to China with his niece, she would divorce him. The couple had come to the mediator to determine what to do; meanwhile, they were living in separate houses.

I met with each side alone in a brief session. The husband's story, told with little visible emotion, explained a lot of his grief and loss issues as he narrated his stowaway passage to America, filled with fear; his isolation in a new land; and his feelings of incompleteness and shame at his lack of filial piety in not returning to China on his mother's death. He needed to come to emotional closure on these issues before it was his turn to die, and his own mortality was becoming more real to him. He felt impelled to make this trip now, before anything else could prevent it, and so he was firm in his position that he should go, even if it cost him his marriage, which also would bring feelings of shame and remorse. As he perceived it, he was stuck in a lose-lose situation.

The solo session with the wife revealed a very different view of the dilemma. Not only was she indignant that he had bought such an expensive item without consulting her, but he had further wounded her by inviting his niece. They couldn't take back the invitation, because that would lead to gossip and shame, yet if the niece went instead of the wife, there would be rumor and speculation that the husband and niece were having an affair, bringing even greater shame on the wife. Her emotional stance was one of vitriolic silence, stonewalling, and indignation that came out in put-downs, discounting the husband, and sarcasm. She didn't really want to divorce him, but if he persisted, she would be forced to do so to keep her standing and reputation.

It was clear at the end of the separate sessions that the real issue was not whether to divorce but how to deal with the trip in a face-saving way for the wife, an honorable way for the husband, and a way that did not further disgrace either of them or distress the larger family unit. Divorce was the final solution if they could not resolve the real issue. The husband's cultural stance of not showing his deeply held emotions and needs was making the situation worse, as was the wife's lack of understanding and empathy brought on by her perception of loss of face.

In joint session, both husband and wife had requested that I serve as arbiter of the dispute, and both kept repeating, "Just tell us what to do." I explained again my role as an impartial neutral who does not make decisions for clients, but every few minutes, they would again show distress at not being told how to act. I realized that in order for the mediation process to be culturally consistent for this couple, I would have to change my usual style of mediation to fit their expectations and provide the much more directive, firm style they were requesting. It was clear that they were giving me only a single-session mandate, and the fact that I was younger than both of them and female was not giving me any extra credibility in their eyes.

I searched for a global goal that would resonate with the cultural attitudes they each still retained. I asked them in joint session to explain to each other what they thought a man owed to his mother and what he owed to his wife. They both agreed that the former was dutifulness and the latter was faithfulness and respect. I then asked the reverse, what a wife owed to her family and to her husband. They again stated the same values. They could agree on their individual and mutual family need to save face.

Taking a more authoritative role than usual, I explained to the husband how this series of events was threatening to his wife. I then reversed this and explained to the wife how deeply her husband held his duty, how that proved his worthiness, and how attending his mother's grave and taking presents to those he had left behind was a duty that he must fulfill and that would add to their family's esteem, not tarnish it. I then pointed out that the reactive step of divorce would taint them both unnecessarily and could be avoided if they agreed to collaborate on finding a way to honor the needs of both sides. Both agreed to these premises. From there, I got both to agree that it was not right for the husband to have made financial obligations or invitations without his wife's consent, and also not right for the wife to treat her husband with such scorn and move out of the shared marital home. Since it was balanced blame, they each could agree. Having established the framework for solving the dilemma and admitting some level of wrongdoing, each could leave the reactive stance and work toward solving the dilemma.

They then started the active agreement process by stating and agreeing to the foundation of their agreement: both had to honor the concept that the husband had a duty and right to go to China at some point, with or without the wife, but both had to honor the wife's original position that she did not want to go and should not be forced or shamed into it at any point. We explored the reality of the urgency and the options: Could the trip be postponed and the delay blamed on some external factor, so that the niece would see the rescinding of the invitation as necessary? Could the niece be told the level of distress over the trip and asked to back out? Could the wife relent and allow the trip if the husband and niece got others to join them, so that they were going as a group, not a couple? Would the wife agree to go if he delayed the trip a year or two on the basis of the sudden downturn of the economy or his health?

Neither felt they could discuss the matter with the niece, because of a sense of personal privacy that was culturally supported. It was taxing for them to share this dilemma with me, and they would not share it with others they knew, which is why they had come to mediation. They both thought that getting a larger group to travel together would be the ideal solution but that the likelihood was small that they could get commitments from family and friends in time to make the trip as planned. The wife still hesitated to commit herself to the trip in the future. The husband still asserted his right to go but agreed that he could postpone the trip for up to a year; he would not lose too much money in the process, just the initial deposit. The husband therefore agreed to the idea of delaying the trip based on his sudden health complications, and telling the niece that he anticipated being able to go in a few years, at an unspecified date, while actively soliciting the rest of the family in order to get a larger group to go later. The wife endorsed this plan, and the husband stipulated further that she would move back home immediately and stop nagging and cold-shouldering him, which she accepted. Then I asked if the divorce was still necessary, and both agreed to stop discussion on that topic.

This case illustrated the need to fit the mediation process to the cultural expectations of the family and to honor the cultural as well as the personal demands of the parties. To do this, I had to be more directive and authoritative than usual without compromising the essential quality of mediation as the clients' free choice. Recognizing my lowered status in their eyes as a younger female, I promoted myself much more than usual, stating again my degrees and years of experience, and keeping a very formal tone and demeanor during the session. I always allowed the man to express his ideas first, because I believed that it could increase his esteem, since he was actually the participant with less power yet would resist as culturally inconsistent and unnecessary any overt attempts on my part to balance power by helping him. The wife could leave her indignant stance when the husband let her have what she wanted, which she communicated through indirectness, silence, and other culturally determined methods. The clients left without a written document, because they wanted no trace that they had even come to mediation, in accordance with their cultural imperatives of indirectness and privacy and the culturally consistent strategy of shame reduction. Through my taking the role of the expert and telling them where to start, they were able to actually do their own bargaining.

GAY AND LESBIAN FAMILIES

Families that comprise two members of the same gender as the primary intimate relationship are becoming more usual, and mediators need not only to become aware of their existence but also to understand the dimensions of these groups as separate cultures. Just how are gay and lesbian couples and families similar to and different from straight couples and families when dealing with family disputes? Should the mediator make changes in his or her mediation approach or methods to better accommodate gay and lesbian families?

Similarities and Contrasts with Heterosexual Families

One of the first truths about gay and lesbian couples is that many states do not yet recognize them as legal marital entities even if there is recognition that they exist as social units. Gays and lesbians are barred from legal marriage in most states, even though several states and many corporations now allow for filing of domestic partnership agreements that confer legitimacy and benefits on long-term same-sex couples, allowing for name changes, insurance benefits, sick and bereavement leave, inheritance after death, and other entitlements formerly only afforded to dual-gender couples. Many same-gender couples are knocked out of the queue for adoption of foster children, infant adoption, and other parenting functions by law, policy and procedure, or personal prejudice of those running the placement systems.

Recognition of same-gender relationships as more social than sexual is an important foundation of understanding, along with acknowledgment of the duration and quality of the relationship without reference to sexual orientation. Would this partnership be seen as healthy and functional if it were heterosexual? Does it demonstrate extremes of behavior that would be problematic no matter who was involved, or is it stable emotionally, socially, financially, and sexually—in the realms of relationship we would use for any other couple or family?

Same-gender couples buy houses and boats together; form and separate; have higher or lower levels of cohesion and fusion, triangulation and enmeshment; parent their biological children and become stepparents and adoptive parents to others; and have disputes that can lead to domestic violence, threats, and patterns that are more or less healthy—just like heterosexual couples. A couple can identify more or less with the gay or lesbian culture, and each partner's social identity continues to evolve throughout their life in the same way that Cross and Fhagen-Smith (1996) described for blacks and that earlier chapters of this book discussed as part of general couple dynamics.

Because same-gender couples get a double dose of the dominant discourse's messages about how they are supposed to be, their sense of voice and place may change over time along with their group and personal identity. Townley (1992) points out that the first thing all gay and lesbian couples have in common is that each person has made at least a private, and sometimes a public, declaration of personal difference; in doing this, they each have had to confront the risks involved in stating their personal reality in a world that is unfriendly at best or physically violent at worst toward those who are gay or lesbian. This lack of personal safety to be who you are is a cost paid by victims of discrimination and prejudice of all types. Risking being labeled as pathological, being stereotyped, or enduring direct censure, threat, or violence just for being a couple is something that many heterosexual couples never experience. Other couples who have experienced discrimination, such as biracial couples or those of mixed ethnicities, can relate to the difficulty of initiating and maintaining a relationship amid the pressure of prejudice. This common experience of discrimination can create a strong bond of us-against-the-world, or it can create an isolated island of acceptance that is hard to leave even when the relationship is not suitable or healthy.

Themes in Gay and Lesbian Families

As with members of other cultural groups mentioned earlier in this chapter, it is imperative that mediators working with gay and lesbian couples and families not only try to understand the common themes in their culture but also personally assess the individuals and the social constructs of the family system rather than making automatic assumptions based on generalizations. The personal and system assessment process in many mediation models should include the level of inclusion and identification each member of the partnership feels toward the range of identities available within their community. It is important to ask the partners how they view themselves and are viewed by others at different points along that range. Some people are more out than others, more comfortable with their homosexual or lesbian identity, or more committed to a particular range of behavior and attitude allowed by that identity. Looking at what role these attitudes play within the structure of that family is the biggest part of determining the dynamics of the relationship, and the systemic view of families described in Chapter One is a lens through which to understand gay and lesbian relationships, using the same principles as for heterosexual couples and their family relationships.

Felicio and Sutherland (2001) point to important themes in the emerging literature about the qualities of lesbian relationships, and they point out that the issues of level of intimacy and fusion, reaction to conflict, and the breakup of relationships are important topics for family mediators to understand when dealing with lesbian couples. They describe how the intense level of intimacy that is often the hallmark of a lesbian relationship has often been viewed as a negative indicator of emotional fusion, the undifferentiated self merging with another to attempt wholeness by creating an enmeshed condition. Recent research has shown greater fusion in lesbian relationships compared with heterosexual relationships, but the major hallmark of lesbian relationships seems to be friendship and closeness or personal engagement before and after the relationship. Lesbian partners tend to have overlapping circles of friends and the same network of contacts and supports, more than do heterosexual partners, who tend to have somewhat different circles and spheres of influence. Felicio and Sutherland report that the issue, rather than fusion, is that the breakup of a couple can affect these shared circles, and disruption in these circles is not counteracted by the strength of other worlds that remain unaffected. As in other small communities, there are few places to hide, and being cut off from one person can mean being cut off from many other relationships. This kind of disruption may have implications for the parenting relationships the former partners may share after the relationship ends and for their ability to form supportive outside relationships.

Another theme pertaining to lesbian relationships is that both partners have been socialized as women in our society to deal with conflict indirectly and to minimize or introject anger into self-harming behavior. Felicio and Sutherland (2001) also conclude that lesbian couples, unlike married couples, do not have institutionalized pressure to stay in bad relationships because of vows or legal entanglements; since the relationships were chosen and self-constructed without the standard role expectations of heterosexual couples, lesbian partners can often leave each other faster or differently than unhappy straight partners, and mediation can be part of this process. Felicio and Sutherland report that angry lesbian couples seem to fight in similar patterns to heterosexual couples and show similar rates of domestic violence, but they may include in their arsenal of control and intimidation the threat of exposing the existence of the relationship or the lesbian orientation of the partner. Thus, dynamics of emotional dependence and control might be areas to watch for in parting lesbian couples.

Because both women of the partnership may be taking care of children they had with male partners or through artificial insemination, and because our society sees raising children as consistent with the typical roles of women, a lesbian mother may not run into as many barriers of prejudice about her role as a parent or the concept of having two moms as gay men who are doing the same thing. Many heterosexual women with children live together after divorce, sharing child care and tasks. People outside the family may not understand the real nature of the relationship or identify the partners as anything other than roommates, but a newly formed lesbian relationship can elicit strong emotional responses from older children who understand the realities, leading to parent-teen conflicts.

Themes for gay male couples can also include issues of prejudice, risk of acknowledgment of one's sexual orientation during couple formation, and threat of public exposure of the partner's orientation. There can be struggles with role division and creating a home life without benefit of many established roles and rules. Another theme of gay relationships is the tension between monogamy and promiscuity when partners are making a transition from an uncommitted gay lifestyle to a fully committed emotional and sexual partnership. Another theme is the ever-present specter of death, due to risks from gay bashing, HIV/AIDS, and past or present risky lifestyle choices. It is harder for two men living together to keep the nature of their relationship private, and even with the increasingly tolerant climate that has emerged in the last few years, there are still many communities and partnerships in which social or physical danger can result from being clearly identified as gay. Just like heterosexual couples and lesbian couples, some gay male couples are struggling with other factors such as health concerns, financial issues, alcohol and drug use, or co-occurring mental or emotional problems, so screening potential mediation cases makes sense.

Although much of gay culture revolves around serial monogamous relationships, the lifestyle for many is a childless household. As in some childless couples of all orientations as they age, a common dynamic is the overresponse-underresponse pattern of caretaking, in which one partner takes a parental, caregiver role while the other maintains a more immature, needy stance, requiring indulgent care and attention. Maintaining negative intimacy through these dynamics and strong enmeshment is a pattern to watch for in this cultural group.

Many gay men have children with female partners or former wives, or become sperm donors for lesbian couples who want the experience of pregnancy. These arrangements are often not made with formal legal agreements and so constitute a realm of potential decisions and disputes that may need the help of a family mediator. As with all parents, gay men's parenting abilities may vary widely depending on their personal development, their parenting legacy, their committed involvement and knowledge, and their access to their children. Gay men suffer the discrimination of being perceived as inadequate parents even when they have already shown themselves to be active and appropriate before coming out and even if they have buffered their children adequately from age-inappropriate revelations or the realities or results of the new partnership. Gay men actively parenting small children may face barriers and stigma from external forces, such as their former or current faith community, as well as from the gay community itself, which is divided about the appropriateness of taking on traditional roles.

Laird (1993, p. 316) describes the issue of whether children who are parented by gay or lesbian families are hampered or harmed by the experience: "Of great interest is the fact that children of gay and lesbian parents appear to grow and thrive as well as children in heterosexual families, *in spite of* the prejudice and discrimination that can and does surround them. Although many of the myths concerning the evil effects of the parent's homosexuality on his children still infect the legal system, a generation of research has failed to demonstrate that gays or lesbians are any less fit to parent than their heterosexual counterparts." In fact, some research noted by Laird (1993) shows that children raised in these nontraditional families have advantages from living with two very active and involved parents who do not model dominance and aggressive behaviors and who are often more tolerant, open, affectionate, and empathic than traditional heterosexual families. The particular strengths, deficits, and family dynamics at work within a family structure may be far more influential than the fact that the parents are gay or lesbian. The wise family mediator would therefore assess the families and parenting within them based on the same criteria that are used for heterosexual family units.

Some questions a mediator might ask himself or herself about mediating family disputes with gay and lesbian couples are the following:

- Do I need to learn more about local gay and lesbian community resources?

- Do I find that I am uncomfortable, or making special allowances, or thinking differently than usual about the presenting problems and options with this case?

- Do I have a trusted colleague or friend who has special expertise in the issues involved in this case?

- In what ways do I think that this couple's sexual orientation or identification with gay or lesbian culture is affecting how they interact or bargain or attempt to resolve their dispute?

- Do I have some concerns about the issues being discussed that are based on my own orientation and socialization? Am I making assumptions based on these participants' orientation or identity that are interfering with my ability to help them?

Case Example: Divorce and Parenting After Coming Out

In May, Bob and Lisa sought divorce mediation. It looked like a standard case: Lisa was moving back to her mother's home two states away, taking the children with her for the summer, and would establish a home there before fall. She had been an at-home wife and mother for the last ten years, since the first son was born, and she wanted to stay that way. She kept telling Bob that how he would support her and the kids was his problem. She was leaving the family home to him, and she didn't care if he sold it or stayed in it. Her demeanor was very brusque and tight, and she seemed to maintain an emotional distance and a hurt, indignant stance in her interactions with Bob, mainly expressing concerns about how he could afford to keep the house and pay for her new domicile as well. Bob seemed sad but amicable, offering to give up his job and move to her new state so that he could remain an active parent for the boys.

It was only in solo session with Lisa that the real issue surfaced, elicited by the mediator's use of a more therapeutic model. Bob had just told Lisa that he was gay and could not keep it a secret any longer, since he and his lover, Steve, had been together for three years and wanted to make their relationship permanent, not just a stolen and sneaky thing. Lisa was still reeling from the shock and implications; questions swirled in her mind: Had Bob used her just to have children or to have a home? Did he ever really love her? How could she not have seen? Did Bob have some dreaded disease? Could this revelation be harmful to the boys? What now? Lisa was emotionally incapacitated, but she felt that she had to do something to clear her head and could not stay with Bob now that she knew. She couldn't talk to anybody about how this had turned her world upside down. All the boys knew was that they were going to spend the summer with their grandmother. Lisa wanted to buffer them from trauma as much as possible, and she wanted to bar Bob from having too much contact with them. He had been a good provider, and the thought of his leaving his job and seniority to follow them was ridiculous to her.

Bob told the story of a painful recognition of his sexual orientation; of marrying at nineteen because it was expected in his small farming community; of working and trying to feel satisfied but realizing the flatness of his existence; of a chance encounter that had blossomed into a real and passionate love, not just a furtive and shaming experience; and of the internal turmoil that acknowledging his truth had caused for him. He didn't want to hurt the sons he loved dearly; he was not a pedophile, but he could no longer hide his homosexuality and didn't want to. He was sorry that this was going to change everyone's life, and he needed help to tell the children in the right way. He was sure the boys would like Steve, who liked to hunt and fish, as much as he did if they were allowed to get to know him. Lisa had gone crazy the night he told her, smashing things, calling him names, and hitting him, so he had not tried to call to the home. Her plans to take the children away seemed retaliatory to him, and he wanted to see them soon to reassure them that he wasn't leaving them. His concept of moving with them was a nice idea, but he also knew it was impractical. So now he would have an empty house, still work ten-hour days, and not see his children, all to be honest with himself and Lisa. He didn't blame her, but he hoped she could relent about the children, and he knew that the big dream house they had spent the last five years working on would have to be sold in order to support her. He never questioned that she would have to get a job or career of her own.

The mediator realized that these two, who had been so intimate at one time, were both hurting from the lack of communication that Bob's secret had required and that the healthiest thing would be for the two of them to talk about their feelings, ask questions, and do the emotional equivalent of holding a wake or sitting shivah for their relationship. Because the mediator did not follow a procedural or problem-solving model but used a transformative and narrative approach, she presented the problems to be solved but also the emotional work to be done around acceptance and forgiveness. She asked if they wanted to hold a separate session just to explore the scary territory about how this situation had developed. They both agreed, and the next meeting was an emotionally cathartic session in which each was able to validate the other, to redefine their love story, and to express the true emotions that had been under the surface but unexpressed until then.

Bob and Lisa returned for the third session, having grieved for their losses, which they could now talk about, and better able to create realistic options for division of property and finances without blame, guilt, and powerless rage. Lisa agreed to get more information on children of gay parents from the local gay support network and the Internet, and to get some therapy as soon as she moved, to help her with this huge life transition. Bob agreed to not introduce Steve to the children or talk with them about his other life until Lisa had read more and become less reactive and they could talk to the children together. They still had very real issues to decide, and the focus of the mediation took on a more collaborative approach, especially after Bob got a temporary visitation schedule that allowed him contact with the boys, and Lisa got assurances of at least one year of full spousal support while she investigated her job and educational opportunities in the new state. The mediator then helped them define further temporary agreements and the long-term intentions of both, and the next session, held at the end of the summer by telephone, was very productive. The mediator switched back to a more standard problem-solving/negotiative model to help them make all the decisions necessary to finalize their divorce and plan the session for jointly telling the children about Bob's true situation.

ETHICS AND PRACTICE STANDARDS FOR CULTURAL ISSUES

The field of family mediation has not yet evolved sufficiently to have a lot of materials on cultural issues in mediating family disputes, but because diverse families with family disputes have often presented themselves to counselors, therapists, social workers, and psychologists, there is a lot of historical and recent material on dealing effectively with families that family mediators should review as relevant. Several counseling associations have special interest groups within the larger body to collect journal articles, research, and clinical practice information for diverse families. The American Psychological Association (1990) has guidelines on-line for providers of psychological services to ethnic, linguistic, and culturally diverse populations. These could serve as guidelines for family mediators.

The American Psychological Association guidelines and the new *Model Standards of Practice for Family and Divorce Mediation* described in Chapter Six require family mediators to develop their cultural awareness and adaptations, and urge practitioners to have a conceptual framework that is large enough to understand the impact of these factors on families and individuals. Family mediators should recognize the limitations of their own competencies and knowledge by seeking consultation or making referrals. They should try to become aware of and reduce their own cultural biases and should not perceive individual pathology when a cultural concept being expressed seems unusual. They should respect the cultural roles and rules, honor divergent belief systems, and translate materials so that accurate understanding is possible. Finally, American Psychological Association practitioners are urged to work against discrimination, bias, and oppression in the sociopolitical realm. These seem like excellent working premises for family mediators as well.

In this chapter we have explored three major populations within American society who may need some additional help and support to understand the premises of family mediation or to function effectively within existing models of practice and service delivery. This can be a dialogue that can affect mediators and not just clients. The most recent U.S. Census points to how diverse our population is. We could hope that family mediators practicing with families who may have multiple cultural and ethnic backgrounds will be able to ask the family the pertinent questions that will lead to better, more personalized, and culturally consistent outcomes.

CHAPTER EIGHT

Interfacing with
Other Professionals and Parties

Family mediators do not offer their services in a vacuum, and the family in mediation exists within larger systems that may also be part of the triggering of the dispute, the recognition of it, or the attempt at help and intervention. It is important for family mediators to know which professions, persons, and positions are affecting the mediation participants both in the session and outside it. These other parties may actually be hindering the mediation process and confusing or harming the client inadvertently by giving conflicting messages or putting the client in a double-bind situation, unless they are aware of the mediation effort, in accordance with the basic principles of mediation, and supporting the participants as they undergo the additional stress of the mediation sessions.

Including children in divorce mediation situations is also a contested issue in mediation circles. Children are parties directly affected by the mediation process and outcomes but without direct decision-making capacity unless granted some by the parents or the courts. In elder care and medical decisions, it is often just the reverse: the adult children can overpower and undermine the wishes of the actual decision maker, forgetting that the elder still has decision-making capacity unless that has been taken away by legal action.

Well-meaning advocates or legal advisers who are not familiar with the confidentiality of the mediation process can be overly assertive and unhelpful unless they are coached in how to support their client while not disrupting the mediation session. When and how to involve them is an important practice dimension that this chapter starts to address. Family mediation practitioners need to accept and maximize the best uses of these other sources of support for the clients, while at the same time limiting the distraction and unhelpful behaviors that can develop in their involvement.

This chapter explores some of the most likely issues in working with other professionals and supportive parties, and with those directly affected by the outcome, in ways that can recognize their contribution to a positive process and outcome for the family members involved. Any family mediator who is considering using other professionals or including other parties as part of the range of process options needs to consider the philosophical and theoretical, ethical, legal, social, structural, and logistics issues.

Many mediation models would never consider doing an interview with corollary contacts of any kind, preferring to work only with the designated disputants. In some mediators' view, this narrow approach to mediation does not take into consideration the contextual reality and cultural differences of families where extended family members, church friends, babysitters, live-in partners, stepparents, and grandparents, not professionals, are the shaping forces that the family relates to and who have direct bearing on the issues and outcomes. In the culture of many families, it is not just the parents who get to have input, and in some families, the children, not the father or mother, know best. In order to understand the dilemma and the possible solutions, mediators may need more input than just the skewed self-reports of the disputants. Remaining open to this possibility when the case seems to require it would be a good stance for a family mediator, and then having enough knowledge and skills to pull it off successfully would be the second concern.

Finding the proper balance point of involvement of outside resources, without swinging to extremes of enmeshment and exclusion, is important because it requires of the family mediator the exact skills wished for participants: clear boundaries and enough assertion to maintain them without direct or passive aggression or negative patterns emerging. In this way, family mediators model what we could hope for in healthy family systems: the connectedness yet the preservation of appropriate boundaries.

CONTINUITY-OF-CARE CONTINUUM

Family mediators are often brought into the family dispute only after the family has sought help during their stage of uncertainty from their lawyers, religious leaders, other family members and friends, and other trusted advocates or resources. Most mediation is triggered by the start of a legal case that is diverted to mediation because it falls into a classification that the jurisdiction has declared eligible to receive mediation services as a primary diversion within the justice system. Participants have often been referred or sent to mediation, on a mandatory or voluntary basis, after having consulted an attorney, a therapist, a court clerk, a friend, or a helping professional of some kind.

Perspectives on Referrals

Mediation rests on the interface between the legal world of ADR, litigation, and court and the service delivery system of a range of helping services. It is part of a continuity-of-care system in both the ADR model and the helping professional's continuity-of-care plan that can include a range of prioritized services. When the ADR and justice services world ignores the existence and involvement of the helping system or the reverse, it does not help the client cope with the distress of the dispute and leads to gaps in services and support for the family and the individual.

Making referrals for tangential services or support is very much a part of the therapist's or social worker's case management approach, which sees the individual and family as having needs before, during, and after the dispute event, but making referrals may not be part of a legal perspective, which tends to see the dispute as a discrete event that needs attention and resolution but may not be connected to a larger set of issues. Family mediators need to meld these two perspectives into a service delivery design that does not overreach the role of the family mediator yet provides the appropriate referrals for situations that are beyond the scope of the mediation itself. Because family mediators may be the only professional with whom the family shares the dilemma and because in the intake and assessment stage the family mediator may become aware of additional personal and family needs, the family mediator should take an active stance toward making positive referrals to persons and programs that can help situations that are beyond the scope of the specific dispute or mediation problem definition.

In their diagram of ideal ADR services for divorcing families, Johnston and Roseby (1997) point out how mediation efforts may need to be offered at different levels for different problem types. In their model of service delivery, basic mediation efforts are part of a continuum of services and support to the family, starting with a first level of parent education classes that provide information relevant to the child and the divorce process. On the second level of services, a case would be assessed based on the presenting problems and assessment of the family functioning and the ability of the standard mediation processes to work for that family. They would then be routed to either the mediation process or to collaborative law approaches, which would not include the children.

If this were not enough to have a positive impact on the dispute, then the case would move to additional services beyond the basic mode, especially for families where violence, high levels of therapeutic need, or allegations of abuse or other serious problems warrant a fuller approach. On the third level of services, their multilayered continuum of care would then indicate more in-depth psychological assessment or intervention to evaluate the ability of the parents. Based on that evaluation, the family would be provided the use of the expanded mediation models of therapeutic mediation or custody evaluation services. Both the more extensive therapeutic model of mediation and custody evaluation should be given enough time, resources, and method to assess the situation and then provide adequate intervention. The more expensive therapeutic mediation would be saved for those who had tried the more usual problem-solving/negotiative mediation process but failed.

At the fourth level, the family's needs might indicate ongoing services, such as supervised visitation and exchange, monitoring of the visitation, ongoing parenting coordination through specialized services, or arbitration through special master's programs. This would also include referral to ancillary services such as mental health, substance abuse, domestic violence, special education, legal services, and financial help.

This has been called the *360-degree service delivery model* of social work practice; it sees the children and family as a unit needing specific services for problems that continue to affect the functioning of the family and the child. In this way, ADR and mediation services are but a thin band in the spectrum of service delivery systems, and they need to work with the other helping systems to ensure the best result for children and families. Continuity of care and services, whether we think of it as a multidoor courthouse with different ADR options or a spectrum of services that need to be coordinated for the clients, is the pressing issue when the family's dispute indicates higher levels of distress for children and their parents or dysfunction that can continue to harm, or when standard models of mediation do not seem to be working.

Making Effective Referrals

Making referrals is not just telling the family member that she needs a particular service and then giving her the names or telephone numbers. Referrals to additional ADR programs and services or auxiliary services that augment the needs that surround the dispute need to be done in an active, responsive, dialectic way. The family mediator has to explore with the family member what the needs are, prioritize them, search for appropriate resources, make the referral, and monitor the participant's responsiveness to it.

The mediator needs to find out barriers to accessing the service, both mental (shame and minimization) and physical (lack of transportation, inability to attend during working hours). Making a referral that the participants can benefit from can take lots of time and effort and require more of a case manager approach. This role may be different from the service model of private practitioners or former attorneys who set their parameters of service and then provide only that which they contract to do, letting the consumer of services find any additional help.

This more active stance of seeing family mediation efforts as part of the family's ongoing process and system will lead to a greater awareness by family mediators, in both private practice and public service, that they should be active referral agents who help create more adequate, differentiated service paths for families needing different levels of service. Providing assertive care in systems with alternatives and levels of service during and after mediation can help develop the role of the family mediator from one thin band of color in the spectrum of services to a necessary part of that rainbow.

INVOLVING CHILDREN AND OTHER PARTIES

People who are not given legal or social authority to make the decisions in a dispute are often referred to as third parties, or second-level stakeholders; they will be directly affected by the outcome of the dispute even though they have no apparent input. Because children have such direct impacts from the decisions that their parents make, many family mediators include them in the mediation process, either routinely or as needed, especially in divorce and separation cases, modification of custody and access, grandparents' rights, and some out-of-home placement decisions. Extended family members, who often derive their involvement through the primary parties to the dispute, may have vital input about the reality of the situation and problem and the participants' true interests, capacities, and credibility, but they often lack a forum for participating, leaving them feeling excluded, angry, and anxious. For example, stepparents have no direct legal authority to make decisions, but their lives may be radically changed by the outcome of the mediation.

The dilemma for family mediators, who want and need this input to understand the situation and help the parties formulate appropriate and workable options, is how to include parties who have vital information without changing the clear hierarchy among the participants and without unbalancing the equality between the participants. If a family mediator chooses or lets the participants choose whether to include new partners, stepparents, grandparents, or other relatives who want to influence the outcome, the rules of their involvement and the impact of their input need to be discussed completely ahead of time.

Risks of Including Children

Another part of the concern is the effect on children who provide the input to their parents or guardians, only to have their elders deny, disregard, or misinterpret what the children say for their own tactical or emotional reasons. Rather than including children in a joint mediation session, mediators may want to shelter children by interviewing them, stepparents or grandparents, babysitters, and others directly but separately and then feeding the input back to the primary participants. Because it comes from the more neutral source of the mediator, in positive ways that allow the participants to hear and understand without undue defensiveness, this indirect inclusion of children's information can buffer them from any recriminations. Interviewing children separately and then passing on what they say as an intermediary process is complicated and can border on the more evaluative process of custody evaluation unless there are some safeguards, such as written statements from the children, questionnaires, and self-reports. It is important that talking to children or other family members be done as part of the mediation effort and not as a co-opted process that allows the mediator to determine what information to pass on to the mediation participants.

Preparing the Others

A family mediator who wants to be able to get additional information from others must inform all primary participants, secure written release-of-information forms prior to any interview with those sources, and explain and have written signatures on a document to the primary participants and the source as to exactly what is confidential and what will be shared. Without this, major ethical breaches can occur, which could endanger the source or the participants. Such agreements should be voluntary and the role of the mediator again confirmed. Since the notes from those interviews or contacts are part of the mediation effort, it should be clarified in writing that the notes from the interview and the subsequent telling of the information as part of the mediation effort cannot be used in any subsequent action like a custody evaluation study, because they are covered by the same laws that govern confidentiality of the mediation process and records of it.

Clearly, based on the ethics of client self-determination, a family mediator should allow the participants the right to refuse such input or interview process, even if he uses such interviews and contacts as standard in his model of mediation. The mediator not only has an obligation to explain why he wants to have this information and what could be gained, but also the risks of allowing such an interview. Those risks include getting information that refutes the participants' own bargaining position, triggers the reporting of abuse and neglect, or provides the other participant with more ammunition to use during mediation or in subsequent processes like evaluation. Information changes at least the perception of the problem, the people, and the process needed. Therefore, including information from other sources either supports and corroborates or reveals further discrepancies and concerns that then must be part of the problem definition and outcome. The pros and cons of interviewing children as part of mediation should be fully explored before the decision to do it is made by the mediator and the participants.

Rationales Beyond Cultural Orientation

Donald Saposnek (1998) has written about the rationale for inviting children to be part of the mediation effort that will directly affect their lives. Each family has a unique culture that stems from their larger social learning and their own unit's values, and this can affect their view of how much children are allowed or encouraged to have some voice in their own life decisions. In some families, children are told what to do by a benign dictator; in other family cultures, children are in a more democratic system that allows them influence or even full participation in decision making. It is important to look at the preexisting culture of inclusion of children before the dispute to see how consistent the decision to include children in mediation would be.

In looking at the cultural variables that may come into play regarding whether children can and should be allowed to give direct input to decisions that affect their own well-being, Saposnek (1991) pointed to four conditions that he believes provide a strong rationale for including children in mediation for custody or access disputes, no matter what cultural expectation of child involvement the participants maintain:

- When the child has been expressing through one parent a strong preference for or abhorrence of a particular arrangement and there is a question whether the parent is speaking for the child or from his or her own set of preferences, interviewing the child allows for this discrepancy to be clarified and allows the child to hear the issue from the neutral mediator rather than the other parent.

- When a child specifically requests to meet with or speak to the mediator to express his opinions, values, and feelings and this is not a manipulation of the child by a parent but the child's own deep concern, the mediator should try to honor the request.

- If the parents are oblivious to the destructive effect on the children of their continued hostility, then children who are ready to give firsthand feedback to the parents can break through the denial and minimization by directly stating to both parents their experience. Parents can no longer maintain a facade of ignorance when this is done as part of the mediation effort.

- All adolescents, due to their abilities to conceptualize their increased independence that is age appropriate, and clear preferences based on realities of their responsibilities, activities, and schedules.

Children can be interviewed separately as an augmentive session, and the results of that special child interview session can then be reported back to the parents or participants in mediation. Another way is to have the children directly involved in the joint mediation session, talking directly to the participants rather than having what they say filtered through the mediator. In the first situation, the mediator provides a climate in which the child may feel more or less comfortable in sharing what is really going on, depending on whether the mediator is able to establish enough rapport and the child feels comfortable and permitted to talk about what is of concern. In the second case, confronting parents can be uncomfortable; it may go against the hierarchy of the family and therefore might not be culturally acceptable. It can also be more stressful, since both parents are together. Children who are going to be made part of the session should understand the expectation and be emotionally ready for the experience.

Models of including children run along a continuum, from simply bringing children in to hear the final outcome, to consulting with them early in the mediation or periodically as new options seem to emerge, to formulating options that are more acceptable to them, to full exposure to the entire process as their own witness and advocate. Mediators who use the interview method can use an analogy of the children being like an advisory committee to the parents or mediation participants, who are the board of directors with the final decision. Children need to understand that they cannot be promised their desired outcome, but they can be given the opportunity to have empowerment and recognition in some way in the process.

Planning Prior to Child Involvement

Mediators who feel knowledgeable and comfortable in interviewing children can gain a lot of useful information by observing the interactions of the family members in the waiting room, as well as gathering the direct statements of the children. Prior to conducting the interview with the children or third parties, the family mediator should have written permission from all participants to proceed and should record the rationale for the interview. Mediators should reflect on the following questions prior to the child interview or involvement.

- What information am I looking for specifically? What is the rationale for talking to the children?

- Are there disputed topics that the children or third party could speak to that seem crucial to the development of the options and transformation?

- What are the differences expressed by the narrative of the primary participants? What does the mother say that is different from what the father says?

- What would be indicators that the persons being interviewed had been provided a script or had been told what to say to support one person's view or position?

- What have the interviewees been told about how their information will be used?

Conducting the interview requires the family mediator to take in the objective and subjective experience as well and then distill this information into what is usable for the mediation effort. For example, if the family mediator sees the child kick the parents when they are trying to get them ready to leave, that behavior is objective information because it was an external event that could have been observed by anyone. If the impression of the family mediator is that the child or stepparent is holding something back or being overly nice, that is a subjective impression of the family mediator, based on the mediator's thoughts, feelings, and impressions. Both can be valid but need to be separated before they are merged into a sense of meaning or a direction for intervention.

Structuring Child Interviews

If a family mediator has decided and gotten permission to hold child interviews, she should ensure that they will be structured enough to give guidance to the process and reduce an overload of subjectivity or claims of unfair or undue influence or bias by the mediator during the process. Many family mediators who interview children do a three-part process:

1. Record subjective and objective observations.
2. Conduct a structured interview using standard questions.
3. Provide an age-appropriate vehicle for self-report by the interviewee or child.

For small children who are not yet readers, the form of the self-report may be modified to have the child draw pictures of the family, his room, what he does at one house or with one part of the family, and what he does at the other home or with the other family member. The interview process can then have the child tell about those drawings, with the family mediator not overly interpreting. Some family mediators get training or opinions from art therapists or child psychologists in interpreting these highly meaningful statements by the young child.

Although separate interviews of each child give good-quality information, bringing all the children who live in the family together as a group is a good way to start the process. This group session provides them the comfort (or irritation) of being part of the group and gives the mediator some idea of the dynamics: who speaks for whom, who dominates, who differs. Some family mediators refuse to interview children under five years old separately but include them as part of the entire sibling group to observe the interaction among the children.

If a child refuses to attend, refuses to communicate, will not separate from the siblings or the parent, becomes uncontrollable in the waiting room, or will not take correction from the parent or the other children, these actions are meaningful in themselves and may have a bearing on the issue in dispute or the natural affiliations within the family that can and should be honored in the ultimate plan for the family. The mediator should record the objective and subjective experiences of this group interview in documenting the interview process.

The mediator needs to reconfirm what is confidential and what is not with the children or interviewee at the start of the session. Before it concludes, the mediator needs to ask the child or interviewee once again, "Is there anything you have told me that you don't want me to share with your parents [or other mediation participants]?" The mediator models the integrity and the permission being granted the children to speak openly yet have their own confidentiality upheld within the usual limits.

Logistics for setting up and providing these separate child interviews can be difficult. They are time-consuming and need to be set for at least ninety minutes for families with more than one child to give enough time for each to speak separately. Children need to come after school and often have activities that make it difficult to schedule one time when a parent can bring them all. Sometimes both parents insist on bringing or sitting with the children in the waiting room, which can lead to uncontrolled family distress, so many mediators require that only one parent bring and stay with the children. A family mediator who is conducting this process should set up procedures that ensure safety for the children and the parents. At the end of the interview, the parents or other participants may try to pump the mediator for information, but it is best not to allow this to take place on the same day or with only one parent because of concerns about maintaining neutrality and the repercussions of the information.

When the parents or other participants have the next joint session, they both need to hear the mediator's report about the interview. The mediator may want to use objective information and direct quotes from the children rather than start with subjective impressions, so that the participants understand that the mediator's job was to collect information and deliver it to the parents without the usual communication interference or discounting rather than to influence the outcome unduly.

Because the information can change the credibility of the participants' bargaining position, both may need some private time to think and reformulate their stance, to process where this leaves them, or to react emotionally before. Asking them separately in caucus or solo session, "What difference does this information make for you?" can help them start this process of reformulating based on the information. From a narrative perspective, the participants must integrate this information and then individually and collectively co-create a new narrative about what is important and what needs to change.

In a private-pay setting, the biggest negotiative issue about interviewing children or others may not be whether the information is useful, or the mediator skilled enough, or the children willing, but who pays for the mediator's time to do the interview. Many times the parents will agree to allow and want the children to be interviewed but do not want to pay for it, seeing it as the responsibility of the identified "problem parent" whose behavior has initiated the dispute and the mediation.

Sometimes neither parent nor other mediation participants can afford to pay the extra cost of interviewing the child. In this situation, interviewing the children and others is a luxury they cannot afford. In some public sector venues, the payment issue is less of a problem, because the case is allocated a maximum number of hours that will be covered by the fee arrangement or subsidized by the court, and the mediator can get a signed statement by the participants that they authorize the use of the mediator's time in this way. Until the jurisdictions or mediation services have unlimited service capacity or full funding for all the effort needed, this will continue to be an issue that must be addressed before child interviews are conducted.

Interviewing children and others within the family as they define it is challenging, so family mediators should consider their stance based on their model of mediation, their expertise and comfort with children and multiple parties, the limitations of their time, and funding. Mediators should consider this issue as a policy concern, then map out ahead of time their specific procedures and interviewing processes, create forms, and check confidentiality issues. When these are well handled and wanted by the family, they can make a major difference in the information base that is being used to make decisions. In many ways, this is part of a full disclosure and fairness component that can be used when needed. When all potential risks and benefits are related, the participants understand the financial and positional consequences, and they are allowed a fully informed choice in the use of input from children and others, then this can lead to ethically consistent, helpful mediation process.

WORKING WITH ADVOCATES AND ATTORNEYS

Families who are experiencing disputes often turn to friends, organizations, and specialized services that may want to be part of the continuum of care for the family. Family members under stress rely heavily on such advisers and advocates, and they frequently want to bring them into the mediation effort with them for morale and direct advocacy. Because mediation is still triggered as a response to the filing of a legal action, many families have consulted attorneys before coming to family mediation, and these represented clients need to know the limits of the role of their legal representatives during subsequent mediation efforts.

Family mediators need to set appropriate boundaries so that the help that these outside resources can give is available to the participants without altering the essential quality of the mediation process. Mediation requires direct voice and active participation by the disputant and direct agency and advocacy by the family members themselves rather than by surrogates, helpers, and others. This direct process ensures that the participants themselves are making the active choices and giving informed agreement to proposals and solutions rather than being intimidated, coerced, or overshadowed by the very people who want to help. The tail should not wag the dog, and the avenging advocate should not tell the tale of the disputants as if the disputant is not there.

Attorneys as legal advocates can and should serve their clients by acting as counselors-at-law, who help their clients understand the legal dimensions, rules, and consequences involved in the dispute, start the initial legal actions that may be tied to the dispute, establish their clients' initial legal standing and positions, then put the case on hold to enable the mediator to work with the client. Whether or not the participants are represented, family mediators should find out from the disputants if there are preexisting or pending legal cases or temporary orders between the participants before starting to mediate, because the participants may be reacting in mediation more to statements and allegations made in earlier legal documents and less to what is actually being said during the mediation session.

As legal advisers and advocates, attorneys usually accompany their clients to any meeting to provide legal advice and counsel and to protect their clients' interests. When the dispute is referred to mediation, there are mixed views of the role of the legal advocate in the need for this level of active representation in session. A 1994 study conducted with a sample of the Florida Family Law section of the Florida bar (Harrell, 1995) found that while a majority of these attorneys approved and used family mediation because of its increased likelihood to bring about settlement, its time and money savings for the clients, the avoidance of litigation, and the tempering of clients' emotions, over half said that they attended the mediation sessions rather than let the clients attend alone. They believed in the process of mediation as effective and helpful, but did not want their clients to go there alone.

The reasons the attorneys gave for attending the mediation sessions were primarily to help bring about an agreement and to protect the clients from themselves, the other client, and the opposing client's attorney. A third reason was to control their own client, and about a fourth of those interviewed said it was standard for them to attend such sessions in any civil case, so they just applied this to the mediation context. Less than 20 percent said they attended to ensure the mediator's impartiality or to assess the mediator's ability. These results led the author to conclude that there is still distrust of the mediator and a misunderstanding of the legal advocate's role when the parties are engaged in the mediation process: "If attorneys attend mediation sessions and act as traditional advocates, they can easily control the process by limiting their clients' communications. . . . A mediation that is controlled by advocates and assists the parties in avoiding responsibility for their own problems may indeed avoid a trial, but only temporarily" (Harrell, 1995, p. 374).

A study of Indiana lawyers (Medley and Schellenberg, 1994) also found that attorneys saw five distinct advantages of mediation for their clients: reduction of time, encouragement of personal responsibility, agreements that are more durable and long lasting, client expression of concerns, and better understanding of the strength or weakness of their case. Despite these apparent benefits, these attorneys also expressed concerns about mandatory mediation and the abilities of the mediator. They did not express concern about unauthorized practice of law or redundancy. Generally, advising attorneys are positive about their clients' use of mediation.

When clients are lacking the important premediation information that a legal advocate can give, the family mediator may be tempted to provide the first set of information without actually advising the participants about their particular best case, and certainly without the capacity to set into motion any legal establishment of temporary stabilizing orders from the court. Family mediators are often the first and only source of reputable information regarding the dispute, and they can safely provide legally related information without crossing the line into unauthorized practice of law. Family mediators who provide this information and education for their mediation participants must know when they do not know and make appropriate referrals to attorneys when in doubt. Family mediators should never try to interpret the participants' likely outcome if the matter goes to court or use a subsequent ADR process, nor should they advise any participant about his or her unique legal standing.

Guiding the Advocate During the Session

Advisers should be available to provide their advice and counsel prior to the core of the mediation and throughout the mediation effort. The mediation participant rather than the advocate should be the one talking, and the fact that one or more participants in the mediation have an adviser should not in any way jeopardize the balance and equity between the parties during the mediation session. Advocates and advisers who prepare and coach their mediation attendees before the session with the most helpful questions to ask, the topics to cover, the needs expressed by the participant, and finally the positions they can or should take to solve the dilemma are the best kind of advocate. They know that in mediation, the participants themselves must do the work, prompted and encouraged by the advocate, not the other way around.

Having the advocate attend mediation sessions brings up two major issues: the confidentiality of the mediation process and balance and equity for all participants. If one disputant has enough financial and emotional resources to have several advisers (attorney, spiritual adviser, special program representative, or others) but the other disputant does not, the family mediator needs to balance the equation so that the former has access and the latter is not intimidated or made more powerless or hopeless. Requiring that mediation participants consult with their advisers only before or after sessions can minimize the perception of intrusion or power plays while maintaining a perception of fairness during the session, but it begs the issue by ignoring the fact that one party has a resource that the other does not.

Short of a major overhaul of our legal system, it seems unlikely that all civil cases will have equality of access to basic legal information and advocacy. Depending on the jurisdiction and problem type being mediated, over half of the cases will have neither party receive any legal advice. Nevertheless, the mediator can attempt to help the unrepresented client find legal and other supportive resources that he or she might not have known. Helping a participant find and pay for appropriate advice that equalizes relative power and bargaining may need to be the first negotiation of the mediation effort, particularly in disputes where the decisions reached are permanent or profound.

Another procedure that mediators can maintain is that the participants of the mediation must approve the inclusion of any and all advocates and that the participants or the mediator can ask and expect them to remove themselves if they are interfering with the interactional process or the mediation model being used. Mediators may have to make that judgment call rather than allow participants to do a strategic, passive-aggressive tactic of objecting or preventing otherwise helpful advocates. Because I believe that the mediator is ultimately in charge of the structure and efficacy of the procedures of mediation, I prefer to see decisions made consistent with not only the participants' wishes but the mediator's professional judgment of the usefulness versus the harm of inclusion.

Examples of Effective Advocacy

In the case of a woman who had experienced a stroke and some short-term memory loss but who could cognitively function sufficiently to mediate directly, the client requested permission to bring a friend of the family familiar with the family dispute and history as her "external memory" to help her stay on track and remember her concerns and not let her waffle on points about which she felt strongly. The other participant recognized the advantage of having such a person in the session and agreed. The mediator structured the expectations that the informal advocate was to cue the woman, not speak for her, and to sign a confidentiality agreement. Because she was instructed by the mediator about her role during and after the session, she was a wonderful resource who allowed the woman to be a full participant and the mediation to be an equalized process. The friend-advocate continued as a resource after the session to help the woman remember and keep to her agreements.

In another case, the client was an Iranian woman who came to the woman mediator only after very cautiously making telephone calls and attending a solo first session with the mediator. There had been no physical abuse or violence, but the woman presented as a female very used to male domination who culturally was not yet in an equal position with her estranged husband, who used his male dominance entitlement to withhold money and threaten her with loss of his visitation or loss of custody of the children. This woman needed an advocate who could empower her to speak for herself during the sessions. The mediator spent several telephone calls building trust and rapport with the woman and realized that any further solo work might create a perception of bias toward her and lack of impartiality needed to mediate fairly. The mediator helped the woman identify a more acculturated Iranian woman she knew who could help her with the language issues and who also was involved with the Americanized equality of women. This woman would act as an advocate to prevent undue pressure, leaving the mediator free to conduct the session as a helper to them both rather than worrying about the adequacy of the woman's response to bargaining.

The husband agreed to the unequal inclusion of a third person as advocate, partly because he was also socialized to see women as needing help and support and often acting as part of a sisterhood. This suggestion was culturally consistent for him as well, and since he did not have to pay for it, as he would have had it been her attorney, he recognized that this was a good situation all around. The couple was able to mediate with the advocate present, and she stepped into the discussion only when she feared her friend was falling back into a submissive stance. The mediator let them work as a team. Legal and supportive advocates can be a tremendous resource if they understand how and are willing to be supportive rather than assertive.

INDIVIDUAL AND MARITAL THERAPISTS

Many family disputes arrive in the family mediator's office with an entourage or trail of individual and marital therapists for each family member, possibly referred to mediation by the most recent therapist. In other cases, the family has never had a therapist despite astoundingly complex family problems, only some of which can be adequately handled by the family mediator. Children with attention deficit disorder, eating disorders, drug and alcohol problems, mental illness and situational stress, medical and disabling conditions requiring adaptations to life, work and parenting patterns: all of these and more can be complicating factors in the family mediation dispute that could benefit from referral out for concurrent services of therapists and specialized programs. Referrals to and from therapists are now more common for the family mediator.

Because the therapist's responsibility is to either one member of the family or the family as the unit of service, it is important for the family mediator to find out the history of therapy for each participant and the current connections they have to the therapist. As a general rule, it is wise to let the therapist know that a client has presented for mediation services by having the mediation client sign a release of information with either the mediator or the therapist. The purpose of this contact is to let the therapist know of the increased likelihood of stress for the client and to give the mediator some idea of the signs of stress that might indicate a need to return to therapy or an immediate concern. By linking in this way, the family mediator becomes a part of the continuity-of-care system of support that the individual or family may need.

Many therapists are unwilling to be an advocate during the mediation session because they fear the involvement will bring them into legal trouble with their own confidentiality. Some are willing to come to provide emotional support for their client while not saying much. For example, a teenager who had been living at a residential treatment program for high-risk youth wanted to come to the father's treatment program to mediate the terms and conditions under which she was willing to see him again. His drinking and criminality had been the source of the tension in the family, and the teenager wanted to talk about what new rules she needed to have with the father and to set new boundaries. The daughter's treatment staff agreed to the mediation session, and the father's family therapist, who was familiar with mediation, agreed to hold the session as a mediation, not classic therapy. There would be a single session, and the treatment staff decided to send her therapist, who would act as advocate during the session.

The therapist prepared the teenager by helping her think of what she needed, how she would deal with the emotions, and how to remind herself to stay calm. On the day of the mediation, the therapist and teenager both went to the father's facility, and the therapist sat quietly while the father's therapist, acting as mediator, conducted the mediation session. The teenager was very capable of saying what she needed to say, and the father and daughter negotiated new agreements about information, his addiction, and the quality of relationship they would have. The therapist for the teenager provided support just by being there and debriefing the teenager after the session.

In this chapter, we have reviewed common issues that family mediators find in working with other professionals, all of whom want to try to help the family in dispute or crisis. Service delivery systems are trying to adapt to the systemic nature of these family disputes and create more ways to work collaboratively with the other family helpers when they run into limitations due to the scope of their expertise or agency definition. Including children and family members directly but with proper coaching as to their role and confidentiality requirements can help bring additional support and realistic information and help balance the mediation that might otherwise be weighted against a participant.

We have very little family mediation literature that describes cases where referral to other services or inclusion of children or supportive advocates or attorneys had made the critical difference, and yet we know that expanding the mediation models and processes to allow this will be culturally consistent and helpful for some families. In the next ten years, the ideas in this chapter will grow and be examined through good field research.

Readers now have the fundamental concepts and processes in mind to look beyond into the specifics of practice. Part Three moves to the specifics of different types of disputes that family mediators encounter and in which there is specialization even within the family mediation context and setting.

PART THREE

SPECIALIZED PRACTICES
IN FAMILY MEDIATION

CHAPTER NINE

Marital Mediation, Conciliation, and Prenuptial Agreements

Before courts had ever heard of using mediation for divorce and separation, many court-connected services or jurisdictions themselves provided conciliation: short-term couples counseling to determine if divorce or separation was really necessary. These conciliation services were developed in the mid-1970s to respond to the increased number of domestic relations filings as no-fault divorce and a more liberal social sense increased the numbers of divorces. States had an interest in both licensing marriage and in determining that all remedies to the relationship had been provided in order to prevent unnecessary ending of those marriages they had granted. Conciliation counseling was offered to help couples determine the problems and see if they could renegotiate the understandings between wives and husbands, mothers and fathers, to prevent parting, which often brought disruption of economic and social structures for adults and their children.

CONCILIATION: MEDIATING THE PROBLEMS OF STAYING TOGETHER

Conciliation, as it has often been practiced in these court-connected settings, is a form of marital mediation because it allows both participants the same capacities and processes as divorce mediation. The participants get to define

the problems and concerns from their own perspectives and work collaboratively toward a resolution or management plan. The outcome and goal of the
process is to develop a set of definable changes and agreements about how to
reconstruct their relationship in order to make it more acceptable. Marital mediation helps intact (or falling apart) relationships reassess their strengths and
weaknesses and asks the participants to determine the outcome. The usual
choices are to remain the same and accept the conditions, have one or both
work to change some conditions, or determine whether the changes, even if
made, would be insufficient, too late, or unlikely to change the basic differences.
Providing marital mediation or conciliation helps the participants really discover
whether the differences are in fact irreconcilable and therefore needing the services of a divorce mediator, or whether with major or minor reconstruction and
renegotiations the marriage can survive and prosper.

In the public sector court-connected programs, mediators switch back and
forth between the role of conciliator and mediator, and so court mediators are
often cross-trained in order to work in both processes. When practitioners feel
equipped to do both functions, there is no ethical or other reason that they may
not do both, as long as they are clear with the client about what they are doing.
Both conciliation and mediation can follow the mediation models described in
earlier chapters.

Because of the difference of goal, though, the mediator who is switching roles
to become a conciliator should differentiate this for the clients. Although the
practitioner may be doing a similar interactive, therapeutic, narrative, transformative, or problem-solving/negotiative style of practice when conciliating as
opposed to mediating, he or she should know and mark the moment when the
role changes. The role of the conciliator, no matter what model or approach is
being used, is to help the participants fully explore what have been the strengths
and weaknesses of the relationship and to determine whether or under what
conditions each person would be willing to stay. The role of the divorce mediator is to help the participants do the emotional, legal, financial, social, and
parental business of parting in ways that will be the most advantageous to them
and their children.

Marital mediation can be provided by therapists who are doing classic couples or family counseling, before any mention of divorce or separation, or by
divorce mediators when a divorce or separation action has already been filed
but the participants would like to try to work things out rather than going
through with the divorce. Since so many couples are not legally married, this is
a bit of a misnomer, because it certainly may and often is provided to couples
who are living together. For many mediators, conciliation is a preliminary step
to providing mediation and can be offered in the public sector, or even required
in private practice, to ensure that the need to separate has been fully covered

and decided by the participants. Seen this way, it is a premediation intervention to ensure that a clear and firm decision to leave the relationship has happened by one or both before starting with that assumption in divorce mediation work.

MARITAL MEDIATION ASSESSMENT

Like all the other forms of family mediation, marital mediation requires some level of evaluation and assessment of the people and the issues as part of the beginning stage. The primary questions that the participants in marital mediation or conciliation must answer for themselves are the same ones that mediators should ask as part of the assessment:

- Are there any conditions or agreements that the other person could make and fulfill that would make it more tenable or satisfying in the relationship?

- Are there absolute requirements that must be met before reconciliation and return or before renewing the commitment to stay in the relationship (for example, entering into drug or alcohol treatment, stopping an affair, or staying on medication)?

- If the other person did those things outlined, would the one requesting the changes really accept them and feel ready to go forward? Is there a need not only for being held accountable and apologizing but also for-giving?

- What likelihood is there that these or other equally unacceptable conditions would reemerge? What steps are each partner willing to take to ensure that these or other problems will not reoccur?

- Are the partners saying to each other, "This really must change," or are they saying, "This really must end"?

Many marital and couples problems are structural in nature, based on external forces that become personalized. When these problems become a pattern of interaction, the participants have only three choices: accept them as unchangeable, reject them and try often uncomfortable and enlarged behavioral responses, such as leaving home and filing for divorce, or renegotiating. Because so many relationships just happen and evolve from each person's set of expectations, a family mediator cannot assume that even long-term partners have ever openly negotiated the rules and expectations about how they will be in their partnership.

Marital mediation helps the participants sort through and legitimize their complaints about each other and their mutually constructed life. Using R. J.

Rummel's view of conflict, the marital mediator or conciliator helps partners sort their concerns and complaints and translate them into at least the following categories:

- *Interests:* Mutuality of interests but different ways of achieving them; nonmutual or discordant interests, some of which might be changeable; lack of any mutual interests
- *Capability:* Each partner's ability to handle the complex tasks of family life—economics, parenting, sexuality and intimacy, communication, and interdependence
- *Credibility:* How much each partner believes he or she can trust the other to live up to and carry out responsibilities, tasks, and expectations

In conciliation and marital mediation, the mediator helps the participants renegotiate their roles about belonging to each other as partners and belonging to this social unit as a family. As Emery (1994) has pointed out, the process of making a firm decision for divorce and separation is predicated on a belief that change is unlikely, impossible, or unwanted. As part of the predivorce condition, the partners need to declare that change and acceptance are not likely or not wanted. Then as part of the divorce process, the couple must renegotiate their family structure by looking at the complaints, concerns, and strengths in two major areas: the intimate, interpersonal couples relationship and their activity as parents, potential parents together, or parents with others outside this relationship.

One model of couple formation indicates that all relationships start with and evolve through different levels of intimacy, passion, and commitment. A marital mediator or conciliator helps the partners discuss all three of these factors in the historical and current context. Although Karen Kayser (1993) used a very small sample, her research indicated a typical progression of disillusionment and disaffection, accompanied by particular thoughts, feelings, and behaviors in each one of the progressions by spouses who need marital mediation and conciliation. Typical stages along this continuum indicate when an individual within the couple unit moves from disillusionment through hurt and anger, to total disengagement and disaffection. These stages of disaffection indicate the level of disruption and disaffection the individual and the couple as a unit feel and can also function as self-evaluation by the participants.

Sometimes one or both persons' score on this self-report indicates that the partner may have declared the relationship dead without trying the resuscitation efforts of marriage counseling, conciliation, or marital mediation. The marital mediator can use this or other self-reporting instruments to help each individual discover and be honest about how bad the relationship really is. The role of the marital mediator is to help the participants sort through not only the disillusionment but all aspects of their relationship, including their levels of intimacy, passion, and commitment, in order to help them determine whether change is possible, acceptance is necessary, and remaining in the relationship or leaving it seems to be in their best interests.

Because marital mediation or conciliation is a separate process more akin to typical marriage and couples therapy, many mediators who use a problem-solving/negotiative approach have been hesitant to employ this process, and mediators who have done traditional marriage counseling or couples or family therapy might feel better about offering counseling or therapy in cases where there is any hope for reconciliation. Compared to the more traditional approach of many counselors and therapists, marital mediation is very agreement oriented. Like all other mediation efforts, it attempts to help the participants define the problems, search for workable options, and make choices that get recorded as outcome agreements, something that is not usually done by most marriage counselors.

Marital disputes may be over the fate of the relationship as a global concern or may be focused on one particular problem in the relationship with no concern about the ultimate fate of the relationship itself. A single issue can make the relationship itself seem unacceptable or can create tension, and the resolution of the conflict through marital mediation can release the tension and allow the couple to continue more happily. Marital mediation or conciliation may take much less time and money than more typical therapy approaches because the need to establish rapport is minimized. Marital mediation is often held as a single joint mediation session or a very short series of two to six sessions. In comparison, marriage counseling or couples work can often take several months and require extensive rapport with the therapist before the issues or problems are revealed. Marital mediation may be the overture that sets the stage for subsequent deeper therapy that is needed.

A Marital Mediation Example

A husband and wife presented their dilemma at a local court-connected divorce mediation program, which also offered conciliation services. They were members of the same Foursquare church, and each valued church attendance every Sunday for themselves and their children. They went to both morning and evening services, with Bible study and visits to family and friends between the services. In the last few months, though, the husband had been coming home during the week to find dinner instructions taped to the refrigerator, the children at various friends' homes, and the wife gone to attend evening meetings connected with the church. The frequency of the wife's meetings had mushroomed from one per week to one almost every night. The husband was distressed for his children and the quality of his home life, which he believed had suffered. No amount of talking seemed to make a difference, and in total frustration, he had painted himself into a corner by telling his wife that he would divorce her if she didn't want to act like a married woman and stay home.

The wife's view was that her husband was being unreasonable, since she felt her activities positively modeled their shared values. She was hurt and confused and, more important, angry that he had mentioned divorce, which their beliefs discouraged for any reason short of grievous abuse or other major and continuing problems. She felt that her husband was trying to get her to chose between him and God, something she didn't want to be pressed on, since her faith told her in which direction she would have to go.

Both partners wanted to stay in the marriage for reasons of values, economics, and parenting, although there were obviously problems they needed to work through, such as why she was not listening to the distress of those she cared about and how he felt being cast in the role of Victorian papa demanding his dinner. Neither of them, however, wanted to go into the more emotionally laden realm; they both resisted offers by the mediator to take them to that level, preferring to stay with the problem-solving orientation of negotiating a more acceptable church involvement on the part of the wife. The wife and husband reaffirmed their commitment to the marriage and each other, and the wife agreed to a schedule that the husband proposed: no more than two evening meetings during the week, no afternoon activities when the children were home from school, and a full program as usual on Sunday.

The mediator had a therapeutic background and hoped to deal with the underlying power and control issues and unvoiced complaints, advising the couple that disputes like this often resurface in other ways even when there has been a good negotiation and agreement. But the wife was relieved, the husband satisfied, and the conciliation effort sufficient to reduce the threat of a divorce that neither partner wanted. The mediator reminded them that they could return for a series of more standard couples counseling sessions, but both partners were content with the thin band of conflict resolution, which, in their words, had "saved their marriage," and they left. The conciliation or marital mediation was all the participants wanted or needed at that time, according to their self-determination of the process; and the mediation process used a straightforward problem-solving/negotiation approach, rather than the therapeutic or transformative model the mediator usually used, since this model fit the participants' needs and was most comfortable for them.

Defining the Problem Differently

Marital mediation can be used for many disputes that are now resulting in unnecessary divorces and separations. For example, stepparents who are having difficulty dealing with the children and the biological parent regarding their role may not seek the help of therapy and counseling professionals because they have deep suspicions about being labeled or because they have realistic time and money constraints. Marital mediation offers the family the advantage of a shorter time frame, a problem and solution focus, and a strength-based approach that keeps the power and control over the process in the hands of the participants. While good therapy also does this, going to marital mediation for a dispute sounds and means something different to the participants from going to therapy for personal or family problems. Marital mediation or conciliation destigmatizes the need for conflict resolution in the couple or marriage, and it makes it more acceptable to have the conflict.

Mediators who are considering offering marital mediation need to have enough understanding of marital dynamics that if a dispute turns out to be part of a deeper, more serious set of concerns, they will become aware that the problem needs to be redefined and offer appropriate help or referral. For example, it would be inappropriate to mediate a marital dispute in which the problem was defined as "how to get my wife to obey me" or "how to get him to stop using methamphetamine."

If the clients are not willing to go through the process of redefining the problem to acknowledge the larger marital problem (power and control issues and possible domestic violence in the first case, and substance use needing treatment in the second), then the conciliation or marital mediation approach is not only doomed but also inappropriate. The parties need a referral to more appropriate resources. Marital mediators need to understand the limitations of the mediation process alone when trying to solve deep family systems problems. They need to resist allowing the mediation process to be co-opted into triangulation, an unholy alliance, or a process that will help maintain severely problematic behavior.

Marital Issues That Should Not Be Mediated

A marital mediator who is also a therapist or well-trained mediator familiar with systems theory should be able to detect which issues are inappropriate for the mediation process. Issues of continuing infidelity and sexual addiction, incest, childhood sexual abuse that is being uncovered, compulsive behavior in general, and eating disorders affecting the relationship may not be best served by the more agreement-oriented approach of marital mediation as the first course of therapy. The limitations of defining the issues in these dynamics as simple problems to be negotiated continue the process of denial and minimization that often accompanies these concerns.

After referral to other specialists and more specific, often longer-term individual therapy, the marital mediation process can often be helpful in negotiating the terms and conditions under which the spouse will continue to be supportive during and after treatment. If the therapist-based mediator is going to provide this, he or she needs to contractually redefine the work as therapy, not mediation or conciliation.

THEMES OF ATTACHMENT, LOVE, AND TRUST

It is sometimes confusing to beginning mediators that marital partners describe each other in such terrible terms and with such vehement resentment and vituperation, yet will not consider separation or divorce at all. The contradictory statements of "He is a terrible person, and let me tell you all about it," while at the same time stating, "I can't [or won't] live without him, and I won't leave this relationship" seem so ambivalent and antagonistic that mediators must have some explanation of what is underneath the paradoxical simultaneous positions. Many mediators see these as cues that the person is dealing with anxious attachment, often left over from childhood or early dating or sexual experiences. Anxiously attached couples cannot stand to be with each other or parted. They do not even like the person they are with, and certainly the love has gone away, but they still want the relationship, because something, even a negative relationship, is better than being detached, isolated, and lonely.

A marital mediator working with a couple who do not like each other and do not want to stay together but will not part could ask the couple some questions about how they got together. Often, the creation of the relationship was an attempt to find or create in this partnership the love, attention, and nurturing that was not in earlier relationships. The foundation and creation of the relationship is also sometimes opportunistic; perhaps one or the other needed a place to live, was on the rebound, wanted a sexual but uncommitted relationship, or other situational circumstances that prompted the relationship to make a leap before it was emotionally ready to undertake the step.

Because insecure attachment means that the person has a hard time dealing with ambiguity or changes in the relationship, these couples are often troubled by continuing concerns about trust, commitment, and whether love is present. They keep setting each other up to "prove their love," and they feel slighted when the partner does not notice, which makes them more insecure and thus starts a cyclical pattern of interactions that enhance rather than reduce the anxiety.

Marital mediators can ask the participants to review the formation of and the major changes in their relationship in front of each other and develop the discrepancies between their views. By doing this, the marital mediator is helping bring to the mutual awareness of both the patterns of each. The couple as an entity is usually not aware of its own patterns, even when an individual within the couple is very self-aware. By bringing out patterns by use of questions, externalizing conversations, and other means (depending on the mediator's model and methods), the couple sees itself as an entity, often for the first time. Marital mediators are mirrors who help the participants see the issues and concerns from the view of the unit rather than from their own individual framework. Helping the couple focus on their interactional themes and patterns demystifies and depersonalizes the conflicts and problems they are having. It helps the couple understand without having to use blame, judgment, or attribution or projection.

As an abstract concept, trust cannot be mediated, but the participants can define for themselves and each other what trustworthiness would look like in concrete behavioral terms. Then the marital mediator can help them agree to those behavioral choices and changes. For example, a partner with anxious attachment may be worried, though with no particular cause, that the other partner is sexually cheating on him. The sharing of this worry can often create more conflict rather than bring about the relief that it was meant to elicit, because the one who is assumed to be cheating often feels unjustly accused and secondarily angry and confused. Neither correctly interprets this as a bid by the worried partner to gain reassurance that his fears and projections are needless.

When the marital mediator can explain this process of anxiety projection to the partners, they can then agree in classic problem-solving ways on how to handle the need for reassurance differently in the relationship. Their mediated agreement might be that the partner who is feeling concerned or anxious will share the feeling, not the projection of bad behavior by the other, and the other partner will try to provide more attention and reassurance without having to get angry or fend off labels and accusations. In this way, the marital mediator does more than just help the participants see the pattern; the mediator secures agreements, but after providing the forum for discussion about an issue that is part of the anxious attachment and intrapersonal response of one or both of the parties. Is trust mediable? It can be when it is redefined and made into observable, measurable behavioral statements that can then be agreed to or modified as the participants make sets of agreements regarding their current and future responses.

DEFINING THE RELATIONSHIP BY AGREEMENT

Most couples never fully discuss with each other their concept of marriage and partnership, even when they have attended religiously based premarital classes. Some jurisdictions are experimenting with requiring partners to undergo a premarital class before issuing a marriage license, and in some of these classes, the focus is to ensure that the participants understand their legal, financial, and social responsibilities toward each other and any offspring. This really leaves a wide-open arena for the marital mediator to add topics to the discussion and to have the couple define the "us" by determining the set of shared understandings and agreements.

Couples need to define for themselves a number of common topics in marital mediation:

- *Bottom lines:* Have the partners defined for each other the "shall and shall not" conditions of staying together? Have those changed?

- *Decision making:* Will this marriage be equal in all things, or will one person make the decisions on some things? If she wants car tires and he wants a new couch, how will the decision be made?

- *Communication:* How much of the couple's business will be shared with others, and whom? How often and in what way will they talk to each other?

- *Work and financial matters:* Do both contribute by working outside the home? Do they pool their resources or retain private money? Do they have spending allowances without checking with the other? Who organizes the finances, pays the bills, deals with insurance, and prepares the taxes?

- *Parenting:* Is one person expected to leave work to care for children? Do they make the parenting decisions together and back each other up, or do they undermine each other?

- *Household tasks:* Does one person do all the work? Is it shared in ways that make sense? Is it gender determined?

- *Outside influences:* Can each of them retain their former friends? Do they have time to maintain these relationships? Is someone's hobby, activity, or group involvement requiring the couple to reformulate everything around it?

- *Involvement with in-laws:* What is expected for holidays? Is there too much or too little involvement with his or her relatives? Does the couple feel comfortable around the other family members?

- *Former relationships:* Have these been acknowledged? Are issues (child support nonpayment, children coming into the family, abuse or threats, inconsistent parenting) affecting the relationship?

When a couple knows the answers to these and many other questions and issues, they have a more clearly defined sense of themselves as a socially constructed unit—as "us." They can fill in the blank when asked to define themselves by description when given the lead, "You are the Joneses, and you are the people who _____ [do this, and do not do that]." All of these items are negotiable and may change over the course of the marriage or relationship.

When each person has a different understanding about these and other items, the couple is open to many conflicts, some of them interest based, some data based, and some values or structurally based. When these conflicts remain unmanaged or unresolved, they lead to relationship conflicts that can seem irresolvable and irremediable, and thus grounds for divorce and separation. If society is really sincere about preserving marriages, it will offer low-cost or free marital mediation at the beginning of the relationship and also from then on, to provide conflict prevention as well as conflict resolution.

CREATING APPROPRIATE CONSEQUENCES

As pointed out in the wonderfully rich, easy-to-read, and easy-to-understand book *Growing Up Again: Parenting Ourselves, Parenting Our Children,* by Jean Clarke and Connie Dawson (1998), all people, and therefore all couples and families, need the right level and type of stimulation, nurturing, and structure throughout life. The authors also point out that natural consequences are what will happen automatically as a result of our actions, but logical consequences are those responses we set up to deal with contingencies and to hold appropriate boundaries with others.

Marital couples need to create their own levels of structure, to know what are negotiable and nonnegotiable rules between themselves, and when there have been violations of those boundaries, they need to set these logical consequences with each other. Because this is not a natural way of talking or thinking about the couples relationship, many marriages have struggled for years with violations of their own covert or overt rules and expectations, but do not have a system in place that they built to deal with providing logical consequences. This is work that the marital mediator can help the couple determine by mutual agreement.

Consider a couple where the one partner keeps spending money being saved for a vacation by playing video poker. They are not only dealing with a gambling addiction; they have had numerous violations of their own structure and have experienced natural consequences (the money was spent, so they did not get a vacation). They need to acknowledge the gambling addiction and get the partner the therapeutic help he or she needs, but they also need to know what will happen to the relationship if the treatment is or is not successful.

Many spouses find it very difficult to lay down ultimatums and logical consequences because they have no practice, or because they do not perceive they have the right to do so. Sometimes they hesitate because they fear that it will be perceived by the other spouse as a threat and intimidation, or a confrontation that might threaten the entire relationship, or they have no communication forum or process in their relationship to do this kindly but firmly. The marital mediator can help couples who need to do this work with each other by providing the venue they need, with support and encouragement, and with the capacity to ensure that the consequences that are selected are not over- or underresponding to the situation.

When the need for having known consequences is seen as a mutual task of the couple relationship, the onus is taken off the person who needs them as well as the one who is requesting them. Providing known responses to predictable situations is part of the contingency planning that family mediators do in most settings, and in marital mediation, it becomes very important. By setting up these predictable, logical stair-stepped consequences, the couple makes the situation and the likely contingencies a lot less anxiety producing. They can provide the anxiously attached spouse the reassurance that they will not file for divorce or end the relationship because of a single behavior or event, and yet it provides an opportunity for increasing the consequences for continued problems. This alone can help a partner with a problem relax and do what he or she needs to do without fear that the marriage will crumble, yet with assurances that there will be positive and negative sanctions for their choices.

PRENUPTIAL AGREEMENTS: MORE THAN MONEY

Couples tend to go to lawyers to get help in drafting prenuptial agreements regarding issues of personal and real property, money, investment, control of businesses, and inheritance matters. These have often been the province of only the wealthiest, who have the most to lose if something goes wrong in the relationship they are considering. Standard prenuptial agreements arrange for the disposition of assets before the wedding, so that items that should not become jointly held or controlled are left out of what becomes the joint marital holdings. By doing this before the marriage takes place, the assets are preserved in case the marriage ends. Most prenuptial agreements cannot be written in such a way as to predict divorce, but there can be sheltering and personalization of resources that are kept out of the joint assets that would become divisible during the divorce.

Given that a majority of people in the United States have more than one marriage or long-term relationship during their lifetime but that 75 percent or more of our population really own nothing other than their personal and household belongings, the issues of wealth are less important in the majority of people's lives than the interpersonal dynamics between the family members of the former and current relationships. Now more than ever before, people need help sorting through their expectations before they become involved with additional families and children. As more and more young elderly—those in their sixties to seventies—remarry, concerns of their adult children about family heirlooms, traditions, and personal items that have great sentimental but little market value become topics for discussion not only by the couple themselves but by the extended families of each member of the couple. Marriage and domestic partnership by gay and other nontraditional couples and long-term cohabitation by nonmarried couples who have very different work and financial lives can also lead to new uses for these prenuptial agreements. Perhaps it is time to bring the terminology from the legal to the personal, to reconceptualize, and perhaps even relabel these as *prepartnership agreements.*

Marital mediators who do prenuptial or prepartnership agreements find that they need to market to a more modest clientele and include the softer issues of heritage, lineage, status, and acknowledgment, along with the harder issues of currency. What is a nonmarried partner who is trying to parent the other partner's children called? The person is not technically a stepparent, because the couple is unmarried, yet the children may think of this person as a stepparent. What does a man call his brother's live-in gay partner ("my brother's domestic partner")? Simple matters like what the person, who is now considered family, will be called and what the new expectations are will become critical to the survival of second marriages or relationships. Prepartnership agreements, talked about openly by a trained marital mediator, can go a long way in helping the forming couple prethink the issues that could be contentious or that they never realized were part of the package.

Second relationships have stressors that first relationships do not have. By definition, there have been prior losses through conflict, divorce and separation, abandonment, death, or disillusionment in a prior relationship for at least one if not both of the parties. They often need to have strong assurances that the problems and issues they dealt with that led to the demise of the first relationship (or a series of relationships) will not be reduplicated in the new relationship. Many times, the prior relationship has provided the awareness of what must and what cannot be part of the new relationship, and expressing this openly as negotiated agreements in mediation can help alleviate the tension of worrying or trying to discuss these issues independently.

As marital mediation evolves with the needs of the population, we may see much more work for marital and family mediators to first draw up prerelationship agreements between the members of the couple themselves, then hold joint sessions with extended family members who may be directly or indirectly affected by the relationship. These mediated agreements may not be ratified by the court or be legally binding, but may be socially explanatory, helping the new couple create and impart the understandings of their unique relationship to the others with whom they are connected. The basic premise of mediation as a practice is that the participants should be self-determining.

The development of new forms of mediation that help support the responsible development of interpersonal contracts and covenants of the parties themselves may start a return to a concept where public announcement of something very personal like marriage or cohabitation is symbolic of levels of commitment and responsibility, although not necessarily legally sanctioned by the state. These mediated agreements could provide families with some shared understanding without needing a state government to determine fairness and obligation. Couples who use inexpensive prerelationship mediation services to define their understandings and then later use marital mediation and conciliation to deal with unforeseen conflicts will be practicing the most responsible way of taking on their new relationship: knowingly, willingly, by mutual agreement, and in written form that can be shared with others.

॰॰

What is old is new again. Marital mediation is perhaps the oldest form of family mediation, since it is derived from the early conciliation court efforts, yet it might be the new service boom for nontraditional and reforming relationships in which the partners contract openly as to the construction of their relationship. Premarital or prepartnership agreements about terminology, lifestyle, parenting of children who are social but not legal responsibilities, extended family obligations and expectations, and inclusion of others in the relationship are but a few of the topics that can be included in the discussion and agreement process during mediation at the start of relationships. Given the likelihood of problems, they can set expectations of behavior that can contribute to more enduring relationships by providing a conflict resolution process that serves as a model of a mutual and shared power relationship. Marital mediation can help create strong foundations and prevent problems from overwhelming marriages. In the next chapter, we look at the other major use of mediation: dispute resolution during and after divorce and separation.

CHAPTER TEN

Divorce Mediation

The most common use of mediation for family-related disputes concerns divorce. Mediation has become the required or preferred alternative whenever divorce or separation has been mentioned. All of the previous chapters in this book are basic to the understanding and practice of mediation for divorce and separation events, and so this chapter assumes that readers have not started here but have absorbed all of the prior information to integrate into this specific dispute use. For this reason, this chapter will not highlight some of the topics covered in some mediation texts, such as face-saving, negotiation, family dynamics, child development and needs, and other extremely relevant and critical knowledge that the wise divorce mediator should have.

Adequate training for divorce mediators should include comprehensive knowledge and skill-based training in four major areas (Taylor, 1994):

- Conflict resolution processes in general and mediation process in particular

- Legal and financial information specific to the mediator's practice regarding legal divorce and finances

- Adult, child, and family development, both normal patterns and special adaptations for different populations

- Basic professional skills, such as clinical interviewing, referral, case management, collaboration with other helping systems, documentation, and appropriate interaction with clients, attorneys, and other family members

This chapter cannot provide all the information that practitioners need in these areas, and the skills are built by practicing mediation with good supervision and feedback. This chapter is oriented toward practitioners who have started their own path toward excellence and have reviewed and developed these fundamentals as the foundation of their practice. The focus therefore is on what is special about the practice of divorce and separation mediation beyond the understandings needed to work successfully with any other family-related mediation case.

Although divorce is a legal event that is triggered by a legal request at a specific time to the court, the process of parting is an ongoing series of events that can transpire over years. It may have had several stages of reaction and interaction by the participants, all of them relevant to the current mental, emotional, and legal status of the family members. Mediators may be called into the picture at any point by one or both of the separating spouses or couples or by the systems they affect and try to access in their process.

THE DIVORCE MEDIATOR'S ROLE

Many couples, married and unmarried, who want to separate and do the right thing by the children and each other voluntarily come to mediation services in the public and private sectors. They are looking for help in sorting out the issues and making well-considered decisions regarding the parenting, financial, social, and other issues involved in parting company, and they do so as an alternative to the adversarial litigative process. For others, the concept of parting throws them into such emotional turmoil that conflicts between the couple and the child start immediately. They can be severe and ongoing, and they often escalate into the category of high-conflict divorce articulated by Janet Johnston and Vivienne Roseby (1997). In some ways, mediation before, during, and after divorce may be crisis intervention, conflict resolution, conflict management, simple decision making and problem solving, problem prevention, and future planning simultaneously or sequentially, depending on the state of the separation and the response of the participants.

The model of mediation that the mediator adopts will determine how and in what way the mediation process will proceed. Despite very different models, approaches, and methodologies, there seem to be some common features of what mediators working with separating and divorcing families do for and with their participants:

- *Facilitating.* When there is no overt or covert conflict, the divorce mediator acts as a facilitator who guides the discussion to the topics that must be decided and creates the collective memory by recording decisions that the participants make.

- *Creative problem solving.* When there have been or are conflicts or difficult and complex topics and choices with different options, the mediator acts as a creative problem solver. The goal is to help the participants understand the issues and concerns of each person, help them develop a sufficient understanding of all the alternatives and their consequences, and then directly negotiate those differences.

- *Third-party negotiator.* When there are major conflicts between the participants, the divorce mediator serves the family by acting as a third-party negotiator, guiding discussion and negotiation, helping everyone understand their own concerns, ideal situations, anxieties, positions, and possibilities. The mediator then tries to help both communicate more effectively with the other.

- *Objective observer and mirror.* When there are deep feelings and patterns, the mediator is often acting as an objective observer and mirror to thoughts and feelings. He or she serves as a therapeutic ally, reality check, or communication filter who is interested and involved but is a more objective observer of the total family dilemma than the participants are.

- *Temporary communication linkage and interpreter.* When there are incomplete communications, the mediator acts as a temporary communication linkage and interpreter for the participants. He or she sharpens the differences, neutralizes the messages, and separates content from delivery to see if the participants themselves can mutually determine what is negotiable and what is not or whether they must be referred to other dispute resolution mechanisms, like custody evaluation, attorney negotiation, or litigation.

Because most separations and divorces will involve all the types of dilemmas in different parts of the separation discussion, the divorce mediator needs to be ready to do all types of functioning, using the perspectives and methods of their model or approach to guide and inform their practice.

MANDATORY AND VOLUNTARY MEDIATION

Divorcing couples who have been told that they must mediate are set up to resent, distrust, and resist the help that the divorce mediator may be able to give them and their family. This is the situation in which most divorce mediation starts in the United States due to the increasing use of mandatory mediation in the public sector as a first recourse before the case can be heard in court. To require mediation efforts as the least intrusive and costly dispute resolution mechanism makes sense as social and fiscal policy, but it immediately creates a potential conflict between the mediator and participants.

When a case is mandatory or ordered to mediation, the first task is to reconfirm the levels of power and control that the participants actually have in order to reduce the suspicion, distrust, and resentment they may feel that could prevent the active use of the mediation process for one or more of the participants. Whether mandatory or voluntary as far as referral to or entry into mediation, the participants should always know they have a right to end the mediation or opt out if they feel that mediation is inappropriate or unhelpful. In this way, even mandatory services retain the ethical stance of client self-determination.

The mediator who is working in a mandatory system needs to share the rights that clients have to be self-determining. Many families, especially those from minority populations, street cultures, or lower socioeconomic groups, hold negative views of the justice system and can start with negative attributions about the mediator's being part of "the government" or "the system." Those who are from the upper economic or educational brackets can also be resentful of having to use what they see as demeaning, too public, or less than top professional-quality public services. Mediators can reduce these negative attributions by defining their own credentials and integrity and explaining immediately the participants' rights to opt out, get private services, or get independent advice. Acknowledging this tension can reduce it. In the public sector, mediators work for two bosses—their service delivery system and their clients—and both must be served equally well.

In private services, the clients who are paying the private mediator a steep fee need to be reassured that they are getting their money's worth; that the mediator has a style, method, or skill that makes the cost of the services worthwhile; and that the needs that bring them to the sessions will be attended to by the mediator. Those needs might include the need for extreme privacy and confidentiality, due to their celebrity or exposure, the need for special expertise in the area of the dispute, or the desire to have a style or method of mediation that is consistent with their values and preferences.

In many jurisdictions across the country, public sector mediation was not available until recently. This was often the case in smaller jurisdictions, more rural areas, or areas whose bench and bar were not enamored of mediation and had refused to move in that direction. Private mediators charging fairly high fees per hour, rather than low-cost public sector mediation services, were the only option for mediation services in those rural areas, if they were available at all. This too is changing, with more private mediators than paying clients in some metropolitan areas. In the private sector, it is always important to remember that divorce mediators work for the participants as well as themselves, and both need to be comfortable with the process. Most states have now moved to ubiquitous and more uniform statewide public sector services, although some of them are housed, staffed, and administered by a social system other than the court, such as the mental health system, dispute resolution centers, social services, or the corrections system.

Another major difference in this public-private schism is that in the public sector, divorce mediators and their clients do not choose each other, so there may not be a good fit, but there may be options to shift the case to another mediator within the agency or system if the relationship is not working. In private practice, there is an economic disincentive to do such appropriate shifts to other competing mediators in the area, although in the long run, such cooperative agreements may be the best way to operate for the clients and for the mediator.

Another important issue is that public sector mediators often have a different range of presenting problems, reality factors, levels of conflict, and disruption in the families they are working with than do the private sector mediators. Each can see a very skewed population. Private sector mediators are often dealing with the problems of overabundance of resources, choices, and potentials, while public sector mediators may be helping clients who have few, if any, resources, choices, or potential for getting them. Neither situation is harder; they are just different and cause the families to have to strategize differently. This affects many decisions in mediation, from whether they can afford to contest a concern, hire an attorney to advise them, create options regarding work and structure, and determine how money must be used to meet basic needs. I have mediated with the issues of both scarce resources and overabundance and find that the different families struggle just as hard, although the numbers of choices and options available to them vary.

Private sector mediators have the right to accept or dismiss their clients, just as the clients have the right to select and dismiss their mediation practitioner. Although this must be done in accordance with ethics and standards of practice, it certainly is an option for private sector mediators who find that they do not like, trust, or want to work with the clients for whatever reason or who do not believe they or their model is functioning well for the clients. However, in public sector mediation systems, often neither the participants nor the mediator can select or dismiss each other on any basis. To head off manipulation by one client, some agencies have the policy that it requires both clients to request a change of mediators, something that many clients, who are already distressed, may not have the emotional resilience to do, even if they have the desire.

Public sector mediators often do not have the luxury of being able to disqualify 20 percent of the cases that come to them as inappropriate (as is noted in the therapeutic family mediation [TFM] model) in order to practice a model of mediation they prefer. Instead, they may have to have more than one model to serve the differing needs of the clients they are required serve. This is a major difference in the type of mediation approaches that may be available in mandatory versus private sector divorce mediation. Some models do not fit with the external requirements of time, money, and number of sessions the case is allotted by the funding mechanism, and the mandatory clients may not have the private resources to supplement this, add needed sessions, or switch to private mediators for expanded services.

For these reasons, many public sector mandatory mediation services are provided in fewer sessions, with less individual work, and often with much less attention to therapeutic issues, emotions, or the cognitive or family restructuring that needs to take place for the separation process to be the best it could be. A typical court-connected service may offer divorce and separation mediation in one to four sessions, as either one marathon session or several sessions, where some models in the private sector look at sets of individual and joint sessions that can be double and triple the time and cost.

It is less likely that court-connected or mandatory mediation services will directly include the children as part of the mediation effort. In fact, the limits of time and the focus on outcomes of mediated agreements within a certain time frame to prevent further litigation can force the divorce mediator to use models and methods that can actually undermine the basic intent and foundation of mediation. The wise divorce mediator working in such a setting will be wary of such structural conflicts within the setting and will work to alleviate them.

In most regions of the United States today, most couples considering divorce have the option of either low- to no-cost public sector mediation services or private practitioners who offer specialized services, although sparsely populated areas may have little choice in practitioner, style, or completeness of services. No matter whether they are private or public, divorce mediators need to operate from their best practices and resist attempts by the clients, bureaucracies, court policies, ideologies of model and approach, funding crises, and other external forces to dictate the way in which they offer mediation. Whether operating in the mandatory court-connected or government-contracted services, or as private practitioners, divorce mediators' highest duties are to the clients' needs and their own professional ethics. Each policy and decision made by the mediator needs to reflect this perspective.

MARRIED VERSUS UNMARRIED SEPARATIONS

Separation of a couple as an emotional and social process is often very similar between married couples and unmarried couples with children, and yet they can be treated very differently by jurisdictions and systems. One emotional difference between married and unmarried couples might be the level of intimacy and commitment each partner felt for the other during the relationship. Sometimes unmarried partners agreed to have children together even though they had not made a firm or lasting commitment to each other as partners. This commitment to parenthood rather than partnerhood can lead to very different dynamics between the parting couple and the extended family.

Our system of divorce mediation is still predicated on the now false assumption that the majority of couples are granted the benefits and responsibilities of marriage by the state, which then has the responsibility of determining fairness and parental responsibility when they part. Yet parents are often unaware of the need for determining and filing a legally binding set of parenting understandings with the court at the time of parting if they were unmarried. Courts and jurisdictions often had a funding mechanism for gaining fees for services based on marriage licenses and divorce filings, but have had to create new funding sources for providing mediation services to unmarried parents who may have never filed a filiation action even to establish paternity and initial responsibility for their mutual children.

When the relationship has been informal, nonlegal, and nonbinding by choice, it is often confusing to the parents as to why they should mediate or create legal documents. They need to understand the benefits of making the ending of such relationships and the parenting formal and legally binding. Divorce mediators may have to be able to help unmarried parents come to terms with this paradox before they can get to the content of the dispute.

My clinical experience with unmarried couples who are leaving each other is that the circumstances of the pregnancy are very relevant to the dispute over child custody, parenting time, or child support. If one partner never wanted to be a parent and requested abortion or has inadequately parented the child, this automatically becomes relevant to the legitimacy of the dispute in the minds of the participants when they have parted. The unaddressed issue of claiming responsibility or fatherhood of the child, of taking active and legal responsibility, and the resulting resentment and disaffection that resulted becomes the first task in mediating these cases.

Because many couples' relationships have been informal, short-duration partnerships and liaisons or even noncohabiting brief affairs that produced children, the level of understanding of each other as persons and as parents is often very small. These are people who really do not know each other and who are required to try to cooperate with each other for the children for at least eighteen years. When they are longer-term, cohabiting, more emotionally involved relationships that are just lacking the legal status of marriage, they function interactively much more like most marriages and other parenting systems. Legal marital status, or lack of it, will not give the mediator the true understanding of the relationship. Asking each of the partners to tell their love story (separately or together, based on the mediator's model of practice) may help the mediator and the participants themselves recognize the fullness or limitations of their understanding of each other as partners and as parents.

Once the true level of emotional and social interconnectedness and relationship is determined, all of the other issues of divorce mediation seem to apply for unmarried parents. They, like all other separating parents, need to determine not only the legal categories of custody, residence, and parenting access schedules and child support but also how they will interact with each other. They

314 THE HANDBOOK OF FAMILY DISPUTE RESOLUTION

have to renegotiate their levels of involvement and communication, like all other separating families. However, the difference is again felt when they need to submit these mediated understandings to the court for its approval. Prior legal work of establishing paternity, which then grants them standing to have parenting rights and responsibilities, may need to be done before the parenting understandings are accepted by the court.

Socially, the unmarried parent may need to do some prior work before the separation takes place. Due to the loss of the other parent, this person may need to announce or acknowledge the child to grandparents and the extended family in order to engage their help and support as part of the family system. Mediators who have the understanding of family systems can help unmarried parents figure out how to do this important work with the extended family, particularly if the unmarried parents have been socially isolated from the larger family for reasons of age, geography, religion, or culture.

A Case of Unknown Partners

One case comes to mind that illustrates the ambiguous status and lack of personal knowledge of the unmarried partner. In this case, the father was a student from Iran, and the mother was a local resident who had been estranged from her family of origin until the end of the brief affair and her pregnancy promoted a new closeness to her own mother, with the new grandchild as the third member of the triangle. The father had announced the birth of the child to his extended family, who promptly sent the little girl a set of earrings (a cultural sign of acceptance of the child by the grandparent). The separating couple agreed on custody and parental access, but they were in dispute over the father's desire to take the child to Iran to meet the grandmother. Part of the mediation was determining how the parents would allow the child her Persian heritage as part of his large extended family in Iran without disrupting the newly forming bond with the local grandparent, who was supplying the family with needed child care.

Because they did not understand each other's cultural expectations or norms and did not understand each other's unique personalities and needs as people, these parents found the mediation very difficult. They had so little shared experience other than their two years off and on together that each did not understand what was important to the other. The divorce mediator tried to help both parents to understand each other's personal and cultural needs and interests, as well as to make age-appropriate decisions about their child and delay her having extended time away from her important adults in order to gain other loving relationships and know her heritage. To minimize the risk of harm to the child, the mother agreed to take the girl to Iran herself after she was five years old, if the father maintained his own relationship with the child and bought the round-trip tickets. This agreement was a necessary compromise on the mother's part.

Gay and Lesbian Couple Separation

As noted in Chapter Seven, gay and lesbian people are as likely as heterosexuals to form and live in couples, but they cannot legally marry in most states; therefore, gay and lesbian relationships are similar in dynamic to the description for unmarried heterosexual couples. No formal legal permission to part can be granted by the court, although many states have gone to a process of legal declaration of domestic partnership, which confers certain rights on the declared partner. Since the state's interest in preserving marriages in order to ensure continuity of care for children is not usually involved in gay relationships, the increasing numbers of gay and lesbian couples who are raising children—their own biological ones or those they adopt together as a couple—could make this same state interest rationale more compelling for gay and lesbian couples over time, especially if they have taken on the added dimension of parenting.

Some gay and lesbian couples may have had intentional statements made on paper at the time of a joining ceremony or through prepartnership mediation, and these serve as the basis of expectation for the couple. Joan Laird (1993) notes that "gay families, like heterosexuals, vary tremendously in how they live and story their lives" (p. 291). Many gay couples are very intentional about their couples dynamic and have been explicit with each other as to their legal, social, and personal relationships. Many recent books on forming or becoming a couple are written from a gay couple perspective, because there are few automatic assumptions in effect as the couple creates their own reality.

The issue of personal coming out is also a theme that is intensified when the couple publicly acknowledges itself as a long-term couple. The traditional assumptions of family life stage and development do not always hold for homosexual and lesbian couples, since there are many variations depending on the identity development of each of the partners, the age and stage of their own family development at which they recognized and outwardly acknowledged their orientation, and the stage of life when they created the current partnership.

As with all other relationships, the issues of level of personal commitment to the partner and level of personal knowledge of the other person are still the primary concerns at the point at which the couple has decided for separation. If this has been a long-term, devoted, personally committed relationship, there will likely be grief, loss, blame, and responsibility issues that must be worked out, and most of the couple dynamics patterns described for heterosexual couples may also hold true for the gay or lesbian couple. The couple's relative inclusion within the larger extended families must also be considered, as well as any parenting decisions they must make and the readjustment of expectation of care for a former partner.

If it was a brief relationship with many negatives such as outside affairs, lying, substance abuse, or other concerns, the parting may feel like more of a relief than a deep pain, and yet there may be entanglements of finances, child rearing, pet ownership, or other shared areas that need to be negotiated in order to part fairly. Concepts of promiscuity and monogamy within the relationship are important dynamics. Although there are some cultural themes in the larger gay and lesbian culture that may be more tolerant of multiple partners or even unemotional sexual relationships, the AIDS epidemic, health coverage and medical issues, the emergence of domestic partnership status and benefits that must be discussed in order to achieve or change them, and the mixed social acceptance and opposition to gay rights have contributed to a climate of increasing intolerance for disloyalty in a committed personal relationship.

Family mediators should not make automatic assumptions about any couple they encounter, gay or straight, but must ask about the particular issues involved in the construction of the relationship, the changes that have taken place, the attempts made to repair the relationship, and the goals of deconstruction for that particular set of people. Family mediators should continue to be aware of the new family research being done about the sameness and variances between these couples and heterosexual couples, which can help them shape the response to mediating their separations and parting.

COMPLETE DIVORCES OR PARENTING ISSUES ONLY

When they first began in the 1970s and 1980s, court-connected public sector mediators dealt only with parenting-related issues during divorce, and the advising attorneys dealt with the financial aspects of the divorce. At the same time, divorce mediators in private practice were willing and able to do complete divorce decision making, leading to a less divided, more integrated experience for those who were willing to pay the added cost.

Recently, jurisdictions have experimented with bifurcation of the case when it first comes to the attention of the court, with the financial issues arbitrated and the parenting issues mediated. Some jurisdictions have also let divorce mediators do property settlement, child support calculations, and spousal support negotiations if the participants requested or allowed it. Other jurisdictions have found the local bar associations strongly opposed to allowing public sector mediators to do financial aspects of divorce; they argue that such mediators were often not lawyers themselves, did not necessarily know the relevant case law and statutes, and would be doing the unauthorized practice of law if they were to do this function.

Part of the rationale has always been that parenting decisions are always changeable and therefore can be handled by mediators, but the final marital property settlement and spousal support generally cannot be reversed and so requires the knowledge and expertise of attorneys. However, this rationale for not having mediators do complete divorce decision making or mediate financial decisions breaks down when one considers that most cases of divorce do not have separate advising attorneys, and there is no provision to provide them to citizens who cannot afford it. Public sector mediators are often providing the only services most separating parents will get. Would it not be better to have at least one pair of professionally trained eyes look over the financial arrangements, even if those eyes were those of a mediator rather than an advising attorney?

In fact, computerized programs now automatically calculate fair and equal monthly spousal support and appropriate child support and taxes, based on updated state laws and plug-in figures, so the issue of who can do this work has become a moot point. Some jurisdictions are requiring this kind of computerized statement as proof of accuracy and full disclosure as part of every case heard, and mediators are able to use these programs as well as attorneys and judges. As the technology of these aids improves, their accuracy increases, and whether the mediator has a legal or a human service background becomes less of an issue in providing clients with accurate, fair problem solving consistent with the laws and procedures of their state. With this technology, even a mediator with little financial or legal training can help families make fair and workable agreements.

Similarly, all states must provide a system of child support guidelines that complies with the national Uniform Child Support Act; therefore, they now use formulaic methods to calculate scheduled child support rather than leaving this to the judge in a case to determine. While there is some latitude in the guidelines for unique circumstances, the goal is to ensure that children are treated fairly and the decisions are equitable no matter where children live or which judge hears the case. Some states (Oregon is one) have their forms, guidelines, and even self-calculating child support forms posted on their Web sites, so clients can calculate their child support payments whenever their economics change. These new technological advances can only get better. This level of sophistication in anyone's ability to produce a fair and legal set of options and outcomes means that the rationale of having only one type of professional with this capacity is outdated.

Financial Issues

In the majority of court-connected cases, the participants own nothing yet owe something, so the issues of parting are often about fairness and capacity to service a debt load based on possible income through work rather than dividing complex assets. Consumer credit counseling, low-cost legal services that teach law students how to do bankruptcy actions, and other related financial services may be more the issue for many cases. In my clinical experience in public sector work, where I often worked with poor to middle-class families, as well as in private practice, I was rarely dealing with dividing abundant resources.

Helping families get connected to public resources, social service agencies, and other financial aid systems was much more common, since divorce requires an increase in living expenses at a time when some people have the same or even less ability to provide financial help.

To help my clients learn about their true financial picture, I created a simple self-calculating budget sheet, using a copyrighted program available to most home computer users. This budget sheet looked at the current reality and also had space for the likely (increasing) future costs of living separately, returning to school, getting therapy, and dealing with the unique costs of doing the divorce. (Appendix E provides a sample budget planning sheet.) Much more advanced programs no doubt do or will exist that can help clients determine their own financial and property issues and options.

Properly trained divorce mediators who have the same computer tools and financial information and training as attorneys and their staff can generate the same quality of outcome and fully advise clients. Wise divorce mediators who are going to do complete divorce decision making should invest in their own training and continuing education and use the same tools as advising attorneys. These tools will become more accurate, easier to use, and perhaps even standardized within jurisdictions, so that both private mediators and public sector mediation programs can offer poor and legally disenfranchised citizens some of the same help and support that they would get if they could afford legal and financial services. This then serves the concept of equity and fairness for all clients, one of the important ethical considerations of the field of mediation.

John Haynes (1994) has described in detail how he mediated family financial issues to help families have complete divorce decision making, pointing out not only the financial issues (according to New York law where he was practicing) but also the mediation-related aspects. He points out that mediators are free to help participants make choices that are not what would have been imposed if they went to court but what they themselves feel is fair and equitable:

> So, we need to know the law but not to be bound by it. If we become bound by the law, mediation becomes a paralegal process that imposes the same outcome on the clients as a court would. Mediation is an empowering process that gives clients the right, the ability, and the process to determine what is right for their family. The mediator's role is to manage the issues that emerge for each couple as the property is divided. The more coherent and organized the process, the easier it is for the clients to arrive at solutions that are appropriate to them. [p. 92]

Based on my experience in the private and public sectors, I have found that participants are often eager and happy to have a mediator help them understand exactly what their current financial reality is, without fear that such a discussion will explode, become more divisive, or be a way of creating conflict and churning the case to create larger fees. Most people in long-term relationships have not been acting as the business partners they are, and so often one person has all the financial information, expertise, or concern. By talking about these issues in mediation, both participants can at least debunk the myth that someone is getting a financial upper hand. This discussion can reduce the often unrealistic and paralyzing fears of being left penniless or being taken advantage of by the other person. It minimizes the competitive stance many have begun.

Starting with Parenting Rather Than Money

Although John Haynes indicated that in complete divorce mediation cases, he would start with the marital property division, I have found that parents need to start with the parenting understandings and then move on to child support, both of which affect monthly income and expenses. If that discussion is successful, then we finally mediate the property settlement, which is usually based on larger, less usable assets and debts. This order is important for two reasons. First, if they start with parenting plans and schedules and the needs of children on a daily and weekly basis, the discussion may indicate which parent needs what specific resources. For example, the parent with two children needs the minivan, while the other parent with one child can probably get by with the two-seater truck.

The second reason I start with parenting concerns is that if the participants cannot cooperate about meeting each other's need and focusing on the best interests of the children or if they are only partially able to do this type of negotiation with uncomfortable, tension-filled acrimony, it is unlikely that the financial mediation is going to be easy or productive. If they are totally frustrated with each other by the end of mediating the parenting issues, the mediator can again ask whether they would like to stop mediating and go to attorneys and advisers instead. If they leave mediation at that point, at least the mediator has been able to help them solidify the parenting relationship issues, which are less clearly defined than the financial issues. They will have done their best work in mediation and can rely on the other systems to give them fair outcomes to the harder issues of money through standard calculations. Complete divorce mediation may need to be broken into these parts and left conditional on the participants' willingness to continue to the next part once an issue has been settled.

Universal Themes in Divorce and Separation Cases

Five major themes must be covered for every divorce or separation case, no matter what model or approach is used.

1. *Ending the personal relationship.* If there is any doubt or hope in one partner's mind that the divorce needs to happen, it is best to explore

that before going any further. Many couples have not talked, have given ambivalent messages by telephone or letter or innuendo, have not yet made a personal decision, or have been relying on the other person to make the final choice. Taking personal responsibility and holding themselves and the other accountable for what did and did not happen that led to the demise of the relationship is important emotional work during divorce. When the decision is clear but the rationale is not strong, it can lead to remorse and rethinking. If the decision is clear but the partners have never shared the reasons, they need a forum to do this in a firm, respectful, and healing way. They need to grieve this loss before they can tackle the business of planning the new life for themselves and their children.

2. *Redefining what continues.* If they are parents of mutual children, they must confront the paradox of finding a way to both end and continue with each other. If they have been actively parenting a child but have no legal relationship (they are stepparents or live-ins), they need to discuss the options for continued involvement, perhaps decreasing their involvement to that similar to a favored aunt or uncle or increasing involvement due to distress by the child. If they want to stay friends, they must figure out in what ways that is different from what they had when they were together. What new boundaries do they have to have with each other, for example, and what can't they do any more?

3. *Taking on new life patterns.* Partners who have been economically supported must make choices about careers and jobs to be more available. They must be willing to change their patterns of interaction with the partner, the children, their work, and their other activities. They have to start rebuilding a new life economically, socially, parentally, and emotionally without the other partner and, it is hoped, without prematurely attaching to others in a new dependency relationship.

4. *Making urgent or temporary changes.* Because divorce as a process can take months or even years to accomplish, they need to set deadlines for events such as becoming economically self-sufficient, selling or refinancing assets, moving to separate quarters, and physically separating and acting as if they were already divorced.

5. *Making long-term plans.* If they need to sell the former marital home, how long might it be before they can buy another house? If they will not be done with job retraining for two years, what will happen then? How will they afford college for their children as they planned? How do they plan to interact with each other over time?

Just as the entire mediation has a beginning, a middle, and an end, so does each session within the larger mediation process. Remembering that the participants need to give opening remarks at each session and have time to finish and understand what they have accomplished and what more they need to do is part of conducting the mediation. Beginning mediators often rush these important rituals of starting and ending because they do not have containment skills, or they respond to the urgency or manipulative processes of the participants, or they do not manage the time allocation of the session or respect their own boundaries of starting and ending on time. These are errors to avoid in setting up and managing the mediation process.

The Crucible of Conflict

In his book *Passionate Marriage,* David Schnarch (1997) notes how each couple with sexual or marital problems creates a "sexual crucible," that is, they keep creating the sexual dilemma in order to be changed inside it. A similar process happens in family and divorce mediation if the mediator allows it. The family dispute becomes the vehicle for personal and family change processes and so has meaning, worth, and importance. Until the couple or family is able to change sufficiently, they must remain in the crucible of conflict.

Mediation participants who are divorcing or separating go into the mediation crucible when they hit their seemingly irreconcilable differences while trying to co-create the new parenting system. They in effect recapitulate their conflict and crisis in the mediator's office and run headlong into the same interactional problems that have led them to declare the marriage so damaged that they need to end it. At this point, many participants hit the wall of the conflict that created the need for mediation. Here was the challenge for change, the precise moment they could never get beyond in their marriage, the specific issue they each and both need to work on, the point where transformation of the self and transformation of the interactional system they have co-created happens. They will keep recreating the same dilemma or an evolving but similar dilemma that features the same interpersonal dynamic or pattern until they can find another way to deal with it. This is a dangerous but spectacular moment when the potential for personal and system change is at its height. The challenge of divorce mediation for the participants of the dispute to interact differently lies in this moment with its potential for change within the crucible of conflict.

This change point in mediation, which can happen in any session, is when the deep interactional pattern of conflict reemerges in all its complexity. When this happens, it allows the levels and type of conflict within the individual and couples system to be more fully understood and dealt with in a way different than they had ever done before, although each person usually tries the same old pattern of interaction. The job of the mediation process is to intervene in the old ways they had of behaving with each other (for example, bullying, pouting, complaining, blaming, resisting, or denying). By having the mediator stay in the interaction with them, naming and reflecting everything that is happening, they can see the problem and deal with it differently. In this process, they create those personal and interactional reformulations or transformations.

Sometimes participants hit the wall of conflict but do not know what to do differently. They may be ready to accept some coaching, feedback, or new ideas. Some need to go home and think about what has happened and come back changed. Others recognize that they are hitting the wall but are not willing to change their attitudes, beliefs, behaviors, or interactions at all at that moment or later, after reflection. These critical moments in interaction can often be determining factors in whether the participants will be able to continue to mediate at all.

DESCRIBING A CASE USING AN INTERACTIVE MODEL

Divorce mediation as I practice it, whether complete with financial considerations or limited to parenting-related concerns, has always had some sense of beginning, middle, and end, with some common themes but much that is unique to the individual people and problems as they present it.

I tend to mediate complete divorce mediation cases in the five-topic sequence listed above, blending emotional tasks with financial and parental issues. Families and couples do not tend to divide their lives into neat boxes, so I do not try to keep them from doing the work they need to do. A typical sequence for my mediation practice is to have one to six sessions, each lasting sixty to ninety minutes. Each session has a smaller version of the beginning-middle-end pace, since going much over ten minutes late compromises the next scheduled appointments. I write case notes reflecting each session as documentation and keep track of decisions made on a worksheet that helps remind me of common issues and choices that must be made.

Each session needs to focus both on the content of the negotiations and the process and interaction of the participants, both separately and together, with me and with each other. In some sessions, content or process could predominate, or there could be a flow between them. My general belief is that good content will not result if there is negative process, so my mantra is *process precedes content*. This means that as a mediator, I intervene to create the kinds of conditions in interaction that facilitate making healthy content decisions.

During and after each session, I reflect on these questions:

- Are these parents disputing because they are attempting to meet their own needs or because of how they define the needs of the child in question?

- Are they consciously and intentionally trying to sway the other, or are they operating out of an old pattern that they are unaware of?

- Are they open to any input from any source? If not the other parent or me, what could be persuasive to them?

- Are they arguing about deep principles or merely their own preferences?

- How characteristic is this dilemma for them as a couple? What does it say about their power balance?

- What help does each participant need from me in order for the other to hear him or her?

Session One: Climate, Concerns, and Commitment

The first session typically is spent getting to know the people and the problems and starting to determine the process that I think might be necessary. I give the participants some feedback on how they are coming across to each other and me during the interaction. This session is more structured than subsequent sessions, since it is up to me as mediator to explain the process and provide the agenda yet leave room for their concerns and needs to show through. (I often liken this to the first session with a physician, where the patient describes the problems and the doctor does basic tests to help rule in and rule out certain diagnoses.) The participants will already have completed a fairly extensive checklist that indicates what they each think are problems and concerns and outlines the past parenting system. The concrete content in the first session is getting a written agreement to mediate, explaining all the requirements outlined in our standards of practice, and assessing the case for domestic violence and intimidation concerns by having at least a few minutes separately with each.

In my model of mediation, I spend twenty to thirty minutes separately with each person during the first session, because I believe that participants need to know their own best and worst case, goals and intentions, and fears and processes in order to bargain with each other out of strength. Because the majority of my clients have not and will not be seeing advising attorneys prior to active mediation, I help them assess their own knowledge, debunk myths, and provide equalizing information, as well as sort through their aspirations. The separate time allows them to be open and is productive in understanding each of them as people, their construction of the dispute, and the potential for ending it.

In terms of process, I also use this first session to model the type of interaction that is productive, notice their style of interaction and assess where and how to intervene, do some defining of boundaries between them and with me as the mediator, and if there is time, set some expectations for them as divorcing parents. I always assume that they are evaluating me as much as I am evaluating them and that they will decide if they can trust and work with me. By the end of this first session, they are also deciding if they could work with the other participant and trying to establish how they would deal with situations during mediation.

Ahrons and Rogers (1987) point out that parents who go through the divorce and subsequent remarriage process tend to fall into a continuum from Perfect Pals to Cooperative Colleagues, Angry Associates, Fiery Foes, and Dissolved Duos, each with a different style of interaction with each other. These descriptive terms, based on the data they found, still seem to be relevant to divorcing parents, although they can be restrictive if imposed rather than used as convenient groupings. I often use this five-part schema to get the parenting couple to tell me what they want and where they think they are on that continuum. By creating the meta-goal for the divorce or postdivorce relationship, they are both actively co-creating the new narrative about how they might be successful in the future. If they had very different goals or are still operating from a need for negative intimacy, fearing loss due to insecure attachment issues, or wanting revenge for past injustices, I bring these emotional issues to their awareness and help them start to accept this as a starting condition for their process and see if they are able to make personal and interactional change on these issues.

If either of the participants indicates a hope for reconciliation, I bring that to the awareness of the other in joint session. If the hopes of remaining together are dashed right there, I help that partner decide how to deal with his or her emotions by taking a few minutes in separate session or by referring out to support people or therapy. If one person is unwilling to be clear in his or her determination to part, then the next agenda is to return to discussing the meaning of staying together versus parting, holding the hard discussion about whether parting is necessary, and attempting to co-create a reality of staying as well as parting. In other words, they have to do some conciliation (marital mediation) to resolve this issue before anything can be accomplished in mediating.

The exception to this pattern of mediation is that although I primarily stay with parenting issues first, I try to have them do some planning for temporary financial and social needs for the immediate future (between this session and the next or for the current month) regarding household expenses, bills and money, visits, and other items. We mediate these temporary decisions to provide order and stabilize the status quo long enough for them to return for the next session to discuss whether they are in fact parting and what it would take to stay together. In my experience, parents cannot focus on idealized parenting or long-term issues or permanent choices if they are facing immediate pressing needs, are scared about money, or have no current plan for dealing with children, housing, and bills. I sometimes assign undecided couples the task of doing a worksheet adaptation of the work by Karen Kayser (1993) on the process of marital disaffection to determine where they are individually and as a couple.

Assuming I get confirmation that they are willing to return to mediation, I try to set an agenda for the second session based on the issues I have heard individually and collectively in this first meeting. Because I believe that personal

professional reassessment, I believe in the power of homework assignments,

Depending on each person's concerns and issues, I sometimes suggest some selected chapters from Isolina Ricci's (1997) wonderful book, *Mom's House, Dad's House*, about the emotions of ending the relationship, long distance issues, and parenting plans. If there are concerns expressed about inadequate or abusive or neglectful parenting or about what children of different ages can handle, I suggest that one or both parents read in Jean Clarke and Connie Dawson's (1998) book *Growing Up Again* about the specific ages and stages of their child and their concerns about the other parent's nurturing or structure (or lack of either). Parents who need to understand the emotions and options of divorce will find these resources helpful. Their decision not to read this or similar material gives me insight into their motivation. Those who use complaints as roadblocks or red herrings in bargaining might find that they cannot be as successful in maintaining their negative stance; when they have been required to use outside information as a legitimate standard for making decisions, the choice to ignore it allows the other parent to gauge the reasonableness of the options and demands, as well as the true level of child-centered decisions each parent is making.

At the end of the first session, I also help them do a very small traded mutual assurance or solve a very small problem—something that would be of concern between then and the next time I saw them, such as visiting the children, paying a specific bill, or having access to tools. Making a decision can ease tension, and it also gives me a lot of information about how they do or do not work together. If the small bargaining is successful, they walk out having made at least one concrete decision together, which gives hope for future mediation. If not, the way they tried to negotiate and their lack of success becomes a topic we talk about in terms of their process during the next session.

This first mediation session is the most critical to establishing the kind of process that could be acceptable to them. Each first session is both formulaic, in that there are definite tasks of contracting for mediation and determining what will be mediated, and unique for the couple based on their personal concerns, process dynamics, and needs. Finding out what is really in dispute and discovering the underlying concerns, emotionality, and individual needs of the participants as well as their negotiation style and conflict orientation always makes the first session challenging.

Session Two: Refining, Reframing, and Redirecting

The second session needs to start with the question, "What has happened to each of you since I last saw you?" Because of the fluidity of the emotional and social changes that can take place, it is not surprising to find that the participants have attempted a sexual renewal and decided to reconcile or that the agreement they made at the end of the first session did not happen, leading to further anger, estrangement, or problems and credibility concerns. Other people take the new information from the readings and discussion to heart and make major positional or personal transformation, which can either reduce or exacerbate the conflicts. Whatever has happened, I assume that the participants must reconfirm or reshape this in the light of their mediation effort. They must use what worked and did not work for them and base new ways of responding on this understanding. This process of readjustment and redefinition helps the participants and the mediator reframe the issues, the alternatives, and the commitments. If the situation has gotten worse, I have each person describe this to the other during joint session narrative and then break into some individual time to find out what further meaning and conclusions they have drawn from this joint information. Returning to joint session, I invite the participants to share their thoughts and then mutually remake the agenda, rule options out, or refocus attention on an issue that has become more primary.

When these new understandings have been discussed, I then focus the parents on the topic of their plans for parenting, stopping whenever they disagree to understand the concerns, fears, or history of the issue. If their process is positive and they are ready to start discussions and decisions, they do this about the legal and social issues of parenting, while I record the decisions, remind them of other topics they need to decide, and help them interact.

Parting parents need to discuss and make informed decisions about the following typical topics regarding parenting during the second and subsequent sessions.

- *Legal custody*—the authority to make major decisions about the child and the level of decision making the noncustodial parent has in small daily matters.
  - *Sole*—100 percent authority to one parent, who makes all decisions.
  - *Joint*—parents must consult with each other to make mutually acceptable choices and agree on the decision.
- *Physical custody*—the residential pattern of where the child stays.
  - *Sole*—the child primarily resides in one household and has parenting time with or access to the other parent (that is, the child lives with one parent).
  - *Split*—multiple children are divided, so that each household has at least one child who primarily resides there (for example, one child resides with the mother and one with the father).
  - *Shared*—each parent has each child a significant portion (usually 35 percent or more) of the child's time at his or her residence, so that the child is living at both places at least periodically (for example, nine months with the mother and the summer with the father, or the

child moves from one household to the other on a scheduled rotation basis).

the parent (and any other children) he or she does not live with, may be modified to require someone else to be present (supervised visitation).

- *Access to or by extended family members*—expectations regarding grandparents and other family members can be determined rather than leaving it to the other parent.

- *Holiday, birthday, and vacation planning*—including which holidays the child will celebrate and who will make that happen and how family birthdays and vacations from school will be handled.

- *Communication, information sharing, and telephone and e-mail access*—frequency, topics, and modes of communication between parents, parents and child, and child and extended family members. If parents are going to be joint legal or physical custodians, how often will they hold parenting meetings to exchange information prior to making mutually acceptable decisions?

- *Relocation of child or parent that affects the parenting plan*—notification of the other parent, provisos about not unduly disrupting the educational process or school attendance, and reworking the physical custody or parenting time if distance is a factor.

- *Transportation to facilitate parenting time*—if there are costs, who will pick up and deliver children, whether a neutral site is needed, and safety when transporting.

- *Discipline techniques*—parenting style, unacceptable and preferred methods of providing structure and nurturing, reporting of events between parents, and consistency needs between homes and parents.

- *Substitute care*—when a parent must be gone from home for illness, work responsibilities, family, or fun, who can be in place of parent, what happens if this is becoming too frequent, and payment responsibility.

- *Child's cultural, religious, and sports activities, and friends*—which activities and settings the parents want to promote or inhibit no matter which parent is supervising and who will pay the costs.

- *Introduction of new people*—expectations between parents regarding lifestyle and new partner choices of the parent that could affect the child's moral or social development.

Most of these topics are social expectations and understandings that must be individually designed based on the interests, needs, capabilities, and past problems in parenting. In some ways, even if one parent is designing the new parenting system as a top-down single decision maker, the process of discussing the likely decisions of the sole legal custodian leads parents to more predictable, less anxiety-producing understandings of the new parenting system. The noncustodial parent during mediation is empowered to voice concern or support, something he or she may not be able to do after the court awards the sole legal custody.

Some parents have one absolutely critical issue and relax their stance on all other topics if they can secure assurances about that issue. The more fully the parents can discuss these topics and make mutually acceptable decisions during the divorce, the more likely it is that they will avoid future problems and conflicts. If the parents cannot agree on the needs of the child, the benefits of one option over another, or even the need to have some rules or expectations about a certain topic, those issues present into a series of small conflicts during the mediation. These can be resolved individually rather than as one huge fight about custody with winner-take-all stakes.

If parents are basically in agreement about these parenting topics, this second session usually produces the majority of parenting-related decisions needed to renegotiate the family structure and role division. If they are not, it helps sharpen the specifics of disagreement, with time for parents to research other options, opinions, and support. At the end of the second session, I have the participants recap the discussion, acknowledge and empower the commonalities, point out the discrepancies, and again assign each person something to think about or research relevant to their reaction (process) or the conflicted issue (content) before next session.

Session Three: Crisis, Climax, and Denouement

The third session is often a watershed time, partly because of the fact that in a typical public sector domestic relations mediation agency, public funding will be running out and the participants will have to decide whether they can complete the mediation effort and whether they are willing to commit to further sessions and pay for them. Even if the sessions are all fully subsidized or are paid for by the clients, this session is still a meaningful midpoint. At this point, each participant has usually run into at least some roadblocks or some resistance to personal preferences or is suspicious as to the ease with which they are negotiating together.

The focus during this session must be on the process, suspending the concerns about the usefulness of mediation and being open about whether each is still willing to continue the mediation effort given what they have experienced so far. Like a novel, this newly co-constructed mediation narrative has or should be reaching a crisis that the characters must resolve successfully. Unconflicted parents are usually able to do most of the major decision making or at least develop some options for further reflection and discussion during the second session, so this third session often becomes less about the content and more about how they are treating each other. The focus often shifts to their deeper values conflicts, the lack of trust and respect they have for each other carried over from the ~~rough relationship~~ ...

... change from a ~~situation~~ ~~... in style, problem solving, and ~~an~~ ... approach dealing with the content of the decisions to be made to a more therapeutic mode. I invite both parents to look at their own unmet needs, plus those of the other parent, their child, and the entire family system. It is here where deep interactional patterns around power and control, attachment, response to conflict, culturally supported negotiation styles, unexpressed emotions, and each individual's capacities and intrapersonal patterns can be getting in the way of the interaction.

When these patterns are deeply ingrained or are part of a mental or emotional health issue, sometimes referral to individual therapy is needed. Sometimes consultations with advising attorneys, child development specialists, or other persuasive information can create a face-saving change in attitudes, beliefs, or behavior during the session. The uniqueness of the individuals and the particular issues involved in their family system make this session of mediation very personal.

Session Four and Beyond: Change and Decisions

The mediator's role as an intervener on the old system and as facilitator to creation of the new interactional system is to create a constant feedback loop for the participants. The goal is to provide insight as to what is happening in their interaction and to translate to the other participant the issues, processes, and concerns they may not have been able to hear from each other. Constantly moving between content (positional statements about parenting wishes) and process (how they were going about trying to get what they wanted, what they were doing), I try to mirror and also shape the discussion in ways that highlight those critical moments.

Sometimes this point is characterized by classic distributive bargaining. Occasionally, to intervene on a nonproductive moment, I separate them and have individual time to enable them to talk out loud without ruining their bargaining with each other. Sometimes I intervene with pieces of information about child development or parenting plans that might provide them with a third option that they could develop further and mutually accept. Sometimes I stay strictly in the realm of the process dynamics between the individuals, acting as a reporter and mirror, asking them what they personally want to do to make change, rather than the old question about what they want the other person to do or not do. This part of mediation, which is not a stage but a process development that can take place anywhere during mediation, seems to reflect Rummel's idea, noted in Chapter Two, of conflict as powers meeting and balancing. This deeper conflict process is the crucible that has the potential to change everything and help create a whole new way of interacting for the family system.

In this interactional model, I allow myself the option of doing power balancing for a participant whom I feel is compromised by old patterned responses, lack of verbal ability, cultural or systemic disenfranchisement, or physiological handicaps. Often I find myself encouraging and supporting each participant by saying something to the effect of, "If you can get through this issue successfully, you can get through all the others." I believe that the "stuck spot" is exactly where mediation should lead them, and it is characteristic of their need for self and system growth and development. If they are able to do this now and here, they will always be able to do it. If they make that courageous leap, I try to support the new changes by marking the moment. If they cannot, I talk to them separately about what it will take for them to do this in the future and what help they need now given that they are so stuck. By becoming part of the temporary interactional system but maintaining my own grounding as a counselor, mediator, and helper, I believe that the discussion between them is always different than it would have been had I not been there.

Moments like I am describing are intense, absorbing, and energy depleting. I often feel that I am caught in their tornado, that their vortex of conflict cannot and should not pull me in entirely, since I and they need me to hold on to my own place and continue to provide help and support for what is changeable and recognition of what is not. Sometimes in order to break the feeling of vortex, I provide an interrupter, such as a story that they can focus on, or I end the session a little early, with specific assignments of things to think about differently. If they are able to resolve this conflict without giving in or giving up, there is usually noticeable tension reduction in the room.

Assuming that the participants recognize and are able to do one thing differently either during the session where the deep, characteristic interactional problem surfaces or later, in between sessions, the participants return either feeling hopeless and unable to make change and agreements or willing and able to resolve the remaining issues, having successfully tackled the biggest issue: their way of interacting. Often these next few sessions are very speedy, detail oriented, and content laden. It is a matter of cuing their attention to the topics that need decisions and letting the new interaction between them find the answers for themselves.

If the process issue has not been resolved or the person who made change lapses back into his or her old patterns and processes, I believe that in the interactional model, it is the job of the mediator to bring that to the participants' awareness and ask if they can continue using the new methods. The mediator becomes a process recorder who notices and calls attention to the times when the dynamics change. The mediator helps the participants do the content tasks they need to cover but helps them, like a coach on the sidelines, to play the game according to the new rules and with the new game plan in effect.

If this has been successful, the participants will continue to negotiate the discrete decisions they need in order to part and reconstruct their parenting, social, and economic issues, such as calculating child support, assessing marital property and debt, and making lifestyle decisions. They will often have another topic that will bring about the same response and interaction, but the mediator will make them aware that this is another opportunity to follow their own new ways. Smaller or even larger conflicts can be negotiated based on the newly constructed paradigm of interaction.

Participants may need several more sessions to go through all the information, discussion, and decision making necessary for complete divorce or separation. This often feels like an urge to get it over with, and some participants get anxious to end mediation efforts and return to the adversarial adjudication stage, since they have difficulty maintaining the new order of interaction and wish to be relieved of that responsibility. This so-called flight to agreement can lead to some ill-considered or hasty decisions that should be reviewed and either ratified or modified by advising attorneys or other support people. Participants at this stage have either strengthened their resolve and believe that fairness and good process is possible between them and they can successfully complete the mediation, or they find a single issue to use as the scapegoat and justify leaving the mediation process by continuing to blame, vilify, or remain in the old interactional pattern, forcing the other participant to end the process. Just as each person contracts to be there, each can end that contract and withdraw. Not showing up for sessions, asking to change mediators, or other dodges are often an indirect way of showing a vote of no confidence in the process, the changes, or the newly constructed interactional requirements.

Because real events can intervene, I do not assume that I know what is happening when someone does not show up for a session, and I talk to them to find the reason. Because it is so hard for some participants to voice their level of dissatisfaction with mediation or with their own ability to adapt to the new system that is being created, it seems important for the mediator to reach out once to the client who does not show up, but constant telephone calls can be too pressuring. I believe in the right of clients to be self-determining, and therefore it is important not to take away from their responsibility to cancel by direct action. Selective forgetting of appointments is meaningful but should not be overinterpreted.

In these subsequent sessions, I record the discussions held and the options being considered, making referrals so the participants can get necessary information and helping compile these into the final document that will summarize what they agree to, as well as a list of topics that they discussed but did not make agreements on. Because some participants go on to have advising attorneys who must negotiate or litigate the unresolved items, it can help those attorneys to have both lists.

Things to Remember About the Middle and End

The mediator should write up the mediated agreements in language that reflects the participants' understandings but foreshadow that many generalized directives made in mediation may have to be negotiated further or secured by further attorney-submitted procedures. For example, a divorcing couple may agree in mediation that the gambler should take on the entire gambling debt, but the attorney may need to prepare a bankruptcy action before or as part of the divorce action. Mediators in this phase of mediation efforts may need to advise participants to get legal advice as to the legal and financial consequences of the decisions they made in mediation. Mediators should not be helping their clients make decisions that are illegal, unconscionable, or impractical.

Just as clients can opt out, mediators who have been working their best for clients who are demanding, unreasonable, and unfair and are seeking unworkable agreements may need to end the mediation process. Of course, mediators need to maintain a fair, nonintimidating climate at all times, and due to the sudden rush to get done, they may be pressured themselves by clients during these sessions to forget certain important decisions, topics, or a full view of all options before making agreements. Whenever this happens in mediation, it is the mediator's responsibility to resist such pressures in order to preserve the fairness and climate of safety in mediation.

INTEGRATING CHILDREN INTO THE PROCESS

When parents are undecided about whether some parenting plans will work to meet the needs of their children, when children have expressed strong reactions to the divorce itself or to an option, either positive or negative, or when there are concerns about the appropriateness of what a parent is unremittingly bargaining for, it helps to have the child's direct input in the mediation session, but without making the child choose, betray a parent, or get stuck in a loyalty conflict. Another situation in which this can be extremely helpful is when the child tells one parent a strong preference but will not tell the other parent, forcing the first to become a conduit for information, which is often seen as tainted by that parent's self-interest.

Mediators who have expertise in child development and direct work with children in interviewing and therapy may feel prepared to offer this to their clients as a way of providing a neutral, professional view of the needs of the child. If a parent is suspicious of the other parent's motives ("They want this option only so that they can have larger [reduced] child support, not because this is best for the child"), the mediator, acting as a child interviewer as part of mediation, can help assess the child's level of attachment to each parent and the amount of disruption the proposed situation would cause.

It is important to distinguish between interviewing children as part of mediation, as opposed to the process used in full-scale child custody or visitation evaluation processes. The latter is not a confidential part of the mediation, and it requires specific expertise under state laws of who can testify in court as an expert witness to defend the conclusions and recommendations that are reached as a result of evaluation. Interviews with children conducted as part of a mediation between the parents should be contracted for separately from the mediation (some jurisdictions allow parents to agree to use their subsidized or allocated mediation services for this purpose). They also should be consented to by both parents, since custody has not yet been determined, and the results will not be helpful to the parents if they were not in favor of the process.

Children who are interviewed should be used as you would an advisory committee, with the parents (or the courts if they continue to disagree) acting as the board of directors who will make the decision based on the input from that committee. Children should never be in the position of making their own custody or parenting system decisions. That is the job of the parent, and to alter this creates a role reversal that can lead to feelings of neglect and abandonment or the equally troubling problem of parentification of one or more of the children.

Interviewing children as part of mediation efforts also can run risks. The children may be very open, communicate well, and remain hopeful that their parents will listen to them. But if it turns out that the parent is still operating out of his or her power needs and totally disregards the children's wishes, they feel doubly used, hurt, undermined, and unsupported. They may also never tell another professional anything true again, which will defeat the next process of evaluation that can make a difference. The message the rejecting parent may give is the very negative parental abdication that reinforces that the parent cares only about himself or herself and not the best interests of the children. Similarly, children who have unrealistic plans or who have created imaginary options can suffer yet another disappointment, frustration, and powerlessness when they cannot achieve what they want.

The third major harm is that the parent can become vindictive and retributive toward a child who disagrees, ruins his or her position, or says hard truths, setting the child in harm's way of a negative response that can even entail abuse and violence. It can make things worse for children unless this is accounted for with safeguards. One case comes to mind where this happened, to my dismay and regret and the child's harm. A father was placing claim to all three children—the oldest in early elementary school and the youngest in preschool—claiming that the mother was not fit. She argued back that she had raised them all so far and that all was well with them. To help them with this perceived competition, I interviewed the children together and separately, and then gave the information back to the parents in a subsequent session.

The oldest boy disclosed that his mother often flew off the handle, hitting him and the others many times. This was reportable child abuse, so I had to make the report to child protective services, which investigated but did not find probable cause to remove the children at that point. As I was telling the parents together about the child's statements and the need to report, the mother denied the allegations. She did not show up for the next mediation appointment, and I heard from the father that she accused the child of "ratting her out," got enraged at the child, and hit him, leaving marks. The father now had the evidence he needed and had called the state protective services, which had intervened and given him temporary custody. The child had been harmed for telling the truth, the mediation stopped, and the situation got worse for the children as a result of that interview. This should serve as a cautionary tale for any mediator who takes on child interviews.

When they are done well, child interviews can add a poignant voice to the equation and help the parents deal with the reality of the child. In one family, the mother was leaving the family home to move to a bigger city and wanted her fourteen-year-old son to move with her to a rental situation with a woman roommate. The mild-mannered father had been trying to tell her that he did not think that was a good idea. The interview with the intelligent, articulate son brought up the fact that he was very connected to his sports team and thought his father was not standing up to his mother to help him. He was not rejecting his mother, just trying to break even in his own life, but her continued insistence was ruining what regard he had for her.

The young man wanted and needed a place and way to say this to the parents, and when I asked if he would like to be part of the next joint session, he jumped at the chance. He stated his anger and frustration and defined his needs and plans eloquently and strongly. He did such excellent work in conveying his needs and interests and refuting the weak arguments that were being used as a rationale that the parents immediately revised the plan to have him stay in his home with his father, visit extensively with his mother during the summers, and maintain his interests and college orientation without having to act out to get what he needed. This was an exemplary tale of interviewing, made possible by the capacities of the child to tell and the parents to listen and respond appropriately.

There have been only a few articles in journals and books about how to conduct child interviews as part of a mediation effort, but many of the excellent books and materials on custody evaluations give an idea of the thoroughness and methods for interviewing children. Many court-connected mediators in the public sector do both mediation and the separate function of custody evaluation, so they need to be clear with their clients on exactly which function they are doing. Children younger than age five may not be able to understand, and five- to seven-year-olds may need to have other siblings in the room for comfort and support in keeping them occupied. It is always interesting to me to see how the siblings interact with each other and with the parent. It is best to let younger children make drawings about their family, their room, and what they like to do with their parents and then ask questions about the drawing.

Following are the suggestions I make in helping mediators assess when it is (or is not) appropriate to interview children:

- Have you secured written permission from both parents, and do both understand the process, the potential gains and risks, and the way the information will be used?

- Have you reviewed what each parent has said and why you are going to interview the children? What questions are you hoping to have answered?

- What difference will the children's input have on the bargaining, the parenting system, and the creation of the new parenting plan? Are the parents likely to respond appropriately when they get the information?

- What harm could arise if you do this interview? How secure is the information? Do you know the limits of the children's confidentiality, and have you explained this to the parents and the children?

- Is your waiting room child-friendly and safe from hazards? Do you have some toys or books to amuse the children who are waiting? Do you have paper and colored pencils for younger, nonliterate children to use for drawing?

- Do you have self-reporting forms for different ages of children (primary, middle school, high school) based on different reading levels? Will you be reporting their exact words or using your own words and interpretations?

- What is the youngest age child you are comfortable interviewing? Can you do this in family-friendly hours so the children do not miss school or activities?

- Do you have lists of good-quality referrals if the children are experiencing distress, need therapy, or seem too scared to talk?

- Have you started and ended the session with understandings about what you will and will not tell their parents? Can you keep your promises to them?

Interviewing the children in a family can provide significant firsthand information that can be directly relevant not only to the content of the dispute but also to the history of the dynamics of the family. Having children draw pictures of who is in and who is out in the past and current family is always revealing. Weighing the pros and cons of interviewing children should be done beforehand, never as a spontaneous response, since it requires preparation. Interviewing children helps bring home the fact that the stakes of the bargaining are not objects but boys and girls who must cope with this difficult change in their lives.

POSTDIVORCE CONCERNS AND MODIFICATIONS

Postdivorce problems cover a wide range:

- Noncompliance or breakdown of the original decree or mediated plan
- Inclusion of new people or ending current relationships (such as stepsiblings, remarriage, cohabitation, or a second separation or divorce by a parent)
- Unsuccessful postdivorce transition, resulting in continuous upheaval and dislocation for the children
- Specific events of overcontrolling, abuse, neglect, or lapses of judgment by the parent or others affecting the children
- Drug or alcohol abuse or mental health concerns of a parent that are affecting the children or might in the future
- Financial problems that have affected trust as well as income
- Relocation that will affect the parenting plan
- Changes in the developmental needs of the children that require revision of previous parenting decisions

New Needs of Parents or Children

While state law may require a substantial change of circumstances in order to file a motion for modification, many mediated agreements specify the use of mediation as a first recourse when parents no longer believe there is a goodness of fit or conflict ensues. Because of the cyclical nature of conflicts and the need for renegotiating family dynamics whenever there are events that affect the family, mediation is a preferred option for postdivorce changes, since it gives greater flexibility and a wider range of remedies. I have practiced at one place long enough to mediate a family's first divorce, the postdivorce trauma, the second marriage, and the second divorce and seen firsthand the levels of disruption to child development that postdivorce developments can have and the need for continuity in the chaotic process.

Dynamics of Postdivorce Disputes

One of the ironies of divorce is that parents who were already stressed when together may find the postdivorce world even more overwhelming, with a new or increased need to work for the increased financial needs of running two households, housing concerns, dating and sexual issues, as well parenting. They may be receiving less empathy from support systems and former relatives than they had before the divorce. Their totally restructured life can lead to isolation and concomitant social and emotional problems, which further erode the new structure. New partners can provide either temporary relief or new sets of problems with children and ex-spouses. By providing mediation for postdivorce disputes and parent-teen mediation (see Chapter Eleven), parents experiencing these disputes can often resolve them before they harm the new parenting system.

Postdivorce disputes can have the same or even higher levels of emotions and the same or different family dynamics, but the major difference is the level of involvement that the parents have with each other as postdivorce parents. Some dynamics get worse, because the repetitive nature of the pattern cannot seem to be controlled by the one who does it, and the other feels even more resentful about being disrupted by the person who has been disconnected emotionally for some time.

One of the important questions to ask about any postdivorce conflict that is triggering a mediation is, "Are these new life events to which the parents are attempting to respond appropriately, or is this an unconscious process of reengaging with the former partner as a form of negative intimacy?" Isolina Ricci (1997) explains that the retreat from intimacy and the new business-like relationship explain a lot about these dynamics. Ricci's book can again be offered to clients as useful reading if this dynamic is occurring, or they can be referred to individual therapy.

If the mediator and the family worked together on the initial divorce and are fortunate enough to work together for the postdivorce dispute, the mediator has some idea of what is going on and so is not starting with an entirely blank page. Nevertheless, it is important for the mediator not to assume but to ask and let them tell the narrative as they are seeing it, while the mediator adds his or her own formulation and hypothesis. If they are not former clients, they may need a mediator but have leftover prejudices about mediators, the process, or each other as participants. The mediator needs to get a very detailed understanding of the mediation process they have already experienced because not all mediations are similar.

Postdivorce disputes also have another feature: the motivation to solve the problem can vary wildly, whereas divorce disputes ostensibly have the external motivating force of wanting to conclude in order to progress to completion of the divorce. Postdivorce disputants do not have this motivation, and their ability to use coercive methods if mediation is unsuccessful are limited—that is, there is often not a good BATNA (best alternative to this negotiated agreement; see Fisher and Ury, 1991).

Motivation to Mediate Postdivorce

Parents whose parenting time is being withheld by the other parent for spurious reasons often lack inexpensive, speedy legal processes to respond effectively to the condition. The longer this situation lasts, the more the withholding parent can gain an unfair tactical advantage. The courts and judges may be unwilling to further traumatize a child who is adapting to the new condition. When concerns are about poor parenting or uncomfortable situations for children but do not meet state definitions of abuse or neglect, there is little leverage the concerned parent can bring to bear on the situation. If the mediation within the jurisdiction is voluntary and not required by the terms and conditions of the original divorce, this can lead to incomplete, single-session mandates or mediation efforts that never start or that end without any accomplishment.

To combat this propensity, some attorneys, judges, and jurisdictions have created mandatory remediation clauses or programs that subsidize these services. When one or both parents have no genuine interest in the problem, the need for change, or the children themselves, postdivorce mediation cannot automatically instill it. For those who do recognize a dispute, conflict, or concern, postdivorce mediation can provide the forum for the discussion even if the desired outcome is not forthcoming.

Postdivorce mediation can work much faster than original divorce mediation. There is less investment in "being nice" to the ex-spouse, there are often single or clear issues and options, and there is usually a desire to get it over with as quickly as possible. These pluses can be harnessed to provide some driving force even when willingness to collaborate with the other parent is minimal. It is not uncommon to go through all the phases of mediation in one or two sessions as opposed to two to eight sessions or more in the original effort.

It is crucial to find out all that has transpired between the end of the divorce and the start of the new postdivorce case. Changes such as live-in partners, problems such as drugs and alcohol, or processes such as layoff and retraining may have happened during this time, affecting the family system and the members' expectations. Because the number and severity of problems and conflicts after the divorce is so highly associated with children's postdivorce adjustment problems, the mediator should be assessing the situation for the hallmarks of high-conflict divorce, parental alienation, and other serious and harmful patterns. Is this an isolated event or one of a series of things?

Contrasts Between Postdivorce Disputes and Initial Divorce Concerns

Another difference with postdivorce disputes is the number of people who may need to be part of the joint mediation sessions. If both parents have remarried and the issue revolves around the stepfather's discipline methods or the stepmother's reliability and responsibility for children when their father is on a business trip, then probably the mediator may need to get all four parenting adults in the room.

Some families have gone through wave after wave of temporary parental figures who did not stay in the picture, so that the children are now banding together into coalitions that were not present in the initial divorce and are discouraging to any potential new partner. Children often become blasé about a parent's multiple partners and "pseudo-siblings" who occupy their home until the couple's fights and problems end the relationship and crisis or conflict dominates the home, leading to multiple breakups. This multiplicity of children and environments that the original family has had to encounter after divorce can lead to very different power dynamics within the family as a reaction to the chaos and disruption.

I believe that the biological parents should be the first ones in the room together, even when the stepparents have been very active in the dispute formation or could be helpful in its potential resolution. They should look at the role of the stepparents in maintaining the conflict or dealing with the alternatives proposed. If either ex-spouse sees that the process dynamics are directly or indirectly serving a function of negative intimacy or other old pattern with the ex-spouse, or believes a stepparent is fomenting the conflict, or if the biological parent is advocating one response and the new partner another, then I hold two separate sessions. Each new social unit—the mother and her new partner, and the father and his new partner—have some solo time to acknowledge the concerns and role of the step- or new parent and the existence of the new social unit. I try to see if they can become one bargaining unit, or whether their new relationship has rifts and problems that must be dealt with concurrently or prior to the issues presented in the dilemma by the first parents.

If either parent minimizes, discounts, or even disallows the existence of the new social unit or refuses to participate in mediation if the new partner is part of it, I let them decide whether those are acceptable terms for their participation. Often this is a power play by the former spouse to regain control, or is interpreted in this way, and the mediation effort ends. At this point, the mediator may refer the case to whatever legal or other social service might be helpful but leaves the door open for a return by mutual agreement.

When the situation remains unbearable, both parents often realize that the need for mediation is greater than the need to control. They can then capitulate to the terms of mediation, which require full and open discussion with those most primarily involved first (the biological parents), then conditional inclusion of the secondary parties (new partners), if the biological parents are able to frame some possible options or if they can agree completely and want to explain the new parenting system to their new significant others.

After the necessary contracting and securing of recent past history, the mediator will probably be told what the problem is and how each parent wants it solved. Often the cure becomes worse than the original problem: parents suggest alternatives that over- or underreact to the situation or create more rather than less disruption to the children and the new binuclear family systems. For example, the parent who is tired of the other parent's being a slacker and coming late or not at all to pick up the children on his (or her) weekend suggests that the solution is for the slacker to change places and immediately take legal and full physical custody of the children, even when this would mean uprooting children from their schools and activities. This is like hitting the nail with a sledgehammer and indicates a level of vindictiveness and lack of empathy for the children, as well as the thinking errors of immediacy and dichotomous thinking on the part of the parent proposing the "final solution." It also indicates the level of desperation and powerlessness that parent feels.

Holding separate solo time and reflecting the feelings, legitimizing the concerns, and trying to get more reasonable and less disruptive options can often be done as part of the first joint mediation. Often in those closed individual sessions, the true motivation comes out. Perhaps the mother wants to remarry and have time to herself and is still resentful of the heavier load of parental responsibility she got (or took) at the time of the divorce, or perhaps the father's drinking has increased and the stepmother is doing far more of the parenting than the father is.

This is another characteristic of postdivorce disputes: they often have high levels of intrapersonal conflict and personalized distress reactions as the parent struggles with the dual needs to get on with life and stay in the parenting role for the children. This internal conflict comes out in the negative interaction with the former partner, which leads to further interactional conflict. For many couples, the decision to divorce is clear and the divorce mediation unencumbered by anger, just sadness and regret; but the postdivorce disputes seem to reek of power and control tactics, dirty tricks, and tactical maneuvers.

Sometimes, the old pattern of learned helplessness (*if I fail miserably in my assigned role, I will be relieved of my responsibility and someone else will rescue me and do my job for me*) turns to icy anger when the new partner does exactly what the communication was conveying. When the new stepparent takes over the active parenting function and becomes closer to the children than the biological parent, it creates a threat of loss and a subsequent insecure attachment reaction by the parent, who reacts to the threat of loss and feelings of jealousy with power-over controlling behaviors to regain face and attachment.

One postdivorce father had stayed on the family acreage during the divorce and had let his new wife do most of the parenting of the children when they came every other week as part of the original week-week parenting system. But when the older daughter stated that she wanted to stay permanently with her mother in a nearby apartment and no longer do the weekly alternation, the father started bribing both daughters (the enticement for the older daughter was a car and for the younger daughter a horse).

The Role of the Mediator in Postdivorce Disputes

With postdivorce disputes, as with all others, the mediator needs to assess the intrapersonal and interactional dynamics and what positive function they serve for parents and the children. If it is truly a new and unforeseen event that needs response or just housekeeping to guard against problems as conflict prevention maneuvers and the parents have low levels of defensiveness, the issues usually can be mediated quickly, and the parents part having reinforced their new parenting system as functional and responsive.

When the parents are there to deal with hard issues that border on abuse, neglect, emotional abandonment, and other highly negative events supposedly done by the other parent or their new partners or in their environment, the dispute is characterized by intense frustration, powerlessness, and vindictiveness, which can become physically dangerous in the mediation session. For these reasons, many mediators want to get some idea of the problems before they schedule the appointment and, especially if there has been any history of violence, hold separate sessions to assess the appropriateness of mediation at all, given the concerns.

Postdivorce mediations are more widely varied and can add interest and challenge to a full-time mediation practice. They also require adequate safety precautions, a full array of potential referrals for different kinds of related services, and a solid understanding of the dynamics of postdivorce lifestyle and stresses.

※

This chapter has addressed some of the common concerns of family mediators dealing with initial separation or divorce of couples. We have looked at the issues common to all mediators and to a view of the pace, sequencing, and typical flow of a case through a mediation effort based on my own model, which includes the use of solo time and a blend of the problem-solving/negotiative and interactional models. We have explored the dynamics of postdivorce disputes, which may have very different levels of personal distress and vindictiveness from the original divorce because of new partners, multiple other prior relationships, family stress, and the perception of intentionality of the dispute. This chapter shows only one model and is perhaps not characteristic of divorce mediation that employs different models, settings, or methodology. Nevertheless, it provides a sense of the crucial issues of practice, the topics for discussion, and how to conduct mediation sessions for families with these disputes. The next chapter examines a different set of disputes within the family: parent-teen disputes and the use of mediation to help manage or resolve them.

CHAPTER ELEVEN

Parent-Teen Mediation

F amilies with teenagers find themselves involved in many conflicts; some are very minor, and some are so severe that the young person's entire life course can be affected by the process used and the outcome. Unresolved or unmanaged conflicts between parents and children can result in high-risk situations for the teenagers, including truancy, running away from home, living on the streets, and involvement with drugs, prostitution, and other criminal behavior. These reactive responses by the young person harm the larger community as well as themselves.

Parent-teen mediation is the term used to describe programs of conflict resolution that specifically target typical problems between parents and their older children. These programs have been developed from different helping systems that work with youth and families, such as schools, social service programs, volunteer community mediation programs, juvenile courts, and family courts, to respond to the need for quick and effective problem prevention and management. In some jurisdictions, the use of mediation for parent-teen problems has been incorporated into the criminal justice system as diversion programs for minor criminal offenses or status offenses (violations that are directly related to the special rules for minors, such as curfew). Depending on which system has set up and oversees the program, it may emphasize some common problems or not deal with certain types of disputes.

Common problems and disputes between parents and teenagers tend to fall into the following large categories:

- Household rules, tasks, and expectations—what the teenager is expected to do
- Structure, discipline, incentives, and consequences—how the parent tries to impose rules and deal with violations
- Identity issues—sexual identity, dress and behavior, groups, and gang involvement
- Behavioral problems at school, work, or other settings—bullying, suspension, or expulsion from school
- Drugs and alcohol—use, covering up, treatment
- Dating, friendships, and activities—too much time spent, choice and influence of people
- Divorce and separation, postdivorce issues—relationships with stepparent or stepsiblings, refusal to go with other parent, maintaining conflict between parents
- Status offenses and minor criminality—curfew violations, shoplifting, graffiti
- Life choices, goals, and direction—joining the military, choice of career, dropping out of school
- Leaving home and restructuring of expectations and responsibilities
- Crisis, trauma, and medically related issues—problem pregnancy, exposure to HIV, victimization by others, resistance to medical care, suicidal, self-mutilation

Although these topics are the manifest problems that serve as the catalyst or trigger event for the family to define it as a dispute or conflict, the concern about the behavior may have been circulating in the family for some time. The manifest conflict, though, is only what the participants are willing to declare the problem to be; it often masks the true interests and concerns of the participants, which form the underlying conflict they are covertly having. The issues of power and control are at the core of almost all parent-teen disputes. At the heart of most of these conflicts are the twin developmental demands of creating autonomy and differentiation for the teenager, while the parent maintains appropriate structure and nurture yet is reducing the level of parental dominance in favor of the teenager's increasing responsibility for self. Also part of most of these conflicts and disputes is an internal-external tension between familial norms and peer influence and group norms.

Because the task of teenagers developmentally is to create independent identity while maintaining connection with family and friends, they need to pull away, do things differently, and establish a separate identity through their choices. Parents who themselves have problems with power and control, loss, trust, and insecure attachment or who have parented their child using some of the negative parenting styles of rigidity, overprotectiveness and overindulgence, discounting, or criticism will have particularly hard issues to face with their teenager as they go through this process of setting new and more age-appropriate boundaries. Either the teenager or the adult is attempting to establish fairness, right process, and positive adaptation, while the other is trying to cling to established patterns.

In families where abuse, neglect, or abandonment has been part of the picture, the child as the indirect or direct victim of the unacceptable condition may have developed coping mechanisms; they may have been helpful to the child's survival but are now interfering with the parent's ability to have control. These teenagers may have become hostile or aggressive, a process of social learning and response explained in Chapter Two. Mediators must understand issues of undiagnosed mental illness, substance use, and hostile or aggressive behavior and the need to report past and current child abuse before beginning mediation efforts—unless, of course, mediation is inappropriate given these features or the severity of them.

The most usual feature of parent-teen mediation is that the mediator is attempting to help the dyad (and later the larger family system) understand and redefine the conflict and attend to the underlying issues of the need for change. Although the outside forces that have made the referral or requirement to attend may classify the case based on the presenting problem and the type of dispute, parent-teen mediation cases often are representative of larger issues that have not been able to be discussed in any other forum.

Consider a teenager who has run away and is using drugs. His problems may stem from his parent's unresolved issues—perhaps parents with unresolved marital problems or their own issues with drugs, alcohol, or abuse. The entire family system may require intensive family therapy or a range of services because the teenager is not the only one in trouble with the law, engaging in abusive or violent acts, or needing referral to other helping, community justice, or correction systems. The acting-out behavior may be a symptom of the larger systemic problems in the family that have not yet been acknowledged or dealt with. The child can become the "identified problem person," and this can divert attention from the other dysfunctions within the family. The first issue in parent-teen mediation is to ensure that the case has mediable issues and no issues that would be a contraindication for mediation efforts.

SERVICE PROVISION CONSIDERATIONS

Parent-teen mediation is most often offered in a single marathon session or can be held sequentially within a short period of time, using one to three separate joint sessions. Because it has often been an outgrowth and expansion of the community mediation models and systems, one or both of the mediators may be community volunteers. Because of this historical, structural, and conceptual background, parent-teen mediation can often involve a team mediation approach rather than just a single mediator.

The family mediator or team receives the referral from the court, school, attorney, or therapist or the self-referral by a family member, then contacts the family members in order to determine their willingness to participate or in order to explain the requirements and procedures, depending on whether the mediation is voluntary or mandatory. Assuming that the identified disputants are willing to come to a joint session, the mediator sets the appointment, conducts the joint mediation session, and writes up an informal mediated agreement document based on decisions made during the session.

Some parent-teen mediation programs allow or even require some solo time with both the parent and the teenager to allow an opportunity for either of them to expose any past, current, or potential future abuse, violence, intimidation, or retaliation. Like all other mediation approaches, standards indicate some level of contracting by the participants, review of the process and confidentiality, the relationship to other systems, the level of confidentiality according to state and national laws, and the need for both disputants to be able to remain safe and coequal to speak and make mutually acceptable decisions that are unforced and noncoercive. Exploration of the presenting problems, plus the underlying issues, for both the adult and the teenager is the basis of the mediation process.

Having been influenced by community-based mediation models, some parent-teen mediations follow the usual process of procedural and problem-solving models. Because of the emotional levels that these conflicts can engender, many family mediators have been applying the newer models and methods of therapeutic, transformative, narrative, and interactional approaches during the sessions.

In the study of a parent-child mediation program in New York in the early 1990s by Michael Van Slyck, Marilyn Stern, and Lori Newland (1992), participants were given a standardized test before and after mediation to determine the efficacy of the parent-child program for making change in their family interactions. The families had been referred to the mediation program on the basis of reported problems, usually pointing to the adolescent as exhibiting disruptive, out-of-control behavior or attitude. Although the data showed a positive impact on the family, especially the parents, and a reduction of dysfunction from the pretest high levels, plus satisfaction with the mediation process, the authors noted the nearly 50 percent noncompliance with the mediated agreement by one or more members of the family after mediation. They concluded,

> A more accurate view of parent-child disputes may be that the adolescent's behavioral/attitudinal problem is symptomatic of a larger family problem. A clearly related finding is that parents and adolescents have highly divergent perceptions of the causes of and the responses to the conflict. This further suggests

that the view that the conflict results from adolescent misbehavior alone is simplistic. [p. 85]

Another finding of note was that the high levels of conflict intensity in these cases actually related positively to successful mediation outcome—the reverse of most other types of disputes. The high conflict actually serves as a motivation to resolve the conflict rather than a deterrent to the effort. To guard against the inherently unfair presupposition that the teenager is the problem, one model for providing parent-teen mediation as a separate grant-funded program out of a family court service structure emphasizes the need to have a well-trained community adult who understands family systems theory and a paid teenage mediator who work together as the mediation team. This teenage mediator can act to balance the perception on the part of the adolescent disputant that the adults are running the show and that they are not coequal in the mediation process. The teenage mediator can also serve as an interpreter for the teenage disputant and provide a comfort zone and trust factor. By having in the room another teenager who is perceived by the parent as positive but who can "voice over" or act as spokesperson for the adolescent's perspective and normalize the teenager's peer culture, the parent can often hear their son's or daughter's concern differently, without the interference of the complex long-term relationship and past interactions. This model encourages positive teenager role modeling and has been well accepted by the adults and teenagers it serves.

Christine Coates and Kon Damas (1997) described their parent-teen mediation program in Boulder, Colorado, which has followed the common pattern of starting as a separately funded youth service grant that has been taken into the city's community mediation service as a part of its comprehensive approach. That program also describes using a co-mediation team approach of a trained adult with a teenage mediator and as a voluntary program to deal with truancy and school problems, family disputes involving communication, out-of-control behavior, disobedience, and behaviors that affect the larger community, such as running away from home and curfew violations.

They averaged four sessions of two hours each and noted that written agreements are reached in 60 percent of their cases. They note that although mediation almost never makes the situation worse, one-quarter of their cases end unresolved, with the mediation being ended by one or both of the participants and referral to other community resources. This figure is not surprising given the complexity of family mediation in general and the hidden family patterns that mediation alone cannot resolve.

Another perspective in reviewing success data is that one would expect, just by the predictive value of the standard deviation curve, that the upper 25 percent of cases will always successfully mediate no matter what mediators do, the lower 25 percent may never successfully mediate despite mediators' best efforts, and the major impact of the mediator's skill and model will likely affect the ability of the middle 50 percent of the curve to be more successful or achieve some, if not all, of their aims.

A collaborative program by the college of law at Toledo University, the juvenile courts, the schools, and the community in Toledo, Ohio, has been successful in diverting youth who are experiencing difficulty from the adjudication system to mediation approaches. Deborah Mostaghel, Stephen Ripps, and Robin Kennedy (1996) reported their development of mediation services to prevent costly delays in the judicial system while providing families with much more flexibility and tailored services through mediation. Their program of diverting appropriate cases of status offenses has helped troubled youth avoid stigmatizing labels, family trauma, further impact of dealing with the justice system, and additional costs to the community.

They note that their model of mediation, based on the adult victim-offender mediation models and restorative justice concepts, had some flaws that they became aware of when they evaluated the program. Concerns lie in three areas: the joint-only format is too restrictive to allow for full disclosure by the teenager and the parents; the issue of coercion to use the process can lead to false outcomes and negative reactions to the process; and the selection process of cases can lead to the referral of some inappropriate cases.

Their solutions to these concerns lie in adapting the mediation process to include at least some solo time with the teenager separate from the parents, so that the underlying issues and power dynamics do not lead to these conclusions. The advantage of allowing or requiring the mediator to have at least some solo time with each participant is that it enables each person to tell the mediator team about information that could be vital in understanding the dynamic or screening for appropriateness of the case or need to report to prevent harm. All of these reasons lead to a conclusion: the family mediator team needs to have some way to get unguarded information from each side during the intake or the actual joint mediation session.

POWER DYNAMICS DURING SESSIONS

Parent-teen mediation implies a structural power difference between the participants. Parents have legal and social authority and power over the adolescent minor, yet the teenager does not have similar power over the parent. And although both have the power of the court over them, the reality is that noncompliance with mediation affects the participants differently. A teenager who does not comply with the mediated agreement faces further negative sanctions and legal and social involvement through out-of-home placement, the juvenile justice system, and social service agencies; a parent who does not comply but who does not violate the law has no other negative sanction or enforcement process that can be used to enforce compliance. As Mostaghel, Ripps, and

Kennedy (1996) state, "If a child feels coerced, there may be an imbalance of power that could result in a mediation agreement that is one-sided and that may not adequately represent the child's interests. Somewhat as a victim of spouse abuse may be too intimidated to participate fully in mediation, a child may be too intimidated to reveal important needs" (p. 257).

Family mediators working with parent-teen cases, whether they are voluntary or mandatory diversion by the court, must be careful to note any intimidation, power and control tactics, pressure, or passive-aggressive behavior on the part of the parents toward the teenager or the teenager toward the parents, as well as the structural problems and pressure that may be inherent in their own referral system. They must not assume that the teenager's reluctance or resistance to mediation is a personality or psychological flaw or diagnostic condition such as oppositional defiance, but must question whether it is based on structural imbalances. Mediators must not fall for the trap of labeling their participants or falling in with the "blame the kid" game that the parents may be playing. Keeping the child as the "identified patient" helps the parents defer and deflect the inquiry off them, and they may be using the child in a very unhealthy game that provides a cover for their own problems.

The other unconscious area for concern is the inherent bias for adults and against teenagers that the adult mediator may have. In noticing interaction during sessions, family mediators should consider whether the teenager reminds them of someone they know (their own child perhaps, or themselves at this age). Wise family mediators will watch for and balance power differences by letting the teenager go first in answering or narrating the story and suggesting options. By leading the teenager to a place where he is no longer reactive to the parent but fully active himself, the mediator can subtly change the power dynamics to create the power-with concept in the room. Being aware of the automatic assumptions and treating the teenager with scrupulous neutrality will go a long way to providing the kind of climate in which the teenager can say what he needs to say.

SPEAKING NATURALLY

Another way in which mediators can allow this free expression is to suspend the usual social rules about communication to allow teenagers to express themselves in their own vernacular. Many teenagers use profanity, crude terminology, and sarcasm as part of their street and youth culture, yet parents and mediators may react and clamp down on it as disrespect for or toward them. If the word choices are not directed at the parent and are not direct intimidation or threats or name calling, allowing this self-expression might be a way of equalizing power in the mediation to allow teenagers the right to speak in their own way. The presence of another teenager usually mitigates the need to re-create self by doing this; the teenage mediator is enough of a representative of the youth culture.

Another reaction for adult mediators to avoid is trying to align with the teenager falsely, to "show her how cool I am," and to try to gain rapport with the teenager through name dropping, helpful hints that border on advice, or self-revelations. This approach can create more problems with power than it solves in rapport enhancement. Teenagers in mediation need to trust that the adult and teenage mediators are fully differentiated themselves and will not try to manipulate them, curry favor, or create artificial relationships. If the mediator is giving away his or her own power (the power of silence, of expertise) to either the adolescent or the parent, the teenager will not trust the process. Teenagers who are in trouble with the law, with their school, or with their neighbors or family are wary of trusting adults. But when they see that the mediator or co-mediation team is treating them with respect, equality, and true nonjudgmental interest, they may join in more fully.

PRACTICE DIMENSIONS

Most parent-teen mediation is offered in specialized community-based programs, some of which use volunteers rather than paid staff. Many of these programs have funding sources through grants, municipal and community programs, government, and justice systems to offer free or very low-cost parent-teen mediation. Because private practitioners must charge enough to cover their own costs, parent-teen mediation has not been a growth industry by itself in family mediation private practice. Instead, it has been a practice builder or augmentative service that a private practitioner may want to receive specialized training in and advertise as an additional expertise and service. However, there may be an increasing use of this model in private as well as the public sector, especially when the sessions are held in conjunction with other forms of mediation that the family may need. A well-rounded family mediator should be able to provide parent-teen mediation along with the other dispute types and applications as part of a more comprehensive approach to family dispute resolution.

The following examples, composites of real cases put together to illustrate the process and the service delivery aspects, show how family mediators can integrate parent-teen mediation into a practice that has been primarily based on divorce and custody or other types of interpersonal mediation.

CLASSIC PARENT-TEEN MEDIATION: PAM AND SUZIE

Suzie, in the summer between seventh and eighth grades, is rebellious and uncooperative at home, volatile, and scary when she gets angry. Her mother, Pam, has begun to suspect that her moodiness is not due to normal teenage emotions and hormones but drugs, and she fears that Suzie may have been experimenting with sex too.

The week before school started, Suzie wanted a sleepover with her friends to celebrate her birthday, and that seemed normal enough. The four other girls were friends from elementary school whom Suzie had not seen much during the summer. Pam, a divorced mother, was happy that Suzie had some good friends and was not inviting some of the other kids she had been seeing during the summer. The plan was pizza for dinner, playing makeup, watching some videos, and finally bed at 11 P.M. for the girls and Pam, the supervising mother at the party.

The girls' parents were shocked when they got a call at 2:00 A.M. from the city police, who to "scare them straight" had picked up all the girls, shoeless and wandering around town, booked them on curfew charges, handcuffed and fingerprinted them, and put them in the holding pen downtown until the parents could be called to pick up their daughters, one by one, with stern warnings from the police that the next time the parents would be fined $250 for not knowing where their children were. Pam was apologetic to the bleary-eyed parents and angry at her daughter, and she vowed she would get some help. It turns out that Suzie had planned it all; she was out to meet some boy who had not shown up. Each girl was sent a letter offering a police-sponsored diversion class that presented programming on out-of-control teenagers and "tough love" parenting instruction (how embarrassing!) and explaining that if no future offenses occurred, the event could be erased from her record. Neither Pam nor Suzie thought this was what they needed, but both agreed that they needed to do something.

Pam's private therapist suggested parent-teen mediation by a private practitioner she knew and trusted, so Pam contacted the parent-teen mediation program. They told her that the subsidized service consisted of one to two sessions, each lasting up to no more than three hours, scheduled on a school night after dinner. The case finder, who took the information and would turn it over to the co-mediation team, talked briefly to Suzie, who said she would be willing to participate.

Mother and daughter went that week to a single mediation session, at which the co-mediation team explained mediation process and rules and then had some solo time with both the daughter and the mother. During the solo time, Suzie admitted that she had been doing other things that would get her in trouble, but her mother had not found out about them yet. In fact, the night she got caught, a boy from across town was due to meet Suzie and her friends. No drugs, alcohol, or harm to self or others was involved, so none of the behavior was so risky that the co-mediators needed to break the confidentiality of the teenager and inform the mother or other systems, but the teenage co-mediator urged Suzie to tell her mother. During her solo time, Pam told a tale of increasingly feeling that her daughter was doing things without consulting with her. Pam wanted to tell Suzie how worried she was. The adult co-mediator encouraged her to consider doing that as part of the mediation.

When they all returned to the joint session, the co-mediators had Suzie and Pam express what they thought the problem was. Both said they needed to have a clear understanding between them about the rules and consequences. Then Suzie started crying and expressed her fears that Pam did not understand her or listen to her. Pam then shared how awful it had felt to get a call from the police in the middle of the night and how worried she was for her daughter.

Pam and Suzie both talked from their hearts and shared the concerns. Suzie shared other things that she had done, including shoplifting. Pam was able to state her shock at the criminality and reconfirmed her own values: she would not allow this to happen and would turn her in because illegality was not nego-tiable. Suzie was contrite and secretly pleased that her mother would hold the line, even if she could not. Although the session sometimes rocked back and forth between accusations with raised voices and mutual tears, the co-media-tion team kept them on track, listed the issues on the board, reframed concerns, directed their communication, and highlighted the normalcy of this struggle and the need to come to agreement. The co-mediators kept turning complaints into specific requests and having Pam and Suzie talk to each other rather than to the mediators. Having expressed the formerly inexpressible thoughts and feelings, having relieved themselves of fear and guilt and secrets, and having listed sev-eral things they agreed needed to change not just in Suzie's behavior but in the way they interacted, they were ready to negotiate new terms and conditions.

Pam agreed that she would bring her concerns directly to her daughter and not keep them covert; Suzie also agreed to the meta-goal of more open com-munication. They both pledged to talk more directly and more often, and Suzie agreed not to leave the house after curfew. Pam agreed to ask, and not assume, and Suzie agreed to tell more and to respect the reasonable limits her mother set. They agreed to hold a weekly family meeting to discuss concerns, and both agreed they would turn complaints into requests. After a two-hour session that ended in hugs, they left, a written agreement in hand that the co-mediators wrote and printed out before they left.

The co-mediator team debriefed the case for a half-hour after the clients left and wrote up notes from the session (a check-off list of topics), described the power dynamics and interventions done during the process, attached it to the mediated agreement, and left. At the routine follow-up made by the mediation center a month later, Suzie and Pam reported that the issues that had brought them into mediation were better and they were very satisfied with the result and the process they experienced. A six-month follow-up telephone call also showed that the family was doing well, and the issues of the mediation had not come up again.

SEQUENTIAL FAMILY MEDIATIONS: THE KENTS

One of the advantages of having family mediators do parent-teen mediation is that they may be able to provide sequential mediations for divorce and parent-teen mediation or make the referrals to in-house programs or other mediators even if they do not want to mediate both types of problems themselves. When family mediators in a court-connected service or a dispute center are qualified to do family mediation and understand the systemic perspective and process of working with families and units within a larger family structure, they are the ideal professionals to recommend or provide the mediation of complex family issues by doing mediation in sequence or tandem. This example illustrates how a divorce mediator may want to do only one part, then hand the parent-teen dyad and conflict to another service, and return to the mediation between parents, as sequential mediation events.

John and Martha Kent had been married for fifteen years, and John worked as a policeman. Their daughter Chelsea was fourteen, and their daughter Zoë was nineteen. Two years ago, Martha divorced John. The custody and property battle between them was bitter and protracted. Both wanted full custody of Chelsea. John negotiated for joint legal custody and 50 percent of Chelsea's time, but Martha was unwilling to agree, and their state's law provided for joint legal custody only with mutual agreement. Divorce mediation was attempted but failed, and the subsequent court order gave Martha legal custody and primary physical custody, granting John parenting time with Chelsea every other weekend, every other spring break, and two weeks during the summer. It had never worked this way, and John requested postdivorce mediation with Martha to discuss it. She reluctantly agreed to come for one session only.

During the solo time with the mediator, Martha told a tale of John's constant low-level intimidation of her and child support payments regularly late by a week—just long enough to create problems but not sufficient to create problems that support enforcement would deal with. She said that John showed no genuine attachment to the two girls and instead related to them as possessions. Zoë, now living away from home and attending school, would not see her father at all, and this frustrated him immensely. He was, in Martha's opinion, putting undue pressure on Chelsea to soothe his own ego, not to provide the child what she needed. He was rigid and dogmatic and had alienated his children himself by not allowing them to have friends over or go to their friends' homes or other activities during his parenting time.

Martha swore that she had always encouraged the girls to go with their father, but in the past six months, Chelsea would invent psychosomatic illness right before she was due to go and constantly asked her mother to get the visitation reduced. Martha had resisted doing anything, since the original situation had been such a battle and she did not think John would listen. Her opinion was that he had brought this on himself, that this was not her issue with him but Chelsea's issue, and she wanted no part of anything more than this one mediation session. She had come only to show that she was not resisting anything and was being honest and cooperative; this was his problem with Chelsea. Her role was to let and even encourage them to work it out, and then support whatever they decided together.

When it was John's turn for solo time, he told a very different story: of a mother colluding with their daughter to defraud him of time, of colluding to concoct a fake illness, of undermining him and poisoning his relationship with Chelsea by speaking ill of him around her, and of encouraging her to resist her parenting time with him. He said that Chelsea and he got along fine during their parenting time; she seemed to enjoy herself, so not showing up was unacceptable to him. He loved his daughter and wanted to have his time with her as the court had provided.

When they got back into joint mediation session, the room was icy with Martha's stonewalling and John's red-faced impatience with the process. The mediator reflected the very different stories each of them had told, then asked if either of them had told the story differently from how it was heard when filtered through the mediator. Both parents were staunch in their initial positions. The mediator then asked if they wanted what was in the child's best interests, and they both agreed. Asked if they wanted to coerce their child, they both said no. Asked if they would allow the mediator to speak to the child to gain her view of the dispute, Martha agreed, and reluctantly so did John. The mediator reviewed their legal options (an expedited hearing on the parenting time dispute was available for forty-five dollars within forty-five days if mediation efforts ended or were unsuccessful). The mediator reviewed the child interview process, which gave complete confidentiality (short of abuse reporting requirements) to the child, set that appointment, and ended the joint mediation with the parents.

Chelsea was a bright, articulate young woman who was eloquent in stating all the ways she did not like to visit her father. Her reasons were exactly as Martha had stated, yet it truly sounded as if they were Chelsea's own words and ideas and that she had not been unduly influenced by her mother's perspective. This was not a case of parental alienation but rather a case of a disrupted relationship between a parent and a child. Chelsea described the lack of connectedness to her father; she thought that if he did not force her to stay with him for such long times, she would be much more willing to continue contact. The harder he pushed, the more she wanted to withdraw; she had seen her older sister grapple with the same issue and was looking forward to escaping from this through graduation and college in a few years. For now, she wanted a reduced package of time and was willing to tell her father directly if she had help. She did not want her mother to speak for her, and although she thought her father was somewhat intimidating, she did not think he would harm her in any way. She had tried to talk to him before, but he always blamed her mother. Asked if she would be ready to tell him directly in mediation, she said she wanted to try, but with some help and support. The mediator ended the interview and reviewed the situation, writing notes that listed the subjective and objective issues involved in the child interview.

In the mediator's view based on the information they had all given, the dispute seemed to be located more in the parent-child dyad than in the parent-parent postdivorce realm, although the one certainly had an effect on the other. John's insistence on dealing with Martha was not allowing her the boundary she had set with him as a postdivorce parent, and the mediator did not want to perpetuate the unhealthy triangulation this family did that kept the child in the middle between two parents. Redefining the issues and referring the case to parent-teen mediation would reduce the unhealthy negative intimacy John was gaining, reduce the stress Martha was feeling by being back in the middle of something she had no power to correct, and would provide Chelsea the opportunity to speak directly to her father in a way she had never dared to do before, making the communication within the family more direct and clear.

The mediator called each parent separately, explained the process of parent-teen mediation service, and asked if they were willing to be referred for that process. If they were, they would put the parent-parent dispute on hold long enough to see if this would be sufficient. John happily agreed, because he believed that he could finally get the real story from his daughter without Martha's influence; Martha agreed because she thought Chelsea would be glad of a chance of help, although she did not have much hope for actual reconciliation between John and Chelsea. Because Chelsea had already agreed to do this, the mediator referred the case to the parent-teen mediation program. Had this program not been available, the mediator could have asked the parents if they were comfortable having the divorce mediator do the parent-teen mediation or whether they wanted a referral to another mediator. It would have been ethical for the mediator to change to the parent-teen mediation as long as there was an appropriate change of contractual understandings between them.

The parent-teen mediation program coordinator called, based on a written referral, and set the joint session between John and Chelsea. That session started with the standard procedures explaining the process, the confidentiality, and the role of the co-mediation team. The team acknowledged the referral and what they knew about the case from it: that the manifest problem was the postdivorce parenting time and the relationship between them. They then asked first Chelsea and then John to explain what each thought were their issues and concerns and restated these back. John again put forth his concern that Chelsea was being brainwashed by her mother, and Chelsea was able to tell John that the issue for her was the lack of quality and flexibility during the parenting time.

Chelsea finally was able to speak her truth to her father. John at first was in denial, arguing with her and trying to convince her of his belief, but then slowly, seeing his daughter upset but sincere, he was able to talk on a different level with her than he ever had before.

Prompted by the mediation team, the two of them described their feelings: hers of isolation and discomfort, wanting to please him but feeling left out of her social life and activities by his insistence on "his time," his of wanting to know her and please her but feeling like a failure. John was able to express remorse for having put her in that position and to share his desire to have a positive connection with her, whatever it took. Chelsea was able to describe to John what her vision of a good parenting relationship with him would be. Chelsea moved from anger and blame to understanding, and John was able to move from the old thoughts of "his little girl" to new respect for his daughter's needs for more independence and a change in his parenting style, rules, and how he responded to her.

From Chelsea's emotionally charged work of redefining herself as a person with her own needs and power in the relationship, John realized that his use of power and control tactics would not get him what he wanted, and he asked Chelsea what changes she wanted to make. She described a parenting time system where she and John negotiated at the beginning of the month the days she would be with him, so that it could better accommodate her sports activities. She explained her desire to have a girlfriend occasionally come with her to stay overnight so he could see her life and friends.

The mediator team pointed out that the actual schedule of parenting time would have to be negotiated between John and Martha in the parent-parent mediation, since Martha as custodial parent would have to approve any ideas they generated or the court would have to approve if the parents could not. Chelsea understood this and was willing to have those ideas marked off into a separate category of "shared recommendations to parents" as long as they would deal with it soon. Chelsea continued to suggest ways that she and John could relate differently during the parenting time, such as having an activity they did together and brainstorming what that could be. The teenage mediator, who happened to be from a divorced family, reinforced the normalcy of Chelsea's feelings and requests, calming and helping Chelsea turn complaints and blaming statements into specific requests in ways that John could hear.

For example, Chelsea requested that John allow her to do some of her favorite activities (use the Internet to chat with her friends, stay up late, and get up late) when she stayed overnight. John was able to hold on to the requirements he wanted: not faking illness to prevent coming over, a telephone call from Chelsea if she wanted a change from the planned parenting time they would agree on, and letting him know whenever she was feeling uncomfortable again rather than complaining to her mother. They both agreed to leave Martha out except for the ways in which she was legally responsible as the custodian yet to keep her aware of what they were planning before it happened. They planned to spend two weeks in the summer on a trip to see John's relatives rather than stay at home, which Chelsea thought would be boring. The co-mediation team wrote down what they both agreed they would be willing to do and the other category of what the parents or court would have to decide.

By the end of the session, John had made concessions but had won back the affection of his daughter, and Chelsea had spoken for herself and been rewarded instead of stifled. After much crying and raised voices at the beginning, the session ended with hugs and a plan to have the parents meet as soon as could be arranged to try to finalize the part that was theirs. Each took home a copy of the mediated agreements and their recommendations for the parenting mediation. The co-mediation team then sent a message back to the original mediator that the parent-teen mediation was completed.

The original mediator contacted John and Martha, both of whom were pleased that the parent-teen mediation had helped John and Chelsea find a new start, and set another joint appointment for the parents to clarify the parenting time schedule. John and Martha were still very formal with each other, but they were able to agree to the ideas that had been generated, including the concept of the monthly scheduling between Chelsea and John. Martha's only condition was that the schedule be put on the calendar and that any changes be made at least eight hours ahead of time so she could plan menus, transportation, and money. They agreed to submit it as a mutually acceptable stipulated agreement to modify the original divorce order, and John agreed to have his attorney draw it up and to pay the costs. The mediator sent them copies of the mediated agreement, and they authorized the mediator to send a copy of the agreement to John's attorney.

This case illustrates the usefulness of parent-teen mediation in resolving issues in postdivorce families where the disrupted parent-child relationship is the source of the parent-parent conflict. Such work can be done only if the child is ready and the parents have established enough trust to allow the conflicted dyad to work independently, without jumping back into the conflict through triangulation. Another necessary condition is enough differentiation and emotional distance on the part of the parent in conflict. Had John been unwilling or unable to make changes that showed a good-faith effort to Chelsea, or had Chelsea been too intimidated, immature, or self-assertive to be able to know what she wanted and state it, this case may not have come to conclusion in the way it did. If there had been a history of abuse or violence by the father or the mother had been unwilling to allow the child to disentangle by engaging in direct discussion with the father, this parent-teen mediation may not have been appropriate at all.

VICTIM-OFFENDER YOUTH PROGRAMS: THE NGUYENS

All of us live in many different levels of involvement at all times: our internal relationship with ourselves, the interpersonal relationships we have with our family members, and the levels of interactions we have with the larger world of school or work and community. Our conflicts, as a part of us, inhabit those various layers of our life. Young people often have deeply troubling intrapersonal conflicts; if they are left unresolved, they echo into their relationships at home, at school, and with other members of society.

Because our helping systems have usually been defined and confined to each setting, programs and systems tend to function only for their own sphere rather than provide a troubled young person a more systemic, comprehensive approach. A young person who appears to be struggling may be referred for personal counseling or therapy to deal with the intrapersonal warring sides of self, will be dealt with by the school for any interpersonal problems displayed there, and usually gets more comprehensive services only if the behavioral problems become so bad that crimes are committed and the young person becomes part of the justice system.

Parent-teen mediation is being used more in the context of diversion of situations away from the juvenile justice system to prevent teenagers who are essentially having intrapersonal or family-related problems from being more victimized and stigmatized by having those problems criminalized. Also, when teenagers have been involved in minor or first-offense crimes, the experience of mediating with their victims, as well as subsequent mediation with the family to prevent the conditions that lead to the negative behavior, can provide the restorative justice that the community needs, along with the conflict management the family needs. In the next example, a hypothetical case moves through an idealized combination program that starts first with the healing of the intrapersonal and family rifts before dealing with the way the conflict has affected individuals within the larger community.

Sixteen-year-old Bruce Nguyen, the only son in a Vietnamese family, was very smart but very troubled. His family, which had immigrated five years ago, was struggling in many ways. Bruce, his mother, his grandmother, and two sisters worked hard at part-time jobs to make economic ends meet; his father had developed a major disability that prevented him from working. Bruce's mother, whose lack of English prevented her from progressing into more lucrative work, had responsibilities to care for her ailing husband and mother. Times were difficult, and yet the family expected great things of Bruce, and all the children were expected to do well in school in order to advance.

In the neighborhood they lived in, many of Bruce's Vietnamese friends were part of a gang that required the members to prove themselves by selling drugs and doing small crimes. Bruce did not want to be part of this and tried to avoid the gang but had recently been roughed up by a few gang members. The pressure between the easy money and status of the gang, and the family's values of hard work, thrift, and honesty, were becoming a huge internal conflict for Bruce, who did not feel he could talk with anyone inside the family or at school. When his grades fell, his parents had clamped down on him, requiring him to spend more time studying after he came home from his after-school job. The school had noticed the shift in Bruce, but he covered over the problems when he was referred to talk with the school counselor.

The next week, an incident took place on school property, with gang members who had dropped out of school coming to school to try to beat up Bruce, who tried to push them away. A small scuffle ensued on school property and spilled over to the lawn of the house closest to the school. The elderly couple who owned it found their rose bushes trampled and their house pelted with eggs that ran down the siding. The campus police were called, and Bruce was suspended for a week, according to school policy. Then the city policeman assigned to the school arrested Bruce and one member of the gang (the rest had escaped in a car). Bruce was taken to juvenile detention and charged with property crimes for the damage to the neighbor's yard, where he was held until his mother could get him. Because this was his first offense, the case was referred to a probation officer, who determined that Bruce wanted a chance to do the victim-offender mediation program (VORP) with the neighbors. If he completed it successfully, he would have a suspended sentence that could be expunged at age eighteen. A chagrined Bruce was released to his mother and returned home.

Before the school suspension was over, his mother met with the school counselor. During this meeting, she explained in her minimal English the terrible privation and trauma during their emigration, the pressure of the gang in their neighborhood, and the economic issues the family faced. She was open to the idea of being referred to the local parent-teen mediation program to help the family work things out, since the tension around the house was almost unbearable.

The local parent-teen program was organized in such a way that they were able to respond to this as a crisis mediation session and even come to the family home when needed. This was particularly important because the father's mobility was so impaired. They were also able to contact a volunteer interpreter, who came along with the professional staff mediator and the teenage mediator volunteer. All three managed to squeeze into the small apartment and to hold a parent-teen mediation session with Bruce and his parents. During this session, Bruce was finally able to tell his parents how difficult life was for him: although he very much wanted to help his family, he had no time to rest or play, and resisting gang involvement was very difficult.

The father was able to talk (in his native language, interpreted for the staff mediator) about the shame and frustration he felt at being such a bad head of household and having to rely on his son and about the guilt he now felt for being too harsh toward the boy, whom he knew was trying to do his best. The mother sat silently until asked by the mediation team to speak (which was difficult for her culturally). She said very little except how greatly it hurt her heart to see her husband and son not talk in the previous few days and how much she wanted them to reconcile.

The staff mediator, familiar with the social services in the area, suggested some options for economic, social, and medical support for this family and made it clear that this would facilitate the family's value of maintaining their son's education by freeing him up from too much work. The teenage mediator was able to reassure Bruce that although the gangs were very strong in this neighborhood and school, social and school support and protection were available. The teenage mediator was also able to acknowledge to the parents that Bruce was not alone with this struggle and that he would be respected, not shamed, by the incident, since he had not succumbed to the gang. She was the voice of reality of the youth world Bruce needed to inhabit in order to get through school. This cathartic session developed a set of agreements about what each person would do while honoring the father's role and the family's values; more important, it had opened lines of communication between the family members.

Bruce then went with his mother to the victim-offender mediation session with the neighbors whose property had been damaged. Bruce took responsibility for his part in the fight, explained that he did not mean to cause problems, offered his remorse, and apologized. The neighbors told him how frightened they were at seeing the fight and worried for their own safety and property. They were unable to climb ladders to clean off the dripped egg.

They accepted Bruce's apology and requested two things: that he help them replant the roses and wash the egg off the house. They had also requested this same solution from the other gang member. Because of the gang member's adult status and larger past criminal history, he was not diverted to this VORP program but instead did standard probation, restitution, and supervised community service working on a job crew on roadside cleanup, so no direct help would be coming to them from the actual miscreant. The neighbors felt that Bruce's contrition and restorative action constituted a positive ending, as did Bruce and his mother. They negotiated a day and time when he would do this work, and the VORP session was concluded. The judge was notified of the mediated agreement and again after completion of the work by Bruce.

When Bruce returned to school after the suspension, the counselor spoke to him about the antigang programs and safeguards and asked that Bruce let him know of any more pressure or incidents. Because the school also had a peer mediation program run by students (the teenage mediator had been trained by that program), the school counselor reminded Bruce that he could ask for help if any currently enrolled students were bothering him, gang members or not. The school counselor asked Bruce about both types of mediation (since each was confidential, it was up to Bruce to decide what to share about them). He stated that he thought they were helpful and that he wanted to move on. The school counselor then contacted his teachers and helped Bruce find ways to improve his grades. Because of the intervention with the family, the internal and family tension subsided, and Bruce was again able to focus on his school and work. The school counselor (who had 420 students on his caseload and was unable to do this kind of work himself) touched bases with Bruce periodically and maintained some rapport and monitoring without intruding on the family's business. The mother called three months later to say how much she had felt things had improved at home and how grateful she was for all the help.

This example shows how even if the mediation system is disjointed or provided by separate agencies and systems, those who are in a position to refer and provide mediation services can work effectively, together or separately, to deal with the complex problems many young people are facing. The parent-teen mediation as the first stop helped the disputant deal with his internal conflicts and family issues, and the community justice system was able to bring about a more fitting and appropriate solution to those affected and an opportunity to make amends and reduce stereotyping and unnecessary fear. The family and the community saved money, time, and energy, and it brought about a more integrated solution to the entire spectrum of issues involved.

✺

Parent-teen mediation seems like an obvious addition to a family mediator's repertoire of services, especially if the family mediator understands and uses models of mediation that support a more holistic, systemic approach. Along with this, adding parent-teen mediation efforts to existing VORP, juvenile justice, or court-connected domestic relations services makes sense as part of a total system of dispute resolution that works with the impact of multiple systems on a multilayered family problem. Dealing with complex family and behavioral problems can best be done by adding this service for continuity.

The next chapter looks at highly distressed and chaotic families where mediation efforts are being used as part of a continuum of social response to complex concerns of parents who are dealing with the shattering effects of major dysfunction on the placement of children due to abuse, neglect, and incapacitation of a parent with untreated substance use.

CHAPTER TWELVE

Adoption, Abuse, and Placement Cases

When families are changing their membership voluntarily by adding another person through adoption, or when trauma and problems have happened that force society to intervene and make decisions on behalf of the children, conflicts are common between the family members themselves and between the family as a unit and the larger institutions that are trying to help them.

These cases are called different things depending on the perspective taken. Sometimes they are filed under different statutes or legal terms, such as *dependency cases, termination cases, child protection cases, temporary or permanent guardianship or placement, state wardship,* or *foster care.* The field of mediation does not quite yet know what to call these cases, so references are often listed obliquely. For mediators, these cases all involve children whose care and control is in dispute or being changed or reorganized as a result of voluntary or mandated processes, and perhaps that is the best way to think of them.

These family events are often marked by continuing conflict if the underlying issues of power and control, true intentions, and capacities of all the participants are not taken into consideration. Mediation is the perfect conflict resolution method for opening these issues in a safe and fair way, examining the concerns of all the participants, and maintaining the integrity of the family's values while making specific structural and behavioral changes that will lead to the benefits for children and adults within the system.

Although each of the situations is different, they all share one common theme: the perception, if not the reality, of loss and detachment felt by at least some of the participants and the need to maintain appropriate safety, boundaries, and structure. Another reality is that family mediators working with these cases need to know the legal rights, responsibilities, rules, and requirements placed on each of the players in the family drama, as well as the outside agencies, laws, and procedures that must be followed in order to ensure a fair process and a legally binding outcome.

Often, participants in these cases are angry, indignant, upset, or in crisis over things that are nonnegotiable and cannot be adequately mediated. These conflicts often arise out of the multiplicity of the people and entities involved, so it is very important that the family and the conflict are viewed from the systemic perspective rather than as a dispute between two parties. If naturally occurring families are complex, the structure of many families in these situations is even more complex. These families often have many persons who can and should be seen as secondary stakeholders, potential power brokers, and corollary contacts who can be important to the process and the outcome. Determining who should be involved in the mediation effort requires a wide-angle lens and often a series of separate mini-mediations among the different factions and units involved.

This chapter looks at the basic concepts of mediating disputes within families and between families and the systems that attempt to serve them in these cases. All of the previous discussions about the theory, models, and methods are relevant to this application. Most practitioners, many of them highly skilled and experienced mediators with expertise from the divorce field, find this to be perhaps the most frustrating and challenging arena for them. The challenges stem from the complexity and sheer numbers of people and agencies that need to be woven into the process and the level of intensity brought about by the time frames for resolution demanded by the law and the permanency of the decisions.

Unlike divorce mediation, where parenting decisions can be rethought and reworked and modified whenever there are significant changes for the children and the parents, the situations of termination of parental rights, adoption, and placement decisions made by child protective services in conjunction with the courts are usually permanent and cannot be redone, modified, or overturned except in very rare conditions of inadequate or illegal process by the agency or legal technicalities. Subsequent continuing conflict left over from the decision-making process can mar the postdecision environment and prevent proper functioning of the new family system.

The goal of mediating in these situations is not only to explore all alternatives and come to a decision that everyone can tolerate, but also to prevent continuing conflict by helping participants understand the full ramifications of events before they happen. These participants are often the most bitter and least willing to collaborate.

Three major issues in the mediation of these cases must be addressed: the nature of the dispute compared to the model of mediation being used; the confidentiality of the mediation context, given that some parts of the dispute are public record and may involve public agencies; and the major power differences that can exist between the disputants in these cases.

FITTING THE MODEL TO THE SITUATION

Not all families involved in adoptions, child placement, or child protective cases are the same, and so it makes sense to create a formulation of the cases by assessing the people and the problem and then matching the mediation process and model to the needs of the case. If the case doesn't involve parents or children with special issues, such as violence, child abuse, or mental illness (see Chapter Five), then the standard problem-solving approach is appropriate, and it is simply a matter of creating an adequate formulation of the case, based on the people involved, the dimensions of the problem, and the process used, as outlined in Lang and Taylor (2000). Some families who are fostering or adopting or are having postadoption or continuing problems with foster care or adoptive children are highly differentiated, motivated, and articulate for their own self-assertion and cooperative in process. The problem is not the parents but the behavior of the child, which is attributable to the child's past abuse or neglect, physical or emotional condition, or other factors beyond the current care of the placement or parent. Defining the problems and who is contributing to them is the first step.

Many out-of-home temporary foster or child protective cases involve one or more participants who are less emotionally differentiated and function at the highest or lowest levels of the evaluation continuum described in Chapter One. They may be functioning at a lower level in terms of self-care or parenting skills, or they may have special problems or a dual diagnosis of mental health and substance abuse problems. Many have major power and control problems with their domestic partners and children that have led in the past to abuse and violence. They may also have great difficulty with authority figures in the legal and helping systems due to past involvement. It is impossible to talk in generalities about these cases other than to say that they require excellent assessment and intervention skills on the part of the family mediator.

Rather than taking a standard problem-solving/negotiative approach, where the mediator is strictly neutral and allows the negotiation to go whichever way it will, adoption and placement disputes may call on the mediator to be far more therapeutic, interactive, or transformative. This is a very sensitive blend of a natural parent who often feels resentful, guilty, and angry at the system, trying to put his or her needs and wishes across to an adoptive parent or agency representative who may be unconsciously dismissive and who has a lot of power and control. Both are trying to understand the complicated needs of a child who may have specialized requirements because of post-traumatic stress syndrome or physical, mental, and emotional distress that is creating behavioral problems or issues of consistency and stability.

Family mediators functioning in these situations need a rich blend of basic mediation and negotiation training. They also need a firm understanding of standard child development and the specialized issues of attachment problems, the responses to sexual and physical abuse by children, and the best and most recent research in parenting adoptive children, many of whom need long-term therapy and specialized educational and social structures to do well despite a positive new home environment.

CONFIDENTIALITY AND PRIVILEGED COMMUNICATIONS

Confidentiality during these termination-adoption and protective placement cases is particularly complicated, since the issues may be framed from the perspective of a public agency mediating against a private individual. The court finalization of an adoption is a public record, and the documentation of the conditions of abuse or neglect or probable cause of endangerment to the child that is necessary to pull a child out of a home into temporary foster placement must be shown to the legal standard in a court proceeding, which also may be public record.

If a client is scrupulously honest during the mediation effort, there may be new or further admissions of abuse or neglect, which may need to be reported. Obviously, family mediators and the mediation process should not be used as a fact-gathering mission, and truthfulness in mediation should not be compromised by fear of further trouble; yet the mediation process should not be compromised by becoming a safe haven for reporting crimes or concerns without the usual consequences. Family mediation in this arena runs the fine line between over- and underprotecting the parties to the mediation, as well as the children who are the basis of the mediation effort.

Because each state has different statutes regarding the privacy issues and legal requirements for confidentiality and privileged communication in mediation, there is no single standard in place about the release of information that has been gathered in these mediation cases involving child protection issues.

Mediators are generally considered to be mandatory reporters of any allegations of child abuse or neglect and must report to child protective services (CPS) any information about past abuse or current protection issues that come to light during a mediation effort. But what if the mediation case was generated or referred by that very agency? The initial reporting of suspected abuse or neglect has already been done, and the agency has already investigated and acted to protect children, so what would be a mediator's obligation to report further or allow the information about the nature and extent of the abuse or neglect to be further distributed?

Couldn't further information generated during mediation prejudice a disputant's chance to be considered for permanent placement? Wouldn't it change the bargaining power and credibility of one or more of the parties to the dispute if information gathered during this mediation effort for placement were used in subsequent proceedings of the CPS agency, or if the details being discussed in the supposedly private forum of mediation were to be allowed into subsequent legal proceedings? Might it not even be a major conflict of interest or equality-of-power problem for an agency to be a participant in the mediation, only to have the right or obligation to provide information to future hearings, legal proceedings, and even the public? How can the mediation process maintain its ethical requirements of fairness and client self-determination under these conditions?

The essential nature of mediation efforts could be jeopardized if mediators of these child protection or placement cases cannot maintain the confidentiality of the work that is being done during the session. Which is the greater good: preserving the integrity of the mediation process or allowing subsequent disclosure? Is it impossible to maintain true confidentiality in these cases? Should the family mediator have privileged communication so that the material discussed is protected from subsequent consequences?

Arguments can be made on both sides of this dilemma. Child advocates and those who promote offender accountability believe that the information gained as part of the mediation effort must and should be available to those who will place the child, so that no further harm is done and the offenders will receive appropriate sanctions. Those on the other side of the question find that to promote honesty in mediation processes so that the real capacities and issues come forward, the threat of future negative consequences from revelations or admissions made during mediation should not be used against those who made them. They hold that the mediation process fundamentally requires the safe harbor of complete privileged communication by the mediator and the parties in order to maintain its integrity. While this has been an ongoing debate and concern for all family mediation, it is in these cases of child protection, placement, and termination-adoption where such issues are best illuminated.

Uniform Mediation Act

Gregory Firestone and Dennis Sharp (2001), noted specialists in the area of child protection mediation cases, have recently reported in the Association for Conflict Resolution (ACR) newsletter about the development of the Uniform Mediation Act (UMA), a recent attempt to create more uniformity among the states regarding fundamental aspects of mediation, such as confidentiality and privileged communication for the mediation process and the mediated agreements that flow from them. The UMA is a product of three years of intensive work to resolve the issues and concerns of the mediation community and the legal community. It has been a joint effort of the Section of Dispute Resolution, a subcommittee of the American Bar Association (ABA), and the National Conference of Commissioners on Uniform State Laws. Because of the ethical and legal complexity of these cases, having such a unitary understanding of the mediator's rights and responsibilities for maintaining confidentiality and privilege would be extremely helpful to the field.

In the first versions of this proposed legislation, there was no provision for making privileged communication for mediators in cases such as these. In the May 1, 2001, draft, confidentiality of the process of mediation was strengthened as a general rule, to include not only subsequent legal proceedings but also nonlegal processes. The UMA has been revised to define the scope of mediation more narrowly, so that a judge or judicial officer who does a mediation-like process but still retains the ability to make an actual ruling or report to one who does is not acting as a confidential mediator under these rules.

The third major revision of the UMA clarifies the mediator's need to report information about child abuse and neglect in most mediation cases as opposed to cases where release of information from the mediation of a child protection case could create a dilemma for the clients in subsequent proceedings with the public agencies. The final draft of the UMA, which was adopted in August 2001, allows in Section 7(a)(5) that in most mediation cases, any admissions of abuse or neglect made during mediation can be released by the mediator in subsequent legal and administrative processes in order to prove abuse or neglect, but if the case was referred to mediation after abuse had been determined, further reporting to the child protective service would not be required, because the abuse would already have been established. In other words, if a family mediator operating under the UMA were to hear of unreported child abuse during the mediation effort, the need to report to the CPS agency would still be in place, trumping the need to keep the process confidential.

Potential Ethical Dilemmas

Often the parties to the mediation effort include not only the abusive or neglectful parent or relative but also the same public agency that is responsible for determining the factual evidence of abuse and then turning that information

368 THE HANDBOOK OF FAMILY DISPUTE RESOLUTION

over to the courts for civil or even criminal proceedings. There is an inherent risk with these cases that mediating without proper protections of the mediation process can lead to further harm of the parties, an ethical dilemma for the mediator who must "first do no harm" to anyone who is a party or a secondary party to the mediation effort. The final version of the UMA solves this problem by stipulating that when the court or CPS agency has referred a child protective case to mediation, the mediator would retain privileged communication, so that statements made during the mediation effort could not be used in subsequent proceedings.

This clarification in the final version of the UMA may help prevent problems for participants and ethical dilemmas for mediators in these situations and is intended to address other exceptions to the general rule of confidentiality of the mediation process, such as how to function when there is a duty to warn of potential violence and threat. Each state will still need to adopt the UMA into state statute, leaving the situation ambiguous nationally until this is accomplished. It should also be noted that even the most finely crafted new legislation may not provide sufficient guidance to mediators handling cases of dependency and placement in which abuse or neglect is central to the issues being mediated. We can hope that family mediators will unite to demand from the laws, the subsequent court cases that will interpret the laws, and their professional societies the clearest definitions of the mediator's responsibilities regarding these very difficult ethical and practice issues. In the meantime, it is imperative that family mediators fully understand their state laws and CPS systems, their own ethics, and the likely dilemmas they may face when attempting to mediate these cases.

As guidance to the drafters of the UMA, the Association for Conflict Resolution (2001b) drafted its own set of eleven principles for the development of any uniform mediation laws. Principles 9 and 11 state that any such legislation or revision should

   9. Adequately address how mediators, parties and representatives are to comply, if at all, with mandatory reporting requirements, that may be required by law or professional ethical standards. . . .

   11. Take into consideration the special concerns raised when the threat of violence is present. [p. 18]

These cases are difficult not only because of multiple parties and needs but also because the family mediator must maintain awareness of rules, reporting requirements, and potential ethical dilemmas that are constantly changing. Until we have definitive, unitary national standards for mediator privilege and confidentiality and until new mediators are adequately trained in family mediation standards of practice and experienced mediators are updated on these important changes, it is important for mediators to work collaboratively to determine standard procedures for mediation within their existing laws and requirements.

Family mediators taking on these complex dependency and placement cases need to clarify these issues when accepting case referrals. By framing common issues in forums with CPS and referral sources, many potential concerns can be prevented by creating safeguards in agency policy and procedure and the mediator's contracting practices and disclosure to the disputants. The duty of family mediators is to keep up with new national and state developments that can affect their mediation process and legal requirements, as well as their personal liability.

POWER DYNAMICS IN PLACEMENT CASES

For many families caught in abuse and neglect that has led to out-of-home placements and the disputes about appropriate permanent placement, the issues of power and control between the parents and between the parents and "the system" are huge. The CPS agency holds the power of information about the legal processes and requirements and the power of law and the force of society behind it. The same is true in adoption cases, where the adoption agency often is the party responsible for telling the birth parent and the prospective adoptive parents what their choices and options are.

In situations of foster placement and dependency, the agency can have private information about the parties, while the parties have little or no access to the caseworker's notes or information on the caseworker's perspectives or past involvement that might show a trend in their recommendations or handling of the situation. The parents can feel automatically at a disadvantage even when the system, agency, caseworker, or other parent is trying to be open and clear.

Power Between Family Members

Mediation efforts require the participants to stop engaging in the form of power behaviors they have developed as power-over, which comes from a hierarchical, dominant-subordinate, winner-loser, command-obey mind-set, where the only choices are to comply, resist in some way, or possibly negotiate. The collaborative process in mediation is about power-with, an acknowledgment of each participant's forms of power and acceptance of the need to be a co-contributor to the solution and that each side of or unit within the dispute needs to be part of the creative composite solution. If the parents are convinced that the agency is an opponent, the mediator will not be able to elicit a problem-solving approach to the situation. The thinking errors or distortion about the nature of the perceived power base need to be addressed openly rather than remain a covert message.

Often each participant believes that all the others have all the power in the situation. For example, the birth parent believes the adoption agency and the adoptive parents have all the power, while the adoptive parents believe the agency and the birth parent have the power in the situation.

Susan Carruthers (1997) points out that there can also be major power imbalances between the parents due to past spousal abuse issues that continue to maintain a perception of threat or inequality. She recommends appropriate screening for past and current concerns about domestic violence between the family members and suggests that mediators have sufficient training and skill to control the mediation environment to prevent further intimidation or threat. She points out that mediation of these placement decisions between the parents and the state may be inappropriate for the parent if that person is incapable of advocating for his or her own rights, let alone the rights of the children, and some persons who have been subjected to domestic violence over time have become incapacitated in this way.

In some cases, the extent or the involvement of the domestic violence issue may make the case inappropriate for mediation efforts. As Carruthers (1997) points out, "A danger exists if the spousal abuser has created the reason for which the CPA [child protective agency] involvement was required initially. In these circumstances, the abused mother's interests and how she would like an agreement to develop may be diametrically opposed to those of the abuser" (pp. 115–116).

Family mediators who have a therapeutic or systemic view of families and the issues of abuse and neglect that have prompted the dispute or need for mediation will find these cases more comprehensible. They can often see beyond the construction of the abusing or neglectful parent as evil, wrong, or criminal to the often wounded person he or she is. This compassion can help the mediator deal with the person, who often exhibits offensive or defensive behavior and can be difficult to relate to. Because there is so much tension in many of these cases, family mediators who have a background in conjoint family therapy or are used to working with multiple party mediations may feel more comfortable and ready with small group skills to manage the complex joint mediation sessions.

Institutional Power and the Family

The agency, parent, or other entity that does have legitimate authority or power to take certain actions needs to clarify that, and the options that are ruled out by legal requirement, rule, or ethical or standard process need to be discussed early in the process, so that everyone knows the power balance in the situation. For example, federal legislation requires state agencies to hold family decision and reunification meetings in order to have a permanent placement for the child within one year of the action to remove of the child from the home. If state law or state agency policy and procedure stipulate the topics that must be covered or the process that must be used during the family decision meeting held by the CPS agency for the development of the temporary or permanent placement options, then these rules need to be clearly stated to all participants. The same is true with the mediation effort. If the family mediator must comply with specific timelines or processes or must produce certain outcome documents as a result of convening a mediation case, these need to be fully covered as part of the preamble to mediation.

In CPS cases, the parents whose children were removed from the home assume they have little power compared to the CPS agency, which they view as monolithic and intimidating; in fact, the agency is often aware of how many legal and social rights parents have even when they have done direct harm to the child. Grandparents and interested and involved family members can also assume they have no power to affect the outcome, yet they may have a very important role during the mediation and after the final decision. When the mediator has the different units describe their perceived lack of power and uses the information to change those perceptions, the situation is often transformed.

Susan Carruthers (1997) points to the two types of power imbalances that tended to show up in child protection mediation cases in the experience of the Nova Scotia Family and Children's Services Division. She indicates the power imbalance between the parents of children who have been removed from the home and the CPS worker and system. She notes that the power differences tend to result from the low socioeconomic status of many of the cases; often the parents have lowered education, language, and communication skills, which can contribute to this perception of lowered personal power. She indicates that mediators who are working between the parent and the agency must provide adequate safeguards to ensure that parents with these deficits are not coerced or taken advantage of.

Using Advocates and Advisers to Mitigate Power Problems

The use of advocates and advisers can change the perception, if not the reality, of the power balance between the units. When a parent arrives at a family decision meeting with a large number of family members and treatment staff who will speak on behalf of his changes and he has been advised adequately by an attorney, he stands on a vastly different power level than if he does not have these supportive resources. The same is true with a pregnant teenager who is considering adoption placement after the birth of her child. When that birth parent is provided independent information other than that given by her own parents and the adoption agency, she often sees her power differently.

The mediator is often brought into the situation after the power-down condition has become intolerable, but also after the dispute has established at least initial power balances between the units. The task in balancing the power in these situations is to do this without jeopardizing the neutrality of the mediation effort. Relying on reputable information that can be brought into the mediation, having information sharing prior to mediation efforts, and balancing the information base reduce the data conflicts, so that the relationship, structural, values, and interest-based conflicts can better emerge.

CHILD PROTECTION AND PLACEMENT CASES

For parents who have had their children removed from the home and are trying to regain custody through a CPS placement, this situation is often the most heated they have ever experienced. They already feel judged, embarrassed, contrite, and often angry at the way in which they have been treated. They start the mediation effort with much skepticism and even outright hostility toward the mediator and the mediation process, especially if they perceive that the mediator is in the employ of the CPS bureaucracy or the government.

A mediator who is an independent contractor, not a part of the system with which the parent is having the dispute, may find slightly less resistance. The parents are often being forced and pressured by other systems, agencies, and treatment programs to make choices and changes. It is very common for mediators working with these cases to have had much scorn heaped on them and to have to work to create a perception for the participants of a sufficiency of impartiality and helpfulness. As Bernie Mayer (1989) put it, "In most child protection interventions, the involuntary initiation of contact and the need to conduct an investigation, which can lead to placement and even criminal indictment, tend to promote a more alienative compliance orientation" (p. 96). Even a family mediator who is providing excellent help and support may not receive any positive appreciation from those he or she is serving, even if participants do experience more overall compliance and positive orientation to the processes they are experiencing and feel less coerced into the outcomes because of the mediation effort.

Another feature of these cases is the sheer numbers of persons who can and should be connected to the resolution of the dispute. Harry Kaminsky and Rhoda Cosmano (1990) note that potential participants in these conflicts can include foster and adoptive parents, attorneys, court-appointed special advocates, therapists, representatives of treatment centers, probation officers and other justice system program staff, doctors, foster care review board or oversight committee members, and many friends and relatives of both the natural parents and potential adoptive parents.

Notably, this list leaves out the children themselves, who might need to be added as potential participants or consulted if they are old enough to understand and have an opinion. Using older children as an advisory committee or a social unit that should be interviewed and have input as part of the preliminary fact gathering of the mediation makes firm sense from a family systems point of view, even if they are not part of the joint mediation session where decisions will be made. From a negotiative view, this also prevents later roadblocks and other difficulties when children who have not been included resist an option or decision. Even if the agencies, systems, parents, and courts are trying to make the best decisions on behalf of the children, it has been my experience that the children (supported by their therapists and legal advisers) are often the ones who can determine the best solutions and the points of resistance of the participants within the family. I believe it could be seen as unethical practice to do a mediation about children without giving the children the opportunity to voice their own positions. While children may need and have a right to have advice of counsel, they are seldom given their own separate legal adviser due to the lack of funding mechanisms.

Determining Appropriateness for Mediation

Carruthers (1997, pp. 121–122) notes that the Nova Scotia court has identified the following criteria for a child protection case that is appropriate for mediation efforts:

1. No immediate risk to the child.
2. A legitimate child protection concern is involved in the case.
3. The parties have the capacity to participate in the process (that is, no severe psychological, psychiatric, behavioral problems, cognitive impairment, or substance abuse).
4. Participation by all parties must be voluntary.
5. It is clear from the onset whether the communication in mediation is open or closed.
6. The method of reporting is established at the onset.
7. All parties have independent legal counsel available.
8. Both parties have an interest in maintaining the relationship.
9. Other options are less desirable than mediation, and the agency has considered its best and worst alternatives to mediation.
10. There must be a conflict that cannot be negotiated, and it is unacceptable to both parties to not deal with it.
11. The power balance between the parties is capable of being equalized.
12. The situation provides sufficient time to work through the process.
13. Specific issues to resolve have been identified.

The use of individual caucus or separate solo appointments over time may go a long way in reducing this initial dread and hostility and may also contribute to more honesty and better communication. Logistically, it may also be necessary because it is very difficult to do multiple session mediations with multiple parties; finding a conducive joint time can be the biggest mediable issue. As public policy mediators often find, meeting each interested participant in his or her own environment and comfort zone can lead to better communication when the large joint sessions, which are often tense, are finally convened.

Chief Judge Robert W. Metzger (1997) described the experience of judges acting in a mediation capacity in British Columbia, Canada, as using the judges as mediators to lend more credibility to the process rather than having the mediations done by the CPS agency itself, which could lead to concerns by the parents of partiality and apprehension about the fairness of the process as well as power and control issues. The judges, trained as mediators, retain some visual cues of their role as judges, yet attempt to mediate as if they were not the decision makers. They use standard models of mediation, even though they may make a nonbinding recommendation on the case, which is admissible in the subsequent next trial.

This Canadian mediation, which allows recommendation to the court as part of mediation, would not qualify as a confidential mediation process under the newly developed UMA in the United States, because Section 8(a) specifically prohibits a mediator from making a finding, report, evaluation, or recommendation to a court or other authority that may make a ruling on the dispute that was the subject of the mediation. (However, the fact that the mediation took place and the ultimate outcome *is* reportable to the court.) Although there were concerns in Canada regarding process and even appropriateness of mediation, it was felt that mediation was a better option than adversarial litigation. When cases involve members of aboriginal groups, those groups are contacted and may have representatives at the mediation to ensure cultural consistency and provide support to the participants as well as oversight regarding the fairness of the process.

Private Practice Contracting

Although there is an increasing use of private mediators on contract with either courts or CPS agencies to provide mediation to cases that are referred, many such cases are still being handled in the family court service systems and agencies themselves. Private practice mediators who are thinking of adding this type of case to an existing family mediation practice may be disappointed to realize the difficulty of the case and the expenditure of time and effort compared to the remuneration in those contracts. Family mediators who do a wide range of services often say that these cases are the hardest, most time-consuming, and least pleasant, yet they are also perhaps the most important, since the participants often have no other resources available to them.

ADOPTION

Adoption, as a changing of rights and responsibilities from one family system to another, is full of potential conflict, from who has the rights to make the decision to the level of secrecy and protection of the biological parents' identities. In addition, there are issues involved in the finances of the adoption—both initial costs and the ongoing costs of maintaining an adoptive child. During the process, there can be questions regarding the speed and correctness of procedures, and there can be postadoption problems between natural parents and adoptive parents and between adoptees and the adoptive parents or other relatives.

Although it is typical to think of adoption as the result of an unmarried birth mother's "giving up" her child to a married couple, this is only one type of situation. Gay couples are adopting children, and many disabled children or children abandoned at birth or soon after are adopted. Adoption also is often the end result of the child's having been taken out of the home by the CPS agency or the informal placement of children within their kinship or larger family system due to abandonment or financial reasons.

Because of the increase in unmarried, live-together adults who are actively parenting children and the interest of gay and lesbian couples in domestic partnerships in adopting children, new terminology has been selected to be more specific. The term *second-parent adoption* refers to adoption by the partner of the child's legal or biological parent, and the term *two-parent adoption* refers to a situation in which a child is adopted by an unmarried couple. In this chapter, the term *adoption* covers all of these situations. There are an increasing number of informal temporary placements of children with family members due to drug and alcohol use, mental health treatment issues, and other concerns, and these may need to be turned into legal temporary custody arrangements, guardianships, or permanent adoptions.

Adoption can be started deliberately and voluntarily by those who want to increase their family membership or as the end of the cycle of a crisis when a child has been in temporary foster placement due to abuse, neglect, or other trauma in the original family and is now being moved to a permanent custodial and residential placement. The planned approach to adoption by couples or families helps them mentally and emotionally adjust to the idea prior to the actual event, just as pregnancy helps couples get ready for the reality.

Because of the length of time and prescreening requirements for most private and public sector adoptions through agencies and attorneys, conflicts between the couple have often been noticed and dealt with. A family mediator cannot assume this about the crisis-oriented adoption. A family that is trying to get final adoption after formal or informal foster care of a child may feel embattled from all the many conflicts they have endured. It is important to gauge the level of relative power that each unit and person feels as they present for mediation of the particular conflict of adoption they are experiencing.

Common Adoption-Related Disputes

Typical issues of termination and adoption are characterized by a number of issues:

- Claiming the child and knowledge of parental responsibility and rights (for example, the mother identifies the man she thinks is the father who must be notified before termination, but he doubts his paternity; a parent claims the child but has not yet acknowledged this parenthood legally)

- Consent and notification of the putative parent or established parent that the termination or adoption is being considered (for example, a problem pregnancy by a minor where adoption is an option being considered by at least one of the biological parents; refusal of the putative parent to allow the adoption)

- Kinship care—that is, formal or informal placement with relatives to prevent permanent adoption or foster placement

- Potential tribal membership (for example, the biological parent believes the child may have entitlement to be part of a tribe even if the child is not currently enrolled; tribal members are disputing the placement of an adoptive child outside the tribe)

- Disputes between prospective adoptive parents and the agency or go-between, as when slowness, interpersonal issues, or financial arrangements are not working for the birth parents, the prospective adoptive parents, or the agency

- Cooperative and open adoption agreements between biological parents and adoptive parents, where the frequency and type of continuing contact between the child and the natural parent must be fully agreed on in advance or problems with the preadoption agreement arise after the termination or adoption

- Disruptions or dissolution of the placement or adoption due to concerns about the child's behavior, special needs, or the adoptive parents

- Maintaining sibling, grandparent, or other kinship connections during temporary placement and after permanent placement or adoption

- Transracial and cultural issues—that is, maintaining cultural or ethnic identity and cultural practices for biracial or multiethnic families
- Postadoption problems between the adoptee and adoptive parents or family, the need for more resources, or potential problems
- Access to information by adoptees, such as unpredicted contact between biological and adopted children or parents and issues of medical information and releases

Adoption-related disputes are often a series of ongoing conflict management, and having access to mediation efforts by the agency or facilitator need not end with the transfer of the child. Often, adoptive children and families have major conflicts and problems, and adoptive children and their families may qualify for specialized financial help to afford the additional costs of therapy and support the child needs.

Family mediators who are available to the families before, during, and after termination or adoption can help the participants sort through their concerns and options before the positions become untenable or develop secondary conflicts in interaction with the necessary agencies. Because of this, many adoption agencies are cross-training their workers in mediation process, and private mediation practitioners may specialize in these disputes. Some state agencies are contracting out to independent mediators when placement or termination or adoption situations happen, either routinely or only when conflicts occur. These private mediators often have a background in serving as court-appointed special advocates, adoption agency staff, or attorneys who have facilitated a lot of private adoptions, as well as skill in mediation. Although this is a growth area of practice for family mediators, mediators must understand the legal requirements, procedures, and social systems that affect families in these types of crises and conflicts.

The National Adoption Information Clearinghouse has a storehouse of information on all aspects of adoption, and this organization highlights all aspects of adoption in its on-line database. Excellent topics for further research and understanding are listed there. The wise family mediator who is preparing to do any form of adoption or placement-related mediation should look at the updated information on the issues and research in this field.

Jean Clarke and Connie Dawson (1998) address the particular issues and concerns of parenting an adoptive child and speak to the special needs of these children and the issues they present to adoptive and natural parents who maintain contact with them. Since mediation of these cases must take place within the legal and therapeutic frames in which the experience of adoption resides, it is imperative that family mediators working with these cases have enough background information to understand and interpret the concerns and issues of all four major groups involved: the natural parents, the children, the adoptive parents, and the helping agencies.

Termination Prior to Adoption

Prior to any formal adoption, there must be a legal action of voluntary or involuntary termination of parental rights of the biological (natural) parent or parents and then separate adoption proceedings. There is always an ending and severing of the usual social, financial, and legal rights and responsibilities of the biological parent before there can be a beginning of the new social unit, so loss by someone is the first experience of adoption. The termination of parental rights also ends the expectation of any automatic visitation or access by the grandparents.

Grandparents can attempt to intervene legally or through mediation efforts to maintain ongoing contact, based on the level of involvement they had prior to the termination, and they may be granted rights separate from or negotiate separately from the natural parent. At the termination, the child is also separated from any automatic inheritance or legacy from the terminated biological parent and grandparents unless they specifically name the now-adopted child as a beneficiary. The termination prevents the newly adopted child from placing any claim to the estate of the biological parents who were terminated.

Adoption law is different in each state as a matter of statutory law and court interpretation, so the legalities of adoption are particular to the state in which the people reside and must be researched in order to understand the legal frame in which the disputes are taking place. There are also national laws that overshadow and determine the state statutes:

- The adoption and placement of children from Native American tribes (Indian Child Welfare Act, 25 U.S. Code, Chapter 21)

- The rules regarding children from other countries (Convention on the Protection of Children and Cooperation in Respect of Intercountry Adoption, May 29, 1993)

- The role of federal agencies regarding adoption (Administration for Children and Families, Department of Health and Human Services, Code of Federal Regulations, 45 C.F.R., Part 1356; Adoption Assistance and Child Welfare Act of 1980, 42 U.S. Code section 620; and Child Abuse Prevention and Treatment and Adoption Reform Act, 42 U.S. Code, Chapter 67)

- The cooperation of various states and uniform laws between states (Interstate Compact on the Adoption of Children)

- Provisions to remove barriers to placement of children waiting for permanent homes due to race, color, or national origin (Multiethnic Placement Act of 1994, Public Law 103–382; Interethnic Adoption Provisions of 1996, Public Law 104–188)

- U.S. Supreme Court and U.S. Circuit Courts of Appeals decisions on adoption

This means that any family mediator who is seeking to help parents or agencies with problematic, conflictual, or even cordial and mutually agreeable adoptions needs to know the specifics of relevant federal and state law. For example, there are specific legal requirements that are different for children who are clearly members of a Native American tribe or those children who may be entitled to be a member even if they have not yet established membership. The number of days between the signing of the relinquishment papers and the release of the child or the specific provisions of the notification of putative fathers can be different in each state. Family mediators may bargain in the shadow of the law, but they need to know where that shadow is likely to appear. The family mediator who is attempting to do any type of adoption work must fully understand the national laws and their specific state laws so that they are not promoting illegal bargains or misleading the mediation participants regarding their choices and options or the requirements that must be met by the participants.

Because of the legal information and requirements, most adoptions have historically been and currently are done by public or private placement or adoption agencies, which research the laws, ensure that all procedures are followed, and help the natural and adoptive parents meet all requirements. Private adoptions, done with the help of a go-between, usually a lawyer or social worker familiar with the state and national laws, also ensure that the complex web of social, legal, and financial requirements is met.

Some attorneys and social workers have added mediation approaches to their practices in adoption, but it is impossible for mediators to adopt law into their mediation practice for adoption. Each person or unit who has an interest in the process or outcome of the termination or adoption decision may need separate legal counsel and representation in order for the mediator to remain truly impartial and neutral and to coordinate the separate rights, responsibilities, and needs of all concerned. Children can have their own attorneys who represent their legal best interests, often paid for by grandparents or others from the biological parent's family.

Adoption is a legal event, but like divorce, it is not just a legal event; it is also a series of social events that affect people's thoughts, feelings, and behaviors about themselves and each other. As tight as the rules and laws and procedures could be made, ending relationships and starting new ones, with all of the heightened emotions, were areas that sometimes the agencies and the lawyers could recognize yet not deal with. Mediation approaches with adoption and placement were a major change in the 1990s; there are now private agencies that specialize in open adoptions using mediation methods, and mediation is now used as part of the process in agencies when disputes arise.

Open Adoptions

Open adoption, sometimes called cooperative adoption, is the term for situations when the biological parents and the adoptive parents meet directly to discuss their own needs and options and determine the specific set of understandings that will govern their continued relationship, and it is becoming more prevalent. There is an expansion of the use of mediation for these sessions, because the mediation process provides the equality of treatment and the assurance of equity in outcome. Adoption agencies that provide open adoption work between both sides to determine that each side is able to voice concerns and requirements and make mutually acceptable decisions in advance that meet the legal requirements and the emotional requirements of the parents who are experiencing the loss as well as those who are receiving the gift.

Open adoption has become a preferred approach because it allows for the parents who are letting go of their rights to discuss the exact level of continuing involvement they would like to have with the child. For some, becoming more like an involved aunt or uncle and maximizing their participation is the great attraction of open adoption. For others, being able to continue to send birthday cards and photographs, or be available for contact when the child reaches a certain age is the key ingredient of the negotiation they want with the adoptive parents. It helps them reassure the child that they did not abandon or act irresponsibly toward him or her. These efforts can reduce postadoption disruptions.

There are many different patterns of open continuing contact, and natural and adoptive parents can look at the range of these. Because there are risks of overinvolvement, inappropriate involvement, and continuing conflict between the natural parent and the adoptive parents or child, openness should be carefully negotiated for individual cases, and it often relates to the patterns of dysfunction and the skills of each side of the triangle of natural parents, child, and adoptive parents. Especially when there has been past abuse or neglect by the natural parent, the child needs to be protected, as does the new adoptive family as a unit. Too much involvement by the natural parent can lead to problems in postadoption adaptation, leading to disruption or even dissolution of the adoption itself.

Harold Grotevant and Ruth McRoy (1998) cite a recent nationwide study of the concept of openness in adoption that looked at 720 participants from thirty-five adoption agencies in the United States that have been involved in open adoption. Jeannie Etter (1993, 1997) published the processes and findings from studies of the use of mediation when the child protective services agency finds that the likelihood of family reunification is not good and a permanent placement and adoption must be made. This Cooperative Adoption Mediation Project study (Oregon State Department of Human Resources, 1995) showed the efficacy of using mediation processes to create open plans that still allow some level of appropriate contact between the abusive or neglectful parent and the child even though the CPS agency must follow the federal mandate to have a permanent placement and adoption within one year. As a result, Oregon has continued and expanded the use of contracted private mediators in these cases.

The change to open and mediated agreements for different levels of continuing involvement by the natural parent is a trend that is being supported by research in the area of attachment theory, as well as consumer driven by birth mothers and agencies that want to support the larger concept of family and reduce the problems experienced by children after adoption. Family mediators are an important part of the service delivery system and can help parents make appropriate decisions that minimize the trauma of abandonment and incompleteness and are more truly based on the best interests of the children.

Mediating Adoption Consent Problems

The first issue of adoption is who is qualified to make the decision. The mother is the decision maker, unless it can be shown that she is legally incompetent to make the decision or unless the care and control of the child have been given to a specific agency or person temporarily. In some states, the putative father (or the man who has voluntarily taken legal responsibility for the child) also must be given notice, and although he sometimes has the power to veto an adoption, he seldom has the right to initiate an adoption over the objections of the other parent. This creates the structural power difference between the mother and father that can leak over into the mediation structure if the mediator is not careful or knowledgeable about the need and process of appropriate notice.

The structural power and control issues of adoption have to do with an automatic power difference between men and women regarding procreation. Generally, unless the child has been fully abandoned by both parents, we know who the mother is, yet knowing that, putative fathers must first establish themselves legally as the father of record in order to have a voice in the outcome of the child's placement. Based on biology, the mother can hold the power of information over the putative father; she can declare someone the father who is not, and he must disprove the allegation in order to extricate himself from the decision making. Mothers can also withhold information as to the identity of the biological father. This gives the mother greater power than the father, at least initially. DNA scans now provide courts and disputants new ways of mitigating these power struggles, but that often is not sufficient to prevent them from starting.

Case Example: Mediated Open Adoption

A case I mediated involved Beverly, who was intending to marry Colin, who was not the natural father of her nine-year-old child, Josh. Josh had always been led to believe that Colin was his father. Beverly now wanted to have Colin adopt

Josh so that they would be confirmed as the family they had been for the past nine years without the fear that the natural father would return to claim his son someday. To guard against this eventuality, Beverly had never told the natural father, Lloyd, of the existence of the child or his probable paternity. Lloyd had moved to another state and established his home and family on a horse ranch there.

Beverly wanted to mediate the situation, because she did not want Lloyd to stop the adoption and because she was not opposed to the concept of an open adoption. In fact, in preparation, she had told Josh who his natural father was, and he was excited to meet a new father and his horses. Beverly had called Lloyd, who was stunned at the news. He accepted this reality and moved quickly to request contact. Beverly contacted her attorney, who sent the necessary agreement to terminate parental rights to Lloyd as the putative father, which confused and scared Lloyd. It was still a new and not yet bitter conflict, but it could become one soon if something was not done.

The mediation effort included a phone call by me to help Lloyd understand his power position and his need to get legal counsel (which he would not do) and to provide enough basic information to help him understand the concepts of determining and accepting paternity, termination of parental rights to enable adoption, and open adoption and mediation of its conditions. When I explained all of this information to him, he stated that he did not feel a need to establish paternity through DNA or a blood test and would rather accept his paternity on Beverly's word, but he understood that this had to be done as a first step. He did not object to establishing his paternity only to terminate it and allow the adoption. His only concern was that he have some limited annual contact with the son he had never seen. It seemed that there was shared openness to an agreement.

Beverly and I used the speaker phone to hold two joint sessions: one to develop their agreements and the next to review the written agreements they had made, which had been sent by mail. Between the two joint phone sessions with Lloyd and Beverly, both had agreed to allow me to interview Josh to determine what he thought about these events. The boy came to my office, and I conducted the child interview as part of the mediation effort, so that it was protected by confidentiality of mediation.

Josh stated that he was thrilled to have a new person in his life without losing his current father, Colin, and he was very open to contact with Lloyd as long as nothing was forced on him. He was attracted to the horses as much as or maybe even more than the father he did not know, but he also expressed a lot of positives about having his stepfather Colin become his official legal father, since he had always assumed that he was and felt good about his relationship with him. He was close to Colin's parents, who had always accepted him and whom he thought of as his grandparents. Josh felt that this information about Lloyd would not stop them from loving him.

In the subsequent joint telephone session, Beverly and Lloyd agreed to an open adoption plan that allowed Josh some in-person contact with Lloyd and his family members whenever Lloyd was in the same state; Beverly would provide Lloyd with annual school pictures of Josh and allow Josh to make telephone calls to Lloyd if he wanted to. They also agreed to an initial meeting between Lloyd and Josh; Beverly, Josh, and Colin would plan their summer vacation to include a two-day meeting, with the idea that if it went well, Josh could make an annual visit of up to a week. The final version of the agreement was sent to Lloyd to review with counsel (which he said he would not do, on general principle of suspicion of attorneys), sign, and return to Beverly's attorney, who would then redraft the termination and adoption papers to include the mediated open adoption understandings.

The mediation saved money, time, and public exposure of fighting over termination in court and facilitated a good agreement that included the child's wishes and obviated unnecessary litigation. It equalized the putative father's power relative to the mother and gave the child some voice in the issue, while letting the status quo remain.

Case Example: Change of Consent to Adopt

Another situation with power imbalances is the dispute that arises when a birth parent no longer wants to go through with an adoption as planned. In the videotape *Adoption: The Chaos of Changing Consent,* Larry Fong (1995), a skilled mediator, demonstrates how a mediator can work with a messy adoption issue. The adoptive parents, who already have the child, and the biological parent, who is now having second thoughts about relinquishing the child at all if she cannot have extensive access, are in dispute about how much time and in what way the biological mother will have contact.

Rather than pursue this as a breach of contract by the natural mother, who is poor and without the benefit of counsel, Fong helps the participants in the mediation define the personal concerns and issues rather than reduce the struggle to a legal battle. The concerns, interests, and needs of both sides are brought out in the mediation effort, and the differences between the positions of the prospective adoptive parents become more apparent. This serves the birth parent, who is having unrealistic expectations, to gain some power and make more appropriate decisions, while giving the adoptive parents some more options other than to end the adoption or litigate to preserve it. The case illustrates the pitfalls of not specifying what level of openness and contact is acceptable and reasonable before the adoption takes place or a child is taken from the home.

Changing Expectations: Opening Closed Adoptions

There has been an increasing trend to change laws so that even formerly closed or blind adoptions can be opened in order for adoptees to discover medical records or find out their heritage. Because adoption laws are ruled by state law, states can also legislate the limits or process of disclosure or may require that these contacts be made through a central registry or specific agency designated to verify that the legal and social needs of both sides have been met. (A current listing of the specific state rules, requirements, and contact information is available on the Internet through the National Adoption Information Clearinghouse's Web site database or by e-mail to the organization.)

These situations usually have the following disputes:

- Whether the need for medical information is sufficient grounds for releasing the information requested (usually a dispute between the agency and the adoptee)

- What level of continued contact they should have now that confidentiality has been overturned (usually a dispute between the birth parent and the adoptee)

- What level of involvement the "recovered" family members should have (often a dispute between the birth parent and the extended family members and possibly involving the other parent's family)

- What grandparent rights or responsibilities the birth parent will accept now that his or her identity is known (a dispute between the adoptive parents and the parents of the birth parent)

- Inheritance issues (a dispute between the adoptive parents' family and birth parents and perhaps with adoptee and other natural siblings)

- Moral or financial responsibility due to the adoptee because of prior abuse or trauma by the birth or terminated parent (a dispute between the adoptee and the parent who voluntarily or involuntarily released the child to the adoptive placement)

An example will illustrate the use of mediation in a case of this kind. Nineteen-year-old Ashley decided that she was opposed to abortion to terminate her unwanted pregnancy and so chose to go to an adoption agency, where she was given a profile book on prospective adoptive parents. She chose an African American adoptive family, since she was white but the child's father, Atticus, was African American. She felt doubly shamed in the situation because she was not married and the child would be biracial, both of which were unacceptable in the rigidly religious household in which she had been raised. She had her mother and two sisters attend the birth for support; she would not have Atticus there, although he offered.

Under the laws of her midwestern state at that time, the putative or established father had no opportunity to override the wishes of the mother, and he was advised by his family to consent voluntarily to termination of his parental rights, which he did. Ashley never saw the baby after the birth, and the adoptive parents received the child three days later. Ashley demanded that the family members who had attended the birth never speak of it again or indicate to anyone that she had ever been pregnant or had a child.

When the adopted girl, named Elissa by the adoptive parents, reached the age of sixteen, the state laws changed to allow for agency-controlled contacting of birth parents by adoptees who wished to make contact. Ashley, who had since married and had three other children, was contacted by the agency. She wanted to see her daughter, but her husband, Steve, when she finally told him about the existence of the girl, was against any contact with Elissa, on the grounds that it could be traumatizing to their three mutual children, who were barely old enough to understand the concept of pregnancy, let alone a biracial older sister. For him, the shock of realizing that Ashley had kept the existence of this child from him for so long was part of his closed attitude about meeting Elissa, as were a long-standing racial prejudice and a strong religious and moral stance against premarital sex. He felt multiply betrayed. Ashley went into therapy to help her deal with the situation she had tried to prevent. After six months, she finally felt strong enough to ask Steve to enter mediation on this issue.

In mediation, all the hurt, shame, and betrayal issues in their relationship had to come to the foreground before they could deal with the adoption contact issue. Steve was also legitimately concerned that she not introduce someone into their nuclear family unit who was not going to be part of them. But he made the concession that he would consider allowing family contact between the half-siblings if Ashley would first make contact with Elissa in secret, establish a strong enough relationship, and establish the fact that there would be more than a single or unpredictable contact. He wanted Elissa to either step into their family fully or stay out. Ashley reminded him that in many ways, this was her decision, not his, and that she was including him out of respect for their mutual family life. She was willing to make this accommodation, so the mediator clarified the understandings between them and offered to perform a similar function when Ashley was ready to clarify her relationship with Elissa.

Ashley and Elissa met several times, and Elissa explained that her adoptive mother would be fine with whatever they decided: to continue contact or not. Although the adoptive mother was concerned about Elissa's needs and reactions, she did not feel at all threatened in her role as mother; rather, she was proud to share her daughter. Had this not been the case, Ashley might have needed a mediation session with the adoptive mother to establish their agreements and concerns. After several visits, Ashley explained her husband's concerns and conditions. Elissa needed some time to think about this all-or-nothing stipulation by a man she did not know. After several hard weeks for both of them, Elissa finally called Ashley and agreed to the terms, as long as she did not have to commit to a specific schedule for visits and as long as everyone respected her right to maintain her primary household with the adoptive family.

Ashley called the mediator, who now suggested a multiparty mediation session with Ashley, Steve, Elissa, and the adoptive parents, so that everyone could express their views and concerns, and so that all concerned would support any agreements. The mediator first had brief solo time with Ashley and Steve as one social unit, then with the adoptive parents, and then with Elissa alone. This gave each group a chance to discuss among themselves the issues and concerns they had, so that when they arrived at the large session, they could speak with one voice. Elissa had thought of another issue that she wanted to discuss: being part of larger family gatherings and getting to meet her cousins. Her main interest was to bring her existence out in the open and not have to consider herself or be considered a shameful family secret any more.

When they convened in the full group of five, Elissa was cued by the mediator to speak first, so that she could tell all the people she loved what she wanted and was hoping. She wanted their acknowledgment that this entire process of meeting her birth mother was her idea, and she wanted "dual citizenship" and easy passage between households. Both parent groups heard and supported this concept. Having established this goal, they all negotiated on how to accomplish this, so that no one felt as if only one person was dictating the conditions. They left with a plan for including Elissa over the next six months and with a statement they could all accept about what they would tell the younger half-siblings. Elissa has since gone off to college, visits occasionally, and maintains comfortable contact with both families. She plans to have both families sit on her side of the aisle at her wedding.

Situations like these are exactly the types of disputes that blind, or closed, adoptions were supposed to prevent but that have started to surface with the opening of adoption records. Mediating these disputes requires the mediator to understand the nature of family systems and the need to get all of the parties into the mediation effort in sequenced units and stages while honoring the need to use other services such as therapy. Mediation efforts may have to be multilayered, to deal with each dyad separately first, then eventually bring all the social units together to make the final agreements. Timing is crucial, as is orchestrating the mediation in such a way that the family units are preserved and any conflicts within those units are addressed before putting the units together into the larger interaction.

Although there is not currently a lot of information on the mediation of these disputes, we could anticipate some increases as more adoptees seek their roots and try to create the complex agreements that families need to make each person feel honored and respected.

※

Family mediation of disputes involving out-of-home placement of children, parental rights, and creation of new family units through fostering, temporary care, and permanent placement and adoption will continue to be complex, tense, and multilayered disputes. They require mediators to have an excellent grasp of the legal issues, but also the complexities of face-saving, power dynamics, and therapeutic responses in order to provide the type of sequence and level of mediation effort required. In the next chapter, we look at another type of out-of-home placement: placement and care decisions about the elderly and disabled persons.

CHAPTER THIRTEEN

Elder Care and
Family Medical Concerns

A relatively new application of family mediation processes has been created in the disputes that can arise for people who are elderly, ill, or temporarily or permanently physically or mentally disabled. In order to portray the range of people who could benefit from family mediation and to avoid awkward acronyms or terms to describe this broad range of people, in this chapter I refer to recipients of care, such the elderly, the disabled, the mentally disabled, or the family member who has a chronic or acute mental health issue or dual diagnosis, as the affected person, as opposed to the family member who is not experiencing the particular distress or need for services, care, or placement. Additional mediation cases may arise out of federal or state legislation that provides benefits, entitlements, or access, and laws that prohibit discrimination on the basis of disability; because these cases are generally handled by mediators who specialize in these types of disputes rather than family mediators, the reader is referred to other resources beyond the scope of this book. Family mediators should be aware that their cases may also include these concerns and may need to be referred to specialized mediators or other processes for full resolution.

Families increasingly must make decisions that can affect the quality of life for people with chronic or acute medical conditions and difficult decisions about organ or tissue donation during crisis or during the grief and loss stage of death. They must make plans for family members with long-standing needs for supervision or monitoring due to disability or severe developmental delay. They must make hard choices about the placement and care of elderly family members that affect all members of the family socially or economically (or both).

These more personal disputes within families have not always had a mechanism for resolution because they have been seen as essentially private decisions of the party regarding medical treatment, placement, care, and finances that were the responsibility of the person with the identified problem or the person's legal guardian or the one with power of attorney.

The medical and social impact of AIDS, as well as medical advances and processes for treating other medical conditions, such as early Alzheimer's, cancer, and other chronic problems that are now handled through successive rounds of treatment and home care, have created even more of these issues for family members to deal with on behalf of another family member. Many more families than in the past are having to help their family members make hard decisions about treatment, dealing with death and dying, and placement and care for long-term illness, as well as the aging process.

There are often deep philosophical and values conflicts and issues within families, as well as financial, resource management, and logistical problems and institutional requirements to meet. These can lead to bitter disputes at a time of stress for the family, such as when a critical medical condition requires decisions to be made quickly or placement opportunities will be lost if the family does not act to secure them. Other decisions are less crisis oriented, but proceed through a series of disputes within the family—some of which will be resolved and some not.

Because there is not always a legal triggering mechanism, as there is in divorce mediation, there is also not always a clear way for cases to be referred to mediators or for family members who are experiencing these concerns to understand the benefits of mediation for these disputes. As our population continues to age, families are coping more than ever before with these problems. As a society, we cannot afford to solve these problems primarily with civil litigation of family members against each other.

In the near future, we may see more combinations of services to help families cope with chronic, acute, or traumatic crisis and conflict, and this provision of services could help a family that is trying to cope with an aging or medically or emotionally dependent family member. For example, in Oregon, legislation has been recently introduced that would combine helping systems such as Aid to Families with Dependent Children, which administers welfare and financial aid, Services to Children and Families, which administers child protection and intensive family treatment services to families with abuse, neglect, or other major trauma and disruption, and Aging Services, which helps with care options for the aging population, into one unitary social service megalith so that it can provide family members the full range of services needed when the family is in distress. Families going to the unitary service could receive help and financial support, counseling, treatment services, and placement information and apply for benefits and entitlements by having one worker who gathers the needed services for the family based on need rather than having the family contacting multiple agencies in order to get complex needs met. Such moves may make out-of-home placement for temporary or permanent conditions less difficult to navigate and could certainly be a system that could benefit from family mediation perspectives and processes within these combined service conglomerates.

Mediation provides the open forum and assurance of completion that families struggling with difficult decisions need. In fact, this area of applying family mediation processes to disputes or decisions that must be made may be the largest growth area for family mediators. More medical social workers, hospitals, and treatment services are training staff members in mediation techniques because there is often not time for the family to employ a private mediator separately; if there is, then the private mediator sometimes may need to be available on a crisis or on-call basis as the situation changes.

MEDIABLE DISPUTES FOR ELDERS AND ILL AND DISABLED PEOPLE

Like all other disputes, it is helpful to see the levels and types of conflicts embedded in the disputes that are mediable. We can define this area of family practice as dealing with the following types of disputes:

- Crisis decision making for immediate care
- Competency for self versus need for supervision or legal agency
- Placement and responsibility for ongoing daily care
- Selection of appropriate or desired medical intervention for chronic or progressive problems
- Financial responsibility and distribution of debts and assets
- Discrimination and access concerns
- Confidentiality breaches

These issues can play out in disputes that are between the affected person and family members, between the affected person and institutions, between several of the affected persons, between family members but not including the person, and three-party mediations between the affected person, the family, and the institution or organization. Often layers of dispute resolution are required to address all the issues involved or parties affected.

ISSUES OF THE ELDERLY POPULATION

Suzanne Schmitz (1998) notes that elders can also have an increased number of consumer, contract, service agency, and neighborhood disputes because of the increased numbers of contracts and services they use to help them with daily living. Because of their increasing dependency on others for transportation, mobility, food service, specialized housing or housing that is in multiple-family dwellings, and other services, affected people may interface more frequently than nonaffected people with the helping systems to which they are attached, which can lead to more conflicts to deal with. Schmitz also notes that the conflict situations can have embedded values conflicts, with personal and generational values clashing and creating the dual relationship of needing services or help and simultaneously being in conflicts that are perceived as interest based, when in actuality the participants are not competitors for scarce resources or mutually exclusive positions.

The affected person can also become the victim of discrimination and access problems at work and in physical surroundings. Because of the definition of these problems as age or disability discrimination cases, many of these might be referred to community-based mediation programs or to mediators who specialize in the specific type of dispute rather than being sent to a family mediator. This chapter primarily examines disputes where the core of the dispute involves the affected person's relationships within the family rather than their relationship to outside resources and systems.

Although the literature base in mediation is scant and looks primarily·at elder concerns, this chapter generalizes to include those who are dealing with similar issues due to illness and incapacity as well as aging. Younger people too may be dealing with similar issues. Their disputes most often have structural conflicts, because they often revolve around the sources and use of power and around power inequities, either perceived or verifiable.

POWER ISSUES IN MEDICAL DISPUTES CONCERNING ELDERS

Joan Kelly (1995) notes that power imbalances surround the content of all disputes. These power imbalances may include problems with one or more of the following factors:

- The history and dynamics of the disputant relationship

- Personality and character traits
- Cognitive style and capabilities
- Knowledge base
- Economic self-sufficiency
- Gender and age differences
- Cultural and societal stereotyping and training
- Institutionalized hierarchies

Using these categories can heighten the family mediator's awareness of power issues for this population.

History and Dynamics of the Disputant Relationship

Often the affected person who has a need for supervised living or an out-of-home specialized placement, temporary or permanent, also has a long-term history with family members that makes these decisions even harder to make.

For example, if a mother and her daughter have never gotten along or if the father was absentee, alcoholic, or abusive when the children were young, the adult children who are now faced with making hard choices with their parent come to the dispute or mediation with the additional burden of past conflicted and often dysfunctional relationships. If the now-ill person was in a negative interactional pattern before, they must make these decisions with family members with that background in the picture. This situation often stirs up old resentments and can often reinforce long-standing negative interactional patterns. Similarly, an affected person who needs help and support but whose adult children are themselves troubled or have never worked through their past resentments or vindictiveness may find that the only people on whom they can rely are not reliable.

Personality Traits

Historically introverted affected persons may not want to agree to be placed in communal living situations, where they have little privacy or respite from others, as is often the case in nursing homes and retirement living situations, even when they know it is best for them. This situation can then set up the dispute for their relatives, who must wrest legal control or acquiescence from the affected person in order to achieve the desired aim. Gregarious and extroverted elders or disabled people usually will not like being placed in situations where they lose their social contacts, even when they know it may be in their best medical or financial interests.

Similarly, those whose personalities have been rigid and less receptive over the years to change, flexibility, or lack of order will find it extremely anxiety producing not to know all the details or to have to remain unsure or waiting for placements, test results, or other factors. This emotional response difference can lead to increased tension between the affected person and the adult child or the institutional representative. The very nature of the person and the situation creates a dispute that can quickly escalate to a family feud encompassing the extended family members.

Cognitive Issues

These issues can also play around the edges of disputes, since the cognitive style of the affected person can be influenced negatively by the person's medical condition or medications. Nevertheless, it must be a starting assumption that the affected person is capable of processing the information in mediation and should be present at all times, unless there is continuing evidence to the contrary, such as a determination of legal incompetence. The mediator must assess this, as in all other mediations, based on the same premises of the client self-determination required for all mediation.

Suzanne Schmitz (1998) notes that the premises of what constitutes capacity to negotiate have been enumerated by family mediation standards and the American Bar Association, as well as by manuals for disabled persons, and include the following abilities:

- Understand who the parties are
- Articulate their own story
- Understand the role of the mediator
- Listen to and understand the stories of others
- Generate options for solution
- Assess options
- Make an agreement
- Keep an agreement (pp. 76–77)

As in all other mediation efforts, the family mediator trying to set up and conduct mediation with the affected person must assess these behavioral capacities as the mediation effort continues. Strategic use of individual time, conducting shorter and more frequent sessions, and other adaptations may be helpful in maintaining the affected person's capacities during the mediation process.

If there is continuing concern about the affected person's abilities (or the other family members') to negotiate on his or her behalf, a surrogate or designated agent, such as an attorney, a conservator, a guardian, or a member of the family who is granted power of attorney by the affected person or the court, can, depending on state laws, have the authority to participate in the negotiation on behalf of the affected person. Informal surrogates may be suggested, but they run the risk of being invalidated later, so the wise family mediator will review documents to verify the legal capacities of the surrogate.

Sometimes the affected person just wants an advocate for support in their bargaining, and the mediator may find that this is helpful if the advocate understands and respects the limits of this role and authority. This may also be true for medical or financial specialists who can speak to the particular issues confronting the family. The advocate or technical expert should also pledge to the confidentiality rules of mediation that are in force in that state; if they do not feel they can for reasons of professional obligation, they should not attend, although they could offer documentary information that can be clearly subjected to the confidentiality of mediation. This should be outlined ahead, and because the process involves all the participants, the persons selected by the affected person or other disputant should be acceptable to all participants.

Knowledge Base

The differences between the affected person and the other disputants in regard to their knowledge base or information can be great. In this age of high technology in the medical industry, the gap of knowledge between the patient and the medical practitioner and care system can be enormous, even with so much reputable medical information available on the Internet and in support groups.

Some patients are very active about getting the information they need to equalize the bargaining, but some are not. Many elders were raised with a deep belief that no one questions the expertise or knowledge of the professional or the institution, and so they have become patient patients who do what the doctor tells them and maintain this social convention of learned helplessness by doing what the doctor, nurse, administrator, or hospital social worker says. In fact, they do not accept responsibility for their own health, placement, care, finances, or other decisions. This passiveness can undermine the integrity of the mediation process, which requires an active, fully informed choice to be made by the disputants.

Information alone will not automatically change the power dynamics, but at least it provides fairness in the area of full disclosure. The mediator has an ethical obligation to ensure that enough knowledge and information was developed during the mediation process, that full disclosure has been made, and that the affected person or disputant understood enough of the information to make an informed choice in mediation. If there is some question about this, then the mediation is questionable, and the mediator may need to stop the process to assess the appropriate accommodations, such as recessing to provide more time to review information or introduce advocates into the mediation process. As Christopher Moore (1988) has pointed out, data conflicts can be the easiest type of conflict to resolve if the participants are willing and able to take an active role in reviewing the data that are available.

Economic Self-Sufficiency

Because so many affected people feel so powerless in medical and placement issues due to the reality of their economic dependence on government programs, rules, and institutional policies or on their adult children, the issue of economic self-sufficiency is at the core of many of these disputes. Many elders lived through deprivation during the Great Depression, then rationing during World War II, and then rampant inflation while raising families who had increasing needs. They may still feel that they do not have enough money even when they do. Some elders perceive loss where there is none and maintain overly thrifty ways despite their affluence due to these overlearned concepts of scarcity and doing without.

Similarly, people who were used to a high standard of living and have now become elderly, ill, or disabled may not appreciate the realities of their current financial status and may have been assuming a self-sufficiency they really do not possess. A life's saving of $40,000 that seemed grand to them can be used up in one year of specialized care, leaving them economically dependent on children or the state and federal programs to which they may apply. Their economic status will determine their best alternative to a negotiated agreement (BATNA) and bargaining realities.

Gender and Age Differences

Gender and age differences can play out in the family disputes regarding care or placement of the elderly, ill, or disabled. Historically, women have been the caretakers of these most vulnerable family members and may take on or be automatically expected to handle a disproportionate share of their elderly parent's needs. Cultural stereotyping and cultural patterns can be part of the power differences that are noted in these cases, and the mediator's job is to bring these to the awareness of the participants to see if they want to make changes.

In some cultures and extended families, the wife is expected to care for her own aging parents and her husband's. With the advent of dual-worker families, these automatic expectations have to be fully questioned in the mediation process, although the goal of the mediation process is to support the mutually accepted decision, even if it is based on a values structure or view that would not necessarily be acceptable to the mediator. Part of the discussion in these cases should address these gender differences so that if the participants have concerns, they are not glossed over.

Cultural and Societal Stereotyping and Training

Another concern can be the automatic dismissal of the person due to age as well as gender. Can the fourteen-year-old son take care of his grandfather after school until his parents get home from work? Is it an option for the seventy-seven-year-old grandmother to take care of the four-year-old child with mild cerebral palsy?

Should the teenager who was emotionally close to her uncle be allowed to voice her thoughts in the end-of-life decisions for him? Will she always regret that she was not involved more or less? Does the family mediator have all the people who should be making the decision at the mediation? What about the sibling whom everyone keeps discounting in making the placement decision regarding moving their mother to a sheltered living situation? How will that person feel when he or she realizes important decisions have been made without consultation? Often the family mediator is the only one who can bring up the hard topics and notice who is not being consulted or included.

Institutionalized Hierarchies

Another major problem with power in cases involving the elderly, ill, or disabled person is the institutionalized hierarchy of the medical field. Consider a case where the nurse, with whom the patient has great rapport and trust, is indicating something different from what the doctor, with the authority to make the decision or action, is recommending. The nurse cannot override the doctor in terms of her power, but her thoughts can be brought into consideration in the mediation effort in a way that does not jeopardize her position yet provides the family with the information they need to help make complicated decisions.

The service delivery system often knows the rules, regulations, and their own policies because they deal with these on a daily basis, but the family must struggle to comprehend the complex policies and procedures very quickly, often for the first time—a situation that often leads the family to feel vulnerable and powerless in comparison to the institution. They may not know what the law or policy says they are entitled to or may have been told once or signed forms that they did not fully take in. Mediation can slow the process so that those under stress can think through the issues and options in a way that is more sensitive to their needs than just reiterating the rules.

MEDIATING FAMILY MEDICAL ISSUES

The doctor-patient relationship is a historically honored, special relationship that requires truth and open communication to maintain trust on both sides in order to promote the healing process. Protected in law by privileged communication, the boundaries of this relationship are a fundamental understanding of our society and must be honored, yet often disputes arise in this dyad that can and should be given the help of a neutral third party such as a family mediator.

Family medical issues that could be mediable fall into at least the following main categories:

- Charges, billing problems, and treatment by office staff
- Inappropriate techniques or malpractice by the doctor

- Informed consent and full disclosure
- Selection of the most appropriate, newest remedy
- Attention to the patient rather than the disease
- Taking a family member off life-support systems
- Authorization of risky treatment for incapacitated others
- Appropriate doctor-patient relationship
- Organ donation decisions by the family members
- Heroic or unproven efforts versus natural processes
- Pain management
- Overwhelming demands placed on family members due to medical conditions
- Drug or medical device liability

Although illness and difficult medical concerns can strike families at any age, the power issues and concerns for the family remain the same. The difference may be whether the family is still in a shock, grief, or crisis situation at the time they need to make these decisions. People who are dealing with crisis need firm direction from outside helpers. Distracted by the crisis, they often cannot hold multiple options in their minds.

Because of the nature of our medical system, outside private practice family mediators are often not available or even thought about, and hospitals and health care facilities do not always have a trained staff person who can facilitate urgent or crisis conflict resolution when such services are needed. The growth of this area of practice will depend on the cross-training that medical social workers, line staff, nurses and doctors, and clinic staff have. The less immediate and urgent the situation is, the more likely it is that the family will be able to avail itself of the help of family mediators. Often, these situations end up in legal actions to try to prevent particular actions from happening or to get acknowledgment and relief if there has been harm or injury.

Rather than hire private mediators, many advising attorneys might attempt to provide settlement conferences that are mediative but do not deal with the underlying values conflicts, interpersonal relationships, religious complexities, and identity issues. The more that comprehensive mediation models can be used by whomever is selected to deal with the medical dispute, the better the situation will be for the family.

Cris Currie (1998) identifies three dimensions of medical practice disputes. First is a legal dimension. Does the situation meet the legal standards for malpractice, breach of warranty, failure to provide informed consent, misdiagnosis and all its related problems, or physician misconduct? He notes that to win a professional malpractice suit, a client must show that a duty to care was owed to the party, that there was a breach by the doctor of that duty, that this breach resulted in an injury, and that the injury was directly caused by the breach by the doctor rather than by some other cause. He also notes that often the disgruntled patient must frame this type of suit "simply to raise the physician's awareness that a legitimate complaint might exist" (p. 216). Mediation of these complaints can legitimize the patient's multiple concerns without having to reach the legal standards of proof that the doctor was guilty of malpractice, did not provide adequate information, made misleading claims, or otherwise acted improperly.

The second dimension of medical concerns Currie notes is the reality that some patients get sicker from the medications, procedures, or systems the medical care provider recommends. Iatrogenic illness, in which the cure becomes the injury or cause of the problem, is real and means that getting relief from the courts through malpractice suits is often inadequate. Actual malpractice suits may be underused to deal with medical conflicts and situations of inadequate protection or harm, because patients do not have the time, financial resources, or skill to process their legitimate concerns in the legal arena. Even when they do, the injured patient often feels only minimal satisfaction.

A third area of medical concerns is the psychological context—that is, the personal meaning of illness, remedy, and wellness. The doctor or caregiver has a special trust relationship with the patient, which can easily be eroded or damaged even if it does not meet the legal tests of malpractice. Patients who do go through the laborious task of trying to sue their care providers are usually seeking more than financial compensation; they want vindication that something has gone wrong. They want to hold the care provider accountable for their perception that they have been wrongly treated, ignored, or neglected in the relationship, not necessarily in the actual medical treatment used. They want to ensure that other patients do not have to suffer this situation by getting a promise by the care provider to change. They want to hear some personal statements of awareness and apology that will allow them to release the conflict.

This makes sense, especially when we look at the model of conflict described by William Wilmot and Joyce Hocker (2001), who state that conflicts have a four-part nature: the content, the process, the identity, and the relationship goals. Wilmot and Hocker note that identity and relational issues are the drivers of disputes, and that is often true in medical disputes.

In this context of family medical disputes, the content may be about what the care provider did as treatment or said about it, and that can be argued legally in terms of objective standards for proof of malpractice or breach of duty for full disclosure. But often medical disputes are about the relationship and identity issues the patient has with the care provider or the medical system. Malpractice suits cannot fix problems in these areas, so this explains why there are so few such suits.

If a patient feels disrespected by the curt manner of the care provider or no longer trusts the relationship for some other reason, that person may know that the care provider is medically correct but still feel in dispute with the provider, leading to a level of ambivalence to continue or comply with treatment. When the care provider is the only source of that care and given that most patients involved in a medical regime are dependent on the care provider or system, it becomes an intolerable approach-avoidance internal conflict for the patient.

Because mediation offers the opportunity to describe these identity and relationship problems, not just the legally defined content conflict of good or bad medical practice, mediation is an ideal conflict resolution process for dealing with these disputes. Currie urges mediators to go beyond the legally defined issues of whether there was legal malpractice to mediate before the issues have been defined in these terms. He believes that if administrators and health care practitioners of all kinds are better informed about the nature of conflict resolution and proficient in providing mediation at the first level of complaint, it will benefit both the health care system and patients. They can address questions they have not been able to ask and release their anger; the physicians and nurses and the health care systems they work for will be able to dispel misperceptions and presuppositions held by patients and learn from the errors so that they can avoid similar problems in the future.

MEDIATING ADULT GUARDIANSHIP

When an individual's physical health, mental health, disability, or age becomes so incapacitating that the person can no longer care for his or her own daily activities, finances, or decisions, the usual recourse is to fall back on the family first. Adult guardianship is the process of legally giving care and control of an adult to another person or group of people, to enable the alleged incapacitated person to meet his or her basic social, legal, and physical needs. This is one of the strongest legal interventions that can be done to a person; it is just short of incarceration or a finding of legal incompetence in terms of how stigmatizing it can be and the implications for the individual from then on.

These decisions can be made in deliberate decision-making processes, when the family and the individual recognize the problem and the need to make acceptable decisions, or as crisis-driven processes that may have bitter family feuds attached. When families cannot decide, they have historically resorted to the family, domestic relations, or probate courts, which often place the adult in question with a guardian outside the family. This resolves the legal responsibility and authority for decision making, but can often leave the concerned family members feeling extremely angry and excluded.

In order to avoid this, some court jurisdictions, aging centers, and other governmental and social service structures have been investigating the use of mediation for these decisions. Some of these have constructed mediation programs as diversion programs for the courts after the legal triggering of the case when parties file legal motions that indicate the usefulness of mediation. The Center for Social Gerontology (1998) has been collaborating with experts in the fields of law, aging, disabilities, and mediation to create programs that will address these needs better than standard legal approaches do. It received a grant from the William and Flora Hewlett Foundation to create some pilot programs in several states in 1998.

These programs are structured to reflect the social structures in the local areas. In some jurisdictions, the Center for Social Gerontology selected to create a private mediator model of service delivery, with differences between counties of who functioned as the intake coordinator and conducted the initial screening of cases. Sometimes it was the court investigator who functioned as the point person for connecting cases with mediation. In other counties, the court administration itself took on the task, using attorneys as mediators, some of whom had no specific family mediation training or only minimal pilot-related training. In other counties, a third method is being tried: using community mediation centers as the screening and service delivery system.

In some counties, cases were accepted only if they had already filed a petition or motion on a related matter, whereas in other jurisdictions, prefiling cases could use the mediation service without prior legal intervention or filing. Oklahoma established a statewide program that used community dispute resolution centers and a few private mediators as the providers. Although the courts themselves were slow to refer to mediation, the other social service agencies and referral points were actively using the resource. Wisconsin also showed this composite pattern, with several counties having private mediators, while others use their existing community dispute resolution centers.

Spin-offs from this original program have been started in Chicago and Tampa, Florida, and several counties in Michigan, Nevada, Virginia, Massachusetts, and Georgia. A site in Denver, Colorado, modified the program to have it run as a court magistrate system. Ongoing training is currently available. The Center for Social Gerontology's *Adult Guardianship Mediation Manual* (1996) seems to be a complete manual for those contemplating doing this work or setting up systems within their own jurisdictions.

The issue for some programs that require private mediators is the funding for payment. A jurisdiction that chooses to use an already funded volunteer dispute resolution program has the advantage of providing another service with no additional outlay except for any specialized training it might do for staff or volunteers in that area. The downside of this arrangement is that complicated family mediation may be handled using standard problem-solving/negotiative mediation models that do not have the flexibility to allow the emotional facilitation or the systems perspective of families to function effectively during the mediation session. Also, many dispute resolution centers practice a model of mediation that requires only face-to-face joint sessions, without the use of caucus or solo time for each participant. This may be a limiting model for complex family systems, where breaking larger groups into subgroups to caucus separately would be the most advantageous way to bring about changes and facilitate feelings. If the dispute resolution centers can reduce this limitation, it could afford the advantage of providing a valid process without a legal filing requirement.

The opposite is true when jurisdictions want to build service delivery systems that will take advantage of the expertise of private mediators. Then the issue is securing funding that will allow for adequate time to mediate these complex cases. In jurisdictions with financial structures to assess a filing fee that is held in reserve for mediation services, such as the Ohio Court Rule that funds the Court Mediation Fund, there is a base of money that may be sufficient for offering mediation services and paying private mediators to provide it. Some jurisdictions set a flat fee. In 1998 in Ohio, for example, mediators were paid $300 per case, no matter who referred the case. Depending on the private mediator's overhead costs, that reduces to three hours or less per case, which may underserve the case or the mediator, or both.

Joan Nelson Hook (1999) notes that programs that use attorneys as mediators may not find the mediation process any less expensive than a standard court proceeding, since mediator attorneys will generally bill at the same hourly rates as other attorneys, and these cases take a considerable amount of time if each family member is given full attention as a participant. The major advantage is not economic but social. In Hook's state, Florida, the legal process has only three choices to offer a family: appoint a guardian, appoint a limited guardian, or dismiss the case. Mediation of these disputes allows for a fuller range of options and creative solutions, with multiple parties taking on different levels of responsibility. In this way, families can disperse the social and economic load while still preventing a loss of rights. Families can often create dyads or triumvirates that help to make mutually acceptable decisions. These systems can include the alleged incapacitated person until he or she is unable to function altogether.

Yet another issue that came up during the pilot program time is the intermingling of the various judicial responses. If a case is assigned a guardian ad litem, an officer of the court who is usually bound to relay information back to the public proceedings of the court action to protect the legal and social interests of the specified party, but then subsequently the case is referred to mediation, where the process is specified as at least confidential, if not privileged communication, then the issues of confidentiality of mediation efforts can be muddied.

The growth and development of this application of family mediation will require practitioners to review the particular state and local jurisdiction in order to determine how these cases are being handled, the referral and funding mechanisms that may be in place for mediation, and the modification of the local court rule or funding system to secure a confidential mediation environment and yet have the family receive help from court-appointed special advocates, guardians at litem, and others.

As elderly populations increase and as drugs and technology allow increased longevity and mobility for those with debilitating conditions, we may see an increase in the demand for these services. It seems ironic that a family must place a legal claim and pay a filing fee to the court, only to be referred out to a noncourt program the members could have accessed without legal filing. We hope that family mediators can make a strong enough case that families facing these hard choices and intrafamily conflicts need easy access to services at minimal cost, but not at the price of going without adequately trained mediators who understand more than the basic process of mediation.

In the following case examples, based on actual disputes that illustrate the complex human dilemmas of these cases, the use of the mediator is shown, without regard to a specific mediation model, to illustrate how the family mediator might work with the other institutions and help families and individuals with complaints, concerns, decisions, and agreements.

CASE EXAMPLE: OUT-OF-HOME PLACEMENT FOR AN AGING PARENT

Mary is a seventy-six-year-old woman and mother of Robert, Jesse, and Terry. She has been in her midwestern home thirty-five years and has been alone five years since the death of her husband. She attends a quilting group every Tuesday but has no other regular social activities.

Robert, the eldest sibling, is fifty-seven and married, and lives in a town about five miles from his mother. Robert and his wife, Sue, have one son, Thomas, who is away at college. Robert is a successful merchant in town, and his spouse has a full-time job in social services as an administrator. They have been planning an early retirement soon and expect to travel around the country full time in their trailer.

The middle sibling, Jesse, forty-nine, is divorced, living with a divorced woman in California, and is a freelance news writer who travels constantly. He gets paid by the job and always seems on the edge of financial breakdown. He borrowed money from Robert two years ago but has not paid it back.

Terry, the third sibling, is forty-five years old, married to Pat, and has two children, fifteen-year-old Brian and nine-year-old Beth. Pat works part-time as a counselor and teaches part-time at the local university, while Terry works as a school counselor at the high school. They live about four blocks from Mary's house. For about two years, Terry and Pat have been swinging by weekly to check on Mary.

The trigger event that started the controversy occurred about three weeks ago when Terry went over to check on his mother; he found no food to speak of in the refrigerator and the kettle red-hot because the stove had been left on. Terry was clearly worried and felt that something had to be done quickly, so he called Robert. Robert consulted with some friends, who all suggested that he contact someone from the Aging Services program in his town. Robert contacted them, and they referred him to a local private mediator, who had a general practice in family mediation and was often the one the Aging Services recommended when families needed to make decisions or resolve conflicts regarding placement.

Robert contacted the mediator and arranged to pay for the mediator's service, and the mediator contracted to provide services to the family. She described the need to explain mediation to his mother in ways that would not alienate her. The mediator explained her model of mediation and that her style usually involved getting everyone in the same room if possible, after individual telephone work prior to the joint session. Robert agreed to that but indicated that Jesse would probably be out of town on assignment, so might not be available even by telephone.

Prior to holding the joint session, the mediator got the following history from her telephone contacts with Terry and Robert. Mary had been living alone in the family home since her husband died five years ago. The house was fully paid for, and she received Social Security benefits and some pension benefits from her late husband's former work (she never worked outside the home). She had been in relatively good health, but lately had been having some heart irregularities and slowing considerably.

Over the past three months, the siblings had had a series of telephone conversations and decided it might be time for their mother to go to at least a supervised apartment, if not a nursing home. No timetable was made and nothing was arranged, but they jointly acknowledged that things were starting to change for her. After finding Mary with no food and with the danger of burning up her kettle from forgetfulness, Terry, very upset, called Robert and said that something needed to be done immediately. Robert had asked Terry if he would take their mother into his home, but Terry refused, leaving both siblings angry and distressed with each other. They had not spoken to each other since this encounter.

In those first solo telephone contacts, the mediator found out the following starting positions. Robert thought it was Terry's duty to take care of their mother, partly because they had the closest relationship, in both time and distance, and also in emotional rapport. Robert believed he and his spouse could not take her into their home. He stated that nobody was at home much, and he and his wife wanted to retire soon and travel. They were even thinking about selling their house altogether after Thomas graduated from college. Robert admitted that his spouse did not get along well with his mother; in fact, neither liked each other much, and they had always had personality conflicts. He thought that he could perhaps afford to pay for an assisted living apartment for his mother in the next town, about five miles away.

Terry's view was very different. He was offended that Robert thought their mother was solely his responsibility just because he lived closest to her. He reminded Robert the other day that he was the youngest and Robert the eldest, so if anything, responsibility should fall to Robert. Terry was defensive about the suggestion that he and his spouse make room in their home for his mother, and he did not believe that he could take her in; they had no extra or unused room, his marriage was already stressed, and the active household of a teenager and a preteenager and the need to save for college for their children meant that they could not provide much in the way of extra resources.

He also felt highly unappreciated for his past two years of checking on his mother regularly, providing companionship, and having his spouse help her. Terry was very opposed to having their mother placed in a facility. He believed it would be a hassle to drive all the way to that special facility; more important, his mother would not be happy there. Besides, he was not sure she would qualify for a nursing home or other care facility medically, but even if she did, he knew that those institutions are expensive. He asked Robert if could find some other solution, but was hurt when Robert did not seem to respond and just hung up. They had not talked since that encounter.

The mediator then called Mary, explaining that she was going to try to help the situation and needed to ask some questions. Mary at first did not want to answer any questions to a stranger over the telephone, so the mediator respected this, hung up, and called Terry, asking him to call her to tell her it was okay to talk openly, which he did. After this, the mediator again tried to talk to Mary and asked if it would be easier if she came to the house and they could talk briefly in person. Mary agreed that would feel more comfortable, and during that brief home visit by the mediator, she divulged that she believed that her deceased husband had wanted her to stay in the house. She saw the house as her secure and familiar home and did not want to leave it ever. But she also said that she did not want to be a burden to anyone. She loved her grandchildren and wanted to have them come over more often. She was convinced that she could never live with Robert's spouse, so she didn't even want to think about that. She perceived herself to be just fine and did not know what all the fuss was about. She had a lifetime of memories in her house. She did acknowledge some increasing forgetfulness but not the level Robert and Terry were implying. She was concerned that Robert might want to have her move so he could sell the house, which had good market value.

Because of the home visit, the mediator was able to assess the situation of her housing objectively. Although the mediator did see that the house was somewhat messy, with piles of magazines and crowded counters with things that could have been put away, she did not find the kind of conditions in the home that would have required immediate emergency action to prevent harm. She also did not assess Mary as so depressed or emotionally unstable that she would need to be referred to secure other forms of treatment prior to mediation. She found Mary coherent, and there were no concerns about her ability to speak for herself during mediation. Had there been concerns about Mary's competency and abilities to understand and participate in mediation, the mediator would have made some attempt to refer during the session. She shared those concerns with Robert and Terry, reporting to other agencies only if concerns about elder abuse, drug and alcohol use, harm to self or other, or concerns about Mary's mental status and ability to comprehend what was happening were major concerns that required such release.

The mediator then went back to her office and reviewed the information, looking at not only what everyone was saying but also at what was absent from the picture. Jesse, the middle sibling, was being left out of the decision-making process, as was Mary herself. Because Mary was fully competent to make the decisions about her life and home and placement, the mediator could not fall into the trap of minimizing her participation. Although it was clear that Mary may have needed some intervention to help her make new decisions, the decisions were still hers to make. Unless the tension between the adult siblings was dealt with, the family could be fragmented further. The old battles for power and responsibility were being played out in this situation, and the mediator could not fall into unholy alliances or collective amnesia.

Because she had noticed that Jesse's participation was being minimized, the mediator called Robert, explained why she needed at least to attempt to contact Jesse, secured Jesse's pager number, and placed calls until she was able to have a brief conversation with him. Jesse said that his brothers always left him out, and he was rather resigned to having them do whatever they wanted, seeing this as the usual pattern. Given his job and distance, he did not think he could do much at all but was willing to be somewhat available by telephone the day of the mediation session. He wanted to support his mother's independence and see her live in her house as long as was possible.

The mediator then set the day and time for a joint session by first asking Mary her preference but taking into consideration the work schedules of the others. The spouses of the brothers were asked to remain available by telephone. The mediation session was held in Mary's house, with Robert and Terry present. The mediator prefaced the beginning of the mediation as an opportunity for their family to help their mother hold a hard discussion and reminded everyone of her rights to be self-determining and make the final decisions. Ascribing them a positive intention, the mediator also indicated that the adult siblings wanted to serve as advisers, not to force their mother, but to hold the first of perhaps a continuing dialogue among the family members. She stated that the goal was to involve the entire family in a collective process so that no one felt excluded or uninformed. This immediately changed the power dynamics and empowered Mary by designating her as the final decision maker.

The mediator then had each son talk to Mary about the events that had been happening lately and about their thoughts and feelings about those events. Robert was able to share his fears that something tragic would happen that could have been prevented, and Terry was able to use several recent examples of his and his wife's concern. Together, they were speaking from their hearts, and Mary saw the sincerity and frustration.

The mediator then asked Mary what she made of that information. She shared her fear that the boys would continue to fight over this and that she would be prematurely forced out of her home. She was also able to admit that she recognized that she needed some help with the housework. She did not yet feel ready to bring up her concern about the financial gain of selling the house.

The mediator then listed the concerns and the feelings expressed by all and reconfirmed the mutual goals they all shared of respecting and supporting their mother yet starting to make accommodations to changes in her circumstances. She then had each of them repeat their worst fear: the sons expressed it as finding their mother sick or harmed by staying alone. She admitted that this was a valid concern and was willing to accept help but not to move. The mediator then stated that that was the thing they would all work together to avoid. When that reassurance was offered, Mary brought up her fear that the sons were trying to force her out to get the monetary value of the house, but then stated that she no longer thought that was the sons' motivation. They continued to provide her the reassurance that her safety, not their financial gain, was the concern. Dealing with her hidden fears was transformative for Mary, and the emotional tone of the session changed at that point. By moving it out of the binary stay-or-leave option and by reducing the sons' active persuasion, which she saw as insensitivity, the family was able to work together instead of struggle with each other.

The mediator then asked the family members, starting with Mary, to share what they had thought of as ways to deal with the newly redefined problem of how to keep her safe and provide the support she needs and make changes as needed. Mary thought that she could get one of her quilting friends to look in on her once a week, so that there would be other people to talk to and help her. Robert stated that he thought she might qualify for a daily food delivery program that would not only make sure she had adequate nutrition but also check on her daily by delivering the food to her door. He also stated that he could provide some extra money to hire a weekly housekeeper.

Robert said that his son was coming home from college to work during the summer, and he might be willing to stay in his grandmother's home. Terry said that his son, Brian, was willing and able to stop by his grandmother's house to mow the lawn and touch base once or twice a week after school. He could also run any errands or do any lifting. The whole family could come over once a month to do larger tasks, such as cleaning and window washing. Robert suggested that he and his wife and their son would be happy to be a part of that if they could do it after church on Sundays. Together they brainstormed a number of things all of them could do to provide more support, coverage, and monitoring of their mother.

The mediator also acknowledged that Jesse was a part of the family system and might want to contribute in some way, so she called him and relayed all the ideas. He suggested that he often had time gaps between assignments when he could use his frequent flyer miles to visit more often or could route his flights to spend one or two days periodically with her and could help during those times with the bigger tasks. He appreciated being able to find a way he could contribute and being asked to be a part of the care system that was being built.

The mediator summed up all the options that had been developed, and so as not to pressure her or go at too fast a pace, she suggested that they recess the mediation effort at this point, asking Mary to think about the ideas and develop her preferences regarding the help she would be willing to accept for food, companionship, physical support and home management, and ongoing monitoring. She also pointed out that the sons had volunteered their own family members for some of the options and suggested that it would be wise to go home and discuss the options with them to gain their actual support before decisions were reached. She asked who would take on the task of verifying Mary's eligibility for the daily food program, and since Robert had suggested it, he volunteered to research it and facilitate the arrangements. They agreed to meet together in Mary's house a week later to make the final decisions.

When they did, Mary accepted the daily food service, the help from her grandson with the lawn, the monthly family gatherings to provide physical support, and Terry's wife's weekly visits. She was not willing yet to have a weekly cleaning service paid for by Robert, but saw that as an option later if the monthly family work sessions indicated that she needed it. Mary also suggested a new option: having someone contact her by telephone each day. The mediator wrote up the agreements and asked if they wanted to meet three months later for a brief discussion of how it was going, to review any new needs, and to develop new options if they were needed. They all thought that was a good idea, so they called Jesse, who agreed that he would arrange his schedule to attend, and they set a date.

At the three-month review session, Mary's health had deteriorated, and the doctor suggested that she needed surgery. She would need to be hospitalized and then stay in a recovery facility for several weeks, but then could return home if all went well. The family agreed to a maintenance plan for taking care of her home in her absence and to a more involved relay system of care after she returned from the recovery facility. That relay system involved Robert and Terry, their spouses, and the visiting nurse program. For the first month post-surgery, there would also be an in-home nurse at night, which Terry would pay for. Everyone agreed that they would take the doctor's and recovery facility's recommendations for their mother's level of care.

They agreed to meet at the facility again before her release to reconfirm the care plan. They did not need the mediator for that meeting, but all agreed and signed a form to allow the mediator to release information from the mediation to the care facility's staff medical social worker, who would become the family adviser and helper from that point forward. This served as a natural point of transition to the medical world, which would be determining Mary's need for care and the options available as they went along, based on her medical condition. The door was left open for further family mediation, but the mediator was not contacted again.

CASE EXAMPLE:
PLACEMENT AND MEDICAL TREATMENT DILEMMAS

Ralph, an eighty-year-old widowed, childless Alzheimer's patient, was signed into a treatment facility by his eighty-five-year-old sister Ann, who had power of attorney to act in his behalf. He seemed fine, but each week when she visited him, she found that his clothing was missing and that he was dressed in clothing she had not brought or bought, with shoes that did not fit. When she asked about this, the care facility nurse said that he kept wandering into other patients' rooms and putting his clothes in the wrong closets. They did not have the time to go looking through all the closets so dressed him in clothes they had on the premises. Ann found this appalling, but did not feel that she had any choice in the matter, especially in the way it was presented as just part of the process.

When she was told that they had started to medicate him because he was getting into fights with other residents, she asked more about his behavior, since she had never seen him engage in combative behavior. The day nurse Ann talked to indicated that he responded aggressively only when the other patients tried to take his things. They had also strapped him to a wheelchair, because he had fallen several times during his night walks. She indicated that she was not sure this was the best course of action, but had no authority to change the medication, since it was policy to medicate aggressive patients. When Ann responded that she had never authorized this medication nor had the doctor called her to indicate that it was medically necessary, she met with George, the manager of the facility, who produced a paper she had signed at intake that stated the policy.

Worried and upset, she discussed the situation with her two other siblings, who indicated that this did not sound like good care and asked her to "do something." She did not know what to do, so she contacted her religious adviser, who referred her to the family mediation center; she called and discussed the situation with a mediator. The mediator agreed to take the case, and Ann determined that it would be a good use of Ralph's funds to hire the mediator.

The mediator contacted the care facility manager and explained the request for mediation. The mediator requested that the facility manager be the one to attend the mediation, but that in order for mediation to proceed, the day nurse and the doctor who had prescribed the drugs needed to be available at least by telephone the first day of the mediation; both had to agree to hold several smaller mediation sessions rather than one marathon session. The mediator agreed to set up the session at the nursing home conference room, so the manager would not lose time traveling, and she assured them that no sessions would last longer than ninety minutes. She then called Ann, explained the arrangements, and had Ann set out the questions she wanted answered, what she wanted to express to the nursing home representatives, and what she wanted as an outcome.

At the mediation, the mediator started by having both Ann and the facility manager, George, state what each knew of the events that had led to the concern, Ralph's specific condition, and the documents that Ann had signed. They did this and found some discrepancies between what each knew. They were then instructed to share with each other the questions they wanted answered. They then called and put on the speaker phone the prescribing doctor, who explained what the drug did and more about the exact status of Ralph's condition. They thanked him for the information and ended that brief consultation.

Then they asked the day nurse to share her information with them, again over the telephone. The mediator summarized what was known and what areas seemed to be discrepant and asked Ann and George to recess and return for the second part of the mediation in two days. During the two days, they should contact any other resource people they wished to consult. George said he would try to verify with the records and the night shift nurse what Ralph did the night he was first medicated. He would also contact another care facility to find out what it did in situations like this. Ann indicated that she would consult with her other brother and sister to get their opinion. They ended the first part of mediation, the fact-gathering stage.

In the mediator's office, Ann called her siblings on a conference call to discuss the situation and gain some support for the course of action she should take. They were both supportive, reconfirmed her right to make the best decisions that she could, and had a few other questions they hoped she could answer. Had the siblings been at all unsure of her role, expressed doubts, or had indicated other dynamics that could have undermined Ann's authority or confidence, the mediator would have mediated between them, keeping in mind that Ann ultimately had the legal authority to disregard what they wanted but was choosing not to act in that way but rather to come to consensus, or at least do consultative decision making with her remaining family members.

George called a nearby facility, which was set up and staffed with more help during the evening shift. This facility also used medication in cases of aggression, although the patient's individual doctor, not the facility's consulting physician, prescribed and monitored it.

Two days later, Ann and George returned to mediate, and the mediator instructed them to share their thoughts and feelings from the previous session. Ann indicated that although she was still concerned, she was glad they were mediating and that George seemed to be open and willing to look at the concerns. George indicated his continued concern; he wanted to make sure that they found a good solution and that he could answer any question Ann or her family had, so they could avoid any unpleasantness that could create negative press.

Ann then asked all her questions again, and this time George answered them as she asked them. Ann was then invited to say what she wanted the care facility to know, which was that she would have liked to have been consulted before and would probably have consented to the medication but did not have any trust left due to this event. She was left feeling powerless and uninformed when she found out after the fact. She was not comfortable with an on-call doctor's prescribing for Ralph, over the telephone and without seeing him, something that was not curative but strictly for behavioral management. The mediator asked George to share what he found in his further discussions with the other facility, which he did.

They then moved to the development of options. Ann suggested that she would be interested in touring the other facility and asked about the financial and legal arrangements to switch, which George explained. She then requested that they facilitate the transfer and that her doctor be used immediately to consult with Ralph to give a second opinion on the type and dosage of the medications he was on. The arrangements were made to have Ralph transported by a staff orderly to Ann's doctor; Ann would meet him there. She agreed to meet back in mediation after she toured the other facility the next day.

When the third session started, the mediator asked Ann if she had toured the other facility, which was actually closer to her home. She had and she liked it, although it was more expensive and would use up Ralph's life savings much faster. Prompted to tell about the visit to the doctor, Ann noted that her physician had downgraded Robert's condition, indicated that he was going into the third stage of the disease more quickly than they had previously anticipated, and had recommended a different medication.

The mediator prompted them to explore other options. One was that Ralph would stay where he was, with the changed medication and routine visits to Ann's physician. George explained the impracticality of transporting Ralph on an ongoing basis to see this physician. Ann again brought up the option of transferring him to the other facility, with no financial penalty or fees. No other options could be developed between them. The mediator asked Ann if she wanted some time to think the situation over, but she wanted to conclude the matter that day. They agreed to the transfer plan, and George called while she was there to make plans for Ralph to be switched to the other care facility at the end of the week. They signed the documents necessary to conclude the matter, and Ann agreed to go to the new facility the next day to sign their documents. They concluded the mediation session, and Ann felt relieved, as did George.

During the mediation, the mediator was attempting to create a dialogue between both sides but to be aware of the power dynamics of Ann's working with what she perceived as an institution that had all the power. Ann herself was an elder, but seemed to have not only the legal but the personal capacity to act on Robert's behalf and needed only the accommodation of shorter, less physically and emotionally fatiguing sessions. The mediator did not do a lot of prompting of George, who understood quite well the negative consequences of not mediating this effectively; he was a sophisticated negotiator who saw the minimal concessions made in mediation as much less troublesome than litigation or bad publicity.

Allowing Ann time between sessions to consult with her family members to gain support was another power balancing this mediator did. This contributed to her perception that although she had the technical legal capacity to make the decisions independently, it was really a larger family issue that could have potentially divisive effects if she did not handle it correctly. She could have been blamed either way she decided, but by checking out the options and using the other siblings as an advisory committee, no one could say she had acted outside Ralph's best interests.

Could Ann have done this without the aid of a mediator? Probably she could have, but maybe not as efficiently or confidently. Did the mediator work for the best resolution for both of the participants and the indirect party, the affected person? I believe so. This is a case where mediation services, if available at low cost or subsidized by care facility collectives or other helping systems, or offered as a private contractual service, can be extremely helpful.

CASE EXAMPLE:
POSTPROCEDURE MEDICAL COMPLAINT

Rebecca, a woman in her late thirties, decided to terminate an unwanted pregnancy and went through the preprocedure counseling at the clinic she selected. She expressed a clear intention, signed all the full-disclosure forms, and returned at the appointed time, undergoing the procedure. All the medical records showed a perfectly normal procedure, with standard postprocedure care, information distribution, and recovery on-site. She returned, as was the policy, for the after-care medical checkup a few days later.

At that time, Rebecca asked to see the counselor she had seen before. This was arranged, and during this brief meeting, Rebecca told her that the doctor had been "flippant" with her, had been joking around during the procedure, and had "greasy hair." Rebecca was considering filing a grievance against him, perhaps even a lawsuit for malpractice. She had not yet gone to an attorney. The counselor tried to get her to talk about her thoughts and feelings. Rebecca shared that the doctor's demeanor had "made her feel uncomfortable." Sensing that this was a potentially escalating situation, the counselor suggested that Rebecca talk to the facility director about her concerns, but Rebecca would not commit to it, and refused any further help the counselor offered, including holding another counseling session with her to explore her thoughts and feelings more. The counselor reported the incident to the director.

A few days later, the director received a letter of complaint, asking that the doctor be "officially reprimanded"; if this did not happen, Rebecca would file a malpractice suit. The director called Rebecca, telling her that mediation was the preferred first step in the agency's grievance procedure and suggested that the agency pay for a private mediator of her choice from those listed in the state mediation directory, so that they could have a mediation session between her and Dr. Thomas. This mediation session would take place at the mediator's office. She reassured Rebecca that this mediation would in no way prevent her from going forward with her formal grievance or malpractice suit against him but was something they like to offer patients. She also suggested that Rebecca could bring someone else to the mediation session as a support or advocate and offered to send Rebecca a brochure about the use of mediation as an option for medically related concerns. Rebecca authorized her to send it, as long as the clinic name and address were not on the envelope. She said she would think about it and get back to the director.

Two days later, Rebecca called back, saying that she would like a chance to talk with the doctor in mediation and would like the counselor she had talked to at the agency to be the person who sat in with her. The director agreed, as long as everyone was clear that the counselor would not be the patient's direct advocate, but simply a supportive and trustworthy person who might be able to help her communicate better with the doctor. The director said she would schedule a single mediation session for the end of the week with the mediator Rebecca chose.

The director then notified the counselor of Rebecca's request for her attendance at the mediation and the director's permission to attend. But the counselor felt that she could not participate in that capacity, since she would have a dual relationship with the client and with the agency and must withdraw on ethical grounds. The director, who had not realized the ethical dilemma she had created for her counselor, understood and then contacted Rebecca to explain this. She encouraged Rebecca to attend mediation with the doctor and suggested that perhaps she, as the director, could attend the session as an interested person—not as the advocate for the patient or the doctor but as the representative of the facility that had an interest in its clients being well served. Rebecca decided to go ahead under those terms.

The director notified the mediator Rebecca selected and explained the basics of the conflict as she knew it. The mediator's policy was to allow others to attend if all participants were informed and if the role of that person was clearly defined. Because the doctor had a continuing employment contract with the facility, the mediator had to determine the exact level of involvement that the doctor and the director had to ensure that his rights and employment records would not be compromised by her active involvement in the session. As it turned out, she did not have even administrative supervisory responsibility of the doctor, since the selection, hiring and firing, employment disciplinary actions, and all his periodic performance evaluations were done by the chief medical director, not by her.

This clarified, the mediator was ethically free to allow the director to attend, and he stressed the confidentiality of the mediation process. The mediator then contacted both the doctor and Rebecca and made sure they understood the requirements of confidentiality of mediation, and he reconfirmed the director's role during mediation and the impartiality of the process despite the facility's paying the mediator's fee. The mediator went through all the required full disclosure required by the state and national laws and professional organizations' standards of practice with each person on the telephone, indicating that an agreement to mediate containing this information would be presented to all participants, including the director, at the session.

When the mediator convened the session, he started with the signing of the agreement to mediate and a review of the process. They had reserved the morning, and if another session was required, the facility was willing to pay for one more session. The mediator immediately equalized the power of the director and the doctor and started all requests for information with Rebecca.

Rebecca described her feelings that the doctor had "made her feel dirty" by his unkempt appearance and cavalier manner. This had been an extremely hard decision, she had felt very vulnerable, and his manner had been very hard to deal with. She felt it lowered the professionalism that she was led to believe this clinic offered, and had she known this was the way it would be, she would have sought services elsewhere. She was doing this mediation or considering a grievance or legal action only because she had a moral obligation to ensure that no one else was treated as she had been. She wanted assurances from Dr. Thomas that no other woman would experience what she went through that day. Rebecca's tone was somewhat stiff and icy, and her words were carefully chosen; she maintained tight control of her emotions during her statement.

When prompted by the mediator to talk about what this had been like for her and how she viewed herself in this conflict, Rebecca's tone changed, and she became less stiff. She had seen Dr. Thomas's behavior as being about her, about demeaning her stature as a respectable person, and that led her to wonder whether he respected his patients. What she now realized was that she just wanted him to know how uncomfortable she had been that day and how his light manner and joking behavior had not helped. She feared that he had judged her and that he disrespected her, which was why he was implying that this was a casual thing she was doing. Saying this seemed to open something in Rebecca, and the emotional climate in the mediation session changed.

Dr. Thomas was more than willing to acknowledge that he sometimes tried to joke with patients because he believed it sometimes relieved their tension and fear; he had never meant his comments in any way to be demeaning, offensive, or offhand. He felt absolutely respectful of his patients, which was why he continued to work at the clinic, risking quite a bit professionally to provide a safe, medically correct process. He explained that the day he did her procedure, he had come to the facility directly from his forty-eight-hour on-call shift at the hospital and may not have been as fresh as he would have liked, having just done emergency surgery for several hours.

He explained that his first reaction to her information, conveyed by the director, had been defensive, since he felt that her allegations of improprieties had held his professional reputation hostage. He had been prepared to defend himself vigorously if she had pressed on to legal action, but he could not see his level of responsibility in the conflict. He apologized and expressed remorse at having made a difficult personal time in her life more difficult. He expressed gratitude that she had brought this to his attention and was willing to look at changing his style by asking the patient's feedback about what she would find most helpful in reducing tension rather than assuming that jokes worked for everyone.

Dr. Thomas's sincerity and openness and his lack of defensiveness on maintaining his professional stance during the mediation session was helpful in reducing Rebecca's face-saving indignation and advocacy of others. When she reflected on how hard that day was for her, she lost her emotional control and started softly crying. The mediator not only allowed but invited both sides to speak about their emotions, reflecting the feelings of hurt, shame, and defensiveness, covered over by distancing behavior, as very normal reactions to hard situations. He also normalized the doctor's deep devotion to proper patient care and his commitment to the patient's rights. The mediator asked if Rebecca needed to take some time out, but she felt she could continue.

To give Rebecca some time to regain emotional control, the mediator called on the director to speak to the commonality of the postprocedure process for many women. The director spent a few minutes noting that many women had postprocedure feelings of guilt, shame, embarrassment, or distrust and that it was actually quite common for them to want to move away from those feelings by covering them or displacing them. She acknowledged that this was why the clinic had counselors and that she would be happy to have Rebecca do more counseling at the facility or could make some referrals to other therapists and even pay for a few sessions if Rebecca wanted some help in dealing with her life situation, feelings, and responses to this situation. This was something practical that the agency could offer to mitigate some of the discomfort she had experienced.

By facilitating the feelings, relationship, and identity issues for Rebecca rather than staying on the content of whether Dr. Thomas had done some malfeasance, Rebecca was able to see that some of what she had experienced was reality based but unintentional by Dr. Thomas and that she actually did need more counseling. The mediator used the interaction between the participants for emotional catharsis, and the indignation dissolved the more that Rebecca was empowered to describe her concerns. She agreed to the director's offer of some additional counseling but not at the facility. Dr. Thomas again expressed his regret and his being less than sensitive to her, and he made a pledge that he would be more sensitive to emotional needs and identity concerns in the future.

The mediator asked the participants if they needed a written agreement, which they did not, and Rebecca and Dr. Thomas shook hands. The mediator asked if Rebecca knew where she was with pursuing her rights to file a grievance, and she said that she no longer felt a need to do so; this session had accomplished what she had wanted. No further mediation was needed, and since they had been allowed to express their identity and relationship issues in a safe forum, they no longer had the need to pursue the content and legal issues.

CASE EXAMPLE:
ADULT GUARDIANSHIP OF A DISABLED SISTER

Roberta's younger sister, Flavia, was born with mental retardation and physical disabilities and had always had low impulse control. She had attended school, but because she lived in a rural district in Montana, there were not many opportunities for socialization and not many social services to provide the family respite relief. The parents often relied on Roberta to care for her sister when they went to town for shopping or other errands. Roberta did the best she could, but found herself vowing that she would never be stuck having to care for her sister over the long term. Roberta did well in school, went on to college, and got an advanced degree in clinical psychology, and moved away farther and farther in this process. Her parents were now having their own medical troubles and knew that they needed to have a plan in place to care for Flavia. Recently, they had been putting a lot of pressure on Roberta to step up to her responsibilities and be designated as the guardian. They wanted to put their will in order. Roberta had consistently refused, and recently it had come to dead silence on the telephone.

Roberta had established a good job and a serious relationship with her boyfriend; on their last visit with her, the parents agreed to attend a mediation session that Roberta had arranged with a family mediator. This was a surprise to them, but they were willing to cooperate. During this session, Roberta was able to express her desire to be "out from under" the sister who had controlled her life as she was growing up. Roberta was willing to be part of a care system but drew the line at having her sister ever live with her. She was willing to visit and maintain contact as long as she could have her own life. She had investigated facilities in her new city and had found several group homes available.

Her proposal to her parents was that she help facilitate Flavia's move and assume shared guardianship with the local volunteer guardian, a pastor who made this population his mission and who could continue in this role no matter which facility Flavia lived in within the metropolitan area. This was the best she could offer. She was willing to be entirely responsible for the financial arrangements for her sister if her parents were worried about the pastor as a stranger who might misuse the funds.

The parents were dismayed; they had never wanted to put Flavia in a home. They expressed concerns that Roberta would travel and leave Flavia alone and at risk. Gently, the mediator tried to see if the parents had any option other than Roberta's taking care of Flavia at home, and they had to admit that they had never explored any other option because they thought it was Roberta's obligation. The mediator noted that the one option they had suggested was clearly unacceptable to Roberta and asked what part of Roberta's option was unacceptable to them. They were vague for a while, then wanted to know how the different living sites would handle Flavia's outbursts. Roberta said that she did not know but that they could interview the different programs to see the response. The parents then sent several other road-blocking questions toward Roberta, who successfully fended off each.

The mediator reminded all of them that if they went with an assisted or supervised living home, the staff would run the home in their own way and that neither Roberta nor the parents would be able to control this. The mediator then tried to focus the discussion on the identity and relationship issues that were driving the conflict. The parents believed that their family values and identity were manifested in the way that they had always treated their daughter as a member of the family. Roberta was able to discuss how she needed a personal identity and life other than as her sister's keeper. Roberta had created a life that was satisfying to her and was not willing to let it go, but she was willing to be part of a caring and monitoring system for her sister. Then the mediator asked the parties to discuss how this issue was affecting their relationship. Roberta eloquently and angrily explained how she felt they never listened to her, how that made her resentful, and how this resentment was getting in the way of their enjoying these years as a family. The parents also expressed their desire to end this ongoing war of nerves and will, and realized that they needed to respect Roberta in her resolve. This acceptance of the emotional standoff and costs changed the tone of the meeting. The mediator highlighted the fact that their insistence was driving away the daughter they needed and wanted to relate to. But there was another option to consider that could provide each the level of connectedness they wanted while preserving personal freedom. The task of the mediator was to help them develop this third way.

They concluded the mediation session with a plan to think about this new option, see if they could develop others, and research the questions they had. They agreed to a telephone conference call in two weeks. Two weeks later, during the call, the parents immediately started the conversation with new information; they had talked with their friends and neighbors, who supported the concept Roberta was suggesting. They conceded that there really were no other choices and that some kind of care facility seemed inevitable. If Roberta would become the legal guardian but have Flavia live at a supervised living site, Roberta could still be part of the decision-making process, which reassured them. This major concession on their part allowed Roberta to stop reacting and maintaining her indignant stance; she changed her competitive, defensive approach to a more collaborative response.

All three then focused on the concrete tasks and steps of making their plan happen, and the mediator helped them make secure plans and sets of contingencies, including a process of reviewing the facilities, meeting the local resource person, and staying with Roberta the first two weeks after they placed Flavia in the facility so that they could visit her every day and discuss with the staff how the placement was going. If all went well in the first three months, they agreed to make this arrangement permanent and to file the necessary paperwork with the court to make Roberta the legal guardian. If not, they would return to mediation to develop another plan.

This sequenced leave-taking was an emotional weaning process, and the concomitant loss of their way of life, which had so revolved around the disabled child who was now an adult, was an important transition for the parents. Doing it slowly, with an escape clause, gave them enough confidence to let go. It was the assurances about a kinder process that helped them finally accept the inevitable.

❧

In order for people to feel the serenity and acceptance of their decisions on behalf of family members in their care or about their own medical treatment or placement, or, for elders, their final decisions in life, they need the reassurance that all issues have been discussed, all options made available, and the best choices made. Face-saving and change in hardened positions are often best done at home, in the middle of the night, or in between sessions, so sequential sessions facilitate this process. Elders need time to come to peace with their own issues that involve so much loss and change. Those who are dependent on others need to know that their relatives are not left with bitter feuds on their account.

Mediation of these very personal family dramas of necessary loss and care provides the container for the emotions and value-laden identity issues. By fully discussing them, new issues and understandings can emerge. Family mediators, with their understanding of facilitation of feeling and sensitivity for moments when transformation can occur, are best equipped to provide the help and support needed in these decisions.

We can hope that this potentially rich area for family mediation practice will continue to develop and serve the needs of people to deal with pressing social and family crises and conflicts. Family mediation holds many promises to transform and empower the participants and to empower families to be self-determining despite illness, disability, medical treatment, and aging.

Family disputes of all different realms and complexities can respond to thoughtful, sensitive application of the mediation process. Mediation provides the most appropriate process for management and resolution of family conflicts, because it keeps the family members in charge of the outcome and responsible for necessary changes in the family system. Mediation is deeply egalitarian and democratic. It is consistent with the recent change of paradigms in helping systems, which holds that helpers should stress individual and family strengths, not just focus on problems. Mediation in theory and practice is consonant with our legal system, which stresses freedom of choice; our society, which stresses individualism and maintenance of each family's values; and a world that needs, more than ever, peaceful management of, de-escalation of, and ultimately reconciliation after conflict. Families, and the successful balancing of their needs for both justice and harmony, are the wellspring of our individual and collective futures.

APPENDIX A:
HOUSEHOLD MAP

Household Map

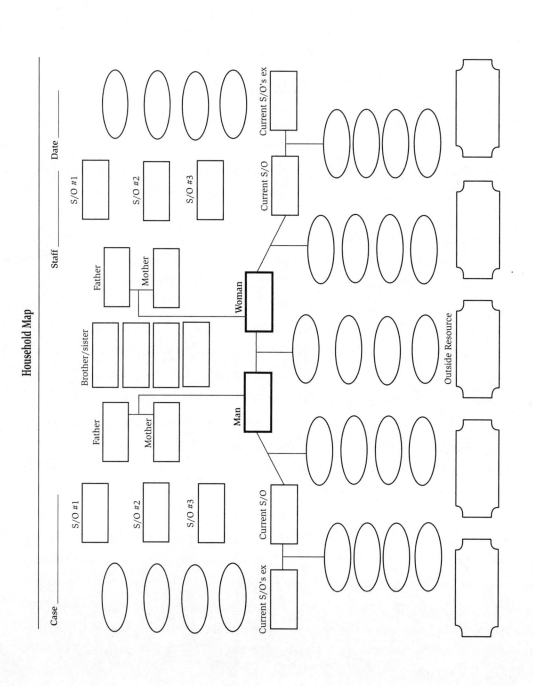

Case _____ Staff _____ Date _____

APPENDIX B:
REPORT OF THE
ACADEMY OF FAMILY MEDIATORS
TASK FORCE ON
SPOUSAL AND CHILD ABUSE

MEDIATION OF FAMILY DISPUTES
INVOLVING DOMESTIC VIOLENCE

Family violence, which is mostly perpetrated against women, and its impact on children, continue to pose serious questions for dispute resolution professionals and the practice of mediation. Women's advocates, mediators, mental health workers, lawyers, and the judiciary are increasingly working together to better understand the complex consequences of family violence. Collaboration is increasing between mediators and advocates from victim's networks.

Some critics consider divorce mediation to be inappropriate in cases where domestic violence is an issue because of the fear of retribution, the absence of trust, and the imbalance of power between the parties. They argue that mediation may not protect parties from coerced settlements and from subsequent intimidation and violence; they believe litigation is preferable to mediation in these cases.

For cases in which there is abuse, a question often asked is whether the legal process—including arrest, protective orders, and litigation—is adequate to restructure a post-separation parenting relationship that will work in the best interests of all involved. This subject continues to be a topic of much debate.

These guidelines address some of the issues involved in determining which cases may be appropriate for mediation and offers recommendations regarding ways to safeguard the physical safety and legal rights of all parties.

Basic Guidelines for Mediators

- Family mediation cases in which there is or has been domestic violence are complicated and can be dangerous to the participants and the mediator. Therefore, beginning mediators and mediators not trained or experienced in dealing with domestic violence should not accept referrals of these cases but rather should refer them to an experienced mediator or to another appropriate resource. Another choice would be for an inexperienced mediator to co-mediate with someone who has considerable professional experience dealing with domestic violence cases.

- If the abuse history or potential for violence is sufficient to jeopardize a party's ability to negotiate without fear or duress, the case should not be mediated.

- There should be no mediation concerning the violence itself. For instance, an offer to stop hitting in exchange for something else should not be tolerated.

- When safety is an issue, the mediator's obligation is to provide a safe environment for cooperative problem solving or, when this does not seem workable, to help the clients consider more appropriate alternatives.

- Above all, the mediator must promote the safety of all participants in the mediation process.

Guidelines for Assessing Whether Mediation May Be Appropriate

A. Prior to commencing mediation, screen all clients for a history of abuse, to determine which cases are inappropriate for mediation, which require additional safeguards in addition to or instead of mediation, and which should be referred to other resources.
   1. Conduct initial screening separately with the parties. This could be done in a variety of ways. For example, screening could take place within a brief telephone or face-to-face interview, or with a written questionnaire. Using a structured questionnaire, basic information that includes details about any history of abuse can be gathered. If screening is not done separately, a victim may be unwilling to reveal the presence of violence or may be placed at risk for revealing the violence.
   2. Screening should continue throughout the mediation process.
B. Whether couples enter mediation voluntarily or because it is mandated by statute, court, or local rule, matters of safety, free choice, and informed consent require special consideration, especially in situations where domestic violence is a factor.

1. Mediators and mediation services have an ethical duty to assure that mediation occurs in a safe environment and that the process goes forward only if both parties have the ability to mediate safely, autonomously, and free from any intimidation. The parties must be capable of reaching outcomes satisfactory to both of them voluntarily and with informed consent. If these conditions cannot be met, mediation needs to be terminated safely and appropriately.

2. In order to assure safety and freedom from coercion, it is important that the courts not view a party's request to waive the mediation requirement as evidence of a lack of cooperation.

3. In jurisdictions in which there is mandatory mediation, it is especially important that there be separate screening. In addition, the following options should be made available:
   a. separate sessions
   b. the presence of a support person
   c. an exemption from the mediation requirement

C. Clients should be strongly encouraged to consult with attorneys prior to mediation and certainly before an agreement is finalized.

D. Mediators must be knowledgeable about domestic violence. Training for mediators should include the following:

1. Issues related to physical and psychological abuse and its effect on family members

2. The impact that family violence (including witnessing violence) has on children

3. Effective techniques for screening, implementing safety measures, and safe termination

4. Referral to appropriate resources in addition to or instead of mediation

5. Sensitivity to cultural, racial, and ethnic differences that may be relevant to domestic violence

E. When a decision is made that mediation may proceed, mediators need to assure standards of safety, voluntariness, and fairness. When mediators have concerns, they should inform their clients that they are not neutral about safety.

The following are recommended procedural guidelines:

1. Obtain training in how to deal with domestic violence and become familiar with the literature.

2. Never mediate the fact of the violence.

3. Never support a couple's trading nonviolent behavior for obedience.

4. Set ground rules to optimize the victim's protection.

5. When appropriate and possible, arrange separate waiting areas and separate arrival and leaving times, permitting the victim to arrive last and leave first, with a reasonable lag in time for safety purposes.

6. Use separate meetings throughout the mediation process when appropriate, necessary, or helpful.

7. Consider co-mediation with a male-female mediation team, as an option.

8. Maintain a balance of power between the couple, and, if this is not possible, terminate the mediation process and refer the couple to an appropriate alternative process. Such alternatives might include shelters, therapists, abuse prevention groups, and attorneys.

9. Allow a support person to be present in the waiting room or mediation session.

10. Terminate the mediation if either of the participants is unable to mediate safely, competently, and without fear of coercion. Precautions should be taken in terminating in order to assure the safety of the parties. For example, the mediator should not reveal information to one party or to the court that could create a risk for the other party.

11. Consider offering a follow-up session to assess the need for a modification of the agreement.

12. Work with diverse cultural and ethnic groups serving violent families to develop appropriate and culturally sensitive options for resolving issues related to separation and divorce when domestic violence is an issue.

APPENDIX C:
CONTROL, ABUSE, AND
DOMESTIC VIOLENCE SCREENER

Control, Abuse, and Domestic Violence Screener

Case: _____ Date:_____ Person Interviewed: _____

TYPE (List all that apply; describe; give dates)

___ Power Imbalance: ___ Overcontrolling:

___ Abuse: ___ Violent events:

PATTERNS OF ABUSE/VIOLENCE (Describe)

___ Ongoing/episodic male battering:

___ Female-initiated violence:

___ Male-controlling interactive violence:

___ Separation-engendered/postdivorce trauma:

___ Psychotic/paranoid reactions:

SEVERITY on abuse continuum

___ Minimal ___ Mild ___ Moderate ___ High ___ Severe/high risk

Describe:

FREQUENCY

___ Single event ___ Past history, not current ___ Past history, recently restarted

___ Increasing ___ Occasional/unpredictable ___ Constant/daily/repetitive

Describe:

LETHALITY

___ Minimal ___ Moderate ___ High ___ Knives/guns used or available

Describe: .

FAPA/RESTRAINING ORDER/POLICE INVOLVEMENT (Describe)

___ Past, with other partner:

___ Past: __ Once ___ Multiple:

___ Past and recent with this significant other:

___ Significant other afraid to get one:

SUBSTANCE USE CONNECTED TO ABUSE

___ None ___ Sometimes ___ Usually ___ Always ___ Addiction __ Treatment

Drugs:

___ Alcohol ___ Inhalants ___ Stimulants ___ Narcotics ___ Mixed ___ Unknown

CHILDREN'S INVOLVEMENT WITH DOMESTIC VIOLENCE

___ None; children didn't witness either directly or indirectly

___ Children involved or witnessed ___ directly ___ indirectly

___ Children directly harmed, threatened, or afraid

Describe:

Control, Abuse, and Domestic Violence Screener *(continued)*

PROXIMITY

	Before Mediation/Recently	*Currently/During Mediation*
No contact (court order, they agreed, significant other required)		
Some contact (living together, access to home or work)		
Stalking, harassment		
Secure home/safety plan		

ASSESSMENT/ACTION PLAN:

___ A: No violence, fear, abuse, or controlling that prevents therapy or mediation:
    ___ Start mediation; use joint sessions

___ B: No violence or fear but some controlling or intimidating

___ C: Some violence, some fear; both want mediation
    ___ Start mediation now; set conditions below
    ___ Conditions met before starting
    ___ Do safety planning
    ___ Referred out (specify to whom, for what):
    ___ Provide special mediation process:
        __ phone only __ advocate __ intermediation
    ___ Mediator set other special conditions (give names/dates/conditions):

___ D: Danger: high violence or fear; inappropriate for mediation
    ___ Return for reevaluation after: (give date, conditions)

Mediator signature/date _____

APPENDIX D: PARENTING PLAN RATIONALE AND MATRIX

Understanding the Parenting Plan Matrix

Alison Taylor, Meg Goldberg

New research on children and divorce is reinforcing the concept that a number of variables and no one single factor influence children's adjustment. Judges, facing overloaded court dockets, and frustrated with parties unable to make agreements that make sense to the family, have resorted to generic supplemental local rules. The result is a court system determining the same outcome for vastly different family situations. New legislation is pushing judges to set parenting plans that specify minimum and maximum amounts of parenting times. Parents are coming to such hearings without advice of counsel.

To help prevent the use of standard "move-to-the-middle" bargaining techniques to establish plans that could be harmful, the authors have developed a parenting matrix that tries to provide a safe starting place for discussion in mediation, advice by attorney, or orders by judges.

As a starting point, we listened to the voice of Hodges (1991). His work has influenced many of us in attempting to help parents develop age-appropriate parenting plans. Based on his research of the literature, Hodges found that *divorce affects children differently at different ages and stages of development.* His books not only clearly delineated his viewpoint, but also made specific recommendations based on the results of research. He took his recommendations and created a list by age that served as a starting point for negotiation. The information thus provided a mediator or therapist working with a family some substantial help, by giving them a firm base to launch the discussion. From his work, we see the important first factor that must be taken into consideration—the age and stage of children. While he also worried that people would take that list as the absolute without looking at extenuating factors, he felt that some differentiation needed to be made for children of differing ages. This then in the chart is where we start in determining appropriate parenting time.

More recently, Joan Kelly, at her excellent three-day workshop on *Children's Adjustment to Divorce: Research Updates and Implications for Practice,* presented the results of her research into the professional literature. Kelly found, as did Hodges, that one of the primary factors research shows is that divorce affects children at different ages and stages of development. Kelly also found that the second important factor to be considered was the *child's attachment to the parents prior to, as well as resulting from, the circumstances of the divorce.* This factor had been documented and researched over the years.

Seminal work in the area of how children build and maintain appropriate attachment was done by John Bowlby back in the 1960s and 1970s, in his three-volume set of books, *Attachment and Loss,* which look at these critical factors; a synthesis of his years of research and the concepts of attachment theory have been integrated into his most recent work, *A Secure Base: Parent-Child Attachment and Healthy Human Development* (Bowlby, 1988). According to Bowlby, there are three major patterns of development, one good, two not so positive, and none of which can be attributed solely to the child's innate temperament, but rather on how the child is treated by those who are responsible for creating and maintaining this critical feature.

The first pattern, *secure attachment,* is what we all strive for, and depends on the child becoming confident that the parent will be available, responsive, and helpful when needed. The second, *anxious resistant attachment,* develops when the child is uncertain whether the parent will be available and responsive when needed, because sometimes the parent was, and sometimes was not. This child becomes clingy, and carries a deep inner insecurity. The third pattern, *anxious avoidant attachment,* happens when the child expects to be rebuffed, reprimanded, ridiculed or just ignored when requesting help. It doesn't always take direct mistreatment, but can be a factor in children who have experienced repeated rejection or who have been institutionalized or cut off from the primary caregiver. This pattern often manifests in later years as delinquency, and personality disorders.

What is important to understand is that most of these patterns are formed before the child has become fully verbal. The pattern that is established in the first year of life is found at 6 years and older. This preverbal understanding of the world, via the caregivers, is like a template that forms the foundation of all other learning. "It is not difficult to understand why patterns of attachment, once developed, tend to persist. One reason is that the way a parent treats a child, whether for better or for worse, tends to continue unchanged; another is that each pattern tends to be self-perpetuating" (Bowlby, 1988, p. 169). While this is generally so, if the pattern of parenting is changed, as from one parent who is not attending to these important developmental needs in the first two to three years of life to the other parent, or if intervention is provided, the child whose attachment is being damaged can reverse the trend and develop healthily. Bowlby's hypothesis was that "the pathway followed by each developing individual and the extent to which he or she becomes resilient to stressful life events is determined to a very significant degree by the pattern of attachment he or she develops during the early years" (Bowlby, 1988, pp. 172–173).

When divorcing, post-divorce, or never-married parents describe months or years of non-contact or abandonment, or being prevented from maintaining contact or access to children, they are describing the conditions, created often by the crisis of divorce reorganization for the family, that can lead to serious problems for children in these critical areas of emotional development. When and how these problems with attachment, separation and loss happen to the child is vital information, and we must ask more questions about how this separation is affecting the child and their willingness to maintain a relationship with the parent. Many parents are very diligent during divorce and their children do not have much loss or separation, whereas other families have a great deal, and so the attachment the child can maintain is affected.

These factors of attachment, not surprisingly, are quite often cross-allegations used by one parent against the other in both mediation and litigation. Attachment, involvement in the parenting function, and the contradictory states of over- or under-involvement that can lead to parental alienation and major disruptions of parenting with children are important assessment factors. Kelly created parenting plan schedules that were based on attachment factors as well as age. Her recent presentations at the AFM conference in San Francisco also looked at the issue of how attachment of the child can be helped or hindered by custodial and access decisions.

Johnston and Roseby's (1997) important new work adds another layer of complexity when high-conflict and domestic violence is part of the family dynamics. Age and developmental groupings also organize their material. They point out that the ability to attach appropriately, a necessary psychological factor for healthy emotional development, can be crucially altered when violence or absence is part of the family dynamics. Since attachment develops differently in different ages of children, and since attachment to a parent is best maintained by *proximity,* our judicial concept of "frequent and continuing contact" is supportable by child development research. The task, however, especially in cases of domestic violence, or mid to high level conflict or parental alienation, is to find a way to maintain contact with children that is safe for all parties.

A third major factor that affects the children of divorce which emerges from a study of the literature is *the ability of parents to effectively parent.* Some parents are more effective and skillful in parenting children, while others need knowledge, exposure, or more information and support. Many divorcing parents will tell their attorneys and mediators that the other parent is "a good enough" mom or dad, while describing specific incidents that show that the other parent is lacking emotional sensitivity to the child or understanding of appropriate parenting expectations for children of a certain age. Others describe the other parent as totally oblivious to the needs and abilities of children. This range has been built into the chart using a very rough scale, of good or good-enough parenting (Chart A), somewhat problematic parenting (Chart B), and major problems in parenting that should not be allowed to continue (Chart C).

What thus emerges from the research and from our experience in court mediation is the importance of taking into consideration not only the children's ages, but also their personal resilience, and their level of past and current attachment to both parents. The other factors rest with the level of attachment of the children for each parent, and the parents toward the child. The third major factor then becomes the parents' parenting ability. All these factors should be taken into consideration when parents and the court are developing parent plans.

DESCRIPTION OF THE MATRIX

Using the current research, we broke the matrix up into components based on the age of the child and attachment issues. Using Hodges' recommendations as a model, we created charts based on the age of the child from birth to six months, infants, toddlers, pre-school, early elementary, middle years, and adolescents. In each of these age groups, we created four types of parenting: Chart A: attached/good parenting; Chart B: problem attachment/problem parenting; Chart C: severe problems requiring limitations; and Chart D: long distance.

Most visitation schedules are flawed in that they only include one of these three major factors—they are organized usually only by age of the child. In developing this matrix, the authors were very aware that "one size does not fit all," and that all three factors need to be somehow addressed in formulating a parenting plan. The needs of the infant are very different from the young teenager. The young father's comfort level and skill in caring for a newborn may be very different from his comfort level of caring for an elementary age child. A family that presents with no history of domestic violence and/or substance abuse is very different from the family struggling with repeated acts of assault, menacing, restraining orders and/or substance abuse.

The matrix assumes that those using it can put themselves into one of the charts to start. If there have been allegations of major drug and alcohol problems by one or more of the parents, you would start in working with the family in Chart C. If there are unsubstantiated or minimal claims of inattention or questionable parenting, or the child has never had opportunities to get attached to a parent due to problems in the couple's relationship, you would start working with the family from the perspective of Chart B. The matrix assumes that parents' abilities and children's attachments may increase or decrease, so it is designed to allow for the growth spurts that happen as the parent becomes more comfortable with his/her parenting function, the child and parent's attachment increases, and the child grows. There is less room to negotiate and there is a stronger need to stay close to the suggestions in each category in cases where the child's needs could be at risk, for example, in Chart C conditions across ages.

For example, take the situation of a young unmarried couple not residing together who are parents of a 6-month-old child. Assume that in this case the father, while wanting to have contact with his child, has had little contact for the past six months. The contact he has had has been for short visits at the mother's home. Due to the age of the child and the father's need to gain more parenting skills, the father will fall under Chart B on the matrix for 6 months to one year.

As father and baby become more comfortable with one another, father will eventually move up into Chart A, and the child will move to the toddler, then the pre-schooler pages, so that the recommendations will increase the time and flexibility of parenting for the father without creating risk or stressing the child past their endurance level to be away from the primary psychological parent. If, however, the father becomes involved in untreated drug or alcohol problems, or has an event that shows an incapacity to make appropriate parenting choices, the parents may well want to return to mediation or court to ask for a reduction of time or an increase in safeguards for the child, and the father would move down to the Chart B or C conditions recommended.

LISTENING FOR FACTORS IN CLIENT'S STORIES

In developing a parenting plan that makes sense for the family involved, it is important to listen for all these factors in client's stories. It is also necessary to assess for factors that may hinder the parent's ability to parent, as well as to build in safeguards to protect the child in high conflict or violent circumstances. Listening for the factors assists the parents in developing a good parenting plan that provides for stability and continuity of the relationship between the child and the parent. It will also help prevent the "one size fits all" box associated with more rigid "visitation schedules."

When parents are self-concerned or distraught about controlling for their own losses during the divorce and separation, they often cannot separate their own needs from those they are stating are the child's. We often see this in mediation. The parent is requesting a half-time arrangement with a child whom they have never had full care of for even a full weekend. They are doing so because the legal system implies that "if I don't get it now, I'll never get it."

Using this matrix model, and indicating a stair-step approach to starting with development of attachment through smaller amounts of time more frequently which can then build to overnights, then whole weekends, can help alleviate this rush to get the ultimate goal before the child is ready to handle it. If both parents understand and agree on the progressive nature of the chart, which automatically gives parents more time *as the child can developmentally handle it,* it can reduce the win/lose nature of a custody or parenting time dispute. Models of mediation that would allow more time to work with a parent therapeutically when they are experiencing separation and loss would be very helpful in reducing these kinds of conflicts between parents.

CURRENT USE

The Parenting Plan Matrix was created by the authors for use by the Clackamas County Family Court Service in Oregon City, Oregon, in 1998. It has been used as a guide for court-connected mediators and their clients. Donald Saposnek, Ph.D., has also shared it with judges and attorneys in California as part of their continuing legal education training. As a first attempt to bring complex information into a format that could be more easily used to help provide differential parenting plans based on children's ages, attachment between parents and children, and parenting skills and conditions of parents, it should be updated and modified as more research becomes available.

References

Bowlby, J. *A Secure Base: Parent-Child Attachment and Healthy Human Development.* New York: Basic Books, 1988.

Hodges, W. F. *Interventions for Children of Divorce: Custody, Access, and Psychotherapy* (2nd ed.) New York: Wiley, 1991.

Kelly, J. Lecture and notes from a three day workshop: "Children's Adjustment to Divorce: Research Updates and Implications for Practice." Presentation at the 1997 ABPP Summer Institute, Portland, Ore., June 26–28, 1997.

Johnston, J., and Roseby, V. *In the Name of the Child: A Developmental Approach to Understanding and Helping Children of Conflicted and Violent Divorce.* New York: Free Press, 1997.

UNDERLYING ASSUMPTIONS OF THE PARENTING PLAN MATRIX

The Parenting Plan Matrix addresses the three essential factors (the child's age, the level of attachment, and the parent's circumstances and skills) that must be taken into account in making safe plans that grow along with children. It is based on these assumptions:

1. *Good parenting plans provide for stability and continuity.* They are based on normalizing parent/child relationships after divorce. For example, the Oregon Revised Statutes (ORS 107.101) states: "It is the

policy of this state to assure minor children of frequent and continuing contact with parents who have shown the ability to act in the best interests of the child."

2. *Plans need to consider significant current and pre–divorce/separation relationships, routines, and attachments of the child to each parent.* Some children are equally attached to both parents, while some have a primary parent. Sometimes this has changed due to the divorce.

3. *Plans need to consider the parenting ability of each parent.* Some parents have never had the opportunity to develop their parenting skills, while some have had problems in parenting.

4. *Ages and stages of child development should determine the plan.* For example, infants and toddlers *need shorter but more frequent contact* with the parents they are attached to, in order to maintain their attachment, and can't handle long times away from the primary parent. School-aged children *may* handle more time away, and teens need more flexibility in how much time they spend and what they do with each parent.

5. *If there has been high conflict or violence, children must be protected. Safety* for the children and parents involved and *accountability* of the violent parties override other concerns.

6. *Severe parental problems, such as substance abuse, mental/emotional illness, neglect or abuse, or criminal activity, require major limitations to protect children.*

7. *When parents live far away, special arrangements must be made.* Younger children should not have to travel long distances, or leave the primary parent. Older children can have longer parenting time, and can travel to the parent's new home for blocks of time

HOW TO USE THE MATRIX

The charts are based on the ages and stages of the child. In each age category, the chart lists four conditions. Find the one that best describes the family's situation. Families may have children who are in different age categories, or who have different attachment to their parents. As much as possible, *plans should safeguard the youngest children.* Families may have to have different parenting plans for each child.

Use Chart A if
- Both parents have been active and positive in parenting.
- The child was attached to both parents prior to the divorce or separation, and this attachment continues.

Chart A shows the *minimum* amount of contact needed to maintain good attachment; parents may want to *add* time.

Use Chart B if
- There are problems in attachment to the noncustodial parent (for example, the child refuses to go).
- The noncustodial parent has never had the opportunity to parent the child or is returning after a prolonged absence.
- The noncustodial parent is unskilled at parenting.

Chart B shows the time that will be needed to *build* confidence and closeness with the less attached parent without endangering the child, or requiring them to leave the security of the primary parent for too long at first. This is less flexible for younger children.

Use Chart C if
- There are allegations of parental drug or alcohol abuse, mental health concerns, concern of criminal activities, or other potentially harmful behaviors by the noncustodial parent.
- There is history or current allegations of direct or indirect harm to the child or other parent, domestic violence, control and intimidation or harassment between the parents.
- There are other safety and security concerns in the noncustodial parent's environment.

Chart C is the most *conservative* and limiting to the parent, to minimize risk and ensure the most safety and security for the child and the custodial parent.

Use Chart D if
- The noncustodial parent lives a significant distance away (more than one hour by car).
- The noncustodial parent might transport the child out of the state or country or go undercover.

Chart D shows limitations due to *distance,* with increases in parenting time as the child grows older, can travel alone, and becomes more capable and independent.

Newborn: Birth to 6 months

	Regular Weekly Schedule	Regular Weekend/ Overnights	Summer/ Vacations	Holidays	Conditions
Chart A: Attached/ good parenting	Up to 3 times per week; 2-hour duration	None	Same as regular weekly schedule	Same as regular weekly schedule	In custodial parent's home, or noncustodial parent's home if childproofed and safe transportation is provided there
Chart B: Problem attachment/ problem parenting	Up to 3 times per week; 1-hour duration	None	Same as regular weekly schedule	Same as regular weekly schedule	In custodial parent's home, with custodial parent or other selected person present
Chart C: Severe problems requiring limitations	1 time per week; 1-hour duration	None	Same as regular weekly schedule	Same as regular weekly schedule	Supervised; only in safe environment
Chart D: Long distance	Daily contact for up to 3 hours, when parent is in the area	None	None	Up to 3 hours, when parent is in the area	In custodial parent's home, with custodial parent or other selected person present

Note: This matrix is a guideline to be used only as a starting point for further mediation or negotiation.

Infants: 6–18 months

	Regular Weekly Schedule	Regular Weekend/ Overnights	Summer/ Vacations	Holidays	Conditions
Chart A: Attached/ good parenting	Up to 3 times per week; 3-hour duration	Once per week, up to one 24-hour overnight	Up to 3 consecutive days and overnights once per year	Every holiday, up to 4 hours, to be determined by the custodial parent 2 weeks prior	Can be in noncustodial parent's home or a familiar, child-related environment
Chart B: Problem attachment/ problem parenting	Up to 3 times per week; 1-hour duration	No overnights, but one 4-hour block every other weekend, in the morning or afternoon	4-hour block of time during the day, up to 7 consecutive days, once per summer	Every holiday, not to exceed 3 hours, set by custodial parent	Must be held in custodial parent's home or familiar, child-related environment, with custodial parent or other selected person nearby
Chart C: Severe problems requiring limitations	1 time per week for 1 hour	None	Same as regular weekly schedule	1 hour for each holiday	Child not to be separated from custodial parent at any time; or only supervised visits through a program or relative
Chart D: Long distance	Daily contact for up to 8 hours, for up to 7 consecutive days, when noncustodial parent is in the area	None	Same as regular weekly schedule	Same as regular weekly schedule	Must be held in custodial parent's home or a familiar, child-related environment, with custodial parent or other selected person nearby

Note: This matrix is a guideline to be used only as a starting point for further mediation or negotiation.

Toddlers: 18 months to 3 years

	Regular Weekly Schedule	Regular Weekend/ Overnights	Summer/ Vacations	Holidays	Conditions
Chart A: Attached/ good parenting	3–5 times per week, each for 2–8 consecutive hours (held during child's waking hours, no later than 7 P.M.)	Every other weekend, 1 overnight from Saturday 9 A.M. to Sunday 6 P.M.	3–7 consecutive days and overnights, twice per summer	Every holiday, a block of 4 hours, to be determined by custodial parent 2 weeks prior	Can be in non-custodial parent's home or a familiar, child-related environment
Chart B: Problem attachment/ problem parenting	1–3 times per week, each up to 2 hours	Every other weekend, 1 day from 9 A.M. to 6 P.M.; no overnights	3–7 consecutive days from 9 A.M. to 6 P.M., once per summer	Every holiday, a block of 4 hours, to be determined by custodial parent 2 weeks prior	May be held at non-custodial parent's home or in a familiar, child-related place
Chart C: Severe problems requiring limitations	1 time per week for up to 2 hours	None	Same as regular weekly schedule	1 hour for each holiday	Child not to be separated from custodial parent at any time; or only supervised visits through a program, relative, or other selected person
Chart D: Long distance	Daily contact for up to 8 hours, for up to 7 consecutive days, when noncustodial parent is in the area	None	Same as regular weekly schedule	Same as regular weekly schedule	Must be held in custodial parent's home or a familiar, child-related environment, with custodial parent or other selected person nearby

Note: This matrix is a guideline to be used only as a starting point for further mediation or negotiation.

Preschool: 3–5 years

	Regular Weekly Schedule	Regular Weekend/ Overnights	Summer/ Vacations	Holidays	Conditions
Chart A: Attached/ good parenting	3–5 times per week, each for 2–8 consecutive hours (no later than 9 P.M.)	(1) Every weekend, 1 overnight from 9 A.M. to 6 P.M. the next day; or (2) every other weekend, from Friday 6 P.M. to Sunday 6 P.M	7 consecutive days and overnights, twice per summer (in different months)	Every holiday, a block of 4 hours, to be determined by custodial parent 2 weeks prior	May be held at non-custodial parent's home or in a familiar, child-related place
Chart B: Problem attachment/ problem parenting	1–3 contacts per week, each 2–4 hours (no later than 9 P.M.)	Every other weekend, 1 day from 9 A.M. to 6 P.M.; no overnights	3–7 consecutive days from 9 A.M. to 6 P.M., once per summer	Every holiday, a block of 4 hours, to be determined by custodial parent 2 weeks prior	May be held at non-custodial parent's home or in a familiar, child-related place
Chart C: Severe problems requiring limitations	1 time per week for up to 2 hours	None	Same as regular weekly schedule	1 hour for each holiday	Child not to be separated from custodial parent at any time; or only supervised visits through a program, relative, or other selected person
Chart D: Long distance	Daily contact for up to 8 hours, for up to 7 consecutive days, when noncustodial parent is in the area	None	Same as regular weekly schedule	Same as regular weekly schedule	Must be held in custodial parent's home or familiar, child-related environment, with custodial parent or other selected person nearby

Note: This matrix is a guideline to be used only as a starting point for further mediation or negotiation.

Early Elementary: 6–10 years

	Regular Weekly Schedule	Regular Weekend/ Overnights	Summer/ Vacations	Holidays	Conditions
Chart A: Attached/ good parenting	1 midweek contact, from after school or work until 8 P.M.	Every other weekend, from Friday 6 P.M. to Sunday 6 P.M.	Up to 14 consecutive days and overnights in a summer	(1) Holidays divided equally, custodial parent having half the list in even years, noncustodial parent in odd years; or (2) each parent has 6 hours on each holiday every year	Winter and spring breaks divided equally or alternated annually
Chart B: Problem attachment/ problem parenting	1 midweek contact, from after school or work until 8 P.M.	Every other weekend, from Saturday 9 A.M. to Sunday 6 P.M.	7 consecutive days and overnights, once per summer	Holidays divided equally, custodial parent having half the list in even years, noncustodial parent in odd years	3–5 consecutive days and overnights during spring and winter breaks
Chart C: Severe problems requiring limitations	1 time per week	Same as regular weekly schedule	Same as regular weekly schedule	Same as regular weekly schedule	Supervised contacts through a program, relative, or other selected person
Chart D: Long distance	1 daily contact for up to 8 hours, for up to 7 consecutive days, when noncustodial parent is in the area	Overnight from Friday 6 P.M. to Sunday 6 P.M., when noncustodial parent is in the area	7 consecutive days and overnights, once per summer	Child may travel to parent for 3–5 days, up to 5 times per year	Must be held in custodial parent's home or familiar, child-related environment

Note: This matrix is a guideline to be used only as a starting point for further mediation or negotiation.

Middle Years: 11–15 years

	Regular Weekly Schedule	Regular Weekend/ Overnights	Summer/ Vacations	Holidays	Conditions
Chart A: Attached/ good parenting	1 midweek contact, from after school or work until 8 P.M., unless child's activities prevent	Every other weekend, from Friday 6 P.M. to Sunday 6 P.M.	Up to 21 consecutive days and overnights in a summer	(1) Holidays divided equally, custodial parent having half the list in even years, noncustodial parent in odd years; or (2) each parent has 6 hours on each holiday every year	Winter and spring breaks divided equally or alternated annually
Chart B: Problem attachment/ problem parenting	Phone contact; or attendance at child's activities only	Every other weekend, from Saturday 9 A.M. to Sunday 6 P.M.	14 consecutive days and overnights, once per summer	Holidays divided equally, custodial parent having half the list in even years, noncustodial parent in odd years	3–5 consecutive days and overnights during spring and winter breaks
Chart C: Severe problems requiring limitations	1 hour per week	Same as regular weekly schedule	Same as regular weekly schedule	Same as regular weekly schedule	Supervised contacts only through a program, relative, or other selected person
Chart D: Long distance	1 daily contact for up to 8 hours, for up to 7 consecutive days, when noncustodial parent is in the area	Overnight from Friday 6 P.M. to Sunday 6 P.M., when noncustodial parent is in the area	14 consecutive days and overnights, once per summer	Child may travel to parent for 3–5 days, up to 5 times in a year	Must be held in a familiar, child-related environment

Note: This matrix is a guideline to be used only as a starting point for further mediation or negotiation.

Older Teens: 16–18 years

	Regular Weekly Schedule	Regular Weekend/ Overnights	Summer/ Vacations	Holidays	Conditions
Chart A: Attached/ good parenting	1 midweek contact, from after school or work until 8 P.M., unless child's activities prevent	1 weekend per month, from Friday 6 P.M. to Sunday 6 P.M., selected by the teen	Up to 21 consecutive days and overnights in a summer	(1) Holidays divided equally, custodial parent having half the list in even years, noncustodial parent in odd years; or (2) each parent has 6 hours on each holiday every year	Winter and spring breaks divided equally or alternated annually
Chart B: Problem attachment/ problem parenting	Phone contact; or attendance at teen's activities only	1 weekend per month, from Saturday 9 A.M. to Sunday 6 P.M., selected by the teen	14 consecutive days and overnights, once per summer	Holidays divided equally, custodial parent having half the list in even years, noncustodial parent in odd years	3–5 consecutive days and overnights during spring and winter breaks
Chart C: Severe problems requiring limitations	1 hour per week	Same as regular weekly schedule	Same as regular weekly schedule	Same as regular weekly schedule	Supervised contacts only through a program, relative, or other selected person
Chart D: Long distance	1 daily contact for up to 8 hours, for up to 7 consecutive days, when noncustodial parent is in the area	Overnight Friday 6 P.M. to Sunday 6 P.M., when the noncustodial parent is in the area	14 consecutive days and overnights, once per summer	Child may travel to parent for 3–5 days, up to 5 times per year	Must be held in a safe environment

Note: This matrix is a guideline to be used only as a starting point for further mediation or negotiation.

APPENDIX E:
BUDGET SHEET

	Woman		Man		Current Combined	Children Current
	Current	Future	Current	Future	Current	Current
INCOME						
Gross monthly income						
Net monthly income (take home)						
Child support (+ or −)						
Spousal support (+ or −)						
Usable income total (net +/− support)	$	$	$	$	$	$
MONTHLY EXPENSES						
Basic Living Expenses						
Food and household supplies						
Rent/mortgage						
Property taxes						
Home repairs/maintenance						
Phones						
Water/sewer						
Garbage/cable/wood/other						
House insurance						
Car insurance						
Life insurance						
Car payment/bus/taxi						
Gas and car repairs						
Child care						
Educational costs						
Debt repayment/installments						
Health care						
Clothing						
Laundry						
Grooming/personal items						
Uniforms/dues/work costs						
Miscellaneous						
Subtotal basic expenses	$	$	$	$	$	$

	Woman		Man		Current Combined	Children
	Current	Future	Current	Future	Current Combined	Current
Variable/Optional Expenses						
Social/religious organizations						
Lessons/memberships						
Pets/hobbies						
Entertainment						
Savings/retirement						
Travel/vacations						
Emergencies						
Holidays/gifts/miscellaneous						
Subtotal optional expenses	$	$	$	$	$	$
PROJECTED BUDGET (all expenses)	$	$	$	$	$	$
Usable income—Projected budget	$	$	$	$	$	$
IMMEDIATE EXPENSES						
First/last month's rent						
Security/utility deposit						
Repairs						
Legal/court fees						
Counseling/mediation fees						
Other						
Subtotal immediate expenses	$	$	$	$	$	$

REFERENCES

Ahrons, C., and Rogers, R. *Divorced Families: A Multidisciplinary Developmental View.* New York: Norton, 1987.

Amen, D. *Change Your Brain, Change Your Life: The Breakthrough Program for Conquering Anxiety, Depression, Obsessiveness, Anger, and Impulsiveness.* New York: Random House, 1998.

American Bar Association. Section of Dispute Resolution. *Resolution on Mediation and the Unauthorized Practice of Law.* [www.abanet.org/dispute/resolution.html]. 1999.

American Bar Association. Section of Dispute Resolution and the National Conference of Commissioners on Uniform State Laws. Drafting Committee on Uniform Mediation Act. "Uniform Mediation Act." [www.pon.harvard.edu/guests/uma/]. Oct. 5, 2001.

American Bar Association. Section on Family Law. *Divorce and Family Mediation.* Chicago: American Bar Association, 1986.

American Bar Association. Section on Family Law Task Force. "Proposed Standards of Practice for Lawyers Who Conduct Divorce and Family Mediation." July 1997. [www.to-agree.com/abafam.html].

American Psychological Association. *APA Guidelines for Providers of Psychological Services to Ethnic, Linguistic, and Culturally Diverse Populations.* Washington, D.C.: American Psychological Association. 1990. [www.apa.org/pi/oema/guide.html].

Amundson, J., and Fong, L. "Systemic/Strategic Aspects and Potentials in the Haynes Model of Divorce Mediation." *Mediation Quarterly,* 1986, no. 12, 65–74.

Anderson, V., and Johnson, L. *Systems Thinking Basics: From Concepts to Causal Loops.* Williston, Vt.: Pegasus Communications, 1997.

Association for Conflict Resolution. "UMA Update." *Newsletter,* Winter–Spring 2001a.

Association for Conflict Resolution. "Uniform Mediation Act Marathon Reaches Final Leg of the Race." *Newsletter,* Summer 2001b.

Association of Family Conciliation Courts. Symposium on Standards of Practice. "Model Standards of Practice for Family and Divorce Mediation." [www.afccnet.org/pdf/modelstandardsfinal.pdf]. Aug. 2000.

Augsberger, D. *Conflict Mediation Across Cultures: Pathways and Patterns.* Louisville, Ky.: Westminster/John Knox Press, 1992.

Averill, J. "Illusions of Anger." In R. Felson and J. Tedeschi (eds.), *Aggression and Violence: Social Interactionist Perspectives.* Washington, D.C.: American Psychological Association, 1993.

Barsky, A. "Mediation in Child Protection Cases." In H. Irving and M. Benjamin (eds.), *Family Mediation: Contemporary Issues.* Thousand Oaks, Calif.: Sage, 1995.

Becvar, D., and Becvar, R. *Systems Theory and Family Therapy: A Primer.* (2nd ed.) New York: University Press, 1998.

Benard, B. "Fostering Resilience in Children." *ERIC Digest.* (ED 386 327) [www.ed.gov/databases/ERIC_Digests/ed386327.html]. 1995.

Benjamin, R. "Mediative Strategies in the Management of Child Sexual Abuse Matters." *Family and Conciliation Courts Review,* 1991, *29*(3), 221–245.

Bishop, T. "Standards of Practice for Divorce Mediators." In J. Folberg and A. Milne (eds.), *Divorce Mediation: Theory and Practice.* New York: Guilford Press, 1988.

Bivins, T. H. "Ethical Worksheet." [http://jcomm.uoregon.edu/ ~ tbivins/J397/Links/Worksheet.html]. 2000.

Bowen, M. *Family Therapy in Clinical Practice.* Northvale, N.J.: Aronson, 1978.

Bowlby, J. *Attachment and Loss.* Vol. 1: *Attachment.* New York: Basic Books, 1969.

Bowlby, J. *Attachment and Loss.* Vol. 2: *Separation: Anxiety and Anger.* New York: Basic Books, 1973.

Bowlby, J. *Attachment and Loss.* Vol. 3: *Loss.* New York: Basic Books, 1980.

Bowlby, J. *A Secure Base: Parent-Child Attachment and Healthy Human Development.* New York: Basic Books, 1988.

Boyd-Franklin, N. "Race, Class and Poverty." In F. Walsh (ed.), *Normal Family Processes.* (2nd ed.) New York: Guilford Press, 1993.

Bretherton, I. "Open Communication and Internal Working Models: Their Role in the Development of Attachment Relationships." In R. A. Thompson (ed.), *Nebraska Symposium on Motivation.* Vol. 36: *Socioemotional Development.* Lincoln: University of Nebraska Press, 1990.

Brown, N., and Samis, M. "The Application of Structural Family Therapy in Developing the Binuclear Family." *Mediation Quarterly,* 1986, no. 14/15, 51–69.

Bunker, B., and Rubin, J. (eds.). *Conflict, Cooperation and Justice: Essays Inspired by the Work of Morton Deutsch.* San Francisco: Jossey-Bass, 1995.

Bush, R., and Folger, J. *The Promise of Mediation: Responding to Conflict Through Empowerment and Recognition.* San Francisco: Jossey-Bass, 1994.

Carruthers, S. "Mediation in Child Protection and the Nova Scotia Experience." *Family and Conciliation Courts Review,* 1997, *35*(1), 102–126.

Center for Social Gerontology. *Adult Guardianship Mediation Manual.* Ann Arbor, Mich.: The Center for Social Gerontology, 1996.

Center for Social Gerontology. *Adult Guardianship Mediation Project: Status Report.* [www.tcsg.org/mediation/statusmed.htm]. Sept. 1998.

Clarke, J., and Dawson, C. *Growing Up Again: Parenting Ourselves, Parenting Our Children.* (2nd ed.) Center City, Minn.: Hazelden, 1998.

Coates, C., and Damas, K. "Family Mediation by the Community Mediation Service in Boulder, Colorado." *Mediation Quarterly,* 1997, *15*(1), 29–38.

Cohen, O., Dattner, N., and Luxenburg, A. "The Limits of the Mediator's Neutrality." *Mediation Quarterly,* 1999, *16*(4), 341–348.

Coogler, O. J. "Changing the Lawyer's Role in Matrimonial Practice." *Conciliation Courts Review,* 1977, *15*(1), 1–8.

Coogler, O. J. *Structured Mediation in Divorce Settlement: A Handbook for Marital Mediators.* San Francisco: New Lexington Press, 1978.

Coogler, O. J. "Mediation of Divorce Settlements: Basic Notions." *Fairshare,* 1982, *2,* 8–10.

Cross, W., Jr., and Fhagen-Smith, P. "Nigrescence and Ego Identity Development: Accounting for Differential Black Identity Patterns." In P. Pedersen, J. Draguns, W. Lonner, and J. Trimble (eds.), *Counseling Across Cultures.* (4th ed.) Thousand Oaks, Calif.: Sage, 1996.

Currie, C. "Mediation and Medical Practice Disputes." *Mediation Quarterly,* 1998, *15*(3), 215–226.

Dworkin, J., Jacob, L., and Scott, E. "The Boundaries Between Mediation and Therapy: Ethical Dilemmas." *Mediation Quarterly,* 1991, *9*(2), 107–119.

Eason, C. "Hispanic/Latino Culture Issues." In D. Gooden and A. Galvan, *Mediation with Latinos Survey.* Tucson, Ariz.: Family Center of the Conciliation Court, 1998.

Ellman, B., and Taggart, M. "Changing Gender Norms." In F. Walsh (ed.), *Normal Family Processes.* (2nd ed.) New York: Guilford Press, 1993.

Emery, R. *Renegotiating Family Relationships: Divorce, Child Custody, and Mediation.* New York: Guilford Press, 1994.

Epstein, N. B., Bishop, D. S., and Baldwin, L. M. "McMaster Model of Family Functioning: A View of the Normal Family." In F. Walsh (ed.), *Normal Family Processes.* (2nd ed.) New York: Guilford Press, 1993.

Erickson, S., and Erickson, M. *Family Mediation Casebook: Theory and Practice.* New York: Brunner/Mazel, 1988.

Etter, J. "Levels of Cooperation and Satisfaction in 56 Open Adoptions." *Child Welfare,* 1993, *3,* 257–267.

Etter, J. *Mediating Permanency Outcomes: Practice Manual.* Washington, D.C.: Child Welfare League of America, 1997.

Evans, J. "Resilience: A Multi-Cultural Perspective." Paper presented at conference of the National Association for Children of Alcoholics, San Diego, Calif., 1995. [www.nacoa.net/evans.htm].

Feeney, J. "Adult Romantic Attachment and Couple Relationships." In J. Cassidy and P. R. Shaver (eds.), *Handbook of Attachment: Theory, Research, and Clinical Applications.* New York: Guilford Press, 1999.

Feinberg, R., and Greene, J. "The Intractable Client: Guidelines for Working with Personality Disorders in Family Law." *Family and Conciliation Courts Review,* 1997, *35*(3), 351–365.

Felicio, D., and Sutherland, M. "Beyond the Dominant Narrative: Intimacy and Conflict in Lesbian Relationships." *Mediation Quarterly,* 2001, *18*(4), 363–376.

Felson, R., and Tedeschi, J. "Social Interactionist Perspectives on Aggression and Violence: An Introduction." In R. Felson and J. Tedeschi (eds.), *Aggression and Violence: Social Interactionist Perspectives.* Washington, D.C.: American Psychological Association, 1993.

Firestone, G., and Sharp, D. "Uniform Mediation Act: Are We There Yet?" *Association for Conflict Resolution Newsletter,* Winter–Spring 2001, pp. 17–19.

Fisher, R., and Ury, W., with Patton, B. (ed.). *Getting to Yes: Negotiating Agreement Without Giving In.* (2nd ed.) New York: Penguin, 1991.

Fogarty, T. E. "Systems Concepts and the Dimension of Self." In P. J. Guerin (ed.), *Family Therapy: Theory and Practice.* New York: Gardner Press, 1976.

Folberg, J. "Confidentiality and Privilege." In J. Folberg and A. Milne (eds.), *Divorce Mediation: Theory and Practice.* New York: Guilford Press, 1988.

Folberg, J., and Taylor, A. *Mediation: A Comprehensive Guide to Resolving Conflicts Without Litigation.* San Francisco: Jossey-Bass, 1984.

Folger, J., and Bush, R. "Transformative Mediation and Third-Party Intervention: Ten Hallmarks of a Transformative Approach to Practice." *Mediation Quarterly,* 1996, *13*(4), 263–278.

Folger, J., Poole, M., and Stutman, R. *Working Through Conflict: Strategies for Relationships, Groups and Organizations.* (4th ed.) New York: Addison Wesley Longman, 2001.

Fong, L. "New Paradigms in Mediation: Thinking About Our Thinking." *Mediation Quarterly,* 1992, *10*(2), 209–212.

Fong, L. *Adoption: The Chaos of Changing Consent.* Washington, D.C.: Association for Conflict Resolution, 1995. Videotape.

Forester-Miller, H., and Davis, T. "A Practitioner's Guide to Ethical Decision Making." Alexandria, Va.: American Counseling Association, 1996. [www.counseling.org/resources/pracguide.htm].

French, J., and Raven, B. "The Bases of Social Power." In D. Cartwright (ed.), *Studies in Social Power*. Ann Arbor: University of Michigan Press, 1959.

Gadlin, H., and Ouellette, P. "Mediation Milanese: An Application of Systemic Family Therapy to Family Mediation." *Mediation Quarterly*, 1986, no. 14/15, 101–118.

Galbraith, J. K. "Power and Organization." In S. Lukes (ed.), *Power*. New York: New York University Press, 1992.

Germane, C., Johnson, M., and Leman, N. "Mandatory Custody Mediation and Joint Custody Orders in California: The Danger for Victims of Domestic Violence." *Berkeley Women's Law Journal*, 1985, *1*(1), 175–200.

Girdner, L. "Mediation Triage: Screening for Spouse Abuse in Divorce Mediation." *Mediation Quarterly*, 1990, *7*(4), 365–376.

Goldstein, J., Freud, A., and Solnit, A. *Beyond the Best Interests of the Child*. New York: Free Press, 1973.

Goldstein, S. "Responses of Asian American and European American Mediators to a Conflict Communication Scale." *Mediation Quarterly*, 1998, *15*(3), 181–186.

Goleman, D. *Emotional Intelligence*. New York: Bantam, 1995.

Gooden, D., and Galvan, A. (eds.) *Mediation with Latinos Survey*. Tucson, Ariz.: Family Center of the Conciliation Court, 1998.

Gottman, J. *What Predicts Divorce? The Relationship Between Marital Processes and Marital Outcomes*. Hillsdale, N.J.: Erlbaum, 1994.

Gottman, J. *Why Marriages Succeed or Fail: And How You Can Make Yours Last*. New York: Fireside, 1995.

Gottman, J., and Silver, N. *The Seven Principles for Making Marriage Work*. New York: Three Rivers Press, 2000.

Grebe, S. "Structured Mediation and Its Variants: What Makes It Unique." In J. Folberg and A. Milne (eds.), *Divorce Mediation: Theory and Practice*. New York: Guilford Press, 1988.

Grebe, S. "Ethics and the Professional Family Mediator." *Mediation Quarterly*, 1992, *10*(2), 155–165.

Grotevant, H., and McRoy, R. *Openness in Adoption: Exploring Family Connections*. Thousand Oaks, Calif.: Sage, 1998.

Hairston, C. "African-Americans in Mediation Literature: A Neglected Population." *Mediation Quarterly*, 1999, *16*(4), 357-375.

Haley, J. *Problem-Solving Therapy*. (2nd ed.) San Francisco: Jossey-Bass, 1991.

Harrell, S. "Why Attorneys Attend Mediation Sessions." *Mediation Quarterly*, 1995, *12*(4), 369–377.

Haynes, J. "Power Balancing." In J. Folberg and A. Milne (eds.), *Divorce Mediation: Theory and Practice*. New York: Guilford Press, 1988.

Haynes, J. *The Fundamentals of Family Mediation*. New York: State University of New York Press, 1994.

Haynes, J. *The Elderly Parent: What to Do with Mother*. Washington, D.C.: Association for Conflict Resolution, n.d. *a*. Videotape.

Haynes, J. *Parent/Teen Conflict: Winning.* Washington, D.C.: Association for Conflict Resolution, n.d. *b.* Videotape.

Haynes, J., and Haynes, G. *Mediating Divorce: Casebook of Strategies for Successful Family Negotiations.* San Francisco: Jossey-Bass, 1989.

Henry, K., and Holmes, J. "Childhood Revisited: The Intimate Relationships of Individuals from Divorced and Conflict-Ridden Families." In J. Simpson and W. S. Rholes (eds.), *Attachment Theory and Close Relationships.* New York: Guilford Press, 1998.

Hesse, E. "The Adult Attachment Interview: Historical and Current Perspectives. In J. Cassidy and P. R. Shaver (eds.), *Handbook of Attachment: Theory, Research, and Clinical Applications.* New York: Guilford Press, 1999.

Higgins, G. *Resilient Adults: Overcoming a Cruel Past.* San Francisco, Jossey-Bass, 1994.

Hindy, C., and Schwartz, J. C. "Anxious Romantic Attachment in Adult Relationships." In M. Sperling and W. Berman (eds.), *Attachment in Adults: Clinical and Developmental Perspectives.* New York: Guilford Press, 1994.

Hodges, W. *Interventions for Children of Divorce: Custody, Access and Psychotherapy.* (2nd ed.) New York: Wiley, 1991.

Hoffman, L. *Foundations of Family Therapy: A Conceptual Framework for Systems Change.* New York: Basic Books, 1981.

Hook, J. "Adult Guardianship Mediation." [www.els-flabar.org/newpage2.htm]. 1999.

Hutchinson, E. *Black Fatherhood: The Guide to Male Parenting.* Inglewood, Calif.: IMPACT! Publications, 1992.

Irving, H., and Benjamin, M. *Family Mediation: Contemporary Issues.* Thousand Oaks, Calif.: Sage, 1995.

Irving, H., Benjamin, M., and San-Pedro, J. "Family Mediation and Cultural Diversity: Mediating with Latino Families." *Mediation Quarterly,* 1999, *16*(4), 325–339.

Jervis, R. *System Effects: Complexity in Political and Social Life.* Princeton, N.J.: Princeton University Press, 1999.

Johnston, J., and Campbell, L. *Impasses of Divorce: The Dynamics and Resolution of Conflict.* New York: Simon & Schuster, 1988.

Johnston, J., and Roseby, V. *In the Name of the Child: A Developmental Approach to Understanding and Helping Children of Conflicted and Violent Divorce.* New York: Free Press, 1997.

Kaminsky, H., and Cosmano, R. "Mediating Child Welfare Disputes: How to Focus on the Best Interests of the Child." *Mediation Quarterly,* 1990, *7*(3), 229–235.

Karen, R. *Becoming Attached: First Relationships and How They Shape Our Capacity to Love.* New York: Warner Books, 1994.

Karpel, M. *Evaluating Couples.* New York: Norton, 1994.

Kayser, K. *When Love Dies.* New York: Guilford Press, 1993.

Kelly, J. "Mediation and Psychotherapy: Distinguishing the Differences." *Mediation Quarterly,* 1983, no. 1, 33–44.

Kelly, J. "Power Imbalance in Divorce and Interpersonal Mediation: Assessment and Intervention." *Mediation Quarterly,* 1995, *13*(2), 85–98.

Kottler, L. *Beyond Blame: A New Way of Resolving Conflicts in Relationships.* San Francisco: Jossey-Bass, 1996.

Kreisberg, L. *Constructive Conflicts: From Escalation to Resolution.* Lanham, Md.: Rowman & Littlefield, 1998.

Kruk, E. "Grandparent Visitation Disputes: Multigenerational Approaches to Family Mediation." *Mediation Quarterly,* 1994, *12*(1), 37–53.

Laird, J. "Lesbian and Gay Families." In F. Walsh (ed.), *Normal Family Processes.* (2nd ed.) New York: Guilford Press, 1993.

Landau, J. "Therapy with Families in Cultural Transition." In M. McGoldrick, J. Pearce, and J. Giordano (eds.), *Ethnicity and Family Therapy.* New York: Guilford Press, 1982.

Lang, M., and Taylor, A. *The Making of a Mediator: Developing Artistry in Practice.* San Francisco: Jossey-Bass, 2000.

LaResche, D. "Comparison of the American Mediation Process with a Korean-American Harmony Restoration Process." *Mediation Quarterly,* 1992, *9*(4), 323–339.

Lee, E. "A Social Systems Approach to Assessment and Treatment for Chinese American Families." In M. McGoldrick, J. Pearce, and J. Giordano (eds.), *Ethnicity and Family Therapy.* New York: Guilford Press, 1982.

Lerner, H. *The Dance of Anger: A Woman's Guide to Changing the Patterns of Intimate Relationships.* New York: HarperCollins, 1985.

Levitt, M., Coffman, S., Guacci-Franco, N., and Loveless, S. "Attachment Relationships and Life Transitions: An Expectancy Model." In M. Sperling and W. Berman (eds.), *Attachment in Adults: Clinical and Developmental Perspectives.* New York: Guilford Press, 1994.

Lewicki, R., Saunders, D., and Minton, J. *Essentials of Negotiation.* (2nd ed.) Boston: Irwin/McGraw-Hill, 2001.

Madanes, C. *Strategic Family Therapy.* San Francisco: Jossey-Bass, 1991.

Maida, P. "Components of Bowen's Family Theory and Divorce Mediation." *Mediation Quarterly,* 1986, no. 12, 51–63.

Marthaler, D. "Successful Mediation with Abusive Couples." *Mediation Quarterly,* 1989, no. 23, 53–66.

Martin, M. "How Transformative Is Volunteer Mediation? A Qualitative Study of the Claims of Volunteer Mediators in a Community Justice Program." *Mediation Quarterly,* 2000, *18*(1), 33–53.

Mathis, R., and Yingling, L. "Family Modes: A Measure of Family Interaction and Organization." *Family and Conciliation Courts Review,* 1998, *36*(2), 246–257.

Mayer, B. "Mediation in Child Protection Cases: The Impact of Third-Party Intervention on Parental Compliance Attitudes." *Mediation Quarterly,* 1989, no. 24, 89–106.

McDonald, M. "A Framework for Ethical Decision-Making: Version 6.0 Ethics Shareware." [http://www.ethics.ubc.ca/mcdonald/decisions.html]. 2001.

McGoldrick, M., and Gerson, R. *Genograms in Family Assessment.* New York: Norton, 1985.

McGoldrick, M., Gerson, R., and Schellenberg, S. *Genograms: Assessment and Intervention.* (2nd ed.) New York: Norton, 1999.

Medley, M., and Schellenberg, J. "Attitudes of Attorneys Toward Mediation." *Mediation Quarterly,* 1994, *12*(2), 185–198.

Metzger, R. "Mediation in Child Protection in British Columbia." *Family and Conciliation Courts Review,* 1997, *35*(4), 418–423.

Milne, A. "Ethical Constraints: A Mental Health Perspective." In J. Folberg and A. Milne (eds.), *Divorce Mediation: Theory and Practice.* New York, Guilford Press, 1988.

Minookin, R., and Kornhauser, L. "Bargaining in the Shadow of the Law." *Yale Law Journal,* 1979, *88*, 950–997.

Monk, G. "How Narrative Therapy Works." In G. Monk, J. Winslade, K. Crocket, and D. Epston (eds.), *Narrative Therapy in Practice: The Archeology of Hope.* San Francisco: Jossey-Bass, 1997.

Moore, C. "Techniques to Break Impasse." In J. Folberg and A. Milne (eds.), *Divorce Mediation: Theory and Practice.* New York: Guilford Press, 1988.

Moore, C. *The Mediation Process: Practical Strategies for Resolving Conflict.* (2nd ed.) San Francisco: Jossey-Bass, 1996.

Mostaghel, D., Ripps, S., and Kennedy, R. "Mediating Status Offender Cases: A Successful Approach." *Mediation Quarterly,* 1996, *13*(3), 243–260.

National Association of Social Workers. "Standards of Practice for Social Work Mediators." [www.naswdc.org/practice/standards/mediators.htm]. 1987.

Nichols, M., and Schwartz, R. *Family Therapy: Concepts and Methods.* (5th ed.) Needham Heights, Mass.: Allyn and Bacon, 2000.

O'Connor, J., and McDermott, I. *The Art of Systems Thinking: Revolutionary Techniques to Transform Your Business and Your Life.* London: Thorsons, 1997.

Olsen, D. "Circumplex Model of Marital and Family Systems: Assessing Family Functioning." In F. Walsh (ed.), *Normal Family Processes.* (2nd ed.) New York: Guilford Press, 1993.

Oregon State Department of Human Resources. *Cooperative Adoption Mediation Project.* Salem: Oregon State Department of Human Resources, Children's Services Division, 1995.

Parker, R. "Mediation: A Social Exchange Framework." *Mediation Quarterly,* 1991, *9*(2), 121–135.

Pearson, J. *Child Access Projects: An Evaluation of Four Access Demonstration Projects Funded by the Federal Office of Child Support Enforcement.* Syracuse, N.Y.: Center for Policy Research, 1996.

Pearson, J. *Divorce Mediation and Domestic Violence.* Syracuse, N.Y.: Center for Policy Research, 1997.

Pearson, J., and Thonnes, N. *Final Report of the Divorce Mediation Research Project.* Madison, Wis.: Association of Family and Conciliation Courts, 1984.

Pinderhughes, E. "Afro-American Families and the Victim System." In M. McGoldrick, J. Pearce, and J. Giordano (eds.), *Ethnicity and Family Therapy.* New York: Guilford Press, 1982.

Pope, S. G. "Inviting Fortuitous Events in Mediation: The Role of Empowerment and Recognition." *Mediation Quarterly,* 1996, *13*(4), 287–294.

Regina, W. "Bowen Systems Theory and Mediation." *Mediation Quarterly,* 2000, *18*(2), 111–128.

Retzinger, S. "Mental Illness and Labeling in Mediation." *Mediation Quarterly,* 1990, *8*(2), 151–159.

Retzinger, S., and Scheff, T. "Emotion, Alienation, and Narratives: Resolving Intractable Conflict." *Mediation Quarterly,* 2000, *18*(1), 71–85.

Ricci, I. *Mom's House, Dad's House: A Complete Guide for Parents Who Are Separated, Divorced, or Remarried.* (Rev. ed.) New York: Fireside, 1997.

Rifkin, J., Millen, J., and Cobb, S. "Toward a New Discourse for Mediation: A Critique of Neutrality." *Mediation Quarterly,* 1991, *9*(2), 151–164.

Roberts, N., and Noller, P. "The Associations Between Adult Attachment and Couple Violence: The Role of Communication Patterns and Relationship Satisfaction." In J. Simpson and W. S. Rholes (eds.), *Attachment Theory and Close Relationships.* New York: Guilford Press, 1998.

Rothbard, J., and Shaver, P. "Continuity of Attachment Across the Life Span." In M. Sperling and W. Berman (eds.), *Attachment in Adults: Clinical and Developmental Perspectives.* New York: Guilford Press, 1994.

Rothman, J. *Resolving Identity-Based Conflict in Nations, Organizations and Communities.* San Francisco: Jossey-Bass, 1997.

Rummel, R. J. *Understanding Conflict and War.* New York: Wiley, 1976.

Rummel, R. J. *The Conflict Helix: Principles and Practices of Interpersonal, Social, and International Conflict and Cooperation.* New Brunswick, N.J.: Transaction Publishers, 1991.

Russell, B. "The Forms of Power." In S. Lukes (ed.), *Power.* New York: New York University Press, 1992. (Originally published in 1938.)

Salius, A., and Maruzo, S. "Mediation of Child-Custody and Visitation Disputes in a Court Setting." In J. Folberg and A. Milne (eds.), *Divorce Mediation: Theory and Practice.* New York: Guilford Press, 1988.

Saposnek, D. "The Value of Children in Mediation: A Cross-Cultural Perspective." *Mediation Quarterly,* 1991, *8*(4), 325–342.

Saposnek, D. *Mediating Child Custody Disputes: A Strategic Approach.* (Rev. ed.) San Francisco: Jossey-Bass, 1998.

Satir, V. *Peoplemaking.* Palo Alto, Calif.: Science and Behavior Books, 1972.

Schellenberg, J. *Conflict Resolution: Theory, Research, and Practice.* Albany: State University of New York Press, 1996.

Schmitz, S. "Mediation and the Elderly: What Mediators Need to Know." *Mediation Quarterly,* 1998, *16*(1), 71–84.

Schnarch, D. *Passionate Marriage: Love, Sex and Intimacy in Emotionally Committed Relationships.* New York: Norton, 1997.

Schwartz, R. *The Skilled Facilitator: Practical Wisdom for Developing Effective Groups.* San Francisco: Jossey-Bass, 1994.

Seligman, M. *Helplessness: On Depression, Development and Death.* New York: Freeman, 1975.

Shon, S., and Ja, D. "Asian Families." In M. McGoldrick, J. Pearce, and J. Giordano (eds.), *Ethnicity and Family Therapy.* New York: Guilford Press, 1982.

Silberman, L. "Ethical Constraints: A Legal Perspective." In J. Folberg and A. Milne (eds.), *Divorce Mediation: Theory and Practice.* New York, Guilford Press, 1988.

Slaikeu, K. *When Push Comes to Shove: A Practical Guide to Mediating Disputes.* San Francisco: Jossey-Bass, 1996.

Slyck, M., Stern, M., and Newland, L. "Parent-Child Mediation: An Empirical Assessment." *Mediation Quarterly,* 1992, *10*(1), 75–88.

Sonkin, D., Martin, D., and Walker, L. *The Male Batterer: A Treatment Approach.* New York: Springer, 1985.

State Justice Institute Curriculum. *Domestic Abuse and Custody Mediation.* Alexandria, Va.: State Justice Institute Curriculum, 1997.

Talmon, M. *Single-Session Therapy: Maximizing the Effect of the First (and Often Only) Therapeutic Encounter.* San Francisco: Jossey-Bass, 1990.

Tan, N. "Implications of the Divorce Mediation Assessment Instrument for Mediation Practice." *Family and Conciliation Courts Review,* 1991, *29*(1), 26–40.

Tarasoff v. *Regents of the University of California,* 17 Cal.3d 425 (1976).

Tavris, C. *Anger: The Misunderstood Emotion.* (Rev. ed.) New York: Touchstone, 1989.

Taylor, A. "Toward a Comprehensive Theory of Mediation." *Conciliation Courts Review,* 1981, *19*(1), 1–12.

Taylor, A. "A General Theory of Divorce Mediation." In J. Folberg and A. Milne (eds.), *Divorce Mediation: Theory and Practice.* New York: Guilford Press, 1988.

Taylor, A. "The Four Foundations of Family Mediation: Implications for Training and Certification." *Mediation Quarterly,* 1994, *12*(1), 77–88.

Taylor, A. "Concepts of Neutrality in Family Mediation: Contexts, Ethics, Influence, and Transformative Process." *Mediation Quarterly,* 1997, *14*(3), 215–236.

Taylor, A., and Goldberg, A. *Parenting Plan Chart.* Oregon City: Clackamas County Family Service, 1998.

Taylor, A., and Sanchez, E. "Out of the White Box: Adapting Mediation to the Needs of Hispanic and Other Minorities Within American Society." *Family and Conciliation Courts Review,* 1991, *29*(2), 104–127.

Thoennes, N., Salem, P., and Pearson, J. "Mediation and Domestic Violence: Current Policies and Practices." *Family and Conciliation Courts Review,* 1995, *33*(1), 6–29.

Thomas, K., and Kilmann, R. *Thomas–Kilmann Conflict Mode Instrument.* Palo Alto, Calif.: Consulting Psychologists Press, 1974.

Townley, A. "The Invisible –ism: Heterosexism and the Implications for Mediation." *Mediation Quarterly,* 1992, *9*(4), 397–400.

Van Slyck, M., Stern, M., and Newland, L. "Parent-Child Mediation: An Empirical Assessment." *Mediation Quarterly,* 1992, *10*(1), 75–88.

Walsh, F. "Conceptualization of Normal Family Processes." In F. Walsh (ed.), *Normal Family Processes.* (2nd ed.) New York: Guilford Press, 1993.

Wile, D. *Couples Therapy: A Non-Traditional Approach.* New York: Wiley, 1993. (Originally published 1981.)

Wilmot, W., and Hocker, J. *Interpersonal Conflict.* (6th ed.) New York: McGraw-Hill, 2001.

Winslade, J., and Cotter, A. "Moving from Problem Solving to Narrative Approaches in Mediation." In G. Monk, J. Winslade, K. Crocket, and D. Epston (eds.), *Narrative Therapy in Practice: The Archeology of Hope.* San Francisco: Jossey-Bass, 1997.

Winslade, J., and Monk, G. *Narrative Mediation: A New Approach to Conflict Resolution.* San Francisco: Jossey-Bass, 2000.

Wolin, S. J., and Wolin, S. *The Resilient Self: How Survivors of Troubled Families Rise Above Adversity.* New York: Villard. 1993.

Wong, R. "Divorce Mediation Among Asian Americans: Bargaining in the Shadow of Diversity." *Family and Conciliation Courts Review,* 1995, *33*(1), 110–128.

Yellott, A. "Mediation and Domestic Violence: A Call for Collaboration." *Mediation Quarterly,* 1990, *8*(1), 39–50.

ABOUT THE AUTHOR

Alison Taylor has been a professional mediator for over twenty years in the public and private sectors. She had a private divorce and custody mediation practice, then served as a mediator and conciliator at Clackamas County Family Court Service in Oregon, where she taught and supervised family mediation interns. She was a founding board member of the Oregon Mediation Association and was given its Award for Excellence in 1996. She was a practitioner member and an approved consultant of the former Academy of Family Mediators, served on the Consultation Committee and the Editorial Board of *Mediation Quarterly,* and provided institutes and workshops at many annual conferences. She is an Advanced Practitioner/Advanced Educator in the new Association for Conflict Resolution.

An Oregon Licensed Professional Counselor, Taylor teaches students and professionals mediation-related courses at Portland State University and Marylhurst University. She provides family therapy and mediation services and supervision as part of the Multnomah County (Oregon) Department of Community Justice in the newly formed Family Services Unit. She provides supervision for mediators and mediation and conflict resolution training for organizations.

She is coauthor with Jay Folberg of the early text in the field, *Mediation: A Comprehensive Guide to Resolving Conflicts Without Litigation* (1984). She has published other articles in *Mediation Quarterly* and *Family and Conciliation Courts Review.* She recently coauthored a text with Michael Lang, *The Making of a Mediator: Developing Artistry in Practice* (2000), which focuses on the issues of personal development for mediators.

INDEX